Evenings On and Off the Roof

FOURTH SUNDAY EVENINGS ON THE ROOF

Fourth Sunday Evening of each month throughout the year, 8:30 p. m.
1735 Micheltorena Street
Los Angeles

(2 blocks west of Silver Lake, 5 blocks east of Santa Monica intersection, above Sunset)

★

1. **Music by BELA BARTOK - - - - - - APRIL 23**
   Second Sonata for violin and piano; selections from four books For Children; Rumanian Folk Dances for violin and piano, arranged by Szekely; piano Sonata.
   Frances Mullen—Orline Burrow

2. **Etudes by CHOPIN and SCRIABIN - - - - - MAY 28**
   Scriabin, Opus 8; Chopin, selections from Opus 10 and Opus 25.
   Volya Cossack

3. **Music by CHARLES IVES - - - - - - - - JUNE 25**
   Second Piano Sonata, "CONCORD, MASS, 1840-60," movements 3 and 4 (The Alcotts, Thoreau); Fourth Sonata for violin and piano, "Children's Day"; Songs.
   Radiana Pazmore—Frances Mullen—Orline Burrow
   "This sonata is exceptionally great music—it is, indeed, the greatest music composed by an American, and the most deeply and essentially American in impulse and implication."—Lawrence Gilman.
   "An amazingly effective person, as his career and above all his complex scores show; of a kind needed on all battlefronts of the world . . . as American as Samuel Clemens."—Olin Downes.
   "The Concord Sonata indeed remains the solidest piece of piano music composed by an American."—Paul Rosenfeld.

4. **Music BEFORE BACH - - - - - - - - JULY 23**
   Galuppi, Purcell, Cornet, Zipoli, Buxtehude, Bull, and others.
   Wesley Kuhnle

5. **Music by BUSONI - - - - - - - - AUGUST 27**
   Program sponsored by Busoni Society, Philadelphia. Second Sonata for violin and piano, E Minor, Opus 36a; Sonatina for piano (No. 1); Kultaselle for violoncello and piano, 10 variations on a Finnish folksong; Turandot's Frauengemach (Intermezzo)
   Orline Burrow—Frances Mullen—Annie Timmner—Volya Cossack

6. **Recapitulation - - - - - - - SEPTEMBER 24**
   Second hearings from preceding programs, additional contributions.

Following six programs to include: Music by MOZART; music by SCHOENBERG; music by ROY HARRIS; music from NEW MUSIC QUARTERLY; music for violoncello; Recapitulation.

Season of 12 evenings, $3.00; single contribution, 50c. This series of programs will be open to the public by the consent of the performers; all contributions of performance or money will be considered as made to a common cause; featured artists will be paid. Programs are for the pleasure of the performers and will be played regardless of audience. All programs are subject to change without notice.

DOROTHY LAMB CRAWFORD

Evenings On and Off the Roof

Pioneering Concerts in Los Angeles, 1939–1971

UNIVERSITY OF CALIFORNIA PRESS
BERKELEY LOS ANGELES LONDON

The publisher gratefully acknowledges the generous contribution provided by the Roth Family Foundation toward the publication of this book.

University of California Press
Berkeley and Los Angeles, California

University of California Press, Ltd.
London, England

Library of Congress Cataloging-in-Publication Data
Crawford, Dorothy L.
Evenings on and off the roof : pioneering concerts in Los Angeles, 1939–1971 / Dorothy Lamb Crawford.
p. cm.
Includes bibliographical references (p.) and index.
ISBN 0–520-08891–3 (alk. paper)
1. Concerts—California—Los Angeles. 2. Evenings on the Roof (Concert series) 3. Monday Evening Concerts of Los Angeles. 4. Music—California—Los Angeles—20th century—History and Criticism. I. Title.
ML200.8.L72C7 1995
780.78'79494—dc20 94–33945
CIP
MN

Printed in the United States of America
9 8 7 6 5 4 3 2 1
The paper used in this publication meets the minimum requirements of American National Standard for Information Sciences—Permanence of Paper for Printed Library Materials, ANSI Z39.48–1984.

This book is dedicated
to Jack,
who has dedicated many of his compositions to me;
and to the musicians of Los Angeles,
whose passion for their art
made these concerts possible.

CONTENTS

ILLUSTRATIONS

PREFACE AND ACKNOWLEDGMENTS

It is common practice for Los Angeles to bulldoze its past cultural accomplishments in the name of progress. In 1984 the late Lawrence Morton, retired director of the distinguished chamber music concert series "Monday Evening Concerts," decided to resurrect the full history of the series from its founding as "Evenings on the Roof" by Peter Yates and his wife, the concert pianist Frances Mullen, in 1939. The change of name in 1954, when Morton succeeded Yates as director, made it easy for the public to forget the common ideals and continuum between the two phases, and Lawrence Morton's conscience had been pricked on that point by members of the earlier organization. He gathered a complete set of programs from 1939 on and began documenting the extraordinary list of world, American, and West Coast premieres the concerts had presented, lists of some one thousand composers and their works, with the names of performers who had taken part in the concerts. He was in his eighties and in frail health. He stated clearly to a publisher that he had no desire to write a history but proposed a documentary treatment, including lists, tables, performers' anecdotes, and photographs. This proposal was rejected in 1985 by the publisher, who expressed interest in a narrative history of the concerts and suggested that he work with someone willing to do the writing.

In the spring of 1986 he brought me into the project and applied for a grant from the Los Angeles City Department of Cultural Affairs to support the work we would do together. Notice of a grant arrived on 1 May 1987. Late in the evening of 7 May Lawrence (a night person) telephoned me in urgent excitement to set up the tasks I should immediately begin, and we made an appointment to meet early the following week. The next day he died.

Without him I had a daunting task, if I were to carry on the project. The grant vanished. I needed to learn everything Lawrence knew. He had gathered a wealth of contacts and experience through his rich but underpaid work in Los Angeles, first as a concert music critic, then as a highly respected writer on music for film, and finally as impresario of the Monday Evening Concerts, the Ojai Music Festival, and, in his later years, the Bing Concerts at the Los Angeles County Museum of Art. His friends and associates were the cream of the concert music world. He had twice won a Guggenheim Fellowship; many composers, including Stravinsky and Boulez, had dedicated scores to him; he had garnered honors and awards from the American Composers Alliance, ASCAP, the American Music Center, the mayor of Los Angeles, and the Arnold Schoenberg Institute and was listed in the 43d edition of *Who's Who in America* (1984–1985).

But he had enlisted me in his project. I felt committed to him, and to it. I have a love of history, a ravenous curiosity, and a willingness to learn. I had recently coauthored one book, *Expressionism in Twentieth-Century Music* (Bloomington: Indiana University Press, 1993) and felt capable of tackling another. I wanted to discover more about Los Angeles, my home since 1970. Of course, it was all much more of a challenge than I anticipated. The book on Expressionism had to be revised and seen through publication. I had to find grants to support my work on the second book, since I could not continue to teach, direct, and perform in my professional vocal chamber group, and at the same time write two books. Just as I was starting the project, serious illness threatened my family.

What kept me going and maintained my excitement was the help of the many, many people who contributed to this book. Some are listed here. Some are no longer living; their deaths gave me a sense of urgency. I felt that in this book I was seeing, and communicating with, the best aspects of Los Angeles.

So my first gratitude belongs to Lawrence Morton for what he gave me by inadvertently throwing me into the water to sink or swim, and for the hours of contemplation his papers provided me into the life he had known and had written about, particularly in his early music criticism. Lawrence's brother, Arthur Morton, allowed me access to Lawrence's programs and concert papers, on loan from the Morton Collection in the Department of Special Collections at UCLA, and granted me permission to quote extensively from Lawrence's writings and correspondence. Frances Mullen Yates gave me her contagious enthusiasm and every possible cooperation in a study that means a great deal to her. Peter Yates's closest friend, the late Peyton Houston, was a powerful spirit behind my work and the generous donor of his rich correspondence with Yates. Mr. Houston's death just as this book reached fruition is a great sorrow to me, and I am grateful for Parrish Houston's help in spite of her recent loss.

I am deeply appreciative of generous financial assistance extended to my work on this project: in the summer of 1988 by the Los Angeles Department of Cultural Affairs with encouragement from Rodney Punt (then its acting general manager); and intermittently from 1988 to 1993, from the Lawrence Morton Fund of the California Community Foundation, with the encouragement of Jack Shakely, its president. In these (and many other) matters Leonard Stein, Heidi Lesemann, and Jeanette O'Connor were my advisers.

My gratitude for essential help in numerous practical matters also goes to Michael Tilson Thomas, Ernest Fleischmann, Kurt Forster, Michael Clyne, Shibley Boyes, William Russell, Vivian Perlis, Steven Fry, Dorrance Stalvey, Marilyn Stalvey, Lance Bowling, Don Christlieb, Mrs. William G. Selwyn, Ara Guzelimian, Betty Walsh, Lea Appleton, Dorothy Norman, Gerald Turbow, and Catherine Uniak.

Laurence Lesser, an alumnus of these concerts who now presides over the New England Conservatory of Music, provided the idea for the final title of the book. Jan Fileman gave me valuable encouragement and help in the selection of the cover art; Tobey C. Moss guided me to Dr. William Moritz, preeminent authority on Oskar Fischinger's life and works and the owner of Fischinger's painting "Yellow Moon." Sheila Tepper, originator and producer of "Backstage at Royce" and "Backstage L.A.," radio interview shows of which I was host for eight happy years, supported and encouraged my inquiry into Los Angeles' musical history. Together we taped three interviews used in this book, broadcasts from UCLA's Center for the Performing Arts on KUSC-FM (the public radio station of the University of Southern California) and on KKGO-FM (Los Angeles' commercial classical radio station).

Further acknowledgments show the international scope of my inquiries and the generous help I was given by the community of musicians around the world who were drawn to these concerts by Lawrence Morton and Peter Yates: my thanks to Mac Babitz, Christina Berio for Cathie Berberian's estate, Marshall Bialosky, Kalman Bloch, Pierre Boulez, Elliott Carter, Sidney Cowell for Henry Cowell's estate, James Decker, Doriot Anthony Dwyer, Lukas Foss, Ellis J. Freedman for the estates of Aaron Copland and Charles Ives, Malcolm Hamilton, Lou Harrison, Marilyn Horne, Grace-Lynne Martin Ingle, Leon Kirchner, Karl and Margaret Kohn, William Kraft, Laura Kuhn for the John Cage Trust, Anne Pecheaux Lang for the estate of Paul Henry Lang, Frederick Lesemann, Melissa Blake Levitzsky, György Ligeti, Natalie Limonick, Anthony Linick for the estate of Ingolf Dahl, Mitchell Lurie, Virginia Majewski, Lawrence Moss, Marni Nixon, Nuria Schoenberg Nono for Luigi Nono's estate, Andre Previn, David Raksin, Wolfgang Edward Rebner, Helen Swaby Rice, William Rosenstiel, Lawrence Schoenberg for Arnold Schoenberg's estate, Eudice Shapiro, Gregg Smith, Karlheinz Stockhausen, Janice and Jeannine Wagner for Roger Wagner's estate, and Leona Weiss for Abraham Weiss's estate.

Wayne Shoaf, Archivist of the Arnold Schoenberg Institute, University of Southern California, Geoffrey Wexler, Manuscripts Librarian, University of California, San Diego, and David Zeidberg, head of the Department of Special Collections, University of California, Los Angeles, were among many who helped my archival research.

I cannot resist mentioning the University of California Press's anonymous readers, chosen to represent the West Coast and the East Coast. Their comments were more encouraging and useful than I can say; they boosted this book off the computer screen and onto the printed page.

INTRODUCTION

THE STORY OF "EVENINGS ON THE ROOF" (founded in 1939) and its successor, "Monday Evening Concerts" (from 1954 to today), presents in microcosm the changing tastes, trends, and battles of twentieth-century art music. The history recorded here is set in the dynamic atmosphere of Los Angeles' growth to cultural maturity from the 1930s to the 1970s and encompasses the concerts' leadership by two men, Peter Yates (1909–1976) and Lawrence Morton (1904–1987). Their vision and tenacity drew from Los Angeles' extraordinarily rich resources of musical talent a dedication and willingness to risk that made these concerts revelations. In fascinating contradiction to the hedonist reputation Los Angeles earned when it was called "Lotusland" by early real estate boosters and, later, "Tinseltown" by the disillusioned, these concerts offer a tale of spiritual and intellectual aspirations, as the most challenging music of the Western heritage (with an occasional but rare excursion into Asian tradition) was taken up by an impressive array of performers, many of whom were, or became, famous. How could this happen with astonishingly limited finances and publicity, in often hostile cultural surroundings? The answer lies in the performers who gave their talent, with little financial return, for the opportunities and prestige the concerts offered; in the composers who contributed their new works, thereby constantly renewing the concerts' process of exploration; in audiences who demanded the challenge of "that which is contemporary" not only in new music but in old music as well; and, in particular, it lies in the persuasive charisma of Peter Yates and Lawrence Morton.

The longevity of the series, now under the sponsorship of the Los Angeles County Museum of Art, makes it the city's second oldest continuing musical organization after the Los Angeles Philharmonic. This in itself is an achievement, for in Los Angeles the history of the arts has been one of constant beginnings, frequent failures, and great difficulty sustaining growth. This book considers the development and vicissitudes of the ideas behind these concerts in their first two phases. (The third phase, Monday Evening Concerts under today's director, Dorrance Stalvey, is contemporary in every sense, and not yet ripe for historical analysis.)

The original idea was a cooperative concept Peter Yates originated in his most impoverished experience of the Great Depression. Impetus for the success of his concept came with the influx of émigré musicians and composers who turned Los Angeles into the capital of the world of art music in the late thirties and early forties. While Los Angeles' young musicians were maturing in the forties and early fifties, they had the benefit of studying and working with many of Europe's musical giants: Otto Klemperer and Bruno Walter were conducting the Los Angeles Philharmonic; Arnold Schoenberg and Igor Stravinsky conducted performances of their own works; and, beginning in 1947, the film composer Franz Waxman conducted a yearly Los Angeles Music Festival. Musicians could study with the composers Schoenberg, Ernst Toch, or Ernst Krenek, the conductors Charles Previn, Fritz Zweig, or Ingolf Dahl, the cellists Emanuel Feuermann or Gregor Piatigorsky, the violinist Jascha Heifetz or the violist William Primrose, the pianist-composer Paul Pisk, or the harpsichordist Alice Ehlers. Fine young professionals were able to perform locally or play chamber music informally with Artur Schnabel, Josef Szigeti, Artur Rubinstein, Stravinsky, Walter, Toch, Heifetz, Primrose, and Piatigorsky. Carl Ebert and Hugo Strelitzer produced opera performed by students. Peter Meremblum's Junior Symphony Orchestra introduced high school instrumentalists to the orchestral literature. Up the coast in Santa Barbara, soprano Lotte Lehmann molded young vocal talent in her master classes. Beyond direct musical contacts there were opportunities to meet Igor and Vera Stravinsky with their friends Aldous Huxley and Christopher Isherwood, to hear Bertrand Russell lecture at UCLA, to attend readings of new literary work at the home of Lion and Marta Feuchtwanger, and to see Bertolt Brecht's *Galileo* produced at the bitter end of his Hollywood stay. In her memoir for the *New Yorker* titled "Pilgrimage," Susan Sontag tells us of her invasion of Thomas Mann's Pacific Palisades home and study in 1947 when she was a precociously intellectual fourteen-year-old. "Oh golden age! It not only was, I knew it was," she writes. "Admirations set me free. And embarrassment, which is the price of acutely experienced admiration. Then I felt like an adult, forced to live in the body of a child."[1]

The layers of culture the émigrés brought to Los Angeles were an enormous gift to the generation of talented musicians growing up in the forties and early fifties. Their sense of a received tradition stands in contrast to the isolation from historical context that characterized their contemporaries, the Los Angeles visual artists who were brought to prominence by the Ferus Gallery in the early sixties. The artist Robert Irwin, for example, remembered his youth oblivious to World War II, and even to criticism about that oblivion: "Look at how it is: calm, sunny, the palm trees. . . . The war was not reality. The war wasn't here. The war was someplace else."[2] The more normal southern Californian pursuits—obsessions with exaggerated cars, motorcycles, sex, and surfing—formed the background to these artists' "Cool School" art, whereas the musicians' experience involved long, harshly disciplined hours practicing, rehearsing, or recording for a pittance of pay, yet finding ample reward and encouragement in active encounters with the luminaries taking refuge in Los Angeles from persecution and war. Young musicians drank in and thrived on the experience of finding themselves in the midst of something important and central to their art.

Before the émigrés began arriving in the early thirties, Los Angeles musicians were also isolated, and largely unaware of modernity in music beyond the works of Debussy. The indigenous musical culture was conservative, as were the politics of the time. In the early twentieth-century genteel tradition, society women, some of them highly trained musicians with few outlets for their talents, held many important musical positions: Alice Coleman Batchelder, a pianist, founded the Coleman Chamber Music concerts in Pasadena in 1904; Artie Mason Carter organized Hollywood Community sings that led to the founding of the Hollywood Bowl Concerts in 1922; Grace Stewart Mullen emulated Mrs. Carter in founding the Redlands Bowl Concerts two years later; the pianist Olga Steeb headed a flourishing music school and performed occasionally as a soloist with the Philharmonic; and Bessie Bartlett Fraenkel, an influential society matron trained as both a singer and a composer, presided over support groups for the Philharmonic. Women's clubs, an outgrowth of the fight for women's suffrage, were the only performing venues for young professional musicians. "A pack of old ladies!" growled the pianist Leonard Stein about performing in the thirties. He asked his teacher, Richard Buhlig, a close friend and colleague of Schnabel's who had studied in Vienna with Leschetizky and performed widely in Europe, "Do you take it seriously? Who do you play for?"[3]

In the mid-thirties, local composers' organizations were formed to resist the influence of European composers. They soon widened into the national Society of Native American Composers, which promoted "Americanism" in music until the society's demise in 1944.[4] The new voices of twentieth-century rebellion, called "Ultramoderns" in music, were perceived by Californian composers as a threat and a danger to human sanity.

Los Angeles was introduced to modernism by the work of architects: Frank Lloyd Wright's Hollyhock House (1920) was followed by the Viennese architect Rudolph Schindler's house on King's Road in West Hollywood (1922) and the houses of his countryman, Richard Neutra. Their combination of outdoor living spaces with interior rooms inspired many Californian disciples. Perhaps reflecting this new internationalism in Los Angeles culture, courageous attempts were made to broaden and deepen the area's musical experience. In 1925 Henry Cowell, the apostle of musical modernism, began his New

Music Society of California at the Biltmore Hotel in downtown Los Angeles, with an aim "to present musical works embodying the most progressive tendencies of this age, and to disseminate the new musical ideals."[5] One music critic, noting Los Angeles' expression of twentieth-century architecture and engineering, and the youthfulness of its film industry, remarked that "its music ought logically to be as contemporary as its other institutions." He predicted that Cowell's organization would launch "a season which may evoke stormy partisanship, but there will be little chance for concert audiences to relapse into a state of placid acceptance—or endurance."[6] About the first concert Isabel Morse Jones, a violinist and part-time critic for the *Los Angeles Times,* wrote that Edgard Varèse's *Octandre* presented "the ungodly noise of New York Harbor in a fog . . . and not overly refined noise at that," yet she was aware that "the concert marked a milestone in the musical life of this city. Here is a right and proper background and encouragement for the new idea in composition. Long may it prosper."[7] Other "Ultra" composers performed were Carl Ruggles, Leo Ornstein, Arnold Schoenberg, Dane Rudhyar, and Darius Milhaud. One critic headlined his article, "NEW MUSIC SOUNDS LIKE TRAFFIC JAM," and called the enterprise "the left wing of the modern musical movement."[8] The battle for progressive music was on; but Henry Cowell soon moved his New Music Society to San Francisco.

Many of the multitude of highly skilled musicians who came to Los Angeles during the depression to find employment in the burgeoning field of radio, and later in the full symphony orchestras formed in Hollywood by the eight major film studios, brought with them a need for higher adventures and aspirations in their art. By 1939—the year of *Gone With the Wind, The Wizard of Oz, Wuthering Heights,* and other classics—films and film music were in their "Golden Age"; musicians had fewer financial worries, but the drudgery of long hours recording anonymously in darkened studios thwarted their training and desire for live concerts.

The influx of refugees meant more talent and raised expectations. The mix of émigrés and Hollywood was anything but the paradise it is often called. Gottfried Reinhardt (son of the great Austrian stage director, Max Reinhardt, who lived for a brief time in Los Angeles) remembered:

> When I think back, I don't believe it myself. I don't believe this conglomeration of European culture within a few square miles, not more than ten or fifteen, all huddled together for a few years and all living and working here, actually took place. And yet it did. The contiguity with their American surroundings did not make for neighborliness. The newcomers lived more or less among themselves. There were two clashing cultures, and there was, of course, also a clash between culture and no culture, because the movies were here, and except for the writers, very little culture inhabited the studios.[9]

In 1936 George Antheil, himself a composer for films, reported On the Hollywood Front for the magazine *Modern Music.* He described his high excitement about "picture music," a new art form coming into its own.[10] In 1937 he noted talk of negotiations with Arnold Schoenberg (who settled first in Hollywood in October 1934, then moved to Brentwood) to score a film for Paramount. Stravinsky (who moved to Hollywood in 1940), Arthur Honegger, and William Walton were other composers talking with studios that year.[11] The conductor Leopold Stokowski arrived in Hollywood to negotiate with Walt Disney, the only filmmaker who planned scores in advance of shooting. (To Antheil, Mickey Mouse films were often "operas in the purest sense of the word,"[12] and such subsequent features as *Snow White and the Seven Dwarfs, Pinocchio,* and *Fantasia* bore him out.) In an article titled "Breaking into the Movies," Antheil advised that composers who remained aloof to Hollywood were at peril of being left behind, "aesthetically perhaps as well as financially." But, he warned, "Hollywood is a brutal city . . . as hard as a diamond, beside which New York seems soft and a veritable rosebud."[13] In growing disillusion with the studios' ignorance of the new musical possibilities available to them, and with growing interest in the influx of old-world expertise, he turned his journalistic attention to other Los Angeles events involving the musical émigrés: the premiere of Schoenberg's Fourth String Quartet at UCLA by the Kolisch Quartet; the sub rosa recording of all four Schoenberg quartets at Universal Studios through the help of the film composer Alfred Newman; the intelligent performance by the Federal Music Project Symphony Orchestra of Schoenberg's *Pelleas und Melisande;* Otto Klemperer's outstanding performance with the Los Angeles Philharmonic of Mahler's *Das Lied von der Erde.* But Stravinsky conducted his *Petrushka* in a ballet performance that Antheil described as routine, produced "in the Hollywood manner," at the gigantic Shrine Auditorium.[14] By the end of 1937 the Hollywood manner had defeated Antheil's excitement over film music: excellent composers had not received contracts; many had returned to the East. Hollywood music was a closed corporation. He asked music critics to turn a searchlight on Hollywood and its "unmitigated tripe" of background music.[15] Through 1938 he continued to lament his disappointments: there were not enough intelligent and forward-looking music directors in Hollywood, and the present state of Hollywood music was very bad indeed. He continued to hope for tremendous improvement, for this crass art "speaks to the largest audience on earth, and has three jumps on radio. . . . No one interested in wider publics, the education of the people, or the general emotional vibrations of the times, can leave motion pictures out of his calculations."[16] By 1939 (though he continued to compose film music into the fifties) the gross commercialism of Hollywood the Dream Factory had soured Antheil, and he gave up the column.

Schoenberg himself expressed the frustrations of a renowned composer, reduced to begging a society matron for her attention while serving her a dish of condescension. In 1935 he wrote, in his newly acquired English, to Bessie Bartlett Fraenkel at her mansion on Santa Monica's Gold Coast:

> I acknowledge how busy you are, and how much of your best time is taken up by the social duties of your position as president of so many important clubs. And therefore I want to propose you to take one Monday evening at 6:30 dinner in my home and to come with us at 7:30 to the class of "Musical Criticism" at the Univer-

> sity of Southern California. . . . I know what I am doing there is of the greatest importance for everybody who is interested in music. . . . There will certainly be in perhaps twenty years a chapter in the musical history of Los Angeles: "What Schoenberg has achieved in Los Angeles"; and perhaps there will be another chapter, asking: "What have the people and the society of Los Angeles taken of the advantage offered by Schoenberg?" Would you not like to have some influence on the answer? . . . I want you and many other of society people among my audience and making propaganda for my work in favor of the musical culture of Los Angeles.[17]

A product of these tensions between the status quo and inevitable progress, between nationalism and internationalism, entertainment and enlightenment, was a temporary loss of identity in musical circles at the time the Yateses began their experiment in presenting chamber music concerts. Los Angeles lacked the cultural cohesion to absorb and utilize so many new influences. "Hollywood" was a market-driven concept, not a cultural center, yet it imparted to the atmosphere of the young city a free-wheeling creative spirit. A problem for all new cultural enterprises was the difficulty of sustaining an effort long enough to make a contribution to the sense of community—which was itself contradicted by the sprawling character of the city's rapid growth. Projects and schemes were transitory. Moreover, the general public in Los Angeles had little interest in the sophistication and more intellectual appeal of chamber music. Symphonic music, as lush as the film scores of the period, was the preferred medium to express the extravagance and glamour demanded by southern Californian consumer culture in the wake of the depression. But studio and Philharmonic musicians were hungry for chamber music, which would give them the chance to shine outside the anonymous ranks of their professional organizations.

It took the bravado of outsiders to provide the vision and catalytic energy for an organization with a musical mission coherent enough to establish and sustain a new identity that would act as a magnet for the neglected intelligentsia of Los Angeles. Peter Yates and Lawrence

Morton were both outsiders: Yates was a Canadian, married to the Californian concert pianist, Frances Mullen, who was well connected to Los Angeles musical circles; Morton, born in Minnesota, came to Los Angeles to join his film music arranger brother, Arthur Morton, by way of professional work as an organist in Chicago and New York. Peter Yates and Lawrence Morton were antithetical in personality but shared many ideals, as well as uncompromising persistence in the face of fierce opposition. In the early years, Yates provided a passionate search for meaning beyond materialism, and such a disregard for market forces that he claimed from the outset that the concert programs "are for the pleasure of the performers and will be played regardless of audience." Both Yates and Morton wrote widely about music. Morton, having been a critic himself, had little tolerance for those local music critics who were unprepared for the adventures these concerts provided. Both Yates and Morton (in their separate directorships and for a few years working together), along with Frances Mullen, gave to the concerts unstintingly of their spirit and strength and seized opportunities to summon from Los Angeles' unfocused conglomerate of performers, composers, and potential audience a unique synthesis; they built a courageously innovative musical community that was envied and emulated in musical capitals around the world. They recognized the genius of neglected resident émigré composers and performers of highest quality whose identity was obscured by orchestral or studio work. They filled their programs with unfamiliar jewels from the chamber music literature. Along the way they fostered young professionals whose brilliance would soon become evident to the world.

By 1953, when Evenings on the Roof were nationally and internationally known but faltering financially, the *Los Angeles Times* music critic, Albert Goldberg, who had not always been friendly to the innovations presented by the series, wrote:

> The things that impart a musical climate to a city are not the visiting virtuosi and the traveling orchestras, opera and ballet companies that flit in on schedules convenient to themselves and depart with whatever they can attract of a town's floating entertainment

> money. A city can have all manner of these things and yet remain a musically arid desert. *A genuinely musical city is one that has its own resources and makes something of them.*[18]

Since 1939 this chamber music concert series had defied social and cultural establishments in Los Angeles, departing from the beaten track to bring Los Angeles to musical maturity. After fifteen years of Yates's management, Lawrence Morton was about to take over the shoestring finances and guide the city's fine performers to new adventures, to be enjoyed by Los Angeles' musical and intellectual community while world renown and influence would steadily grow to greater heights. But to bring off the adventures was always a struggle. The critic knew that and knew that the city needed the concerts.

One

"WE ARE NOT DISMAYED"
1931–1938

"PETER YATES INAUGURATED an age of musical enlightenment in this community," said Lawrence Morton at a memorial concert for Yates in Los Angeles.[1] How could have this been said of a single man in the baffling tumult of this myopic city, by a revered veteran of years of cultural struggle? What was the state of music in the thirties in Los Angeles? Who was Peter Yates? How and why was he interested in musical enlightenment? And what was Lawrence Morton's role in the effort?

The story begins with the concert artist's lot in the Great Depression in Los Angeles. The founding of the concert series Evenings on the Roof bears a resemblance to the origins of Leonard and Virginia Woolf's Hogarth Press; it was an experiment begun at the home of dedicated musical amateur Peter Yates and his wife, the concert pianist Frances Mullen. It began, almost as a hobby, to satisfy Peter Yates's musical curiosity and to counter Frances Mullen's personal discouragement as a performer. It was the right venture in the right place at the right time and captured the allegiance of many highly talented American and émigré musicians who flocked to Los Angeles for their livelihood, only to find their artistic needs stifled.

Peter Yates's ideas came from his habitual practice of questioning, thinking radically, and coming up with concepts or solutions that were quite unlike accepted notions. Though Yates was a boldly independent thinker, his maverick's path was strewn with paradox: he was a born educator, but his classroom was for many years the concert stage; he dauntlessly promoted and fought for musical causes but preferred, as an impresario, to remain behind the scenes; he was always hungry for creativity as a writer yet put aside his plays and poems to publish deeply thoughtful essays on composers, so that his major publications were all in the field of music;[2] he was in every way an uncommon man, passionately committed to individual integrity, who nevertheless toiled in a demeaning government bureaucracy. He was not interested in easy success and thrilled to the challenge of drawing achievements out of adversity. His bête noire was intellectual loneliness; the pain of this spurred him to achievements that gave lasting benefit to Los Angeles.

His greatest desire was to be a poet, but his attitude toward poetry was ambivalent. Though his knowledge of modernism in all the arts was profound, there was much modern poetry he could not tolerate. Because of his preoccupation and fascination with music, he conceived his own experimental poems, plays, and a long novel in musical, rather than literary, forms. He searched for similar qualities in writers he admired. As he read works by Virginia Woolf in January 1934, he commented, "The art of Virginia Woolf is like that of Bach. Never has literature been so constantly used as a means of formal improvisation as it is now. Never have authors been so aware of music." He found Woolf's novel *To the Lighthouse* to be "a prose sonata, the middle movement an adagio on change and recurrence. Change and recurrence, as in music, is the method of her art."[3] But as he helped his wife build her career as a pianist, Yates's interest in music itself became his life, crowding out writing. His extraordinarily energetic and questioning mind dwelt on philosophical values: for him music seemed better able than literature to satisfy this need. "I think for us the best approach to modern thought may come through music," he wrote his college friend and lifelong intellectual companion, Peyton Houston, in 1938.[4]

In music Peter Yates proudly proclaimed himself an "Amateur," always aware that love, the root of amateurism, was the generating force behind the highest human endeavors. Lawrence Morton, the respected music critic who succeeded Yates as director of Evenings on the Roof, remembered that Yates's amateurism "was in many ways more musicianly than the professionalism of many of the musicians who participated" in the concerts.[5] He had an extraordinary ability to inspire the confidence and dedication of extremely talented professional artists, and to draw them into a nonjudgmental community where music came first.

Perhaps the greatest paradox of the many in Yates's life is that his intellectual, creative, and philosophical predilections achieved remarkable results in the anti-intellectual, culturally unfocused Los Angeles of the late 1930s and 1940s, a city described by hard-boiled writers of the time such as Nathanael West and Raymond Chandler as a tough, cynical, crime-ridden, meaningless world of sham and illusion. Yates himself described Los Angeles in a 1934 poem as a "great fat wench recumbent by the waters of the Pacific":

> Enthusiastic as a fat woman in a grass skirt
> Entertaining the boys
> Full to overflowing, voluptuous
> Like a blister raised by the sun.[6]

He later remembered the city of the 1930s as a "veritable Sahara of artistic incomprehension."[7] In the 1940s he called it "a city of small cultural islands surrounded by vacant lots."[8] He had little interest in motion pictures and rarely went to them. Instead he read constantly, widely, and deeply, working his way through all the stacks of the Los Angeles Central Library. His musical crusade in Los Angeles was made possible only by his faith in himself and in others. This faith was matched by the courage of the lovely young pianist whose attractions drew him to California.

Whereas Frances Mullen was born (1908) and bred a southern Californian, with strong ties to the musical community in and around Los Angeles, Yates was born in Toronto to American parents of Dutch and Scottish heritage. His father was an engineer in charge of hydroelectric power in St. Catharines, on the southern shore of Lake Ontario, near Niagara Falls and Buffalo. The fact that he was born in Canada made Peter Yates feel himself an outsider in America, and this accentuated his stubborn belief in individualism. In his early teens he visited his maternal grandparents in Redlands, California, sixty-five miles east of Los Angeles. Yates's grandfather, William M. Cochrane, was one of many who "retired" to California and became caught up in its real estate booms. In the 1920s Cochrane owned and developed Crescent Heights Park in Redlands and, as a prominent citizen of the town, was asked by the musical and society leader Grace Stewart Mullen to join the board of the Redlands Community Music Association.

Grace Mullen was a close friend and admirer of Mrs. Artie Mason Carter, who established the Hollywood Bowl in 1922 largely from such popular efforts as penny-box collections and community sings. In 1924 Grace Mullen founded the Redlands Bowl along similar lines and remained for forty-two seasons, until her death in 1966, the president and musical director of its parent organization, the Redlands Community Music Association.[9] Her daughter, Frances, developed into a fine pianist with a flair for contemporary music, an extraordinary gift for sight-reading, and a determination to be a concert artist.[10] In 1926, when she was eighteen, Frances Mullen studied for two and a half years in Europe with Isidor Philipp and Walter Frey. Frey was well known for his interest in contemporary music and particularly encouraged her work in this field. She returned to California at the beginning of the Great Depression, which dashed her hopes for a broader concert career and confined her to Redlands, where she taught piano and was invited by the informal but innovative Spinet Club to perform in a recital series devoted to contemporary composers.[11] She found herself chafing at the inferior pianos and banal repertoire she encountered as she played concerts for other local musical groups and women's clubs.

Mullen's first meeting with Peter Yates, when the two of them were approximately thirteen and fourteen, was not a success. The Canadian Peter did not play tennis well enough to suit the Californian Frances. Later, dissatisfied with his family's college choice, Yates transferred to Princeton in his junior year on the strength of some of his poetry.[12] His new Ivy League status, along with his ruggedly handsome photograph on his grandparents' mantel (and some matchmaking on the part of Peter's great-aunt Ella), induced Frances to read Yates's poems and to begin a correspondence with him in 1929. She sent him a photograph of herself, taken as she began her professional career. Yates visited Redlands the following summer (1930), and a romance began in earnest. Because of Frances he returned to California in 1931, after graduating from Princeton.

His musical experience had consisted of piano and organ lessons in childhood. He read music, but his musical tastes were confined to hackneyed standards until he entered Princeton in the fall of 1929 (and when Princeton instituted its first music course during his senior year, he was too preoccupied with English major requirements to take it). One October afternoon in 1929 he listened to the inauguration of live radio concerts in successive hour-long programs of symphonic music conducted by Toscanini and Stokowski. Yates's lifelong self-education in the literature of music began that day, shortly before the great stock market crash. He later wrote, "I think the effect of the change symbolized by that pair of [broadcast] concerts went as deep into our culture as the Depression."[13]

His college friend, Peyton Houston, provided a further important musical stimulus. Houston owned a hand-wound, spring-driven portable phonograph, an excellent record collection, and interests similar to Yates's in finding musical models for poetic form (both admired this aspect of T.S. Eliot's long poem *The Waste Land*). The two engaged in a strenuous program of discussing music, literature, and life, which lasted until Yates's death in 1976.[14] In Princeton they found a Hungarian pianist who introduced them to Béla Bartók's *Allegro barbaro* and others of his works. (Bartók's first concert tour to the United States had taken place in 1928.) Mullen wrote Yates that she needed new contemporary piano repertoire for Spinet Club concerts. Yates wrote back, "By all means, Bartók!" She eagerly took his suggestions. "I'd buy whatever he'd say to buy," Frances Mullen Yates remembers; "I was very enlightened, and grateful for Bartók for many, many years, and did a great deal [of his music]."[15] With

Houston, Yates rummaged among Paul Hindemith, Arnold Bax, and Erik Satie but did not favor the fashionable French composers who called themselves *Les Six*. Endlessly the two men argued the merits of the late works of Ludwig van Beethoven versus the B Minor Mass and the unaccompanied violin sonatas of Johann Sebastian Bach. They avidly devoured the few recordings available to them of Mozart, Haydn, and Brahms. Houston remembered that although Yates had no knowledge of musical theory he had a very discerning ear.[16]

When he moved to California in 1931 Yates had no job prospects. Moreover, he rashly married Frances Mullen in November 1932, against both his and her families' resistance, when Mullen was struggling—piano teaching her sole support—to establish herself as a professional performer. At first Yates sold insurance for a small Pasadena company whose motto was "We sell the Earth." He trudged from door to door, raising crippling blisters and meeting "quantities of strange and wonderful human beings."[17] Having no success, he turned to writing publicity, "as close to libel as I am able," for a public relations firm that paid him next to nothing.[18]

When home from work he spent his time helping in the development of his wife's career. He studied the program making of such master pianists as Myra Hess and Walter Gieseking, selected new repertoire for Mullen, and took on the publicity and management of her concerts. At the time of their marriage, she was performing Bartók's *Rumanian Dances* with a dancer trained by Ruth St. Denis.[19] "[Frances] is the most powerful woman pianist I have heard, despite her smallness," Yates reported to Houston,[20] who responded to their programming needs with generous gifts of recently published music he was discovering in New York and Philadelphia. Soon Mullen was exploring works of Henry Cowell and Ruth Crawford; Aaron Copland's Piano Variations, Roy Harris's and Bartók's piano sonatas; and Schoenberg's Six Little Piano Pieces, Op. 19. For several years she performed modern works such as these with a dancer, whose "expressions" of the music (*not* "interpretations," her husband insisted) might help audiences translate difficult works. Yates felt the arts had become "too exclusive, too academic. . . . The dance expression will carry [Bartók's Sonata for Piano (1926) and Schoenberg's Six Little

Piano Pieces, Op. 19] on the [Californian] tour to audiences that could not otherwise enjoy it."[21] After one of her first modern programs in Los Angeles, a solo appearance at the Western Concerts Artists' League in the Biltmore Hotel on 13 March 1934, a critic commended Mullen's courage "in her choice of Schoenberg and Bartók numbers, which still seem like the language of Lapland to the majority of hearers."[22] Yates later recalled that at the end of the Bartók sonata there was an angry protest and counterprotest, "as close to an uproar as our decorous audience has ever created, to my knowledge. . . . [When she played these pieces] there was always fury. There was reproach in the family, from friends, and so on. And there were a few people who would support her."[23]

In these years the impoverished couple could not afford to attend most concerts and plays. On the day of the great Long Beach earthquake of 1933, Yates rushed to the famed Pasadena Playhouse to snap up a cheap ticket returned by a nervous—and practical—patron. The play was Molnár's *Liliom;* "the longest play I have seen," Yates confessed to Houston. As he sat in the center balcony through numerous aftershocks ("one per scene, the last the best"), the rest of the audience fled in panic.[24]

To satisfy his own rapidly growing musical appetite, Yates continued attentive listening to radio concerts and read all the music history and criticism he could find. In his correspondence with Houston he discussed the writings of Romain Rolland on late Beethoven, Richard Specht on Johannes Brahms, Percy Grainger on Arnold Dolmetsch, and the reviews of music critics such as Olin Downes, Paul Rosenfeld, and Cecil Gray. With friends the young couple listened to Artur Schnabel's recordings of late Beethoven, seldom heard in concerts at that time in the United States. Inspired, Mullen began working on Beethoven's late piano sonatas and the *Diabelli* Variations, Op. 120, a work that was to become a cornerstone of her career.

Yates admired performances of Bach by John Smallman, an English choir director, trained in Boston, who had founded the first a cappella choir in southern California at the First Congregational Church in Los Angeles. In the spring of 1934 he eagerly attended Smallman's tenth annual Bach festival, at which the *St. Matthew Passion* was performed, as well as a two-piano version of *The Art of Fugue,* arranged and performed by the American pianist Richard Buhlig, with his pupil Wesley Kuhnle.[25] Yates then began a search for pre-Bach keyboard music for Mullen; they were encouraged and helped by Houston, who had visited the Dolmetsch family workshop in England.

In July 1933 the Yateses heard with excitement Nicolas Slonimsky's iconoclastic programs of modern music at the Hollywood Bowl, including the West Coast premiere of Edgard Varèse's *Ionisation,* which Yates thought "an exact musical parallel to cubism and Gertrude Stein," his favorite poet.[26] He and Frances met and spent intense evenings discussing modern music with E. Robert Schmitz, the French pianist and founder of Pro Musica, an international society for the promotion of modern music, which brought Bartók, Maurice Ravel, Alexandre Tansman, Ernst Toch, and other composers from Europe to perform their own works coast-to-coast in the United States. Schmitz advised Mullen to concentrate on modern piano works, which would "make her reputation as an individual and present technical difficulties in overcoming which she will grow equal to anything," Yates reported to Houston.[27] Through Schmitz, in October 1933 the Yateses came in contact with "the monumental" Otto Klemperer as the great conductor began his first season with the Los Angeles Philharmonic Orchestra. Yates wrote Houston, who was tall, but could not match Klemperer's 6′7″ height, "Klemperer is one of the few artists you would have willy-nilly to look up to."[28]

Klemperer excited Yates's rapt admiration, for (until the conductor's illness and brain operations of 1939) this titanic musical figure, one of the first musician émigrés from the newly elected Nazi regime in Germany, elevated performance standards and musical understanding to new heights in Los Angeles.[29] The quality of intellect Klemperer invested in the musical scene was precisely what Yates had been seeking in recordings and radio broadcasts and could now find in live concerts of the Los Angeles Philharmonic. As he watched audiences, Yates observed: "Everywhere I find people open-mouthed for knowledge, breathing discussion, but unwilling to sacrifice one jot or tittle of their convictions or prejudice. Open ears, closed minds;

ears ajar, souls fisted. The few exceptions are too often silent, listeners."[30]

At the time of Klemperer's arrival in 1933, most of the Los Angeles concert environment was monopolized by the entrepreneur Lynden (Len) Ellsworth Behymer, who continued until his death in 1947 to pursue formulas of commercial success he had initiated in southern California in 1900, when he presented three performances of the Maurice Grau Metropolitan Opera Company (with the singers Nellie Melba, Lillian Nordica, Edward De Reszke, the conductor Walter Damrosch, and a company of 253) in Los Angeles. Behymer began as a salesman and publisher of theater programs and tickets who knew little about music and expected little knowledge from his audiences. In his early years he used ventures in gold mining, oil, and baseball to float musical extravaganzas and mythologized his record as a musical impresario.[31] Although he aided such local efforts as the Spinet Club in Redlands with his bookings, his control of the Los Angeles musical market stifled audience interest in any musical exploration that went beyond the boundaries of what Behymer deemed good box office.[32] The touring virtuosi he imported from New York were tired by the time they reached Los Angeles and in any case played what they had played for years, perhaps even decades.[33] It was natural that Yates would take a position against this attitude of "art for money's sake."[34] "This virtuoso business," he snorted to Houston, "when there is no conceivable reason for the artist being interested in the particular performance, leaves me with a sense of horror, like perfunctory church going."[35]

In addition there was another problem for professional musicians in Los Angeles. For a performer seeking frequent professional opportunities outside the city, Los Angeles' situation as an "island on the land," cut off by barriers of desert, mountains, ocean, and distance from other cultural centers, posed insurmountable difficulties. Frances Mullen often suffered deep despondency about performing, partly because her rapidly developing talent was too confined. Yates wanted her to find pleasure in playing, for he felt that in transmitting that delight an artist "cannot escape a measure of greatness."[36]

Solutions were not to come easily. Not only was money desperately short, but in 1934 a fire destroyed the couple's belongings. After an arduous monthlong tour of the Pacific Coast with her modern program, Mullen became seriously ill in her first pregnancy. She was summoned to her parents' house in Redlands to recover. Yates, alone and with no hope of earning a salary from the cynical publicity office, reached a crisis of despair in July 1934. He described it to Houston:

> Unreasonably married in devotion, unreasonably about to become a father, loving and beloved, reborn of recent years in music, crammed with the knowledge that still chokes expression, facing, hating, and loving an irrational world that judges success by income instead of achievement . . . I do not fit![37]

With no hope of a paying job, he bought a knapsack, put into it *King Lear* and *The Little Flowers of St. Francis* and some heavy black Russian pumpernickel bread, and set out on foot in fierce heat to search for spiritual sustenance from the renowned guru Jiddu Krishnamurti. Annie Besant had proclaimed Krishnamurti the world leader of the Theosophical Society and had established him on one thousand acres in the Ojai Valley in 1922, but in 1928 he had renounced his followers. This independence inspired Yates, who—resting on his way and soaking his blistered feet in a convenient goldfish pond—wrote to Houston, "He shares my impatience of security and contentment. . . . He insists on questioning and denies all authority."[38] The first stop on his weary pilgrimage was a Vedantists' ashram, sixteen steep miles into the San Bernardino mountains, where he knew Krishnamurti often spoke. There he did not find Krishnamurti and decided that the presiding swami, dressed "in white topee, white polo shirt, riding breeches, boots, and cane—very much the Anglo-Indian,"[39] was a "thorough imposter, like most but not all of his kind."[40] As he rested at the ashram, washing dishes and managing to break nearly every rule of the close community (he even had the temerity to sit in the swami's comfortable chair), he began forming theories about "disciplined communal equality, governed by reason or communal faith, not needing oily flattery or the grease" that he observed the swami requiring.[41] Urged by the irritated swami to leave ("He was jealous of my admiration for Krishnamurti," Yates wrote Houston), he hiked, blistered and driven by a "terrible and intimate realization of one's aloneness," over the Santa Susana pass to Ojai, a tiny community in the Santa Ynez mountain range, seventy-five miles northwest of Los Angeles. In Ojai's "blessed haven" he felt master of his soul, intensely alive and happy. (Ojai's lovely mountain valley was to be used three years later as the setting for Shangri-La in Frank Capra's famous film *Lost Horizon.*) Again he failed to find the elusive Krishnamurti.[42] While he recovered from his long trek in a Theosophists' cooperative community, he produced a solution to the musical and communal problems he had been pondering. His experience with Frances's trials as a performer caused his strong reaction "against the formality of the present performance of music, against that separation between playing for recital and for pleasure, and the same with listening." Instead of formal recitals, he advocated opening a house or studio

> once a week or month to all comers, free or at local movie prices, to give an informal recital without bows, entrances, or exits, performing not only unusual music but also such things as the Bartók children's pieces and often repeating a big work in an evening or in successive evenings . . . until both audience and performer have digested it. . . . Outside artists should be invited to perform works not ordinarily allowed them in recital, their fee being the evening's take. In every case it should be impressed on the mind of each player that the primary reason for his performance is his own pleasure in it, that if the audience be small or absent that is no reason for personal disappointment or loss of pleasure. . . . Such is the community idea.[43]

Yates's ideas of July 1934, born of poverty, personal crisis, and his desperate, wandering search for spiritual answers, were to form the basis of the concerts he and Mullen founded five years later.

His unique concept was left to ripen while Yates faced fatherhood. He found a position as education counselor with the Civilian Conservation Corps in the mountains above San Bernardino, where the young family moved after the birth of their first son in November 1934. His job was to teach English to young toughs, quartered in the mountains above the Los Angeles basin, who were cutting firebreaks, digging wells, and installing telephone lines in the rugged terrain. At first he found himself strained and nervous. His superiors were foul-mouthed retired military men for whom he had no respect. When he suggested to a "fat-headed" second lieutenant that he have his mouth cleaned with the toilets, the captain fired him and he was assigned to another company. Ezra Pound's *Thirty Cantos,* T.S. Eliot's *Waste Land,* and music were his solace.[44] Gradually he endeavored to harness his frankness; life and work with such uneducated men were important in the development of Yates's powerful ability to persuade. One of the truck drivers for the corps had been a driver for Al Capone; another was a child-rapist. To gain such people's trust in order to educate them was a personal triumph for Yates, who explained to Houston, "For one who has lived a withdrawn and rather lonely childhood . . . the growing of this power to win over others affords a never-failing delight and the prophecy of perhaps great reward in the future. I may say I have learned a good deal about making friends; the art has not come easily."[45]

In February 1935 the pianist Richard Buhlig gave private studio performances at his home in Los Angeles of modern programs he was preparing for New York concerts. Yates and Mullen heard him play Alexander Scriabin's Preludes, Op. 74, Schoenberg's Three Piano Pieces, Op. 11, Ernst Krenek's Suite, Op. 26, No. 2, Carlos Chávez's Sonatina, Copland's Piano Variations, and Bartók's Piano Sonata. While Mullen had already gained success performing the Bartók sonata and Schoenberg's Six Little Pieces for Piano, Op. 19, and had explored Copland's Piano Variations, this occasion at last enabled her to hear a master in this repertoire. She began study with Buhlig; his influence, sponsorship, and performances were to become important in the formative years of Evenings on the Roof.

Richard Buhlig (1880–1952) made his performing career primarily in Europe. After studying in Chicago, where he was born, Buhlig went to Vienna while still a teenager to study with Theodor Leschetizky. In 1900, after two years with Leschetizky, he and his fellow pupil and lifelong friend Artur Schnabel left Vienna for Berlin, where they gravitated to Ferruccio Busoni's circle. By 1902 Buhlig was in demand as a teacher in Berlin, as well as a recitalist with sufficient acclaim to be invited by the Steinway Piano Company to tour America in the footsteps of the vastly successful, flamboyant Jan Paderewski—whom Buhlig resembled. However, Buhlig's tour was a failure, for even at age twenty-two he stood above fashion and presented late Beethoven sonatas to unprepared, unsophisticated American audiences. After this fiasco in the United States he returned to Europe and introduced Schoenberg's Three Piano Pieces, Op. 11, to Berlin and London. During a wartime sojourn in England he spent a summer with Arnold Dolmetsch at Haslemere, where he doubtless learned about early music performance practices. In 1918 he was appointed to the piano faculty at the Institute of Musical Arts in New York City. He briefly returned to Europe with his pupils Henry Cowell and Wesley Kuhnle in 1923, when Cowell "kicked up quite a stir" in avant-garde circles from Vienna to London with his brash use of tone clusters on the piano.[46] In America, Buhlig's approach to Bach keyboard performance drew considerable attention from the critic Paul Rosenfeld. By the early 1930s Buhlig had settled in relative obscurity in Los Angeles to teach, occasionally emerging to perform Bach with Kuhnle, or Beethoven with Klemperer and the Los Angeles Philharmonic, or to offer such ambitious recitals for knowledgeable circles in New York as the program the Yateses heard previewed in February 1935.[47]

Contact with Buhlig was inspiring and stimulating to both Peter and Frances Yates. The pianist's scholarship in painting, literature, mysticism, and religion intrigued Peter Yates. Buhlig's playing could be demonic, with an enormous range of tone. "Buhlig makes modern speech of modern music," Yates wrote to Houston about the private recital; he also noted that as Mullen began study with him, music mattered more than ever to her.[48] Together, the Yateses probed piano works of Beethoven, Bach, and Schoenberg with increasing intensity. Schoenberg, who had settled in Los Angeles in the fall of 1934, offered a series of lectures in Hollywood in the spring of 1935. His talk on Bach stimulated the couple's study of the *Goldberg* Variations and

The Art of Fugue. Buhlig was a close acquaintance of both Schoenberg and Klemperer and introduced Yates to the works of Mahler through Klemperer's performances. Yates looked forward especially to meeting Schoenberg.[49] With the added stimulation of this exalted circle, musical explorations now became the greatest adventures of Peter Yates's life.

In March 1936, while their friend Peyton Houston was visiting and their second son was about to be born, Yates lost his Civilian Conservation Corps job. He moved his family from San Bernardino to a rented bungalow in the Silver Lake area of Los Angeles, just east of Hollywood, in vain hope of finding a position with the telephone company. The house on surprisingly steep Micheltorena Street had only five rooms and was dilapidated to the point of looking ready to slide down the hill backwards.[50] Houston stayed on for almost two years with the family, helping as the baby arrived, working on his own writing, and contributing to expenses. His phonograph (by now an electric model) and large case of records were the focal point of evenings with the Yateses' friends, who came to the house at 1735 Micheltorena Street to listen together and discuss music.

The area was filled with musicians. With the advent of sound in movies in 1927, performers all over the country had lost theater positions and had migrated to Hollywood, where numerous radio and film orchestras were established. During the depression the pool of musicians grew to include the country's finest young orchestral players, for in the film studios pay was better and steadier: the Musicians Union established a minimum of $30 for a day's work.[51] This aggregation of talent soon proved a magnet to the émigré composers fleeing Hitler. "It seemed quite a waste that all the talent locked up in movie music in Hollywood was not being called on," Houston remembered.[52] Brilliant young performers were dismayed to find their musical tasks in studio orchestras uninspiring, and they missed the response of an audience. The violinist Eudice Shapiro, fresh from considerable New York experience as a soloist in contemporary music, following her training at the Eastman School of Music and the Curtis Institute, remembers playing "footballs" (as the musicians called whole notes) for hours on end in darkened studios. Opportunities for young professionals to grow musically were hard to find.[53]

Peter Yates and Frances Mullen, on the other hand, were encountering new musical experiences at a rapid pace. As Yates put it, he was "more than ordinarily open to new creations, because less than ordinarily able to follow the structure of accepted things."[54] Shortly before the family's 1936 move from San Bernardino to Los Angeles, Rowland Leach, professor of violin at Redlands University, tossed bound copies of Charles Ives's Piano Sonata No. 2 (*Concord*) and his accompanying *Essays Before a Sonata* onto the Yateses' piano as a joke for Mullen, widely known for her sight-reading ability, to puzzle over. Yates devoured the *Essays,* while Mullen began serious work to learn the sonata.

In January 1937, while their musical ambitions grew, the young family—now with two baby boys—faced an ultimatum from Peter's parents, who could give no more financial support: Yates would have to find a job or give up the house on Micheltorena Street and send Frances and the children to live in Canada. Frances wrote in panic to Peyton Houston, who was visiting San Francisco, that she and Peter had only $50 in the bank.[55] For a while Houston took on the rent payments for the house; Frances continued concertizing, and—after contemplating a job with the Atlantic & Pacific grocery chain, or the specter of going on Relief[56]—Yates found himself a civil service position with the California Department of Employment.

Fear shackled Yates to this job for twenty-five years. He gave it tremendous energy, great compassion, and much imagination, but it was a tediously repetitive occupation in a bureaucracy that rejected his philosophy of individualism. He soon took the view he learned from Charles Ives: his creativity was not to be compromised. After office hours he led his second life writing, reading voluminously, corresponding, playing through the complete keyboard works of many composers, planning and administering the extraordinary concert series he envisioned, and dealing personally with some of the greatest contemporary composers as well as with brilliant performers. He constantly listened to, advised, and supported Mullen in her playing, which he vowed was not to be sacrificed to financial pressures.

At first their plan was for her to tackle an East Coast tour, culminating in a New York debut. Yates spurred her on to undertake increasingly challenging works.[57] When she encountered resistance from Buhlig for attempting "too heavy" a program of Beethoven, Debussy, Honegger, Schoenberg, and Bach-Busoni, Yates characteristically retorted to Houston, "We are not dismayed."[58] By February 1938 he felt that Frances's persistence was winning its reward; she was gaining important invitations and endorsements for her performances of modern music. At Yates's request, Houston began a search for East Coast bookings for her special repertoire.

Developing a gift for gathering artists and gaining their respect and trust, Yates solicited the energetic interest of an impressive contralto, Radiana Pazmor, who had sung and recorded Ives songs for Cowell's New Music Society. A friend of Henry Cowell's from childhood, Radiana Pazmor was born in San Francisco in 1898 to a locally well known musical family. Her father (Henry Bickford Pasmore) founded a Conservatory of Music in 1914 in San Francisco and taught her voice. Her sisters formed a piano, violin, and cello trio that toured widely in the United States. Radiana Pazmor performed in London, Berlin, and New York from 1921 to 1935, then settled in Hollywood.[59] The composer Lou Harrison remembered her magnificent contralto voice and dramatic stage presence: "She was several feet higher than everyone else, and wore very long earrings. . . . She was really quite beautiful in a grand and glamorous way. . . . Her concerts were very much loved."[60] Orline Burrow, a young but excellent violinist, well trained by Oskar Seiling (a prominent violin teacher, himself trained by Josef Joachim in Berlin, and soloist with the Los Angeles Symphony, predecessor to the Philharmonic), joined them.[61] Mullen, Burrow, and Pazmor developed an all-Ives program. Yates wrote to Charles Ives, asking for music, and began receiving from the composer a large collection of scores and instrumental parts, as well as deeply grateful letters dictated by Ives (whose handwriting was by then rendered laboriously shaky by illness) to his wife, Harmony. On 6 April 1938 Ives wrote,

> Miss Pazmor is not only a remarkable singer and musician but she has courage and stands her ground and I think your wife must

have similar ways. Strong traits have declined in this world of ours today and music could be a stronger thing if more musicians wouldn't be so afraid of the patronic [sic] box-sitters and the pansy-eared column-drapers called critics (83½% of whom are aural cowards and know almost three nice chords—after dinner).[62]

This correspondence with Ives, begun in 1938, injected more excitement and determination into the Yateses' plans. Gerald Strang (to whom Henry Cowell had sold *New Music Editions* upon his 1937 imprisonment in San Quentin on a morals charge)[63] loaned them his and Cowell's collections of Ives's works. Yates also wrote to Bartók asking for recent works, unavailable in the United States, for an all-Bartók program Mullen was planning with Orline Burrow but received no reply. Radiana Pazmor offered her home for these all-Ives and all-Bartók programs.

With a characteristic burst of confidence, Yates combined the plans for performances of modern works with a vision of comprehensive programs of Beethoven's works, for he felt (perhaps with Buhlig's counsel) that in America "Beethoven is suffering, but I believe the great day for Beethoven will come when he is rediscovered as a composer, not the writer of a few sure-fire pieces. So I am interested to see [Piano Sonatas, Opp.] 22, 28, 10:3, 31:3, and 90 programmed."[64] His energetic interests and ideas attracted enough fine performers that Yates could design an extended series of Beethoven concerts, intended to broaden the public's understanding. Yates's life was now taking on a fuller meaning, although he was frequently exhausted. His letters to Houston hinted at the personal problems he hoped to solve: "Loneliness has gone away. . . . You are all making me, with Frances, my first masterpiece. . . . Although these days I come home too tired for deskwork, I am not tired in creative thinking. . . . My nights are more peaceful than hitherto. I have a world to live in; I am becoming an American."[65] An important spur to his enterprise was his recognition that by 1938, in spite of the throngs of excellent musicians in the city, chamber music had nearly vanished from the Los Angeles musical scene:

> The old Los Angeles Chamber Music Society [which had presented concerts in the Biltmore Hotel] was gone. The local chapter of Pro Musica was moribund. Except for the sturdy Coleman Concerts in Pasadena and occasional series presented to the universities by Elizabeth Sprague Coolidge, *both using imported musicians,* Los Angeles had no chamber music. Elsewhere [in America] the situation would not have been regarded as abnormal. It was abnormal in Los Angeles only because of the large number of resident musicians, most of whom had come to work in the motion picture studios. [For them] Los Angeles [was] geographically isolated, cut off from association with other large cultural communities.[66]

Yates seized the opportunity in this situation. The community's full recognition of local musicians was always a keystone of his concert philosophy, which originated in his deep desire to see Mullen find greater achievement and fulfillment in music.

In March 1938 Yates's great-aunt Ella provided a loan of $2,700, with which they bought the run-down bungalow they had been renting at 1735 Micheltorena Street. They had originally planned to build a piano studio for Mullen in two or three years' time, but, because of the musical situation, in July they hastened their plans, deciding to forgo owning a car in order to build a room large enough for concerts immediately. Because they were in touch with modernism in its every aspect they asked Rudolf M. Schindler, the first of the modern European architects to reach Los Angeles,[67] to draw up plans for a studio that would seat one hundred people.

Schindler was Viennese-trained and strongly influenced by architect Adolf Loos, the Viennese advocate of simplicity and utility. Working under Frank Lloyd Wright, Schindler had introduced modern architecture to Los Angeles in the twenties. As Yates remembered, after conflicts with Wright, Schindler went his own way,

> building small residences for people who couldn't afford to pay much money. . . . He was a man almost without ambition, almost without self-interest. . . . He built very few large places. He built

practically nothing in the way of "show" architecture. He would draw up just sufficient plans to get by the city authorities. Then he would go ahead and improvise on those plans—this house is a very good example—in order to accomplish things which perhaps he couldn't account for to the authorities under the building regulations. . . . He had the Viennese suavity at its best and also the Viennese indifference, in a way, to the ordinary facts of life.[68]

Schindler decided the Yateses' music studio should be erected as a second floor on the roof of the bungalow, overlooking a great sweep of Los Angeles from City Hall on the south, and the Griffith Park Observatory on the north, west to the Pacific. He solved the problem of the cracked foundation at the back of the house by cantilevering the weight of the new second story from its solid front wall. He pitched the ceiling of the studio to imitate the angle of a piano lid, thereby aiding the acoustics of the room. By making much use of plywood (which was not only cheap but acoustically practical), not drawing elaborate plans, and not demanding his usual fee, Schindler kept costs low and exceeded their budget by only $75. The entire cost of buying the 1890s property and remodeling the house was $4,900.[69]

By August 1938 Yates could see the European war on the horizon.[70] He felt an urgency, born of his struggle in the depression, to achieve something unique, and in doing so to live his philosophy. In his determination to come out from under hopelessness in the difficult period of 1935 he had searched for "a new recognition of the values of life" and rejoiced when he thought he could detect "that work is honored, beauty reverenced, the spirit loved."[71] His precarious employment interviewing crowds of the destitute (at the rate of a new applicant for work every two minutes) convinced him of society's evils: "More and more I am a revolutionary, not for causes, but against the deceitful slack-fisted lazy-souled or soulless viciousness of human ways . . . and I too day after day am slugged by this fear, fear of losing livelihood."[72] Yates was completely opposed to authoritarianism and the bureaucratic controls he saw in his office work and in prewar Europe. He despised the excesses of capitalism and, like many others in the 1930s, was interested in theoretical communism; he was reading Harold Laski, John Reed's *Ten Days That Shook the World,* and the anarchist Prince Kropotkin's *Memoirs of a Revolutionist,* yet he felt that the Russian Revolution had been a "violent spiritual failure."[73] Against the atmosphere of restive liberalism, the California Employment Service circulated memos threatening dismissal of employees for "improper political activity,"[74] and Yates turned to defining societal problems in philosophical—rather than political—terms. He came to the conclusion that the problem of art was "to find again the integrating power in a disintegrating universe of superficiality."[75]

As he wrote about the house alteration to Houston, Yates declared, "I must come to earth somewhere. My work must take root, and I have no preference for other worlds, if I may grow here. The essential conditions have been obtained."[76] While the performance studio was being built overhead, circumstances surrounding the Yateses were chaotic: huge holes in the house on Micheltorena Street allowed drafts—along with mounting excitement—to inflict illness on everyone in the family; Grace Mullen suffered a serious mental breakdown and had to be institutionalized; Peter's good angel, great-aunt Ella, aging rapidly, came to live with the Yateses, along with her required nursing assistants; work handling new Social Security provisions at Yates's office was increasingly stressful and fraught with administrative disorganization. As he threw himself into concert planning, Yates began having serious attacks of fatigue, a prelude to the nervous illnesses that would plague him throughout his fifteen years running his concert series. But, in spite of all difficulties, his notion that "the best approach to modern thought may come through music" continued to crystallize.[77]

Although its plywood interior was utterly simple and rough, the new roof studio was to be "a beautiful room, a room to be enthusiastic in."[78] Yates described it to Houston during the final stages of construction:

> The ceiling is peaked at the piano end to make an obtuse angle . . . so that the steep wall will throw out the piano tone along the

> ceiling, without echo or pocketing. Lights on the piano side of the [roof] beam throw a diffused glow down and out from the steep wall. All the best features of a theater and stage are there, but so unobtrusively that it scarcely seems so. A railing divides the head of the [inside] stairs [to the ground floor] from the piano, framing the stage and also containing the built-in heater. . . . What would most delight you is the outlook. . . . The back half of the south side, facing downhill, is nearly all window above a four-foot rail. Three sliding windows . . . above, an enormous triangular window right up into the peak, so that from their seats our audiences will seem to look almost straight up at the stars. . . . The room is so high that not a roof impedes our view, and the big fir at the southwest corner is a thing of beauty rather than an interference.[79]

Each evening, when he came home from work, the Yateses' two toddler sons demanded that their father take them up on the roof, and from their clamor—despite Frances's strenuous objections—he decided on the name, Evenings on the Roof.[80]

Two

"THE WORLD WILL COME TO US"
1938–1945

LOS ANGELES IN 1938 not only lacked performances of chamber music but had no consistent introduction to modern music. Here lay another opportunity for Yates. Otto Klemperer, who had been an outstanding innovator during his scintillating regime at the Kroll Opera in Berlin, was now hampered at the Los Angeles Philharmonic by a precarious financial situation that threatened the existence of the orchestra, so he ventured difficult new works only occasionally.[1] Eugene Goossens, the English conductor renowned for his ability with new works, had played Bartók, Honegger, Prokofiev, Schoenberg, and Stravinsky on visits to the Hollywood Bowl in 1926–1929; Frederick Stock gave the Bowl's first all-American concert in 1932 (performing palatable music by Henry Hadley, Deems Taylor, and Edward MacDowell); but in 1933 Nicolas Slonimsky was unceremoniously ousted from his eight-week conducting contract at the Bowl because he dared expose the populace to works of Varèse, Schoenberg, Harris, and Ives.[2] Frances Mullen and Peter Yates had made the area of new music their own through performance and study. Yates wrote in his first letter to Charles Ives on 28 March 1938, "My wife has a reputation for fearing no labor in order to present the best contemporary music."[3] The "inauguration of an age of musical enlightenment in

Los Angeles" grew out of the couple's fearlessness and aptitude for hard labor and from the beginning encompassed contemporary music in relation to—never detached from—music of the past.

In 1938, as their plans accelerated, Mullen was working increasingly hard. She took on works of Roy Harris, Ernest Bloch, Debussy, Delius, Honegger, Prokofiev, Mendelssohn, Liszt, Mozart, Handel, and Chopin for projected East Coast programs. She and the violinist Orline Burrow prepared an adventurous all-Bartók program, tried it out at Oskar Seiling's studio in Los Angeles and at Mills College in Oakland, and planned to make it their dynamic Town Hall debut program in New York City. Mullen sight-read twenty songs of Charles Ives with Radiana Pazmor, who thought such a feat by a pianist impossible. She performed piano works of Harris, Copland, and two movements ("The Alcotts" and "Thoreau") of Ives's *Concord* Sonata for one of the last concerts of the dying Los Angeles chapter of Pro Musica. She continued her explorations of Schoenberg's piano works (Opp. 11, 19, 25, 33a, and 33b) and began work on Ferruccio Busoni's Sonatina for Piano No. 1, which she found "terrible to learn."[4] Yates described this work as "an amazing thing . . . [a] marriage of Lisztian technique with Mozart style enlarged through Beethoven in streamlined contrapuntal form." Peter's curiosity about Busoni was such that for Christmas Frances gave him a membership in the Busoni Society.[5]

For his part, Yates was also reading music at the piano, getting an overview of Brahms's oeuvre, and making his own catalogue of Mozart's works. A Bach concert in Los Angeles by the internationally renowned Viennese harpsichordist Alice Ehlers (who had studied piano with Leschetizky, music theory with Schoenberg, and harpsichord with Wanda Landowska) stimulated once again his love and admiration for the composer he considered "the Plato of music."[6] By October 1938 he had drawn up projected plans for monthly concerts that were to take place in the new roof studio from April 1939 through November 1941. Neglected twentieth-century masters, toward whose lonely courage and individual heroism he felt sympathetic, topped the list. Programs of all-Bartók, all-Ives, all-Busoni, all-Schoenberg, a program of American composers, as well as an evening dedicated to music from Henry Cowell's *New Music* publications were on his October 1938 list and came to fruition in the first seasons of concerts, along with a pre-Bach program by the local early music specialist Wesley Kuhnle, a festival of Bach, a Beethoven festival, and an evening comparing Chopin and Scriabin etudes.[7]

At Yates's urging, Peyton Houston went to visit Charles Ives in his New York home, to ask for the violin part for the Fourth Sonata for Violin and Piano that Mullen and Burrow were preparing, and for other music, because Yates was actively engaging the interest of Los Angeles choral and orchestral conductors in Ives's music. Ives sent Yates a copy of Lawrence Gilman's "almost apoplectic rave" review of John Kirkpatrick's 20 January 1939 performance of the *Concord* Sonata at Town Hall. Yates felt that this (and *Time* magazine's) belated praise of "the greatest music composed by an American" would boost his and Frances's plan for an all-Ives program, at which she would play the complete *Concord*.[8] Yates himself played the sonata through as he prepared his program notes on Ives.

Through Richard Buhlig, the Yateses began a cordial personal relationship with Schoenberg.[9] Peter Yates's interest in this composer had originally been piqued when he was a student at Princeton and cut class to hear a broadcast of the *Gurre-Lieder*. In 1934 Mullen began performing Schoenberg's piano works, with a gift from Houston of the Six Little Piano Pieces, Op. 19. While they explored whatever works of his they could find, Yates read all the materials available in English on Schoenberg and quoted them at length in his letters to Houston. As he came to know the man in relation to his compositions, he felt Schoenberg embodied the "spiritual integration" he searched for in all art.[10] By March 1939 Yates was meeting Schoenberg regularly in an effort to bring about performances of his works—particularly *Pierrot lunaire,* Op. 21—which remained unknown in Los Angeles.

Yates spent two to three hours at the piano each day in an exhaustive study of Mozart. He wrote Houston: "I find in Mozart more unfinished business than in any other of the classics, and material best suited to mingling with our moderns. . . . Certainly the public is only beginning to hear Mozart."[11] He had an idea Frances could encompass Mozart's entire solo piano repertoire.

He admitted that he was "almost too fierce a taskmaster for Frances," but she was growing remarkably, and fine possibilities were developing for her.[12] Her recitals had taken her north to British Columbia, Seattle, San Francisco, Oakland, Sacramento, and San Rafael. She had given four recitals at Mills College, then the West Coast academic haven for the new in music. In southern California she had played at Scripps College, the University of Redlands, Santa Barbara, the University of California, Los Angeles, and Pasadena. In the spring of 1939, the intense interest stirring in Los Angeles about the coming Roof concerts decided both Peter and Frances against her eastern tour and New York debut. Yates explained to Houston, who was arranging eastern bookings for her, "Frances is doing too well here to go East this season. Our series has given a new meaning to all plans. Now New York [would] draw us from it; we no longer need to get away or to attack. I have never wanted for Frances the horrid inertia of a touring virtuoso. Now I think we can escape it. The world may and will I do not doubt it come to us."[13]

Buhlig began to consider emerging from performance retirement to play in the Yateses' series but first recommended his pupil Volya Cossack (who had recently soloed with the Philharmonic in works of Prokofiev);[14] he said she should play for the Yateses whatever was required of her. She agreed to play the Chopin-Scriabin and Busoni programs Yates had in mind. Buhlig's colleague Wesley Kuhnle proposed a program of pre-Bach composers to illustrate early keyboard performance practice.

Alfred Leonard, who had developed a following as the proprietor of a music shop and a radio announcer, agreed to send announcements of the first six concerts to two thousand customers on his mailing list. While friends and family remained condescending, prominent musicians of the émigré community—among them Klemperer, the composer Paul Pisk, the pianist José Iturbi, and the conductor Richard Lert—were showing interest, and plans were "going ahead with . . . bounding leaps. . . . Such enthusiasm is amazing for LA." Knowing that programs of the "weight and toughness" he intended would be "a new thing in Los Angeles,"[15] Yates stated in his initial publicity announcement that the programs were to be "open to the public by the consent of the performers," as they were intended "for the pleasure of the performers" and would be played "regardless of audience." These precepts were essential to the concert philosophy Yates had developed in Ojai in 1934. Admission receipts would go to the performers, although their income would be negligible, for prices were democratically scaled to the amount for second-run movie admissions. At first—and until 1944—a single admission cost fifty cents. The subscription rate cost half that, or three dollars for the full year's twelve concerts. The concerts were to take place on the fourth Sunday evening of each month, year-round, in the Roof studio. Programs subsequent to the uncompromising first six months of all-Bartók, all-Ives, all-Busoni, pre-Bach, and Chopin-Scriabin fare would include music by Mozart, Schoenberg, American music, and works published in Henry Cowell's *New Music Quarterly.*[16]

Although the first announcement did not indicate the breadth of his musical purposes, from the beginning Yates hoped to establish "a long-term historical series in which a thorough diet of classics may be balanced against a few carefully spaced contemporaries."[17] Along with his ambitions to present a comprehensive overview of Beethoven, Mozart, Brahms, Bach, and pre-Bach composers, Yates envisioned short Ives and Schoenberg festivals. These expanding plans were based on the gathering of a company of enthusiastic performers, whose confidence in Yates's ideas was attracted by his "disinterested integrity," Houston remembers.[18] With them Yates carefully began to build a nonjudgmental musicians' cooperative. He encouraged the musicians to read from music, rather than memorizing, for performances.[19] He remarked to Houston, "I must keep my group of artists small and closely knit for the present, and I must keep complete control." He forecast that he would, "if I don't lose patience, spend a major portion of my life trying to show musicians that the principal worth of musical performance is not money, not fame, not perfection in any sense . . . but simply mutual good-fellowship . . . a self-sufficient purpose."[20]

"Has anyone anywhere ever done anything like this?" Yates exclaimed to Houston as the first concerts began.[21] Very little of Béla Bartók's music had been heard in Los Angeles. Bartók himself had visited the city on a recital tour sponsored by Pro Musica in 1927, but in 1938 no music of Bartók's dating later than 1927 was available in local music stores.[22] Yates realized that much of Bartók's music was "unacceptable" to the Los Angeles audience.[23] Nevertheless, in a gesture that characterized the bold philosophy of Evenings on the Roof, the new series opened on 23 April 1939 with an all-Bartók program: the Second Sonata for Violin and Piano (1922) and the Rumanian Folk Dances (1915, arranged for violin and piano by Székely), played by Burrow and Mullen; songs sung by Pazmor;[24] the Piano Sonata (1926) and selections from *For Children* (1908–1909) played by Mullen. The audience in the Roof studio at the first performance numbered nineteen. With the help of ancillary performances at the California Institute of Technology and Los Angeles Junior College, a repeat of the program at the Roof studio the following Tuesday evening brought in another twenty or so, more than half of whom were male[25]—a distinct shift from the predominantly female audiences of women's club circuits and society-backed concert series the Yateses were trying to escape. In the first three seasons Roof programs were frequently given twice, and many listeners came back for a second hearing of the unfamiliar repertoire; Yates's educational purpose had appeal from the beginning.

Following the comparative program of Chopin and Scriabin etudes (28 May 1939) by Volya Cossack (whose temperament, Yates thought, marred her performance), the all-Ives program, including the *Concord* Sonata, songs, and the Fourth Sonata for Violin and Piano, performed by Mullen, Pazmor, and Burrow, drew a raptly enthusiastic audience, among them, on 25 June 1939, Otto Klemperer. As Yates described it,

> Scarcely had the Ives program begun, with Emerson [the first movement of the *Concord* Sonata], than at the door appeared the massive Otto; I interrupted the program and Frances began over

> . . . [and] instead of collapsing began even better and played magnificently. The room was so full Otto had to balance on the corner of a divan. . . . At intermission he plunged downstairs after Frances calling for the [*Concord*] Sonata, which he studied and declared impossible to play because it has no [time] signature. Then he swung back upstairs to me and began looking into scores. Finding in the Second Set an instrument he could not decipher: Vat iss dat! That, I replied, is a zither. Oh! Oh! it iss impossible, impossible! But I had to drag him from the music. At the end of the evening he plunged downstairs again to congratulate Radiana, who sang as magnificently as Frances played. Until you have heard Radiana sing Ives you ain't heard nothing. Afterwards Otto paced the front walk with me while I sold him the idea that he could play the New England Scenes: they are easier I repeated and repeated. Leaving [with the score] he wondered whether Ives could compose him a new piece; I explained Ives' illness; with that Otto grew very sad—he is not at all well himself—and became more persuaded.[26]

Pianist and Schoenberg-pupil Leonard Stein, who was serving as page-turner, remarked that evening to Yates, "After tonight you can do anything!"[27] The program was repeated, and an exhibit of Ives scores, which Yates had organized at the Los Angeles Central Library, continued for three weeks. Yates mused to Houston, "Schoenberg may have the edge in chamber music, but we have yet to hear Ives."[28] He later observed that the audience offered less resistance to Ives's music than to Bartók's and Schoenberg's.[29]

Yates reported that the all-Busoni program,[30] although impressively performed (on 27 August 1939), brought a small audience. After the Ives, the second most popular program of the first season was the program of pre-Bach keyboard music by Byrd, Bull, Gibbons, Purcell, Cornet, Frescobaldi, Sweelinck, Buxtehude, and Scheidt played by Wesley Kuhnle (23 July 1939). This was also music new to Los Angeles and began an important trend of exploration into the distant musical past in these concerts.

SECOND AND THIRD SIX-MONTH SEASONS: OCTOBER 1939–NOVEMBER 1941

At first California seemed very removed from the European war. Yates, at this time a pacifist who felt that "refusal of war service is the essential heroism,"[31] thought that the world had gone mad and declared Hitler a scapegoat for its own evils. He wrote to Houston: "We would be wise to find out the fanatic in our own souls and expose him. . . . We had better go and pray. That is the only war we can win. We must be fierce with ourselves and pitiful with other men." At the news of declaration of war he turned to reading André Malraux's *Man's Hope*,[32] which was to play an important role in his profession as a writer. (In 1937 Malraux had spoken with great success to a packed Shrine Auditorium—seating 6,300—on behalf of the Republicans in the Spanish Civil War.) Outside of his tedious work in the California State Employment office musical activity demanded all Yates's time. He began drafting essays on music, which would later be used as program notes.

A rush of new plans, including Yates's extended chronological overview of Beethoven's piano and chamber works with violin and cello, accompanied the successful conclusion of the first season. This Beethoven series was planned to take place over the span of a year (October 1940–November 1941) on Monday evenings, overlapping the regular Sunday series, which continued monthly year-round. By the summer of 1939 Yates had gathered enough fine musicians to accomplish this. "I can find scarcely any talk but music," he wrote Houston, urging him to come out to California for the Beethoven series. Nine pianists were interested in playing. Kurt Reher, cellist in the Philharmonic (of whom Yates wrote, "Imagine the best playing you have heard anywhere"),[33] committed himself to the group. He brought along his brother, the Philharmonic violist Sven Reher, and promised to help induce the orchestra's principal clarinetist, Kalman Bloch, to join.

The Reher brothers had had impressive training at the Berlin Hochschule für Musik (Kurt with the cellist Emanuel Feuermann, Sven with the violinist Carl Flesch, the most prominent teachers of their time) and in Los Angeles found themselves in "a musical desert,"[34] relieved in 1934 by Klemperer's invitations to join the Philharmonic. Since the orchestra had a short season and paid only $60 a week, the brothers played in radio orchestras as well. It was frustrating to them that radio performances of serious chamber works, such as Beethoven's string quartets, were never entrusted to Californian musicians but were always broadcast from the East. Their willingness to work impressed Yates. Sven Reher remembered,

> Mr. Yates said: "Now, we don't have any money. . . . There's a war going on and we want to get this off the ground, and we want the cooperation of musicians if we can get it. . . . We're going to give you the chance to perform a contemporary work or something unusual." . . . It grew like topsy-turvy. It really gathered momentum and became one of the most important things in the United States as far as contemporary music is concerned.[35]

The Reher brothers made their mark in chamber music in Roof concerts, playing such challenging works as unaccompanied sonatas by Paul Hindemith and Zoltán Kodály, and world premieres of pieces written for them by Walter Piston, Ernst Krenek, Gerald Strang, Charles Wakefield Cadman, and Ingolf Dahl. Kurt Reher was intrigued by the opportunity to play the complete cello works of Beethoven in the Roof's Beethoven series and worked on them a full summer with Feuermann (who gave master classes in Los Angeles in 1940 and 1941). His performance (at Yates's suggestion) of the Kodály Sonata for Unaccompanied Cello was the product of a year's study and was such a sensation in 1942 it was reprogrammed repeatedly. The brothers' chamber music performances drew such excellent notices that they were soon made principals in the Philharmonic (in 1944 by Klemperer's successor, Alfred Wallenstein), much to Peter Yates's satisfaction and pride. Kurt Reher's first performance on the Roof was with Mullen in Claude Debussy's rarely played Sonata for Cello and Piano, in May of 1940.

In 1940 the clarinetist Kalman Bloch committed himself to the Roof group. The same year he recorded Schoenberg's *Pierrot lunaire,* with Schoenberg conducting. As Yates signed up these fine musicians, he realized that occasional programs featuring a central performer, rather than composer, would strengthen his company's loyalty. The performers were asked to be responsible for widening audience interest by personal ticket sales. Bloch was featured (on 24 November 1940) in a program of music for clarinet that included Mozart and Brahms chamber works, and the first performance in Los Angeles of Alban Berg's atonal Four Pieces, Op. 5 (1913), for clarinet and piano. (The Berg manuscript belonged to Schoenberg, Bloch says, and Leonard Stein, who played the piano, thinks theirs might have been the first performance in the country.)[36] Bloch also remembers Los Angeles as a musically provincial city at that time. It was important to him that the Roof offered the only opportunity to venture into what Yates called "tough" repertoire, for small audiences who listened attentively and critically.[37]

The second six months' season (October 1939–March 1940) started off with music by Paul Pisk, formerly the secretary of Schoenberg's Society for Private Performances in Vienna, along with that of his colleague on the music faculty of the University of Redlands, the violinist Rowland Leach. This was the first program of music by local composers. It was followed by a program of music of American composers published in the thirties by Henry Cowell's *New Music Quarterly.* Gerald Strang, editor of the *NMQ* since Cowell's incarceration, turned arrangements for this program over to George Tremblay, a California composer and piano improviser of genius. There was no printed program, but Yates reported in a letter to Houston (8 October 1939) that Maurice Zam would play piano pieces by Cowell, Dane Rudhyar, and Tremblay; Tremblay would improvise; the flutist Helen Little would play a sonata by Adolph Weiss for flute and viola, a Strang work for flute and piano, and a Wallingford Riegger flute solo; Weiss (Schoenberg's first American pupil) would speak; Radiana Pazmor and Frances Mullen would "tangle with [Elie Siegmeister's] 'The Strange Funeral at Braddock,' that ridiculous piece of nightmarish class-consciousness which sticks like chewing gum after a hearing," and works by Alejandro Caturla and Paul Bowles. On 18 November 1939 Yates reported (again to Houston) that the program was "an unqualified success." Four composers were in the audience for the first performance, Buhlig attended the second. The improvisations by Tremblay "were the best things we heard"; they were done first in a serious, then in a light manner. Frances Mullen Yates remembers that issues of the *New Music Quarterly* were displayed on the walls of the studio.[38]

Leonard Stein, a piano pupil of Buhlig's and teaching assistant in Schoenberg's classes at UCLA (in 1975 he was named the first director of the Schoenberg Institute in Los Angeles), and UCLA undergraduate Emil Danenberg (later president of Oberlin College) joined Mullen as pianists for an all-Schoenberg program, 28 and 30 January 1940. Schoenberg attended this program, which consisted of piano works Opp. 11, 19, 33a, and 25 and *The Book of the Hanging Gardens* sung by Radiana Pazmor. There was a full house, and Yates read his program notes, in which he called Schoenberg "the most consistently progressive intelligence in musical history."[39] Dika Newlin, at the time a fourteen-year-old pupil of Schoenberg's, wrote an ecstatic account of the event in her diary:

> Oh, I've had more joy today than has ever come my way before in my life! . . . It seemed as if everything went together to make this "Evening on the Roof" a perfect one. . . . The site is quite off the beaten track, six blocks east of where Santa Monica Boulevard cuts Sunset, and three blocks above Sunset on a steep hill. The "Roof" is simply an attic studio . . . with great windows stretching across the back of the room and affording the most glorious view of the city lights: an altogether delightful place. . . . The Great Man was there and as merry as a cricket; well he might be, for in my opinion his music was magnificently done. . . . In particular, Frances Mullen's performance of Opp. 19 and 25 was remarkable in its technique, emotional content, and understanding; and as for Radiana Pazmor, she is truly a marvel![40]

The story of Emil Danenberg's struggle against overwhelming odds to perform moved Yates deeply, for he felt the times called for the quality of personal heroism this young pianist exhibited. Danenberg, a teenaged piano prodigy crippled by arthritis, was hospitalized for a drastic operation in the months preceding the Beethoven series, which he was scheduled to open. After two months in a plaster cast ("solid from head-top to waist," wrote Yates to Houston) he emerged in a leather harness. He performed Roy Harris's Piano Sonata and Little Suite in this neck brace on 23 and 25 June 1940 but then suffered a heart attack just before the October opening of the Beethoven series. The day he was scheduled to play

> Emil discharged himself from the hospital more or less by walking out . . . and called to say he would play. Which he did, scarcely able to stand up, played better than he has ever played for us. I had to hoist him up the stairs for his last bow. There was a full house, as usual 50% masculine. . . . Nobody was bored; the Beethoven enthusiasts were transported; most of them will be back. We could scarcely have done better.[41]

Danenberg's performance of music by Roy Harris, on 23 and 25 June 1940, was part of a program devoted to Music by Americans. (In March there had been a program of Music by Germans, Bach, Handel, Mahler, and Reger—presumably to transcend wartime propaganda.) The American program, presented to "a miserably small audience,"[42] included Harris's Little Suite, also played by Danenberg; Aaron Copland's Piano Variations, played by Leonard Stein; piano sonatas by Charles Griffes and the Los Angeles twelve-tone composer Hugo Davise; and a song to a poem of Peyton Houston's ("Descent into Dusk") by Californian Lucille Crews Marsh, whom Paul Pisk described as "quite able as a composer."[43] This event, and the program of works of Americans published in the *New Music Quarterly,* set a tradition of attention to American, and particularly Californian, composers; music by Californian women composers was encouraged, on the very few occasions when such could be found.

The Beethoven series presented, in roughly chronological order, all the piano works with opus numbers, the fifteen violin and cello sonatas, and the song cycle *An die ferne Geliebte.* In his elaborate program notes, Yates dedicated this series "to the genuine amateur, the lover who is not afraid to be himself," who would labor to know the music and use his ears.[44] He read these notes aloud, to the irritation of the audience. His voice—nasal, harsh, and deliberate—was not inviting. He himself enjoyed writing the notes more than the spoken delivery of them and soon abandoned this practice, printing them for the audience on a hectograph. Klemperer, recovering from the brain operations that had forced his temporary withdrawal from conducting, attended the Beethoven series, sitting at Danenberg's elbow to hear his performance of Op. 111 (19 January 1942). Mullen, by now pregnant with her third child and often not well, played Beethoven's immense Sonata 29, Op. 106, the "Hammerklavier," but although prepared she postponed performing the *Diabelli* Variations, Op. 120.[45] When one wonders how she accomplished so much, it must be noted that she followed the practice of not memorizing but reading from the score.

At this time Yates initiated another policy he deeply believed in: a few accomplished amateur performers should play, along with such experienced professionals as Kurt Reher. In spite of frequent rough results, this continued to be Yates's policy—a bone of contention with some players, and often a point of criticism from reviewers—throughout his administration of these concerts. He was determined to live his philosophy that love—amateurism in the best sense—is essential to art. The effect was to encourage performers and audience alike to concentrate on the music itself, rather than merely on performance.

The congruence of plans for the third season of Sunday evening programs (November 1940 through May 1941), the fourteen-program Beethoven series (October 1940 through November 1941), and a three-program summer festival of music by Ives (August–September 1940) posed many difficulties of coordination for Yates. The violinist Orline Burrow decided to marry and left for Texas. ("She has the stuff . . . damn Romance!" exclaimed Yates, who noted that she was also beautiful.)[46] She was a well-regarded performer in Los Angeles, had taken on challenges in Bartók and Ives with aplomb, and was difficult to replace. Sol Babitz, a Philharmonic violinist under Klemperer and a close collaborator and friend of Stravinsky's, played the

Beethoven violin sonatas, Op. 30, Nos. 1–3, in the Beethoven series and took over from Burrow the Ives Fourth and Third Violin Sonatas, with the pianist Ingolf Dahl, for the Ives festival.

Dahl, a composer, pianist, and conductor, had fled in 1933 from the Nazis to Zurich, where he conducted and coached for the Zurich Opera, and fell in love with a young American student from Los Angeles. He followed her to Los Angeles in 1939, married her, and began his American career conducting, accompanying prominent soloists, composing, and arranging music for film and radio studios. (Gracie Fields and Victor Borge made use of his talents in their shows.) Through his friendship with Sol Babitz he became a close musical associate of Stravinsky. Dahl was appointed to the music faculty at the University of Southern California in 1945. His multiple gifts, broad musical interests, and lively personality established him as one of Los Angeles' most admired and loved musicians. Dahl attended the first Ives program on the Roof in 1939.[47] His collaboration with Babitz to edit Ives's Third Violin Sonata for publication was initiated during the Roof's Ives Festival of 1940. He had to cancel his participation in five piano trios for Yates's Beethoven series while he toured as accompanist with Edgar Bergen and his dummy, Charlie McCarthy,[48] but Dahl's serious and venturesome contributions soon became a solid cornerstone of Roof concerts.

The illness of Wesley Kuhnle brought in his place the émigré violinist Adolph Rebner, who had taught Hindemith and performed with Bartók, to play violin sonatas in an all-Bach program on the Roof, 28 and 30 July 1940, and with him Eda Bodanzky, who had toured as accompanist with Rebner in Europe. Eda Bodanzky (the younger sister of the late conductor and director of the Metropolitan Opera, Artur Bodanzky) continued to play in several Roof concerts, giving a particularly memorable exhibition of pianism in Debussy Études (26 January 1941), but Rebner held a post at that time in Cincinnati. (His son Edward later became a well-regarded Hollywood studio pianist, who played often on Roof programs.) Yates later called Adolph Rebner "the quintessence of Viennese style."[49] He admired this "little milkwhite-haired violinist . . . in his day a great musician in Europe, though never known here. . . . I have never known anyone who enjoyed playing as he did. And I have seldom seen an audience more moved than this was by the unostentatious presence of a simple man, who put all his thought into what he played. . . . I wish more of our uncertain, grasping American artists could discover his spirit."[50]

By 1940 Schoenberg, Klemperer, Ernst Toch, Erich Korngold, Max Reinhardt, Aldous Huxley, Christopher Isherwood, Heinrich Mann, Vicki Baum, Richard Lert, Stravinsky, Dahl, Ehlers, and André Previn had settled in Los Angeles, joining earlier arrivals Rudolf Schindler, Richard Neutra, Carl Laemmle, Jascha Heifetz, Galka Scheier, and Salka Viertel. Thomas Mann, Lion Feuchtwanger, Alma Mahler-Werfel, Franz Werfel, Bruno Walter, Bertolt Brecht, Hanns Eisler, Eric Zeisl, Mario Castelnuovo-Tedesco, Artur Rubinstein, Sergei Rachmaninoff, Vladimir Horowitz, and Joseph Szigeti were soon to arrive. Ernst Krenek and Gregor Piatigorsky came after the war. Along with these stars came thousands of others, who were to make their audiences. The consequent intellectual and artistic leavening of Los Angeles' primarily materialistic, consumer-oriented culture was a strong factor in the continuation and success of the daringly uncompromising Roof concerts.

While entranced with his new European contacts, Yates did not lose sight of the emerging cause of new American music. The three-program festival of music by Ives (August–September 1940) was planned from Yates's large collection of scores and provided an important exposure for the isolated composer, who responded to Yates's announcement of the programs with genuine enthusiasm in a letter of 2 October 1939: "I cannot adequately—but I want to try to tell you—how deeply I feel about all you have so generously done in behalf of my music. I realize fully the time, trouble, hard work as well as courage it has taken."[51] Ives offered to have instrumental parts made, discussed the possibility of a recording by Pazmor and Mullen of his songs for Columbia Records, and sent a $100 check to the Yateses (as was always Ives's custom, he asked that the gift be kept anonymous) to use as they pleased to further their interests or the series.[52] The Yateses decided the money would be best used to help "guarantee our artists a minimum of $15 per concert . . . the essential insurance for a series which has depended almost too much on loyalty."[53] Mullen played the *Concord* Sonata four times in the festival; the First and Third Violin Sonatas[54] and a group of songs were each heard twice. Mrs. Artie Mason Carter (founder of the Hollywood Bowl concerts), and others important in Los Angeles musical circles, attended. Nicolas Slonimsky, who had been the first to conduct Ives's works, and Gerald Strang, editor of the *New Music Quarterly*, were present. They had not until that time seen Ives's Third Violin Sonata and invited Babitz and Dahl to edit it for publication.[55] Several members of the festival audiences—"the most enthusiastic we have had"—wrote to Ives,[56] among them Slonimsky, who mentioned the great feeling and understanding in Pazmor's performance of the songs.[57]

At the time of the Ives festival, Yates was asked to write an article to accompany a photographic portrait of André Malraux for John Entenza's monthly magazine, *California Arts and Architecture* (in January 1944 its name became *Arts and Architecture*). Yates agreed to discuss Malraux's writings—"a vital record of the hopes by which men live"—if in return he could write an article on the personal heroism of America's most original and neglected composer. His article on Charles Ives appeared in the November 1940 issue. In it, Yates claimed, "This is our music, and when we find it out we will insist on hearing more and more of it."[58] Harmony Ives soon responded to this article, "Mr. Ives says that "were it 40 years ago he would ride a bronco over the Rockies & shake your hand." She also contributed minor corrections, and one major objection, as far as the Iveses were concerned:

> There was one thing in the article that somewhat depressed us both for a while—when you said that "the chief interest . . . was in making money." Whoever told you that was mis-informed or very unfair. Never was Mr. Ives' chief interest that. Some of his business associates often said that he wasn't interested enough in that side of business. His chief interest has always been music.[59]

More fully quoted, Yates's article had actually said, "The chief interest *of New York City during the early 1900s* was in making money. Ives, not to be outdone by his environment, not only composed great music in defiance of his environment but made money too."[60] The Iveses took this amiss through a nephew's inaccurate report but, after hearing from Yates, two weeks later sent another letter with abject apologies for raising Yates's temperature.[61]

From this time until he left California in 1968, Peter Yates wrote monthly columns on music in *Arts and Architecture.* His erudite program notes for Evenings on the Roof were condensed for many of these articles and spread awareness of the concerts as far as Europe and New Zealand. His writing gradually encompassed broader issues in music and the arts and was widely respected in intellectual and artistic circles, for he took his readers into musical and artistic adventures they might not otherwise encounter.

His second article (December 1940) was on Arnold Schoenberg. His discussions with Schoenberg brought about the performance on the Roof of the first two movements of the composer's newly published Violin Concerto, Op. 36 (1934–1936), which, Schoenberg claimed, Jascha Heifetz had recently told him was unplayable. (Heifetz actually wrote Schoenberg that he could not play the work, which, Yates commented, "was at least more polite than saying it was unplayable." Schoenberg, both disconsolate and proud, said, "[If] Heifetz can't play it, nobody can play it.")[62] In his search to replace Orline Burrow, Yates found Helen Swaby, who was studying with a member of the Philharmonic and had recently placed second in a young musicians' audition at the Hollywood Bowl. Unable to prevail upon other violinists to take up the task refused by Heifetz, with characteristic bravado he persuaded Helen Swaby to tackle the concerto, and ever-heroic Frances Mullen took on the orchestral part. At a coaching session at his home in Brentwood, Schoenberg approved of their playing and was so pleased to hear his work at last that he included a short excerpt of their performance on an NBC broadcast of his music.[63] Schoenberg wrote in Helen Swaby's violin part on 10 February 1940, "Dear Miss Swaby, Now I heard this for the first time and I am satisfied, about you and the composition too."[64]

The all-Schoenberg concert on 25 May 1941, which included the movements of the Violin Concerto, was the last of the regular concerts (excluding the continuing Beethoven series) to actually take place "on the Roof." Helen Swaby Rice remembers that a small audience of about fifteen to twenty attended, sitting informally about the room, some on the floor, some on a daybed in the corner. What was remarkable was the degree of concentration in their listening. She remembered that quality about Peter Yates himself, as well: "He was a quiet man, extremely interested in music."[65]

The 1941 Monday evening Beethoven series was regularly bringing in forty to fifty people. But attendance for the regular season's Sunday evening programs was uneven and reached a low point with Sven Reher's April 1941 all-viola program. Reher had not worked as hard at selling tickets as he had at preparing the music, and only eight attended. The Yateses were discovering some enduring facts about concert giving: musicians preferred practicing to production duties; Sunday night was not a good night for drawing audiences; in addition, lack of organized publicity, difficult access and parking on the steep Micheltorena Street hill, and the informality of Yates's ideas all contributed to a situation in which the concerts could not survive without higher income from admissions. "The ruddy flame of friendly art needs whitening in the impersonal furnace," Yates wrote Houston.[66] Newspaper critics were attending the programs out of curiosity, occasionally announcing coming concerts, but not yet reviewing them regularly. Alfred Price Quinn, music critic of the *B'nai B'rith Messenger,* turned in the first review, of a Monday evening Beethoven program that included a "masterful" performance by Kurt Reher in combination with Emil Danenberg's "strong pianistic gifts" in the Beethoven Cello Sonatas, Op. 102, Nos. 1 and 2, and the Piano Sonata, Op. 101.[67] In a personal crusade for the performance of more "Native American" composers' works, Isabel Morse Jones, music critic of the *Los Angeles Times,* noted Mullen's performances of Ives's *Concord* Sonata; she felt that the influx of famous European composers at this time threatened the nascent movement in American music.[68] (In 1933 Yates had sneered that Isabel Morse Jones was a "second-rate violin teacher, turned critic for a living."[69] He came to respect her more than many of her male colleagues in the press.)

From the time of the first all-Schoenberg program (28 January

1940) Yates began suffering from intermittent attacks of what he called shingles: attacks of high fever, accompanied by a rash that swelled his face, closing an eye. By the summer of 1940 he described to Houston "something more resembling a nervous breakdown through general anxiety exhaustion [*sic*] from handling too many projects than I like to consider or have made public."[70] (The Ives festival was in full swing; Yates had printed up announcements of the following year's regular and Beethoven series, pushed himself to write the "hurry-up" article on Malraux, and was hoping for a vacation. His illnesses often erupted just at the moment when he could at last afford to relax after strenuous overexertion.) Severe and prolonged bouts with exhaustion alarmed and kept him from office work. By the spring of 1941 he was ill enough to reassess his situation. Ever contrary, he decided to risk expanding, rather than withdrawing, the concerts but hoped to inspire the musicians to take on more responsibility. He described to Houston

> the simple and daring plan of presenting at the Assistance League Playhouse [in Hollywood], the best chamber music hall here (370 seats), a series of 12 bimonthly programs, at $3 the series. . . . I have . . . organized the series, composed the programs. . . . The enthusiasm, as you may imagine, has done the rest. From this point on, though it will consult with me, the group will run itself. . . . I hope to sell the series twice, and perhaps part of it again in Long Beach. This would pay the performers about $100 each.[71]

When forced to the wall, Yates's policy was to expand—rather than withdraw—and to legitimize the concerts.

FOURTH SEASON: 1942

At the beginning of the 1942 season there was a solid nucleus of thirteen enthusiastic members in the musicians' cooperative. Yates advertised the concert series as "entirely cooperative, organized and run by the performers themselves—no managers or impresarios. We have faith that there is a larger public for our music. SUPPORT LOS ANGELES CONCERTS ORGANIZED AND PLAYED BY LOS ANGELES MUSICIANS."[72] David Frisina, a Philharmonic violinist (in 1943 he became concertmaster of the orchestra under Alfred Wallenstein), joined the group and formed a strong string trio with the Reher brothers.

Yates galvanized the performers and supporters into action for the move to a public auditorium and garnered 120 subscriptions before the opening at the Assistance League Playhouse (1367 North St. Andrews Place, just west of Western Avenue, between Sunset and Fountain, a neighborhood now cut by the Hollywood Freeway). The playhouse could seat around 350 people. The rent was not high. Concerts now took place Monday evenings, rather than Sunday. The Yateses began printing tickets on their own printing set (a gift from Peyton Houston); the Baldwin piano company offered a free piano. Programs for the season offered a continuation of the Beethoven series with trios and other chamber works. These were mixed with pieces by Purcell and Brahms, and more contemporary seasonings of Kodály, Villa-Lobos, Creston, Barber, Stravinsky, Chávez, Berg, Schoenberg, Hindemith, and Ives. A repertoire policy of two-thirds music up to 1900 and one-third music since 1900 was now established and roughly adhered to until the fifties.

Three music critics reviewed the first concert, 5 January 1942, which was attended by an audience of 150 and included works by Purcell, Brahms, Haydn, and Kodály. The *Times* mentioned the "unusual audience more interested in music than performers."[73] The *Daily News* commented, "This is the kind of music undertaking, without guarantee, for the love of art . . . carried out artistically, which lifts the cultural level of any community."[74] Yates wrote in enthusiasm to Houston about the sudden emergence of Kurt Reher's unassuming genius and absorption in Kodály's Sonata for Unaccompanied Cello, the thirty minutes of which, he boasted, Piatigorsky and Feuermann had not yet played.[75]

In the next concert, 19 January, Ingolf Dahl played Stravinsky's *Piano-Rag-Music* and Heitor Villa-Lobos's *Choros for Piano.* A group of Philharmonic players (with Frisina, the Rehers, and Kalman Bloch) played the Beethoven Septet, Op. 20, and "the audience went nuts.

. . . To the audience it was fresh as new-laid eggs. . . . I think the series is made," Yates wrote in relief, adding that at that point the season seemed paid for by subscriptions.[76] (Among his subscribers in this period were the composer Charles Wakefield Cadman, the conductor Richard Lert, and the architect Richard Neutra.)[77]

Lawrence Morton, who described himself as having "floundered musically [in the 1930s] in the mires of church and radio music and in teaching piano and organ to the untalented," yet having begun a lifelong study of contemporary music, had moved to Los Angeles from New York in 1939, and from January 1940 until February 1949 was concert critic for *Script,* a Beverly Hills biweekly magazine modeled after *The New Yorker.*[78] Although he described the opening program of the Roof season as "better in prospect than in actuality," he found "complete and unmitigated joy" in the Beethoven septet but "could not be won over" by Stravinsky's *Piano-Rag-Music,* which failed "to communicate anything to me except the colossal job of learning and playing it."[79] (This comment is interesting in view of Morton's later relationship to Stravinsky's music; in 1941 he had met but not yet become an intimate of the composer.) He acknowledged the sophistication and critical attention of the audience and soon became a regular reviewer of these concerts, often "acid" (his own adjective) in his comments. But he was hooked, for, as he later admitted, the concerts "were teaching me a great deal about repertoire that I didn't know."[80]

As the risks Yates and Mullen took were rewarded with acceptance, Yates's hope of building a tradition of open-mindedness among performers and audience alike began to pay off. "No large accomplishment is accomplished by small daring," he had written Houston on 23 June 1939. He continued to study thoroughly each composer he considered programming, reading through works at the keyboard as well as investigating scholars' insights before persuading players to take up new pieces. In an expansive mood he negotiated the joint presentation of a five-concert series of Bach's keyboard works with the Bach Festival of the First Congregational Church (on Commonwealth Avenue near Sixth Street) in Los Angeles. Like the Beethoven series, the fall 1942 Bach programs "should provide a safe audience," he conjectured.[81] The programs also helped publicize the monthly Evenings on the Roof.

While the reputation of the concerts was growing, Yates's hope of achieving a truly self-motivated cooperative of musicians in Los Angeles was far from realization. By the summer of 1942, membership in the local musicians' union included "hundreds of the most influential and highest paid musicians in the country,"[82] and in the growing competition to maintain their status in film and radio work, performers often required substitutions for their Roof appearances. They also continued to rely on Yates's ideas and leadership in programming and administration: "I have to initiate, urge, drive policy, design publicity, meet innumerable quibbles, try to persuade the performers they can sell 380 subscriptions—160 will meet maximum expenses, the rest is their profit. . . . They want to know why I do it? what do I get out of it?"[83]

He prided himself on almost never losing his temper, but he was worn by strain and continued to suffer nervous exhaustion and nagging illness. He spent much time and energy cajoling players into tackling works they would not approach on their own. It puzzled him that such highly gifted musicians could be limited in their musical understanding and that this never showed when they played.[84] He discovered that instrumentalists "fear even when they do not hate Bartók";[85] that performers were afraid of Bach; and that program planning sessions, as musician-members sought the spotlight, were often so complex and time-consuming that he was left exhausted and ready to resort to dictatorial methods.[86]

In this period Yates also attempted to find publishers for his poetry and children's stories but received only rejection slips. His fevers, rashes, and swellings were difficult for doctors to diagnose. He read *The Problem of Anxiety* by Freud, vowing skepticism about psychoanalysis and pondering "the presence of God," as he lay severely ill.[87] By this time his stance on pacifism was clear: deep personal conviction made him opposed to war, but this view was not the result of any religious affiliation, and he therefore did not claim exemption from war duty as a conscientious objector.[88] The war, which had seemed distant from Los Angeles while it was waged in Europe, came shockingly close on Sunday, 7 December 1941. Frances Mullen Yates remembers vividly the fear she felt as she sat with their third child, six-week-old John, in the sun on the steps outside the roof studio and heard on the radio that the Japanese had bombed Pearl Harbor.[89] During the same period, after a strange overflight of sixty bombers her husband wrote, "Everybody except Los Angeles blacked out. They seem to have decided that Los Angeles lighted is more confusing than Los Angeles dark. I don't doubt it. Los Angeles under any circumstances is confusing."[90]

By early 1942 Los Angeles was undergoing the greatest industrial boom in its history, in response to President Franklin D. Roosevelt's call for an "arsenal of democracy." Yates's office amalgamated with all other, often feuding, departments of the California Employment Service and became the United States Employment Service, the largest employment office in the world, working on an emergency basis. The aircraft industries abandoned their own employment offices and moved them into the combined service, bringing thousands more applicants. (Aircraft employment alone rose from 1,000 in 1933 to 280,000 in 1943.)[91] Yates's job became a battle for order over human mobs. He now defined heroism as "courtesy under pressure," for he was put on a forty-four-hour workweek and, having attempted to enhance the efficiency of his department, was again facing conflict with an incompetent manager.[92] Yates's employment situation was further aggravated by his awareness that, in spite of wartime need, and in spite of the 1941 Fair Employment Practices Act, "Candidly, between ourselves, we don't hire negroes, no, not Jews. We have many ways to drop them. . . . We need all the men we can get who can do the work, but we won't hire Jews."[93] Because he fought discrimination, Yates was passed over for promotion time and again. In disillusionment, he wondered to himself if "the day of the individual may be passing."[94] Yet the concerts always drew him back to contemplation of higher things, and the fine performances of thought-provoking music he had set in motion gave him deepest satisfaction.

In a March 1942 review of a program of American composers (Roy Harris, Paul Creston, Samuel Barber) Isabel Morse Jones of the *Times* announced, "Evenings on the Roof programs . . . are becoming events of importance in community music life."[95] On the other hand, reviewing the same program, Lawrence Morton reported unenthusiastically in *Script,*

> the dubious pleasure of listening to a program that was uniformly interesting from beginning to end and yet included not one composition of real merit; that is to say, all the music was new to me, and all of it had been written by some of the best second- and third-rate composers in the business. Without doubt the music got better performances than it deserved, with Frances Mullen and Kurt Reher contributing their usual first-rate artistry.[96]

Yates complained, "When reviewers get down to cases they simply can't find the good words to say for our more unaccustomed music. It baffles them; they fight it. Yet they do not suggest in any way that we should do without it."[97]

Only two weeks later (28 March 1942) Lawrence Morton's tone changed. The draft was playing havoc with local chamber ensembles and orchestras. Faced with a prospective drastic curtailment of musical activity in southern California, he now focused on the true community spirit growing around the Roof concerts:

> If you still doubt the morale-building potentialities of music, you should have heard David Frisina and the brothers Reher play the first of the [string] trios of Beethoven's Opus 9. Whatever it is that happens to an audience when good music is beautifully played, it happened here. I do not say that this audience would have been able to stand up to a Panzer division without fear after the performance, but I am sure that it was capable of some unselfish, if not heroic, action.[98]

In an all-Ives program (25 May 1942), Mullen repeated the *Concord* Sonata. Morton, hearing its entirety for the first time, found it "confusing" but glimpsed Ives's sincerity and nobility of spirit.[99] Two weeks later Mullen performed the *Diabelli* Variations, Op. 120, of Beethoven, and Brahms's Piano Trio, Op. 101, with Frisina and Kurt

Reher. It was a brilliant end to the season, Morton wrote, in a review that credited the Roof concerts with "weight and toughness" of repertoire, "[These concerts presented] the most significant and varied repertoire of chamber music that this community is ever likely to have the opportunity of hearing in any one season. . . . [The Roof group is] consistently working in this community for serious and genuine musical advancement." Of Frances Mullen's *Diabelli* (a work that, to the Yateses' knowledge, had never before been performed in Los Angeles), Morton wrote:

> However impressive her skill may be—and she has shown herself capable of great virtuosity—it is in her readings of large and profound works that she discloses the earnestness and sincerity of her approach to music. . . . The demands [of the *Diabelli* Variations] upon the performer's understanding are tremendous. . . . Miss Mullen has found in this music "how deep within the liturgies lie hid the mysteries," and in many of the variations, particularly the slow ones, she disclosed some terrible and awful beauties. Her performance was one of rare penetration and discernment.[100]

Between January 1941 and June 1942 Mullen performed Beethoven's "Hammerklavier" Sonata, the *Diabelli* Variations, Ives's *Concord* Sonata (all taxing works of great length), two movements of Schoenberg's Violin Concerto, his Suite for Piano, Op. 25, much of Bartók's new *Mikrokosmos,* the Busoni Sonatina for Piano No. 1, Ives's complex songs, and chamber works of Mozart and Brahms. She took on more than her usual share of the administrative work of the concerts for six months during her husband's 1941 illness and bore their third son. (Between May 1942 and May 1943, she prepared and played thirty-five separate works, Yates noted in his correspondence with Houston.)[101] The family had the roof studio, the concerts, but still not enough money for a car, and after Pearl Harbor no markets made grocery deliveries. Mullen later remembered, "Friends had to help with food and so on when it came time for me to perform. . . . We didn't have any help. . . . It was pretty gruelling at times, . . . [but] Peter was the knock on the door for me for all kinds of things. . . .

Practically everything I played came from him. . . . I did it all for Peter."[102] A friend remembered her 1942 performance of the "Hammerklavier" Sonata while pregnant with her third child: she was dressed very simply, with a ribbon in her hair, smiling, and chewing gum to keep from being nauseated. "She looked adorable, and played like an inspired and ferocious demon."[103]

The first of a distinguished list of visiting performers, Paul Wittgenstein, the Viennese pianist who had lost his right arm in World War I and subsequently commissioned concertos for the left hand alone from Prokofiev and Ravel, asked to play a special program in the Roof studio. The proceeds for his 8 July 1942 recital of piano compositions for the left hand were intended to establish "the nucleus of a working fund for further Evenings on the Roof," but he could not draw an audience. Yates remarked about this occasion, "Los Angeles was still nearly as much cut off from the musical world . . . as it had been forty years before, when Busoni toured and seemed to think that playing in Los Angeles was the continental low spot of his experience."[104] Other celebrity guests who subsequently performed for Evenings on the Roof were the composers Ernst Krenek (13 October 1947), Henry Cowell (10 November 1947), John Cage, in an early performance of his Sonatas and Interludes for Prepared Piano (23 February 1948), Aaron Copland (5 April 1948); the pianist Soulima Stravinsky (27 September 1948); the violinist Joseph Szigeti, in a benefit concert for the Roof (7 January 1950); the conductor Izler Solomon (6 March 1950); the cellist Joseph Schuster, who played two benefit recitals for the Roof (15 and 22 January 1951); and the early music specialist Suzanne Bloch (10 March 1952).

FIFTH SEASON: 1943

In January of 1943, as the fifth season got under way, Yates's Employment Service office duty was increased to forty-eight hours a week, and his holidays and vacations were curtailed. He was additionally burdened with work on the War Manpower Commission (which entitled him, after a presidential directive of 1944, to draft deferment). At the outset of the war, seeking a way to vent his anger with public policy, Yates had begun terracing his steep backyard with his own hands. He continued through the war years to assemble great boulders for the support and articulation of garden beds, working out in physical labor the negative aspects of his life; "laying," as he wrote in a poem, "for no purpose a pyramid to myself that none will admire."[105] His illnesses seemed compounded by his discouragement about a literary career.

A group of performers and their spouses, perhaps not aware of all Yates's difficulties yet cognizant of the heavy work involved with maintaining the concert series, took over and enlarged the mailing tasks. The critic Alfred Price Quinn announced, at the opening of the season, "Evenings on the Roof concerts . . . have now become the most widely discussed private musical enterprise in the city."[106] In spite of an extremely rainy winter, which cut some audiences to the most devoted, attendance increased as word got around that Los Angeles was producing something done nowhere else. Three hundred fifty people attended the opening concert of the second season at the Assistance League Playhouse.[107] Yates wrote in *Arts and Architecture* of the effect of these audiences upon the performers: "The enthusiasm they brought to the concerts, expectant and intense, stimulated performances of the sort jaded professionals occasionally dream of."[108]

Works of Mozart appeared on almost every program of the 1943 season. (Isabel Morse Jones, in the *Times,* mentioned "a brilliantly performed program of Mozart rarities," such as the Clarinet Quintet, K. 581, and the Duo in B-flat for violin and viola, K. 424.)[109] Schubert and Brahms, Bartók, Busoni, and Stravinsky appeared prominently in the repertoire. An ensemble of Roof musicians presented a concert for Grace Mullen's Redlands Community Music Association in the Redlands Bowl. At the end of the season, the second five-program Bach series at the First Congregational Church (again concentrating on keyboard literature, with a few instrumental works) opened to a packed hall, with many standing, and closed "a big success." Although no admission was charged, and donations were asked instead, the performers each received four dollars for a performance—twice the earnings from the first Bach series.[110] For the regular programs the performers received ten dollars. They were clearly joining the cooperative and playing for other reasons than money.

Word passed around amongst performers dedicated to exploration in their art that these concerts were the place to grow musically. More Philharmonic players joined the group, among them the violist Abraham Weiss, the cellist Joseph Di Tullio, and the bassoonist Frederick Moritz. The Philharmonic flutist Leonard Posella, clarinetist Antonio Raimundi, hornist Fred Fox, and bassist Richard Kelly were occasional participants.

Yates's plan to build a fine string quartet was put in motion when a stunningly gifted pair of Curtis School of Music graduates, Eudice Shapiro, violinist, and Virginia Majewski, violist, arrived to seek their fortunes in Hollywood. They immediately became the first female principal players in studio orchestras[111] and began playing for the Roof concerts. By March 1943, when the draft had taken many male players, Eudice Shapiro found herself concertmaster of both the Paramount and RKO studio orchestras simultaneously, the only woman to hold such a position in Hollywood. Her husband, the cellist Victor Gottlieb—a youthful veteran of the Philadelphia Orchestra under Stokowski, five years with the Coolidge Quartet, and a year with the Pro Arte Quartet—was stationed with the Army's Radio Production Unit at Santa Ana[112] and also began playing in Roof concerts with the new string quartet: Shapiro, Majewski, and Alexander Murray as second violinist. (At this time the quartet had no name; in 1945 it called itself the "American Quartet"; then changed in the fall of 1946 to the "American Art Quartet.") They received such acclaim that Yates added two extra postseason string programs for them in June 1943. The complex schedules of these players caused Yates nerve-wracking difficulties, and even the cancellation of one of the quartet's concerts (when Eudice Shapiro was called to play a Russian Relief program organized by Paramount music chief Boris Morros, who had hired Stokowski to conduct). Players could be called for work at the studios at any time when a film producer was in a rush and were often required to rehearse or record twenty hours at a stretch, as overtime was not yet controlled by the musicians' union.[113] Gradually individual players worked out clear arrangements with their studio contractors, so that they would not have to give up the chamber music performances at Roof concerts that made their reputations in the city.[114]

The same season, the Canadian pianist Shibley Boyes (whom Buhlig called "a genius lost in accompanying")[115] joined the group and became, for nine years, one of its most important members. She was happy to abandon a promising solo career for the challenge of accompanying and learned much of the traditional chamber music literature for the Roof concerts, which in turn formed the springboard to her thirty-two-year career as staff pianist to the Los Angeles Philharmonic.[116] She appeared at two of the 1943 Roof concerts with the California contralto Eula Beal, in a group of Ives songs and in Gustav Mahler's *Kindertotenlieder.*[117] (Beal performed this work and *Das Lied von der Erde* with the Philharmonic under Bruno Walter.) In 1945 and 1946 Beal and Boyes presented songs and cycles by Rachmaninoff, Sibelius, Mahler, Wolf, and Vaughan Williams. Boyes accompanied other Roof singers in Schoenberg, Bartók, Brahms, Mahler, Loeffler, Ravel, and Copland cycles and contributed her own English translations to her performances of Franz Schubert's *Winterreise* and *Die schöne Müllerin.* She took on instrumental repertoire from Bach to Ives and Hindemith with equal success. In the late 1940s she and Ingolf Dahl played a number of four-hand piano works together, and she was chosen to accompany the visiting celebrity guest cellist Joseph Schuster in his two Beethoven recitals benefiting the Roof in 1951.

A new piano trio, formed by Philharmonic musicians Louis Pressman, violin, Joseph Di Tullio, cello, with Maxine Furman, piano (it was called the Philharmonic Trio), played trios by Mozart, Schubert, Ravel, Reger, and Roy Harris. With changes in violin personnel, this group contributed importantly to Roof concerts for years, exploring significant trio repertoire and expanding for piano quartets.

Frances Mullen repeated her performance of the *Diabelli* Variations and, with other works, played Ives's Fourth Sonata for Violin and Piano with Eudice Shapiro. In addition she performed the rarely heard Sixth Suite by François Couperin, using Wesley Kuhnle's theories of ornamental style. The field of early performance practice had caught Peter Yates's interest. He himself spent hours at the keyboard working out ornamentation. He ordered pre-Baroque English keyboard music from England and became deeply absorbed in it. He spent much time discussing the subject with Wesley Kuhnle, who was advancing his studies in performance practice by building a harpsichord, clavichord, and virginal and performing on these. Kuhnle became immersed in studies of tuning and later made a series of recordings on the history of tuning. Yates's interest in Kuhnle's work was the root of the Roof's "old music" activities, which he considered as important as the contemporary music activities.[118]

Stravinsky's works began to appear more regularly on Roof programs, owing to the efforts of Sol Babitz and Ingolf Dahl, who performed his Violin Concerto (in piano reduction) in January 1943 and returned in March with his Divertimento inspired by Tchaikovsky (a transcription for violin and piano by Samuel Dushkin and Stravinsky from *Le Baiser de la fée*) and Babitz's arrangement for violin and piano of the *Circus Polka for a Young Elephant.* From this time on, Stravinsky's music figured more and more importantly in Evenings on the Roof, becoming a pillar of the concerts in the fifties. Stravinsky's relative good fortune in supporting himself in the United States through conducting had postponed Yates's inclusion of his works on early Roof programs, for he felt other composers were more undeservedly neglected and needed to be heard. Soon after meeting Stravinsky, however, he became very fond of him, and proud of the role the concerts played in Stravinsky's creative life.

The composer Lou Harrison came to Peter Yates's attention in 1943. At that time Harrison was studying with Schoenberg and supporting himself as an accompanist at Lester Horton's Dance Studio. The dancers noticed that Harrison could improvise piano accompaniments—even fugues—for dance classes while reading a book propped on the piano.[119] Henry Cowell had introduced Lou Harrison to Charles Ives's music, and it was Harrison's interest that had brought much of Ives's music to the West Coast, including chamber music that found its way (through Cowell and Gerald Strang) to the Roof's library. Harrison wanted to hear Frances Mullen play Schoenberg's Suite for Piano, Op. 25, and Ives's *Concord* Sonata, along with the Couperin she was performing at the Roof concerts. She complied, Yates reported, and

> Inspired he tore off, as is his manner of composing, a huge twelve-tone piano suite. . . . This massive . . . tribute he laid at Frances's feet. It certainly does not show weakness. . . . After seeing the Suite Schoenberg advised him to give up any more studying and get to work. At a quiet evening recently I met Copland and told him about Harrison. . . . Lou is going to New York this month, armed now with introductions from Copland.[120]

By now the Los Angeles music critics were intensely interested in the musical life provided by Evenings on the Roof. Subscriptions and single ticket sales were doubled from the preceding season, and seasons were ending financially in the black.[121] The exigencies of war, the draft, and the studios—while making the enterprise almost impossible administratively—established the concerts artistically. In such a period of stress music had a rare ability to meet the needs of the spirit, and audiences and performers all responded. Peter Yates enjoyed watching the performers backstage "fairly hang out the wings to watch as well as listen." But at the end of the season he again found himself "in the dark valley of exhaustion."[122]

SIXTH SEASON: 1944

For Christmas Yates's parents gave him, in a belated but welcome vote of confidence, an official letterhead for Evenings on the Roof. The year of 1944 began with another change of venue, to a larger studio owned by radio station KFWB in a former soundstage on Warner Brothers' lot south of Sunset (only a few blocks west of the Assistance League Playhouse, but now on the other side of a freeway). Yates later remembered this sixth season as the beginning of "the glamorous period of the Roof."[123] Richard Buhlig agreed to come out of performing retirement to play Beethoven's thirty-two piano sonatas in a special six-recital series coinciding with the 1944 season.

As far as anyone then knew this was the first time Beethoven's sonatas had been presented in their entirety by one player in Los Angeles.[124] Buhlig's first recital was a near sellout; although weakened by exhaustion toward the end of his eight recitals, Buhlig sustained an emotional impact throughout. Klemperer attended with his Beethoven scores. "I have never seen an audience more moved," Yates wrote. "It is because Buhlig's performance is so packed full of all Beethoven was and is and must mean when truly rediscovered and imagined that I set it quite apart from all other performing and Beethoven playing."[125] While agreeing that these were very important concerts, Lawrence Morton caviled at wrong notes caused by Buhlig's too "demonic" attitude toward the early sonatas, and Buhlig shook his finger at Morton for his impertinence.[126]

Although the price of tickets to the regular series jumped in the subscription rate from twenty-five cents to forty-five cents (and nonsubscription tickets from fifty cents to $1.10), the first regular program in the KFWB studio was oversold. (This program, held 24 January 1944, included string quartets by Schubert and Brahms, a piano sonata by Mozart, and premieres of works of the California composers Charles Wakefield Cadman and Lou Harrison.) Yates rented two neighboring sound studios and had the program repeated. The first half began in Studio 4 while the post-intermission half began in Studio 3. The string quartet (now with Alfred Lustgarten as second violin) performed on both halves and had to scuttle back and forth to play each work twice—this after three of the members had spent a long day recording for the studios. "I tell with pride that their last performance was the best. . . . They can compete with any quartet in existence," Yates crowed to Houston.[127]

Brahms's chamber music was a focus of the season's programs. His trios, quartets, quintets, and Sextet (Op. 18) were taken up by the new quartet and piano trio, along with his *Zigeunerlieder* (performed by Beal and Boyes), Songs for Contralto, Viola, and Piano, Op. 91 (by Beal, Abraham Weiss, and Dahl), a Sonata for Cello and Piano, Op. 38 (by Kurt Reher and Danenberg), and a Sonata for Violin and Piano, Op. 78 (by Frisina and Furman). The Santa Ana Air Base String Quartet, of which Gottlieb was a member,[128] assisted in the

Brahms Sextet. By now the quality and numbers of members of the Roof's cooperative group had grown enough to perform quintets regularly, and these chamber groups began to be invited to play in other locations.

Mullen played works of Villa-Lobos, Mozart, Haydn, Falla, Piston, Byrd, the first West Coast performance of Carl Ruggles's *Evocations* ("skilled and thoughtful pianism," wrote Morton in *Script*),[129] and Lou Harrison's new *Gigue and Musette,* along with the twelve-tone Suite for Piano that he had composed for her. Yates felt "the crowd was rather at a loss" about the latter work.[130] Morton wrote that Harrison's Six Sonatas for piano, played earlier in the season by Mullen, "gave a pretty good indication of how today's composers are creating the spiritual climate of their time."[131]

For the final program of the season the Viennese harpsichordist Alice Ehlers played a distinguished half-program of works for her instrument with viola d'amore and viola da gamba (played by Virginia Majewski and Rebecca Haight Hathaway), ending with J. S. Bach's *Capriccio on the Departure of His Most Beloved Brother.* A pupil of Landowska and of Curt Sachs, Ehlers had recorded and performed widely as an early music specialist in Europe. Concert tours brought her to the United States, and, fleeing Hitler's regime, she and one of her daughters settled in Los Angeles in 1938. In 1941 she was offered a position on the rapidly expanding artist faculty of the University of Southern California (USC) School of Music, where she gave classes in eighteenth-century performance practice and attracted outstanding student musicians to the Alice Ehlers Baroque Ensemble.

In his first visit to Evenings on the Roof, Stravinsky came to hear his friend Sol Babitz play a Mozart violin sonata with Shibley Boyes on 6 March 1944. Wesley Kuhnle played works of Gibbons, Byrd, and Purcell, as well as a Haydn sonata on the same program, and won high praise from the composer, who was to make many subsequent visits to the concerts.[132]

Alfred Wallenstein had become conductor of the Los Angeles Philharmonic in the fall of 1943 and appointed the cellist Kurt Reher and the violinist David Frisina first chair and concertmaster, respectively. The conductor was pleased so many of the Philharmonic players were performing in these chamber concerts, which he attended and commended for their "tremendous contribution to the musical life of Los Angeles."[133] The critic Alfred Price Quinn noted "a vast change in the size of the audiences" since the first days in the Roof studio.[134] Yates summed up the success of the concerts to Peyton Houston as "a tribute to my naiveté. Against the entire tradition of concert giving I have presumed that people who really like good music really want to hear good music when good musicians play it, similarly that good musicians like to play good music when people who like good music come to hear it. This simple premise is now filling the house."[135] The season, in which he produced twenty concerts (with a twenty-first at the Los Angeles Central Library), was "damnably exhausting." At the end of it Yates collapsed again with high fever, toxic poisoning, a head-to-foot rash—and an inability to stop work on plans for the next season, which excited him more than ever.[136]

SEVENTH SEASON: 1944–1945

"I may be, as I have always believed, one of humanity's notable cowards, but I'm stubborn," Yates wrote to Houston, as he planned the seventh season, which now shifted to an October–June schedule, and expanded still further to twenty-six concerts.[137] He felt his audience was impressive, and to challenge it he was eager to celebrate both Charles Ives's and Arnold Schoenberg's seventieth birthdays, and, in their honor, to include in the season's programs many other twentieth-century composers. Buhlig was to appear again, in four piano recitals: two programs of works by Schubert, and two of Buhlig's two-piano arrangement of Bach's *Art of Fugue,* with Wesley Kuhnle assisting. Kuhnle offered his arrangement for two pianos of Bach's complete *Goldberg* Variations, performed with Frances Mullen. Alice Ehlers disapproved of this version and insisted on playing the same work in the original version for two-manual harpsichord, "Since she had at last found an audience which deserved to hear it," Yates commented.[138] Morton noted that Ehlers's performance "was the occasion for the Roof's largest audience of the season and for a demonstration of approval and gratitude which would have shocked the gentlemen who run the successful concert agencies from their elaborate offices in [Manhattan's] Radio City."[139] (Perhaps this comment refers to the fact that Alice Ehlers had suffered a shocking rejection by these managers herself.)

Eudice Shapiro, violin, and Kurt Reher and Victor Gottlieb, cello—each with Shibley Boyes—played Beethoven's fifteen sonatas for violin or cello with piano. Dowland, whose Elizabethan songs and lute pieces (arranged for keyboard by Peter Warlock) had already been performed sparsely in previous concerts, was given greater prominence by soprano Alice Mock with Shibley Boyes and Frances Mullen. (Alice Mock, born in Oakland, California, was a coloratura soprano who sang in opera and films. Yates described her voice as having a "thin, clear, instrumental timbre unusually well-adapted to 17th- and 18th-century music.")[140] Kuhnle played frequently, in more works of Bach and other Baroque composers.

Frances Mullen gave her tenth performance of Ives's *Concord* Sonata in an all-Ives program in celebration of his seventieth birthday. Babitz and Dahl played their new edition—deciphered from Ives's manuscript—of the Third Sonata for Violin and Piano, and "The Revival" and "In the Barn" from the second sonata. Lawrence Morton noted about the latter,

> As with so much of Ives's music, [these two movements] were startling in their prophecy of things to come. They are pieces which Aaron Copland could not possibly have known, according to Mr. Dahl who is currently editing the manuscript in company with Mr. Babitz. And yet you hear Copland's musical parentage in a half-dozen passages. The place of Ives in the history of American music looms ever larger and larger. He is never anything less than amazing.[141]

Schoenberg's *Pierrot lunaire,* newly translated into English (in accordance with Schoenberg's wishes), finally received its Evenings on the Roof performance on 18 December 1944, after years of negotiations, in an all-Schoenberg program. It was conducted by Ingolf

Dahl, with relatively few rehearsals. "Schoenberg insisted sixty to one-hundred rehearsals were necessary for any performance anywhere," Yates remembered. The night before the program Adolph Weiss, Schoenberg's first American pupil and now a composer closely associated with both Schoenberg and the Roof, telephoned Yates to say that Mr. Schoenberg forbade the performance of *Pierrot* because it was inadequately rehearsed. Yates wrote Houston,

> I told [Weiss] to tell Mr. Schoenberg that we would perform the work and that Mr. Schoenberg and his family would be expected to be present. It was, I think, the one way to break through Schoenberg's resistance. He took to bed with a fever, but the remainder of the family turned up. Shortly afterwards, that performance of *Pierrot lunaire* was broadcast and received his full endorsement.[142]

Lawrence Morton expressed his dislike for the work:

> [A] spirit of nineteenth-century romantic decadence. . . . the kind of romantic goo that makes one laugh—until he realizes that this stuff has serious intentions. . . . *Pierrot* is . . . a perfect wedding of perverse music to a perverse text. The songs from "The Hanging Gardens". . . were not nearly so objectionable. . . . Obviously I did not find myself richly rewarded by the Schoenberg program. As performance, however, it was most interesting.[143]

Bartók's *Contrasts,* which Yates had been urging upon the clarinetist Kalman Bloch for a number of seasons, was given its first Los Angeles performance by Bloch, the violinist Manuel Compinsky (a former member of the NBC Symphony under Toscanini),[144] and Mullen, with such success that Yates called for an encore. In subsequent seasons and tours, this work became a surefire hit with both players and audiences.

Ingolf Dahl's Music for Brass Instruments (1944) and Adolph Weiss's Concerto for Bassoon and String Quartet were performed, as well as works by Ernest Bloch, Virgil Thomson, Walter Piston, Lou

Harrison, Alfred Casella, Mario Castelnuovo-Tedesco, Leonard Bernstein, Darius Milhaud, and Stravinsky. Paul Hindemith's Third String Quartet received an impressive performance by the still unnamed Shapiro-Lustgarten-Majewski-Gottlieb quartet. Mullen, Babitz, Dahl, Boyes, and Belva Kibler, mezzo-soprano, presented a program of the music of Carlos Chávez at Occidental College, on the occasion of the composer-conductor's visit from Mexico. In other concerts, three Mussorgsky song cycles were performed, along with the 24 Preludes for piano by Dmitry Shostakovich and works of Busoni, Debussy, and Ravel. President Roosevelt was memorialized with Bach chorale preludes played by Mullen at the opening of the program on 16 April, four days after his sudden death.

This season of accomplishment set high standards for the future. Serious interpretations of rarely heard music of the past were juxtaposed with full, thoughtful appreciation of two twentieth-century masters, along with enterprising explorations of works by over seventeen other composers actively building their careers in America. More works by Schoenberg and Ives were performed than had ever been heard in a single American concert series.[145] Ives sent an anonymous gift of fifty dollars to help pay for the expenses of copying Schoenberg's instrumental parts. Klemperer (now well enough from his long illness to return occasionally to the Philharmonic podium) attended the concerts regularly. On his visits to Los Angeles, the pianist Artur Schnabel became interested in the concerts through his close friend Buhlig and fostered them publicly. When he learned that New York's successful Friends of Music hoped to establish a branch in Los Angeles that would rival the Roof concerts, he withdrew his support from the New York organization and urged instead that a newly founded Los Angeles venture, the Music Guild, amalgamate with the artistically successful, but financially insecure, Roof concerts. Schnabel went so far as to make his performing for the new Music Guild contingent on its collaboration with Evenings on the Roof.[146]

The Music Guild, capitalizing on the Roof's efforts to educate an audience in the literature of chamber music, was organized to bring celebrity chamber music events to the city. Although this was a goal in direct opposition to his philosophy, Yates, searching for relief from administrative headaches, saw in this joint venture possible financial benefit to the Roof series and optimistically went ahead with the arrangement. The Music Guild would provide for Evenings on the Roof a prestigious 1,300-seat hall (the Wilshire-Ebell Theater), a fixed sum for the season, and positions for Roof personnel on its board of directors. The Roof series would provide most of the Music Guild's programs, the remainder of which would be celebrity recitals. The aim of both groups, as Yates saw it, would be "to integrate the Los Angeles [concertgoing] public and break up the Behymer monopoly."[147] "We are now a major part of the country's music. People expect a great deal from us," Yates wrote to Houston.[148]

Three

“THE KEYNOTE OF A TRUE MUSICAL CULTURE” 1945–1954

THE WAR PRODUCED A PHENOMENAL change in southern California's prosperity and self-image. Newly powerful industries swung into massive postwar expansion, while thousands of ex-servicemen returned to live in "Lotusland," creating a huge population boom. The arts had proved themselves vitally important in wartime, and, until the House Committee on Un-American Activities stepped up its anticommunist attack on Hollywood in 1947, there was a new confidence among leaders in artistic circles about Los Angeles' cultural maturity and ability to compete with the eastern establishment.

It was a natural time for Evenings on the Roof to ally itself with a larger organization. Yates felt he could no longer continue "one-man government" of the concerts. But many friends and supporters were not sanguine about an alliance with the recently founded Music Guild, for Evenings on the Roof had, after all, originated in anti-establishment attitudes. Lawrence Morton (who had by now declared himself in *Script* an enemy of commercial interests in the concert world)[1] wrote, at the opening of the Roof's eighth season, "The [Music] Guild has extended a helping hand to Evenings on the Roof, by way of guaranteeing its expenses for its eighth season. [So far] it has had the good sense to keep hands off the musical policy of the

Roof. . . . But I cannot help wondering if the commercially sponsored concerts are going to bring storm clouds."[2]

The storm clouds were in evidence from the beginning. The Music Guild's budget was in the $20,000 to 30,000 range. "Our $2,000 . . . vanishes like small change. . . . I haven't been at ease in weeks"; the Roof's lack of financial clout put "our ambition, our idealism . . . deep in debt," Yates wrote Houston in early June 1945.[3] There were long board fights over "the deal," joined by Morton, who was on the Guild's board of advisers, and Ingolf Dahl, who—with Yates—was a member of the Guild's board of trustees. By the end of the summer Yates realized that the smaller organization's principles were threatened:

> I have great difficulty to make the trustees [of the Music Guild] understand the special character of our work. With them the audience comes first, the music second, their performers third. Our rule has been: performers first, music second, audience afterwards. . . . Without [this plan] and the trust and confidence it has created we could never have survived. I have seen the organizations come and go: they raise money; they have full houses; they vanish. Year after year we have no money; we have small audiences; we survive. Public conscience will not let us vanish. And now the audience is gathering around and forming groups to carry forward every part of the work.[4]

In this crucible of conflicts during the 1945–1946 season, a group of influential citizens volunteered to sustain the unique character of the Roof concerts. Among them were Max Laemmle, founder of the Laemmle theater chain (a cousin once removed of Carl Laemmle, founder of Universal Studios), Artie Mason Carter, founder of the Hollywood Bowl (which had itself now fallen into the hands of business interests), and the general manager of powerful Northrop Aircraft, LaMotte Cohu, who sent his public relations director to advise the Roof group, while his wife and daughter joined the musicians' spouses and volunteers to facilitate mailings. Elizabeth Reames Spires, a musician, and her husband, Al Spires, became Yates's chief business assistants. Oscar Moss, a wealthy tax attorney and founding member of one of Los Angeles' largest accounting firms, offered to underwrite the next season's concerts to the extent of $100. "I consider the series one of the most important events in the musical life of Los Angeles. The participating artists and the management deserve much credit for the fine programs you have been giving for the pleasure and growth in music appreciation of the audience," he wrote, on 25 April 1946.[5] He subsequently offered to incorporate and direct the business affairs of an independent support organization that would maintain the concerts independently again, and Evenings on the Roof's arrangement with the Music Guild was dissolved after only one season.[6]

EIGHTH SEASON: 1945–1946

While these negotiations were going on, the amalgamated season was a great success musically. In the celebrity series, the Music Guild presented such stars as Maggie Teyte, Artur Schnabel, and the Pro Arte String Quartet. Klemperer conducted many of the Roof musicians in Bach's Brandenburg Concertos, performances that left Lawrence Morton in "a state of highest exaltation."[7] The Roof's fine string quartet, newly named the American Quartet (now with Marvin Limonick as second violinist), substituted at short notice for the indisposed London Quartet in an ensemble program with Schnabel, which was ecstatically received.

The Roof group's separate chamber music concerts were now presented in two prestigious locations: at the Wilshire-Ebell Theater and at Hancock Auditorium on the campus of the University of Southern California. These were larger halls than had been used in previous seasons (the Wilshire-Ebell seated 1,300). Season subscription rates for the regular series jumped from thirty cents to eighty cents per ticket. Richard Buhlig offered a second series of Beethoven's thirty-two piano sonatas, this time in seven recitals. About these Yates wrote Houston,

> He has grown at least as much more during the two years as Schnabel has declined. . . . Technically he is not and never can

> become flawless . . . but his playing of the "Waldstein" stood the audience on end. . . . Mildred Norton, by far our best local newspaper critic [*Daily News*]: "The most magnificent piano playing I have ever heard in my life. . . . Buhlig's playing, at its finest, partakes of the anguish of creation, and his greatness lies in this tremendous ability of drawing the listener to the very taproot of the music, and its Promethian source."[8]

But Buhlig suffered psychosomatic illness; his health and his concert schedule were precarious, his strength and control hung in the balance. Before his final recital he was in bed with a fever. "It was not his very best performance, but at the end there was an absolute prolonged silence, followed by a standing ovation," Yates reported, exhausted by the ordeal of cosseting this nervous artist through his concerts. "Buhlig spares no opportunity of telling me how grateful he is that I have brought him out," he wrote Houston.[9] Because Buhlig's plans to play in New York were canceled, "It may be the world's fate never to hear him play Beethoven. We who are fortunate to have heard him at his ripest will never forget and will doubtless spend many hours trying to explain to others just how it was."[10] Lawrence Morton, on the other hand, snarled, "Although this almost frighteningly sincere artist has achieved the position of a high priest in local circles, his ministry is one of faith rather than works."[11]

There were eighteen concerts in the Roof's chamber music series; highlights included repeats of Bartók's *Contrasts,* Kodály's gigantic Sonata for Unaccompanied Cello, Beethoven's Septet, and Kuhnle's two-piano arrangement of Bach's *Goldberg* Variations. The first program of the season (15 October 1945) featured the Los Angeles Philharmonic (many of them first desk) players who were members of the Roof group: Shibley Boyes, David Frisina, Kurt Reher, Kalman Bloch, Leonard Posella (flute), Frederick Moritz (bassoon), Abraham Weiss (viola), Fred Fox (horn), and Richard Kelly (contrabass). Shapiro and Boyes played five of Beethoven's violin and piano sonatas, completing the full cycle of ten they had begun the previous season. The contralto Elizabeth Vermeulen and Shibley Boyes performed Schubert's *Winterreise* in Boyes's translation. Ingolf Dahl figured importantly as pianist, composer, and conductor. His Wind Quintet and *Six Variations on a Swedish Folktune* for solo flute (1945) were played. "Ingolf is going places," Yates wrote, proud that the Roof concerts and musicians provided Dahl with the impetus for much of his composing.[12] Dahl appeared as pianist in many works, among them (with Sol Babitz) Ives's First Sonata for Violin and Piano, Harold Shapero's Piano Sonata for four hands, and an important performance of Paul Hindemith's song cycle *Das Marienleben* with the soprano Sara Carter, who had recited *Pierrot lunaire* with great success the previous season. Yates wrote in *Arts and Architecture* that Sara Carter "is the rare combination of a vocally gifted singer with the large-scale intelligence of a first-rate solo instrumentalist."[13]

"Los Angeles no longer eats anybody's dust," Peter Yates exulted to Houston. "You can credit the best part of that to the Roof."[14] Artur Schnabel and Aldous Huxley came to hear Buhlig. Artur Rubinstein, Jascha Heifetz, Isaac Stern, Gregor Piatigorsky, Rosalind Tureck, and Rosina Lhevinne were drawn to the concerts. Many composers came. Peter Yates kept himself out of sight behind the curtains: "I didn't appear on the stage if I could avoid it, except to move the piano or chairs or things of that sort. I always felt that the musicians should be featured, and the impresario should not."[15] He felt the fun of the concerts was backstage, where other performers would watch and listen from the wings. "Unfortunately the orchestra players lack the zeal of the pianists. Life for them is too much tone quality, too little the music itself," he observed.[16]

Following the death of Béla Bartók in New York City, at the end of the 1945–1946 season two memorial concerts were added. Yates was disappointed that audiences for these programs were small, although the occasion presented "probably the largest amount of Bartók's music yet played in one series."[17] Bartók himself had performed several times in Los Angeles and in January 1942 had been the object of long articles by both Lawrence Morton and Yates, yet the city still barely knew this master (as it barely knew Alban Berg's music and much else by the early twentieth-century masters). The two all-Bartók Roof programs included the Second String Quartet, played by the

American Quartet, the Rhapsody No. 2 for violin and piano played by Shapiro and Dahl, the Second Sonata for Violin and Piano played by Manuel Compinsky and Frances Mullen, and Five Songs, Op. 16. As always, Mullen took on many Bartók piano works, including the challenging Sonata for Piano, the *Allegro barbaro,* Rumanian Folk Dances, and selections from *Mikrokosmos* and *For Children.*

Both Yateses had an unusually exhausting year. With the war's end Yates's work with the Employment Service was more chaotic than ever. In addition to his job, he was swamped with new tasks as a member of a committee for the American Federation of Labor. Contention with the Music Guild, nagging worries about the concerts' future, and continual meetings with volunteers made him weary of organizing the concerts and increasingly torn by his desire to write a large novel and to publish a collection of his poetry.[18] Frances Mullen wrote to Peyton Houston, "We are both swamped with the drudgery and details of [the concerts]. I'm finally convinced we will not continue another season if a complete systematic organization has not been worked out for us by next March or April [1946]."[19]

She was now teaching piano at the Sutro-Seyler Studio; she helped establish concerts by Roof musicians in Santa Barbara; and among her larger works for the regular season were Schubert's "Trout" Quintet, Beethoven's Bagatelles, Brahms's Clarinet Sonata, Op. 120, No. 1 with Kalman Bloch, the first performance of an arrangement for two pianos of Schoenberg's Variations on a Recitative for Organ, Op. 40, and Kuhnle's two-piano arrangement of Bach's *Goldberg* Variations. Two of the children were often ill and had to undergo tonsillectomies. Her mother was again in the throes of a mental breakdown. She herself was suffering from manic-depressive illness, a problem her husband had been aware of since early in their marriage. Recovery from her crises was a difficult, lengthy process. Peter's solution to her problems, as always, was novel. He felt that Frances was in better health when she kept up her performing and suggested she tackle the complete solo piano works of Mozart in a series of recitals in the Roof studio the following season. She accepted the challenge.

The experience with the Music Guild proved to be catalytic. The break with the larger organization publicized the achievements by local talent in the Roof concerts. Recognizing the importance of the Roof concerts, the musicians' union accepted the struggling enterprise's unorthodox fee system and made an exception to its rules that was essential to the concerts' survival: no payment was required for the musicians' rehearsal time.[20] Yates had been writing seasonal reports in *Arts and Architecture,* but now he summed up a history of Evenings on the Roof, which he called the *Fourth Report.* He published it with Buhlig's financial help and sent out 4,200 copies to major musical organizations, periodicals, and critics in the United States and Europe.

Beside cataloguing the complete repertoire played in the concerts so far and in those planned for the 1946–1947 season, the report listed the steady members of the musicians' cooperative (at that time thirty-six) and occasional participants (fifty-two more). Pianists outnumbered other instrumentalists on both lists. A chronicle of the concerts was prefaced by a statement of Frances and Peter Yates's objectives in founding the concerts:

> Evenings on the Roof is a unique musical organization, created to help a number of Los Angeles musicians prepare and play good music under better conditions and at less expense than would be possible in separate recitals; to relieve them of any feeling that music should condescend to or try to entertain a merely well-wishing majority of ticket-buyers; and to provide a collaborative means by which individual performers may be guarded against the fruitless spending of the impresario while standing together to meet the competition of imported big-name virtuosos. . . . For several years, hampered by the inadequacies of the standard entertainment recital, [Frances Mullen and Peter Yates] had been trying to find or to create an audience for that class of music which is always contemporary, whether written by the sixteenth-century composers Byrd and Gibbons or by the twentieth-century composers Hindemith and Ives. They had become convinced that an audience for such music does not exist in a fireside vacuum but

> must be created; that listeners who use the radio or buy recordings are more likely to prefer the relatively small number of commonly played "famous" or "great" or "popular box-office" items than to explore on their own initiative the further reaches of the musical cosmos. But they knew that this great body of stalled inertia must contain isolated within it many persons of more eager and more curious interest who actively resent the limitations of the ordinary standard concert and recital programs.[21]

The report included full details of Buhlig's current Beethoven series, with nine eloquent critical testimonies to his playing. It advertised the Roof's chamber ensembles available for engagement and published a plea for financial support for a recording fund, which would "bring honor to the musicians of Los Angeles." Otto Klemperer and Alfred Wallenstein added their strong endorsements to the final page of this summation, after eight seasons, of Evenings on the Roof.

Through the *Fourth Report,* the critics Virgil Thomson, Paul Henry Lang, B. H. Haggin, and many others across the country were made aware of the unique nature of the concerts. Lang responded with praise in the *Saturday Review* for "chamber concerts at a price not far from admission fees of second-run movie theaters, with programs that reflect as much artistic integrity as they do intelligence, courage, and foresight. The performances [are] mainly by able local artists—a system which is the keynote of a true musical culture."[22] Privately, Lang wrote to Yates, "I'm quite sure that only organizations such as yours can change the commercial tendency in the administration of music in our country."[23] Lawrence Morton, in his role as Los Angeles correspondent for the League of Composers' quarterly, *Modern Music* (from January 1944 to the end of 1946 when this important publication ceased), called attention to Evenings on the Roof as "the very ante-room to modern music in this community."[24] Isabel Morse Jones, writing in the *Los Angeles Times,* reiterated Yates's challenge: Los Angeles artists counted first in Roof program-making, and there would be no concession to audiences, who by now were becoming sufficiently receptive to explorations of new music and rare old music.[25]

As he had in 1941, Yates responded to crisis with bold expansion in the ninth season. New Roof ensembles were rapidly forming, and their energy could be used to bring in higher fees ($700 for two string quartet programs) from Arizona and other cities in southern California, as long as presenters would accept a high level of musical challenge. Oscar Moss completed the incorporation process for the support organization, called the Southern California Chamber Music Society, and plans were made for a fund-raising campaign. (By the end of 1946 the concerts, still presented at the expensive Wilshire-Ebell Theater, had run up a deficit of $1,000.) In December 1946 an announcement was sent out, with an appeal for membership in the society, which was intended to establish a permanent fund for the Roof concerts. Max Laemmle was president, Mrs. Cohu vice-president, Oscar Moss treasurer, and Yates executive director.

Evenings on the Roof recordings (produced by Alco Records) of "exceptional performances of extraordinary music"[26] began to appear for sale in October 1946. The first were recordings of Ives, Schubert, and Hindemith, priced at five dollars each. Kurt Reher's recording of the Sonata for Violoncello Solo, Op. 25, No. 3 by Hindemith was listed by *Downbeat* magazine as the best small record of the year. A Roof recording of Ernst Toch's *Chinese Flute,* a work featured on the season's programs, was later used in the famous Japanese film *Rashomon.*[27] Although these 78 rpm recordings were intended mainly for sale to the Roof's local audience, it was through 33 rpm recordings that the concerts' innovative performances would eventually reach a wider public and indeed "bring honor to the musicians of Los Angeles."

The series seemed to the fourteen-year-old Susan Sontag an essential part of Los Angeles' golden age. She and a friend frequently told their parents they were going to the Central Library, when they intended to hear Roof concerts.[28] But in *Script* Morton chided the community for not yet being "sufficiently aware of the many significant events that occur at Evenings on the Roof." Among these in the ninth season, he particularly admired Ingolf Dahl's "profoundly moving" performance of Aaron Copland's Piano Sonata and the "distinguished achievement" of Dahl's new Duo for Cello and Piano (1946), which "spoke out vigorously for the importance of big ideas in music," in its premiere performance by Dahl and Kurt Reher.[29]

Steady members of the performers' group numbered thirty-six at the beginning of the ninth season. The Philharmonic's young second flutist, Doriot Anthony, who had been attracted to the concerts by the Bartók memorial programs, joined and played often between February 1947 and the fall of 1952. In that period her widely varied repertoire included Debussy, Bach, Hindemith, Schoenberg, Mozart, Ravel, and the first West Coast performance of William Walton's *Façade*. "I considered those years in Los Angeles my 'college,' although I had graduated from Eastman," Doriot Anthony Dwyer remembers.[30] In September 1952 she left Los Angeles to become principal flutist and soloist with the Boston Symphony, breaking an important gender barrier: none of the big five orchestras of Boston, New York, Philadelphia, Cleveland, and Chicago then had female principal players other than harpists.

In June 1947 the Music Guild agreed to share the Roof's deficit by matching funds raised by the new support organization, but voted Peter Yates off their board.[31] Three fundraising programs were added to the ninth Roof season in June, to aid a membership drive for the Southern California Chamber Music Society. For these, admission price for a single seat remained the same charged from 1944 to 1952: $1.20 including tax. These events of special interest included the first American performance, by the harpsichordist Alice Ehlers and the Canadian violinist Adolf Koldofsky, of five violin sonatas from Heinrich Ignaz Franz von Biber's series titled *The Passion of Our Lord,* in a new continuo realization by Hindemith. In Europe Alice Ehlers had toured with Hindemith (who played the viola d'amore) in a group specializing in Baroque music. She owned the Biber works in manuscript, for they had not been published.[32] This was one of several programs that the Hungarian violinist Joseph Szigeti attended.[33] He had recently played Berg's Violin Concerto in one of Klemperer's rare guest appearances with the Philharmonic, was now a resident of nearby Palos Verdes, and became an admirer, personal friend, and benefactor to the Roof concerts and the Yates family. The second special program featured works of Virgil Thomson, Samuel Barber, and Ingolf Dahl, played by Kurt Reher and Dahl; as finale, Schoenberg's *Friede auf Erden* (Peace on Earth) was performed by a local church choir. The third of these programs was a full evening of the works of Ernest Bloch, cosponsored by the Jewish Centers Association. At the end of the season, C. Sharpless Hickman (music critic for the *Christian Science Monitor*) wrote that the Roof "made Los Angeles the outstanding metropolitan center of chamber music in the United States."[34]

TENTH SEASON: 1947–1948

After a summer's postponement due to illness, Frances Mullen played the complete solo piano works of Mozart in six programs, from September through November, in the Roof studio on Micheltorena Street. It was now important to Yates that she be "set up" separately from the Roof season. He reported to Houston that she was playing exceedingly well, to overflow audiences; Buhlig commented that she had never played better.[35] In each program she presented works chronologically, from the 1760s to Mozart's final years. The composer Ernst Krenek, recently settled in Los Angeles, attended all her recitals, which ran alternately with the regular programs.

The tenth season was particularly notable for the number of distinguished guests who played their own works on the concerts. With the violinist Adolf Koldofsky (a fine artist recently arrived from Vancouver with his pianist wife),[36] Krenek played his new Sonata for Violin and Piano (1945) and with Kalman Bloch gave the first Los Angeles performance of his Trio for Violin, Clarinet, and Piano. Henry Cowell (released from San Quentin in 1940 and fully pardoned at the end of 1942) played his Sonata for Violin and Piano (1945) with Sol Babitz, and four of his solo piano pieces. He shared the program with the Los Angeles composer Adolph Weiss, whose work he had promoted when they were both in New York in the 1920s and early 1930s. Yates, who described Cowell as "infinitely loveable," found his music now disappointingly outdated, naive, and plain; on the other hand, Weiss's new Sextet for Piano and Wind Quintet, played by the New Music Quintet with the composer as bassoonist and Mullen as pianist, was "the power of the evening. . . . Weiss is a sound, witty composer."[37] Ernst Toch, one of the most successful of the émigré composers in Los Angeles, performed his Piano Quintet, Op. 64, with the (renamed) American Art Quartet. On 5 April 1948, Aaron Copland came to play his Piano Variations on a program to celebrate the twenty-fifth anniversary of the New York–centered League of Composers. Works of American composers Harold Shapero, Arthur Berger, Walter Piston, Richard Franko Goldman, Lou Harrison, Donald Fuller, and Charles Jones also appeared on this program. The league returned the tribute by broadcasting on station WNYC in New York a program of music by the Los Angeles composers Weiss, Dahl, and Tremblay, to honor Evenings on the Roof. Yates had fostered performances of American music since his first program of "Music by Americans," in 1940. On 8 December 1948 he instituted a series of yearly programs featuring Los Angeles composers. The first aired works of Halsey Stevens, Edward Rebner (son of Adolph Rebner, the violinist Yates admired in early days on the Roof), Julius Toldi, Dahl, and another work of Adolph Weiss.

Mario Castelnuovo-Tedesco, Stravinsky, and Schoenberg all received performances in this season. Schoenberg was honored with a full program of his Wind Quintet, the string sextet, *Verklärte Nacht,* and the first West Coast performance of his new Trio for Violin, Viola, and Cello (1946), performed by Adolph Koldofsky, the Hungarian violist Zoltán Kurthy, and the cellist Jascha Schwarzmann. (In 1988 the violist Sven Reher still regretted that the Reher trio—which by 1947 included the violinist Felix Slatkin—had turned down the opportunity to play this premiere.)[38] In order to celebrate the survival of the Roof to its tenth season—albeit with continuing worrisome poverty—and in order to shock a potentially resistant audience into gratitude for one of Schoenberg's most difficult works, the twelve-tone Wind Quintet, Yates inserted Erik Satie's *Mass of the Poor,* a fragmentary work for piano and three singers, before the Schoenberg on this program (10 May 1948). Yates had long been fascinated by

Satie. He had programmed Satie's *Socrate* in an all-Satie concert at the end of the Roof's first full year of concerts (28 April 1940) and repeated it in 1946. About the celebration of this tenth anniversary with a Satie work Yates later recalled, "The effect of this on the strongly Germanic audience was most irritating and frustrating. They had no idea what it was all about, and it was French. They vented all their fury . . . so that when we came on next with [Schoenberg's] woodwind quintet they relaxed . . . and the evening was a great success."[39]

Yates's interest in Satie was one of many he shared with John Cage. Cage's relationship with the Yateses dated from 1928, when Frances Mullen's brother was a classmate of Cage's at Pomona College. Peter Yates met Cage in the fall of 1940 at Buhlig's house and soon began publicizing Cage's innovative ideas in *Arts and Architecture.* On 19 April 1948, a special invitational program in the Roof studio on Micheltorcna Street combined John Cage performing his own recently completed *Sixteen Sonatas and Four Interludes* for prepared piano with Japanese music played by the great master of the shakuhachi, Tamada, a player whom Cowell and Gerald Strang introduced to Peter Yates. Since Japan's attack on Pearl Harbor Tamada had refused to play, because of the relations between his country and the United States, and he considered this private concert his emergence from "death."[40] The day before the performance Cage prepared the Yateses' Steinway piano—with rubber fruit-jar rings, bolts, and washers carefully placed between the strings to create something like a one-man gamelan—so that Peter Yates could have the pleasure of playing it overnight. Tamada arrived at the concert accompanied by the local Buddhist abbot, who drove demons out of the house before his performance took place. Cage returned the following year (21 February 1949) for another performance of the *Sonatas and Interludes,* co-sponsored by Lester Horton's Dance Studio. Yates and Cage remained closely associated after Yates gave up management of the concerts in the 1950s, and Cage's second personal appearance, in 1962 for the Monday Evening Concerts, was also arranged by Yates.

Another invitational concert in the Roof studio was given by Schoenberg's brother-in-law, Rudolf Kolisch, the left-handed violinist who at that time was the leader of the Pro Arte Quartet. Among other works, he played Bartók's Sonata for Unaccompanied Violin.[41]

The regular performers on the series had by now formed six enduring ensembles: two string quartets, a string trio, a wind quintet, a piano trio, and a piano quartet. The ensembles and players were:

American Art Quartet:	Eudice Shapiro and Marvin Limonick (later, Robert Sushel), violins; Virginia Majewski, viola; Victor Gottlieb, cello
New Music Quintet:	Archie Wade, flute; Gerald Caylor, clarinet; Lloyd Rathbun, oboe; Wendell Hoss, horn; Adolph Weiss (the composer), bassoon
Philharmonic Piano Trio:	Maxine Furman, piano; Martin Black, violin; Joseph Di Tullio, cello
New Art Quartet:	Israel Baker and George Berres, violins; Milton Thomas, viola; William Van den Burg, cello
The String Trio:	Felix Slatkin, violin; Sven Reher, viola; Kurt Reher, cello
The Piano Quartet:	Shibley Boyes, piano; Ralph Schaeffer, violin; Abraham Weiss, viola; Mary Louise Zeyen, cello

In all, the tenth season was a triumphant show of accomplishment. Critical tributes were accumulating. With more and more performers eager to be associated with the concerts, there was now relatively little room on the programs for soloists.

Albert Price Quinn, music critic of the *B'nai B'rith Messenger,* suffered a heart attack in April 1947 and asked Yates to keep his column going. Around the same time, the *Times* ousted Isabel Morse Jones for what Yates called "refusing to go along with the right people"[42] and hired as its first full-time music critic Albert Goldberg, from Chicago. Goldberg did not encourage the innovative aspects of Roof concerts. He and Yates were soon at loggerheads. Goldberg detested the music of Ives, and Yates felt he "wrote down" to the Los

Angeles audience.[43] In this dangerous period of anticommunist witch-hunts in Hollywood, when there was extreme right-wing paranoia in California, Yates was secretly proud of the socialist leanings in his concept:

> The Roof, after all, is as radical a project as ever received the unwitting support of the *L.A. Times.* Private enterprise should tremble at the thought of it. Shhh! Make a menace the most obvious part of an enterprise, and it may not be noticed. My best supporters are pillars of private business. And why not! Private enterprise must create and is creating practical socialism, American plan, to counteract governmental supremacy.[44]

In his first article in the *B'nai B'rith Messenger* for Quinn, Yates lamented a threat (not carried out until March 1949) to close down the magazine *Script* and consequently to silence the local music criticisms of Lawrence Morton. He noted the work of Mildred Norton as music critic for the *Daily News* but commented that Los Angeles was severely limited in its number of good music critics. In another article he commented (as Morton frequently had) on the unhealthy state to which the Philharmonic had fallen under Wallenstein. Lack of artistic satisfaction and low pay were causing musicians to leave the Philharmonic for studio work.[45] "It is time for Mr. Wallenstein to become more aware of his responsibilities to the Los Angeles public and to Los Angeles musicians," he wrote.[46] Later, in his oral history, Yates recalled how Wallenstein's arrival in 1943 had been greeted with high hopes,

> because he was an American conductor, and we thought this was a very important thing. We hoped that [his] reorganization of the orchestra would mean closer ties. So we opened [the eighth season, after he had given first chairs to Roof members] with a program featuring the first-chair men of the Philharmonic. . . . We invited Wallenstein and gave the concert in his honor. He told us that he was very sorry, but he would have to be in Palm Springs for the weekend. At that time we could see already developing the estrangement of Wallenstein from the community, which ended in the

> long effort to get rid of him as conductor. . . . He yielded to . . . social persuasions. . . . with the result that he made himself a perfect second-rater . . . and lost the individuality he might have built up.[47]

The *Musical Digest,* a national periodical (sponsored by the Detroit Symphony) that thrived on controversy, asked Yates for an article on problems with the Philharmonic. In an article entitled "Los Angeles: Musical Jig-saw," Yates began, "Los Angeles, one of the most important musical centers in the world, if only because of the number of professional musicians who live and work here, is a center without cultural determination or direction." He pointed to some of the reasons: the Philharmonic was being "whitewashed" by money from the Santa Anita racetrack; Wallenstein's backers refused to give heed to public demand for a change; opera, rather than growing indigenously, was imported from New York, courtesy of the Metropolitan Opera. He concluded, "To grow in culture a city must stimulate and encourage its own creative life, not import it."[48] In a subsequent issue of the same magazine, Albert Goldberg rebutted by sneering at Yates's nonprofessional status and listed local statistics as proof of vigorous musical effort. Yates replied,

> During the last several years patronage and power in Los Angeles musical society have tried to still any voice that would disturb their pleasant inertia. Rebelling against these pressures, that were slowly stifling every opportunity, the local musicians began combining in various ways, without patronage, to make music for themselves. The result has made Los Angeles second only to New York in the range and quality of its chamber music concerts.[49]

Yates waded further into controversy when asked for articles by the *Saturday Review* and *Music of the West* magazine. For the former he wrote two articles on Schoenberg, one of them defending Schoenberg in the battle between the composer and Thomas Mann over Mann's novel *Dr. Faustus.*[50] For the latter, Yates wrote an article titled "Los Angeles: an Unrealized Musical World-Center," in which he challenged business interests to rise to a new cultural responsibility. He attacked what he called the "Chamber of Commerce" attitude in Los Angeles, which continually ignored such local composers as Schoenberg, Stravinsky, Toch, Adolph Weiss, Dahl, Krenek, Strang, and Roy Harris and insisted on importing big-name musical soloists instead of recognizing the wealth of local performing talent. The antidote would be to find a place for the local musician and the local composer; to establish the city's own opera company; to see to it that the Philharmonic played representative compositions by a dozen Los Angeles composers each season and gave Los Angeles musicians at least a third of the bigger solo jobs; and thus to "make the community and world so conscious of Los Angeles musical enterprise that, before we know it, our creative capacity begins to live up to our boasts."[51] In *Arts and Architecture* he wrote, "Los Angeles should take pride in its composers and encourage them as creative individuals. . . . These are the voices of our city far more truly than the complaints, already lost in time, of those who refuse to recognize or understand them."[52] Yates's notoriety now worked against the Roof concerts. He strongly suggested that the Hollywood Bowl perform such compositions as Stravinsky's *Symphony of Psalms* and Schoenberg's *Gurre-Lieder,* and because the Bowl's music director was also the Los Angeles County musical adviser, "the $1,000 we were to have been granted by the County Music Commission has been lost in transit. . . . It is extremely dangerous to look at truth, even more dangerous to be sure that truth is what you look at. . . . If I were cured [of my unrelenting rebelliousness], I should not give a damn about many affairs that now I damn heartily," Yates confided to Houston.[53]

ELEVENTH SEASON: 1948–1949

The concerts were now thriving artistically; the program announcement for the eleventh season quoted *Times* critic Albert Goldberg as saying, "Evenings on the Roof chamber concerts are a restful island in a sea of commercialization." Concerts alternated between the Wilshire-Ebell Theater and the smaller Wilshire-Ebell Chamber Music Hall. Audiences now numbered four hundred to six hundred, but the possibility of deficits threatened each season. These were partially avoided by increasing the number of programs sent out of town, particularly to Santa Barbara and to Tucson and Tempe, in Arizona. The musicians' union made occasional gifts. The new Southern California Chamber Music Society and supporters such as Laemmle and Stravinsky underwrote programs. In times of particular crisis the performers donated their fees, amounting to approximately $1,500 each season, to keep the organization afloat. The musicians' union looked the other way and did not interfere with this infringement of union principles.[54]

In spite of the lack of pay, increasing numbers of musicians clamored to be involved. The requests of performers and composers for special attention, and the complexities of programming, became more and more burdensome to Yates. His unique ideal of a cooperative, noncompetitive group of musicians was strained as new ensembles formed and high-powered artists vied for performances. Although Yates insisted that their interest in the music should come first, some began criticizing others' talent and ability. The fact that contentious egotism had been held in check through the years, and that a constituency of musicians had developed that was dedicated more to art than to popularity, had been essential to the "extraordinary equanimity and frequent serendipity" of the programs, which continued to be developed through prolonged, painstaking dialogue among musicians, composers, and Yates.[55]

Yates's weariness, his sense of distraction due to his daily office job, and his desire to devote himself to his writing were interfering with his ability to keep up with administrative details of the concerts, as they burst into a large enterprise. He had completed ten years of the strain of daily management and now planned a new phase of organization. It was his hope that the musicians would run the concerts independently. After training Mary-Jeannette Brown (a recent graduate from UCLA in musicology and a respected campus music critic) as a volunteer during the 1947–1948 season, Yates installed her, in 1948–1949, as full-time salaried executive secretary, while he became coordinator. (He himself had never drawn any salary from the concerts). Al Spires (a civil-service employee at the Los Angeles General Hospital) continued as volunteer business manager, and Jane Blumenthal (a member of Warner Brothers' story department) was volunteer publicist. At the same time a volunteer Board of Musicians was elected to govern the membership. Ingolf Dahl was the first to be elected chair, with Kurt Reher vice-chair. In March 1948 the Board of Musicians and Yates drew up an agreement that outlined the new organization. By definition, the concerts continued

> for the pleasure of and belong to the musicians, except the title "Evenings on the Roof" itself, which specifically remains the property of the co-founders Peter Yates and Frances Mullen. Use of this title may be withdrawn by Peter Yates and Frances Mullen at any time, after three months' notice.

In order to deal with a projected deficit, newly stringent requirements demanded that "No fees will be paid this year to any musicians, except to non-members. . . . Participating musicians will underwrite all concert expenses of Evenings on the Roof. The Southern California Chamber Music Society will provide advance funds when necessary, and these must be repaid at the end of the season."[56] The fees were calculated at $10 per unit, or piece played, with $40 (for four units) a maximum fee per evening. The result of belt tightening for the fiscal year 1949 was a net loss of only $115.50.

In spite of these financial restrictions, the eleventh season was bigger in several ways. A new organization, The New Friends of Old Music, fostered by Yates's interest in early music, offered a preseason series of four programs featuring seventeenth- and eighteenth-century music. These displayed the work of Sol Babitz and Wesley Kuhnle, self-taught specialists in the performance practice of this music, in their pioneering search for historical authenticity. Babitz used bows of the period from the Arnold Dolmetsch Workshop in England and a private collection and flattened the bridge of a modern violin to imitate an early instrument. The results were at first difficult for audiences to appreciate, as Babitz slowly assimilated the techniques toward which he was working. Kuhnle, who was soon to become a master instrument-builder himself, at first played a borrowed John Challis clavichord. One of the programs made use of the viola da gamba, played by Rebecca Haight Hathaway; another featured compositions of Carl Philipp Emanuel Bach. Alice Mock sang a program of English, Spanish, French, and Italian songs of the seventeenth and eighteenth centuries. Lawrence Morton welcomed this "revivalist movement," which "revealed an area of musical experience that has been nearly closed to us by the passage of time and the changing of fashions."[57]

At Stravinsky's request, his pianist son, Soulima, gave his first solo American recital in the Wilshire-Ebell Chamber Music Hall, 27 September 1948, playing Stravinsky's Serenade in A (1925), his own Three Études (1947), sonatas by Mozart, Domenico Scarlatti, and Beethoven, and five pieces by Rossini. The younger Stravinsky, who had gained renown in Europe as the foremost interpreter of his father's piano music, had recently left France with his family to make a new home in the United States. An all-Stravinsky program opened the regular Roof series at the Wilshire-Ebell Theater on October 4, including the *Duo concertant* (with Sol Babitz, violin, and Soulima Stravinsky, piano), the *Tango* and *Piano-Rag-Music* (1919) (played by Dahl), Concerto for Two Solo Pianos (Soulima Stravinsky and Dahl), Three Pieces (1914) and Concertino (1920) for String Quartet (Compinsky Quartet), and *L'Histoire du soldat,* conducted by Edward Rebner. So began an intensive and fruitful association with Stravinsky, culminated by his dedication of his *Three Songs from William Shakespeare* to Peter Yates and Evenings on the Roof in 1954.

The regular season drew attention, by means of a continuous J. S. Bach festival, to the bicentennial anniversary of this composer's death. Selections from the forty-eight preludes and fugues of the *Well-Tempered Clavier* were played at the opening of each program. The *Times* critic Albert Goldberg "made a point of coming late because he did not care for hearing Bach."[58] By the spring of 1949 Kuhnle had built his own clavichord and played on it three all-Bach programs, including another performance of the *Goldberg* Variations (with Mullen) and the *Capriccio on the Departure of His Most Beloved Brother.*

Roy Harris requested (and underwrote, at Yates's suggestion) a program of his music for the celebration of his fiftieth birthday—"the beginning of his barren period," commented Yates in his oral history.[59] Copland's Sextet for Clarinet, Piano, and String Quartet (1937) was played by the American Art Quartet, Kalman Bloch, and Dahl, in a program that also included a Toch trio (1936), and Dahl's *Concertino a Tré* (1947), for clarinet, violin, and cello. The violist Milton Thomas, who had premiered Dahl's Divertimento for Viola and Piano (1948) the previous season, this season played Hindemith's Sonata for Unaccompanied Viola.

The New Art Quartet, New Music Wind Ensemble, String Trio (Felix Slatkin, with the two Reher brothers), and Philharmonic Piano Trio were all active in this very busy season, which included works by Mozart, Beethoven, Michael and Joseph Haydn, and Schubert. There were premieres of music by Erich Korngold and Julius Toldi—composers whose work Yates did not like but thought should be heard. The yearly program of Los Angeles composers continued; Yates dubbed it an "often grueling evening," but important for composers.[60] Again there was an added series of four concerts in June. In the first, Mullen repeated her acclaimed performance of the *Diabelli* Variations, "at the top of her ability," in better health than in seven years.[61] In all there were thirty concerts, including the regular series, the early music programs, special programs, and the out-of-town programs. By the end of this 1948–1949 season, it was estimated that one hundred fifty performers had taken part in the Roof concerts.

TWELFTH SEASON: 1949–1950

Yates was now turning out a steady barrage of articles about composers and music. He left management more and more to Mary-Jeannette Brown, as he hastily assembled a collection of articles into a book on twentieth-century music, which he unsuccessfully submitted to publishers. He reported to Houston that Herbert Weinstock (reader for Knopf) had commented, "I find your style hard going, your references elliptical, and your general approach a little forbidding." Yates admitted, "I do not know my subject cold, and I doubt that anyone else does."[62]

The concert staff was doing well, yet there were always financial crises. Joseph Szigeti offered the Roof a benefit recital of three of Bach's sonatas for solo violin. Yates wrote, in *Arts and Architecture,* "The courtesy that can bring to the service of a benefit recital for a musical organization he admires not merely his name but the most demanding and the best qualities of his art is in the nature of Szigeti. He can do no more and he will do no less for whatever he admires."[63] This was Szigeti's only Los Angeles appearance in 1949–1950 and brought an audience of eight hundred. Yates wrote to a friend of the concerts that Szigeti had insisted the Wilshire-Ebell Theater be sold out: "He should know when he plays such a program that he also, like the Roof [group], must play regardless of audience."[64]

Izler Solomon, appearing as guest conductor with the Los Angeles Woodwinds, presented Alban Berg's fiftieth birthday tribute to Arnold Schoenberg, the Chamber Concerto for Piano, Violin, and Thirteen Winds (1923–1925), in its West Coast premiere. The Los Angeles Woodwinds were a thriving conglomerate of top studio musicians. At their core had been a quintet gathered in the 1930s by Don Christlieb, bassoonist, to play Hindemith, Schoenberg, and Stravinsky for musical gatherings at the Hancock mansion on the corner of Wilshire and Vermont, where they found that "audience reaction was never neutral or so-so. It was always violent rejection or acceptance. . . . The biggest shocker of all came from some German refugees who said 'There ought to be a law against works like these.' "[65] It was this ensemble (Christlieb absent, because of a film commitment) that had played Schoenberg's formidable twelve-tone Wind Quintet at the conclusion of the Roof's tenth season, and from then on this fluid group of musicians, augmented to become the Los Angeles Woodwinds, played many important performances and premieres in these concerts.[66]

Other highlights of the twelfth season included the world premiere of Walter Piston's Duo for Viola and Cello by Sven and Kurt Reher, who had commissioned it. Vocal works to texts of Gertrude Stein by Virgil Thomson were performed on the occasion of Thomson's visit to Los Angeles. Sol Babitz and Wesley Kuhnle took a seventeenth- and eighteenth-century program to Arizona. Some new performers included the cellist Georg Neikrug, the soprano Marni Nixon, the harpsichordist Carol Rosenstiel, and the Coriolan String Quartet, consisting of the violinists Bernard Kundell and Isabelle Daskoff, the violist Abraham Weiss, and the cellist Joseph Di Tullio. Abraham Weiss recalled, "The name 'Coriolan' was decided upon in 1949. I preferred the name 'Cimarosa,' but being voted down I thought of that beautiful strip-teaser Anne Corio, [and] that was the closest we could get to her."[67]

The seventy-fifth birthdays of Schoenberg and Ives were celebrated with full programs of their works. A second performance (in English) of *Pierrot,* with Alice Mock, speaker, and Lillian Steuber, piano, was conducted by Dahl; Kurt Reher performed Schoenberg's 1932 Cello Concerto after a harpsichord concerto by the eighteenth-century composer G. M. Monn. Yates had long been ambitious to present the world premiere of Ives's Second String Quartet. A West Coast premiere scheduled for this concert by the Compinsky Quartet had to be canceled, as it was still too difficult for the quartet to find its way through Ives's photostatted manuscript. (The Coriolan Quartet picked up the challenge and performed the work the following season.) The soprano Marni Nixon, accompanied by Mullen, substituted for the canceled work, singing songs of Ives; Mullen played the *Concord* Sonata; and the Babitz-Dahl edition of Ives's Third Sonata for Violin and Piano was performed by Sol Babitz with André Previn. Previn and Nixon, young colleagues in the film studios, were performing for the first time on the concerts. About the pianist Previn, Yates reported (in Ivesean down-home style) to Harmony and Charles Ives: "When he had got himself together after that first solo [he] went at it better and better, with a good clanging tone that the music needs and not too much pedal, that Sol talked him out of." Szigeti, whose "unusually engaging and independent mind" appealed to Yates, sat with Yates and Henry Temianka, first violinist of the Paganini Quartet, at the Ives concert. Szigeti had performed Ives's Fourth Sonata for Violin and Piano but knew no other Ives. Yates wrote the Iveses, "During the Hawthorne [movement of the *Concord*

(Above) George C. (Cochran) Yates, Frances Mullen Yates, Peter B. (Bart) Yates, and Peter Yates, 1938. Photo by José Reyes, Hollywood, courtesy of Frances Mullen Yates.

(Left) Peyton Houston with Bart Yates, Los Angeles, 1937. Photo courtesy of P. H. Houston.

1938–1939 construction of the Roof studio at 1735 Micheltorena Street, Rudolph M. Schindler, architect. Photo courtesy of the University Art Museum/Architectural Drawing Collection, University of California, Santa Barbara.

(Above left) Arnold Schoenberg in the 1930s, Los Angeles. Photo courtesy of the Arnold Schoenberg Institute, University of Southern California.

(Above right) Richard Buhlig in 1947. Photo courtesy of Peter Hewitt.

(Left) Ingolf Dahl in the mid-1940s. Department of Special Collections, University Research Library, University of California, Los Angeles.

Kalman Bloch. Photo courtesy of the Music Center Operating Company Archives, Otto Rothschild Collection.

Shibley Boyes. Photo courtesy of Shibley Boyes.

The American Art Quartet, 1950; left to right, Eudice Shapiro, Robert Sushel, Victor Gottlieb, Virginia Majewski. Department of Special Collections, University Research Library, University of California, Los Angeles.

The Gesualdo Madrigalists on Stravinsky's lawn, Hollywood, 1954–1955; left to right, Marilyn Horne, Cora Lauridsen, Robert Craft, Richard Robinson, Grace-Lynne Martin, Charles Scharbach. Photo by Jay Barrie. Department of Special Collections, University Research Library, University of California, Los Angeles.

Peter Yates, Mary-Jeannette Brown, and Frances Mullen Yates in the Roof studio, 1735 Micheltorena Street, 1951. Photo courtesy of Mrs. William G. Selwyn.

Marni Nixon in 1959. Department of Special Collections, University Research Library, University of California, Los Angeles.

Sonata] Temianka said it sounded like Scriabin, but Szigeti said, No, it's bigger and all vital."[68] The concert was broadcast and a tape recording made. Mullen took her performance of the *Concord* to Tucson and Tempe, Arizona.

THIRTEENTH SEASON: 1950–1951

The distinguished cellist Joseph Schuster gave two benefit recitals for the Roof's thirteenth season, playing the five cello sonatas by Beethoven and two by Hindemith, with Shibley Boyes, in the Wilshire-Ebell Chamber Music Hall. The regular series branched into two, the second of which posed a brilliant challenge for the fine string quartet ensembles the concerts had generated. The American Art Quartet, Compinsky Quartet, and Coriolan Quartet participated in this series. In six concerts (titled "Mozart Series"), the string quartets and quintets of Mozart were juxtaposed with six contemporary quartets: Berg's *Lyric Suite,* Ives's postponed Second String Quartet, and quartets by Schoenberg, Hindemith, Bartók, Anton Webern, Miklos Rozsa, and Leon Kirchner. Quartets of the last three were given first Los Angeles performances. Kirchner (who had recently completed his studies with Schoenberg, Ernest Bloch, and Roger Sessions) also gave the first Los Angeles performance of his Duo for Violin and Piano (1947), with Eudice Shapiro.

Robert Craft, a Juilliard graduate with several years' experience conducting modern scores in New York, had been living in Los Angeles since 1948 as Stravinsky's assistant. In his first appearance of many in these concerts, he conducted the Los Angeles Winds and others in first Los Angeles performances of works by Gilbert Grau and Gerald Strang for the Roof's fourth annual Los Angeles Composers program. Leonard Stein performed, after an extended absence due to disagreements with Peter Yates,[69] as one of the four pianists in the first Los Angeles performance of Stravinsky's work *Les Noces,* conducted by Dahl, with the Roger Wagner Chorale. On this outstanding program the Chorale also gave the first Los Angeles performance of Palestrina's *Pope Marcellus* Mass, Monteverdi madrigals, and J.S. Bach's Cantata No. 106, *Gottes Zeit ist die aller beste Zeit* (God's time is ever the best), with Wagner conducting.

The Roger Wagner Chorale had its origins as the Concert Youth Chorus, sponsored by the Los Angeles Bureau of Music, who chose Roger Wagner to be supervisor of youth choruses. He auditioned the best young singers in the city and in 1943 gathered twelve, including Marni Nixon, age thirteen, whom he found at Dorsey High School. Marilyn Horne auditioned when she was twelve and needed to learn to read music. He trained this group to provide the sound he wanted:

> I never let them force. I always [demanded] a forward sound, a yawny sound, and when the sopranos got high I didn't let them shriek. I respected the fact that they were young. . . . With Marni, she could sing above high C, but I wouldn't let her do much of that. She was a superb musician, she was a violinist. . . . [The flutist] Doriot Anthony practiced with Marni Nixon every Saturday at my house, so she could [make her flute] sound like a human voice.

These singers were the basis of the larger Roger Wagner Chorale, founded in 1946. With the chorale he made his first recording, of the *Pope Marcellus* Mass by Palestrina, for Capitol Records in 1949. The recognition and awards it garnered gained him an invitation to perform for the coronation of Queen Elizabeth II in 1953. Wagner was quickly becoming internationally known, but he remembered having to carry the risers for his singers onto the stage at the West Hollywood Park auditorium for the Roof concert. It occurred to him to start a series called "Monday Evenings in the Basement."[70]

The cellist George Neikrug played a full program, including the first Los Angeles performance of Ernst Toch's Chamber Concerto for Cello and Eleven Solo Instruments, Op. 35. Marni Nixon, a seasoned performer at age twenty, sang the first Los Angeles performance of Schoenberg's *Herzgewächse* (with a Hammond organ, as a harmonium could not be found). Her performance in this spectacular work inevitably resulted in an encore, which, she remembers, terrified her, because she would have to repeat the F above high C.[71] Ives's *Aeschylus and Sophocles* and *Hallowe'en* were given first Los Angeles performances. Yates had not regularly documented premieres in his programs,[72] but now that this was clearly an important and natural part of the Roof's adventurous programming policies, an attempt was made to record them.

By this time, Sol Babitz had acquired copies of an eighteenth-century bow and violin, built for him by the Dolmetsch workshop. Albert Goldberg commented in lukewarm fashion about a concert by the New Friends of Old Music in the Wilshire-Ebell Chamber Music Hall: "Old music of this type undoubtedly needs some new friends"; but he found "a gap between talent and genius, both in the performers and the composers." The composers were Henry Eccles, François Couperin, J. S. Bach, Rameau, and Corelli; the performers were Babitz, Kuhnle, and James Arkatov, playing a modern cello. Goldberg continued,

> The violin is smaller than the standard model and must be played without a chin rest; the bow is shorter than the Tourte design used by contemporary violinists and much more loosely strung. As a classroom demonstration the exhibition had its points; chords and various other passages can obviously be much more easily executed on the type of instruments for which they were written, but the small unresonant tone, at least as produced by Mr. Babitz, is scarcely to be preferred permanently to the modern style violin.[73]

By 1950 there were 510 season subscribers for Evenings on the Roof. Lawrence Morton later remarked that the thirteenth season had probably "the attendance record for all time for the sale of season tickets." There were not enough seats for the first program, on which Olivier Messiaen's *Quartet for the End of Time* was given its West Coast premiere by the violinist Joachim Chassman, his clarinetist son Edmund, the cellist Michel Penha, and the pianist Shibley Boyes.[74] The City of Los Angeles Bureau of Music was calling the Evenings on the Roof audiences "among the most musically sophisticated in the nation."[75] But each season was threatened with a deficit.

FOURTEENTH SEASON: 1951–1952

The prospectus for the fourteenth season showed the efficiency and hard work of Mary-Jeannette Brown. Through John Anson Ford, a county supervisor, she arranged free use of the West Hollywood Park auditorium (at 647 North San Vicente Boulevard, between Melrose Avenue and Santa Monica Boulevard) in lieu of the county's financial support for the concerts. This larger auditorium could seat six hundred and was often filled. (A drawback of the county facility was that the national anthem had to be played at the beginning of the programs.) Brown and Yates managed to interest *Time* magazine in an article on the concerts. "They pick their program to please themselves . . . [and] do not give a hoot for the critics," wrote *Time*.[76] There were twenty-three concerts, again divided into two series. A list was printed of sixty-two contributors to the Southern California Chamber Music Society, and over three hundred subscribers to the fourteenth season (a drop, perhaps caused by the change in auditorium). Writing in *The Music Review* (published in London), the critic Everett Helm wrote: "In recent years music activity in Los Angeles has increased and the quality thereof has risen to such an extent that this sprawling Western city now runs the compact island of Manhattan a close second and in one field, chamber music, bids fair to surpass it. Particularly outstanding is the unique organization called Evenings on the Roof."[77]

The opening concert, announced as the 262nd Roof concert in Los Angeles (and covered by *Time*), featured the first Los Angeles performance of William Walton's *Façade,* with the film star Jane Wyatt as reciter. In other programs, Copland's *Twelve Poems by Emily Dickinson* were given a local premiere by the mezzo-soprano Muriel Maxwell and Shibley Boyes. Eudice Shapiro and Shibley Boyes played four Mozart violin sonatas. The pianist Natalie Limonick played the entire *Ludus tonalis* of Hindemith (also a Los Angeles first). The Roger Wagner Chorale and the Occidental College Choir, conducted by Howard Swan, offered full programs, ranging from Monteverdi to Brahms. Frances Mullen, after another year of illness, played a full program: Beethoven's "Waldstein" Sonata, Haydn, Schoenberg, and Maurice Ravel's *Gaspard de la nuit.*

Sol Babitz and Wesley Kuhnle continued to educate the audience in early performance practices, this time giving attention to tuning temperaments. Kuhnle played his own harpsichord, tuned approximately one half-step lower than modern pitch and to mean-tone temperament, in J. S. Bach's *Capriccio on the Departure of His Most Beloved Brother* and François Couperin's seventh prelude from *L'Art de toucher le clavecin.* Suzanne Bloch, daughter of the composer Ernest Bloch and student of Arnold Dolmetsch, performed as solo guest artist in a full program of music from the thirteenth to the seventeenth century for voice, lute, recorders, and virginals.

Robert Craft conducted the first Los Angeles performance of Schoenberg's Serenade, Op. 24, which he was to record for Columbia Records. A California Composers program (of works by Paul Pisk, Andrew Imbrie, William O. Smith, George Hyde, and Mildred Couper) included two Ives quarter-tone pieces for two pianos, since Couper's works were for the same combination. Several programs were sent to Arizona and to Santa Barbara, where Mildred Couper owned a beautiful home called Monteverde, which became one site—along with the Lobero Theater—of touring programs by Roof musicians.

Yates, now deeply immersed in the writing of a large novel that had haunted him for years, retreated further from concert planning but remained in charge of out-of-town contacts. (The novel's title was "University." It was planned in three volumes and conceived in "symphonic form," with use of sonata form, development, variations, stretto, etc.: "A form better suited on the whole to a novel than a symphony. . . . I am very pleased with the result," Yates wrote Houston on 19 January 1953. But the grandiose project was never published.) Lawrence Morton, who had been brought by Dahl and Rebner onto the Board of Musicians, took on the role of coordinator of the concerts, while Yates and Mullen were named founders. Morton was particularly interested in programming. For this fourteenth season he arranged (with the help of Don Christlieb, the bassoonist-founder of the Los Angeles Woodwinds) to have transcriptions of Bach's entire *Art of Fugue* made by thirteen local composers and arrangers—many of them from the film studios.[78] The work was performed at the end of the season by the Los Angeles Woodwinds and Brass, the American Art Quartet, Carol Rosenstiel and Frances Mullen, harpsichords, and Magdaleno Rivera, contrabass, all conducted by Morton. *Los Angeles Times* music critic "W.H." found Bach difficult listening. He gave Morton credit for "tackling so difficult and ambitious a job" but felt that he contributed little to the actual performance. "His mechanical, unimaginative, and undramatic conducting did not help a poorly integrated ensemble."[79] This was the only time Morton conducted for the concerts. Yates called the performance "a hit, particularly with the players, and the sound was wonderful."[80]

FIFTEENTH SEASON: 1952–1953

The fifteenth season started out with a disaster. Planning for each new season was initiated soon after the current season was under way and was usually completed by early spring. Mary-Jeannette Brown had taken increasing responsibility in the organization and had run things with efficiency. In spite of an enlarging budget, she had managed to keep deficits small, even entirely eliminated in the fourteen season. She kept excellent records and managed details so smoothly as to allow considerable expansion. Yates himself was deeply relieved that the quality of the programs themselves remained excellent. His novel demanded tremendous sustained energy. Frances had suffered a mental breakdown in the spring of 1951 and had not played for a year.[81] At the employment office Yates faced an increasing load in an occupation "so physically and emotionally destructive [it] leaves no desire, or little hope . . . of rising beyond the low grade I have held so many years." As "a well-known, unreconstructed rebel," he was bypassed for promotion and given assignments where he could at all times be checked. He described how he felt about his work to Houston: "I meet and reach out to a large part of the globe, body to body, through the dirty, crowded, foul-smelling office where a few of us by an effort of discipline keep standing in long lines the mob that shouted in the coliseum and fed the guillotine."[82]

Two weeks before Yates's 1952 summer vacation, Mary-Jeannette

Brown suddenly announced her resignation. Her reasons were that her salary was not commensurate with her abilities and that, despite her warnings to the Board, the Southern California Chamber Music Society had not succeeded—and seemed unlikely to succeed—in properly endowing the concerts. A deficit was looming. Yates felt Brown was suffering the consequences of the rigidity she had established as her management style. "If she had quit before commencing plans for next season, I would have let [the concerts] go," Yates wrote to Houston, "but she quit with obligations and commitments well along, leaving innumerable problems to be solved." She offered "rosy solutions," such as persuading the musicians' union to pay all performers' fees out of the union's recording fund and finding donors to put up a minimum of $5,000 a year.[83] Yates himself had organized some nineteen out-of-town concerts (in California at Redlands, Santa Barbara, Long Beach State College, and also in Arizona). A four-program retrospective had been organized to memorialize Schoenberg, who had died the previous year. An Art Song Competition, endorsed by Lotte Lehmann, to be judged by the most distinguished vocal and choral leaders in Los Angeles, was in the works, along with another full season of concerts.

Yates reinvolved himself in plans for the coming season, while persuading Brown to stay on until September, when she planned to move to New York. Lawrence Morton wrote to his close friend Ingolf Dahl (who was teaching at Tanglewood), "[The Roof] is Peter's property again."[84] There was growing tension between himself and Yates over control of the concerts. William Hume, a composition student of George Tremblay's who was teaching part-time at Occidental College, took on the duties of executive secretary.

During the summer Yates suffered the illness he had endured each vacation when released from the accumulating tensions: the head-to-foot outbreak of what he called shingles, with fever, depression, and degrading physical exhaustion.[85] To relieve his stress he turned to playing Kuhnle's collection of harpsichords. He placed an order with Kuhnle to have his own spinet made. As their encouragement to Yates, the Board of Musicians presented him with a check to help him pay for the instrument. They expressed, in a letter, "the gratitude and appreciation felt by so many of the musicians of Los Angeles. Your contribution not only to their own development but to that of the city's cultural stature is not easily weighed. It is, however, deeply felt and profoundly realized by us all."[86] Although Yates still wanted to separate himself from the pressures of the concerts, he was again working hard on the difficulties. One problem was expressed in the prospectus for the fifteenth season: "Musical visitors to Paris, Berlin, London, New York, tell us repeatedly how musical people everywhere know and ask about Evenings on the Roof of Los Angeles. . . . Is Evenings on the Roof praised and valued as much in Los Angeles, the community which it directly benefits?"[87]

The season itself was a very important one. The four Schoenberg retrospective programs presented more of his works than had been performed in a series anywhere else until then.[88] This "cultural event of first magnitude," as Morton pronounced it (in his new position as music critic for the liberal magazine *Frontier*),[89] was made possible largely because Robert Craft was unintimidated by difficult scores and able to undertake the rehearsing and conducting of such works as Schoenberg's Serenade, Op. 24, the Suite for Septet, Op. 29, the *Ode to Napoleon Buonaparte,* Op. 41, the cantata, *The Lover's Wish,* Op. 27, and *Pierrot lunaire,* Op. 21. Many other Schoenberg chamber works were already familiar to Roof musicians from previous performances; they felt at home with the music and were now able to enjoy performing it. "There is a wonderful serenity, humor, flow of multi-rhythmed motion in well-played Schoenberg which can be known only when you have heard it played like this," Yates wrote Houston.[90] Robert Craft recorded the Serenade and the Suite for Septet for Columbia records. Stravinsky, his nose in the scores, was in close attendance at rehearsals and recording sessions. This was his first close exposure to much of Schoenberg's work. After the first Schoenberg program, on 15 September 1952 (which included the Three Piano Pieces, Op. 11; *The Book of the Hanging Gardens,* Op. 15; Six Little Piano Pieces, Op. 19; and the Serenade, Op. 24), Yates wrote Houston, "I feel that I have helped to end the long feud between Schoenberg and Stravinsky. Igor has become a devotee of his rival's music, sat the whole evening score in hand following every note."[91]

Craft brought the original manuscript of Pierre Boulez's *Polyphonie X* (for eighteen solo instruments) from Paris in May 1952.[92] Don Christlieb gathered wind players for its first American performance (6 October 1952). During the difficult summer rehearsals Yates asked Houston, "Do you know of Boulez? If not I can only tell you that [the work] is violently post-Schoenberg, with multiple rows in complex arrangement, the musicians hate it, for which I don't blame them, and it is the shocker of the moment in the advanced musical world."[93] To another friend of the concerts, Yates described Stravinsky's reaction to the Boulez work:

> Igor practically took me on his lap. He wished to explain to me what is wrong, aesthetically, with the Boulez Polyphony: it has no continuity. I explained that this is indeed the very purpose of the Boulez-Cage aesthetic as of present information, to break up continuity, to provide a set of discontinuous experiences. He listened patiently and resumed by pointing out that it is of course extremely interesting and marvelously well played, but it has no continuity, it does not lead the ear and mind on.[94]

Later Yates recalled about the performance of this work (which Boulez soon withdrew): "It took three sets of players before the third group finally made it to the stage, looking as though they wouldn't get off again. And when they came off triumphant, it was like the winning football team. It was a very interesting thing to watch." He also remembered that Stravinsky's close friend Aldous Huxley "was very complimentary about the way it was done."[95] On the program with Boulez's first Los Angeles bombshell, Craft also conducted a Bach cantata and two little-known works of Haydn, which received their first American performance. One of these, a *Feldpartita,* required the use of a serpent, an obsolete bass wind instrument invented in the sixteenth century. The ever-enterprising bassoonist Don Christlieb had acquired the Haydn works from Vienna, and a serpent from

England, and created quite a stir by performing with the instrument coiled in front of him.[96]

Luigi Dallapiccola's wartime protest against fascism, *Canti di prigionia* (1941), for mixed chorus, two pianos, two harps, and percussion, received its first West Coast performance (12 January 1953), along with Claudio Monteverdi's *Lagrime d'amante al sepolcro dell'amata,* sung by a chorus from the University of Southern California, conducted by Charles Hirt. Marjorie Low, soprano, and Marvin Hayes, bass, won the Art Song Competition and presented a joint recital. Academic musicologists began taking interest in the work of Sol Babitz, who, Yates reported to Houston, was at last learning to control his violin and bow, rebuilt in the style of 1750, "no mean feat for a violinist who makes his living [in the studios] on a modern instrument."[97]

In the spring of 1953 Craft conducted the first Los Angeles performances of Stravinsky's *Renard* (1916–1917) and *Pribaoutki* (1914). After the concert (30 March 1953) Lawrence Morton reported to Ingolf Dahl,

> Last week's *Renard* was wonderful and made a big hit with an unfortunately small audience. I had to copy 25 pages of the new piano part which replaces the cimbalom [unavailable in Los Angeles]. . . . What a job! Also I translated *Pribaoutki* from the French, but I'm afraid it isn't successful, really. One of the best concerts we ever had. . . . Monday evening with Peter, Oscar Moss, Bob [Craft], and Bill Hume on the subject of Roof survival. Everyone seems hopeful. Bob will have a hundred plums, most of which I shall have to cultivate; Peter will lord-and-master it from Olympian heights; Hume will have no end of drudgery; and I daresay I will have to do a lot of dirty work myself. But it's fun cooking up programs. . . . We shall want you to play Stravinsky's *Piano Rag* and his *Tango* on a wonderful program. . . . It will be Igor's "JAZZ"—the *Ragtime* for 11 Instruments; the two piano pieces; a *Praeludium* for jazz orchestra which was written several years ago but never performed—this will be a premiere, though it's only a 5 or 6 minute work; and the *Ebony Concerto*. . . . If you want to play piano in the *Ragtime* he will rewrite the cimbalom part for us.[98]

The season was of the greatest importance to Stravinsky, for he had reached a crisis point (described by Craft in his book *Present Perspectives*) in March 1952, when he felt he could no longer compose.[99] Craft's enthusiasm for and involvement with the music of Schoenberg roused Stravinsky's creative energies and boundless curiosity; he received crucial nourishment for his composing from the breadth of repertoire in these chamber concerts; and the prospect of rearranging older works for immediate performances by the fine performers at hand kept him at work and productive in the seasons to come.

The fifteenth season ended with a mighty deficit of $3,342, owing in part to a naive system (instituted by Oscar Moss, Lawrence Morton, and the new Musicians' Board) of selling discounted books of coupons, rather than season subscriptions to the concerts. People took advantage of the bargain and brought all their friends on their personal coupons. An emergency campaign for funds to assure another season resulted in a friendly article by Albert Goldberg, in which he noted that Cecil Smith (formerly editor of *Musical America,* and now music critic of the London *Daily Express*) had recently written in his book *Worlds of Music:* "Evenings on the Roof presents the country's most adventurous array of music new and old, played by admirable performers many of whom are otherwise buried in the Hollywood studios." Goldberg admired the courage it took "to depart from the beaten track and make music itself [the musicians'] aim rather than personal glorification." He listed many of the accomplishments of the organization, described its financial plight, and ended,

> The Roof has made a unique place for itself. Its programs have been exasperating on occasion, but far more often they have been stimulating and provocative, and seldom are they just plain dull. They are an asset to music and to the community, and one would not willingly dispense with them. It is sincerely to be hoped that ways and means will be found for them to continue.[100]

Yates expressed his gratitude to Goldberg in a letter, in which he remarked on the adjective "exasperating": "You put it mildly. . . .

Though I've missed completely only one program in the history of the Roof, I've wished myself away from more than a few."[101]

SIXTEENTH SEASON: 1953–1954

In the fall of 1953 Yates gave a talk urging the audience to support ticket sales and asked contributors willing to underwrite the concerts to meet him at the front of the hall after the concert. Only Aldous Huxley came forward, "heavy with sympathy, a hovering compliment."[102] Sadye and Oscar Moss telephoned later to volunteer full responsibility for underwriting the concerts from that time forward. Yates accepted their help, as long as they would have no influence on the programming. This had been a sticking point with other potential donors, but the Mosses agreed. Yates expressed his gratitude in his oral history: "The patron who supports a concert series without imposing his own tastes and wishes on what is performed is the rarest of men."[103]

The printed concert programs themselves are evidence of the power struggle at this time over control of the concerts. Yates was loathe to let go, yet the old order was changing. With Lawrence Morton's time increasingly available for programming and arrangements with personnel, striking changes began in the sixteenth season. Yates's concept of steady membership in a closely knit cooperative was pushed aside, as many new performers came in. Craft began to dominate the programs, and there were many performances of Stravinsky's works. The season opened with Craft conducting a performance of *Il Combattimento di Tancredi e Clorinda,* by Monteverdi (with a sonata for three violins by Giovanni Gabrieli and—in great contrast—the Mendelssohn Octet for Strings, Op. 20). Stravinsky attended, as he usually did for Craft's concerts, and after the concert remarked to Morton, "An organization that puts on a program like that is going to be a dedicatee of my next piece."[104] The concerts reminded Stravinsky of his youthful experiences at the St. Petersburg Evenings of Contemporary Music, where he had performed his own pieces and had heard new work by the most exciting composers of the day. His next work,

Three Songs from William Shakespeare, was dedicated to Peter Yates and the Evenings on the Roof, "as a tribute to their artistic achievements during sixteen seasons of concerts." It was premiered later that season (8 March 1954), with performances of his Cantata (1952), his Septet (1953)—a work directly inspired by Schoenberg's Suite for Septet, recently conducted and recorded by Craft—and Debussy's Sonata for Flute, Viola, and Harp. At a private dinner given by Oscar Moss, Stravinsky presented Yates with a sheet of sketches for the *Shakespeare* songs, with a dedicatory couplet: "For Peter Yates, Who kindled his roof in the Evenings / For listeners so cool in the day."[105]

Earlier in the season (19 October 1953) the era of Stravinsky premieres in Evenings on the Roof got off to a lively start with the Elliott Brothers' jazz band,[106] assisted by many other performers and Craft as conductor, in the half-program of "Stravinsky Jazz," including two works from the forties (*Tango,* newly orchestrated for a jazz group, and *Ebony Concerto*), the recently revised version (with piano instead of cimbalom) of *Ragtime for Eleven Instruments,* selections from *L'Histoire du soldat,* and the world premiere of *Praeludium* (1937), originally conceived for jazz band. Ingolf Dahl gave a memorable performance of Stravinsky's *Piano-Rag-Music.*

Craft also conducted a program of Renaissance and early Baroque music, works by J. S. Bach, and Heinrich Schütz's *Fili mi, Absalon,* in which the bass soloist Marvin Hayes (male winner of the Art Song Competition held in late 1952) and a quartet of trombones made a lasting impression. Preoccupation with music of the early Baroque became important in Morton's programming. The music was a fresh contrast with increasingly complex twentieth-century scores, but it was also difficult to find. Craft recalled, "Musicology had not yet become the heavy industry that it is now, and most of what the two of us knew about old music performance was a mixture of book-learning and on-the-spot practical decisions. Sol Babitz edited most of the Schütz that we performed."[107]

For a program presented 18 January 1954, Peter Yates turned to classical Japanese music of the eighteenth and nineteenth centuries performed by highly regarded musicians of Los Angeles' Japanese community and wrote to Henry Cowell (who was deeply interested in music of other cultures),

> I put on Mr. Eto, Mrs. Nakashima, Mr. Yamaguchi, and Atsuko Yamaguchi . . . carefully prepared for by opening with a neutral, embellished solo cantata by Telemann and followed by an even more neutral duo for two strings by Honegger; then a big Bach cantata. The first four minutes of shock when kotos, samisen, shakuhachi, and artificial vocalization hit the ears of our receptive audience were something to remember, if you listen to the undertone of audiences the way I do. They were ready to run, as some of them ran from our half-evening of Webern. After that it was a triumph. Atsuko and I squatted at the edge of the stage during intermission displaying and talking about the instruments.[108]

The half-program of Anton Webern's songs (Opp. 15–18), pieces for violin and piano (Op. 7), for cello and piano (Op 11), Quartet (Op. 22), and Concerto for Nine Instruments (Op. 24), conducted by Robert Craft on 8 February 1954, was the occasion for a vehement reaction on the part of the film composer Miklos Rozsa, who walked out, slamming the door.[109] On the other hand, Yates reported to Houston that the pianist Leonard Stein, who performed in five of the nine works, complained that "nobody in the audience had let out a boo. 'They can't all have liked it that much,' he insisted. 'Some of them must have hated it; and how much better it would have been for them to boo.' "[110] At the same time Craft recorded his epoch-making set of the complete works of Webern with the Roof performers, and, as Yates described it to Houston, Stravinsky "sat through the rehearsals, his nose in the score. . . . Then he came to the concert and did the same over again. At more than 70 he retains a young man's capacity to hear music the first time, to take it all in as a new experience with all the excitement of discovery."[111] Yates himself, contemplating the new wave of post-Webernism sweeping the avant-garde, confided to Houston his disaffection: "Unless I am to be presently converted, I part company with the present vogue."[112]

Frances Mullen gave her last program at the Roof concerts on 2

November 1953, playing Mozart and Beethoven sonatas, Lou Harrison's Suite for Piano, and, with Manuel Compinsky, works they had performed previously for violin and piano by Mozart and Bartók; in keeping with the new phase of the concerts, they added Stravinsky's *Duo concertant* (1932).

Leon Kirchner, a brilliant pianist, performed his own *Sonata concertante* for violin and piano with Eudice Shapiro, and the two of them recorded it.[113] In its recording, this large piece makes tangible the invaluable benefit composers derived from the Roof and its principles. The piece involves many cadenzas for both instruments. For this performance, Eudice Shapiro remembers the composer reworking the entire piece (which had been premiered the previous year in Carnegie Hall by Tossy Spivakovsky and Kirchner): "We [re-]wrote it as we rehearsed it. We would try out something, and then try something else. We worked together, phrase by phrase: Maybe we should do this, maybe we should do that. . . . He changed a lot of things. It was published in its original form, but by the time we got to recording it—I used his manuscript all the way, as did he—it was completely different."[114] Yates's last large gesture, before turning management of the concerts over to Lawrence Morton, was a concert (11 January 1954) of the music of Ingolf Dahl, recently returned from a Guggenheim Fellowship year in Europe with new compositions. Dahl had attended the Roof programs from their very beginning. He had joined the Roof group to play Beethoven piano sonatas in the first Beethoven festival (1940–1941) and had been not only a faithful and strong performing member of the cooperative group but one who understood Yates's principles. In 1948, when he became first chairperson of the Musicians' Board, Dahl had given a talk outlining these radical ideas from his own point of view. He claimed:

> The musician . . . realizes that "audience appeal" is a false criterion for programming. We become accustomed to what we hear most frequently; deprived of the opportunity to hear, how can we increase our hearing faculties and develop our tastes? And, unless our audiences become more experienced and more discriminating, how can the musician in America find gratification for his artistic as well as his economic needs?[115]

Dahl, a painstaking and relatively unprolific composer, flourished in the atmosphere of the Roof. He, like others, wrote specifically for the brilliant performers with whom he came in contact through the concerts.[116] During the war, at the outset of his composing career, he thanked Yates for writing about his music in *Arts and Architecture:* "I received a great deal of spiritual help through it, and a great deal of propping up and encouragement which I need quite badly, as every artist does in these discouraging and inimical times . . . helping me in my very own struggle against isolation and defeatism."[117] A remark by Edward Rebner (a fine film studio pianist who had studied piano with Schnabel, composition with Hindemith, and conducting with Szell) sums up what many performers felt about Evenings on the Roof:

> You ask what "E. on the R.," cultural bulwark against commercialism, has meant to me? Spiritually it was my home; economically, my hobby. It assured me that I had a profession, not just a job. And it seemed to justify sacrificing my childhood practicing the piano. Performing for critical listeners, who can judge a work as well as its interpretation, is a great privilege and one of "E. on the R.'s" most valued aspects.[118]

Letters from Peter Yates to Peyton Houston show the emotional toll taken of both the Yateses as they left the organization. Frances Mullen had been the mainstay of the concerts in the early years, playing the largest repertoire of any performer, sweeping the pine needles from the steps to the Roof studio and getting the children to sleep before concerts in their home, mailing innumerable announcements and tickets, hosting untold numbers of meetings and conferences. It was for her that Yates had formed his first ideas for the concerts. Now she felt a distaste for the effort of learning new works and suffered an emotional breakdown so acute that she required shock treatment, the prescribed remedy of the 1950s.[119] Yates was devastated by her illness. He felt the keyboard had "been put in the background by our burgeoning, indeed overblown, creation of chamber music. . . . It seems odd that in trying to make a place for her I have made a greater one for myself. This was not intended."[120] Yates was clearly feeling exhausted and torn by his need to write, yet he recognized that his "fighting persistence and devoted fury" for the Roof "may be . . . or has been my life's work. How or when am I to give it up? or for what?"[121] Few were aware of his passion for early music—at that time gaining wider recognition as a field for fruitful endeavor—which made him wish for a new start in music. As for contemporary music in 1954, he wrote his friend Peyton Houston:

> I do feel that music, temporarily, has reached a dead point where nothing reverberates. . . . but conscience reminds me in a wifely voice, you have ridden the peak of a tide at the crest of a wave and are a little breathless after being banged flat on shore. . . . Oh but to do it again! To join tide and wave together at the crest . . . so boating back out on my plank I meet the revival of the older music coming in and am off again, though I know it can never be the same.[122]

Four

PETER YATES AND THE MUSICAL MODERNISTS

"I HAVE A PROPHETIC STREAK in listening to music," Peter Yates observed in 1966.[1] His espousal of the music of Béla Bartók, while he was still in college and Bartók was practically unknown in the United States except to his American piano students, was a weather vane pointing to the future. (Ralph Hawkes, Bartók's publisher, remembered encountering apathy and aversion everywhere when promoting Bartók's music in the United States in 1940–1941.)[2] If young Frances Mullen had not accepted Peter's very first repertoire suggestion to her—"By all means, Bartók!"; if Yates had not been convinced that an all-Bartók recital would be the way Mullen should attack her eventually aborted New York City debut; and if the same program had not seemed to him the best way to open Evenings on the Roof, this enterprise might not have engaged the interest of the "articulate and worthwhile audience" Yates hoped for.[3]

The Yates-Houston correspondence presents the unfolding of events in Yates's encounters with the new music. In 1934 Mullen, "with rage in her eye," tackled Bartók's Sonata for Piano (1926). Artie Mason Carter sent a program of one of Mullen's programs to Bartók. After Mullen and Burrow took an all-Bartók program to Mills College in 1938, Yates himself wrote Bartók—without results—to ask for more music.[4] As the Roof concerts opened with the all-Bartók program in April 1939, Yates feared that Bartók's personality "is too well expressed by his music to be at once accessible."[5] In May 1940 he and Mullen obtained all six books of the recently published *Mikrokosmos.* Yates wrote Houston, "It is probably his most permanent contribution to the art. . . . Several are the tightest pieces of thinking in music. . . . No problem is repeated; each reintroduction of the same problem involves an entirely fresh difficulty in relationship."[6] He published an article in *California Arts and Architecture* in April 1941 on Bartók's "basically fresh approach to the use of the keyboard instrument."

He hoped to invite the composer to the Roof for an evening of his own music, if he should come on a concert tour to Los Angeles. "Certainly he'll find no one else in this country who has presented more of [his music]," he wrote Houston, when he learned that the composer and his pianist wife had settled in the United States.[7] On 5 December 1941 Bartók did come to play a piano recital, mostly of his own music, with some eighteenth-century pieces and one piece by Kodály, at the Wilshire-Ebell Theater. He was welcomed by the mayor of Los Angeles; Hungarian girls in peasant dress offered him flowers, but a mere handful of an audience was present. Yates and Mullen gathered their accumulated programs of their Bartók performances and waited for the composer after the concert backstage at the Wilshire-Ebell, having brought along their friends and colleagues to make up a good number of the small audience. Yates wrote about the concert and Bartók's music in a second article on the composer, titled "Béla Bartók Plays," for *California Arts and Architecture:*

> It is thinking but it is not intellectual music. . . . Whoever calls Bartók dissonant damns his own ears for laziness or incompetence. . . . Played by him his music returns to the eighteenth century and to still earlier days. . . . [His] later music will originate a new study of the speech of music. . . . Like Ives and Schoenberg he teaches us in music, music of our own unrecognized harsh, sweet idiom, to think like contemporary human beings.[8]

Only in 1953, well after Bartók's death, was Yates able to confess what happened at the December 1941 recital:

> My only meeting with Bartók resulted in the most thorough snub I have received from any human being. . . . We stood in line happily . . . love beaming as we thought unmistakably from our eyes and faces, yet ashamed to have heard Bartók playing to so many empty seats. . . . We drew near. He was very small, weighing even less than a hundred pounds. . . . He seemed all head, all sprite, all sparkling, alight intelligence, radiantly gathered above the articulate jaw, the straight stubborn lips, the sharply directed nose, in the unforgettable personality of his eyes. . . . I held out my hand to him trying to find in my mouth words to say that might reflect something of the devotion which had been so long in my mind; and in my other hand I held out the envelope containing the little bundle of our programs. Nothing passed between us but the bundle, which he accepted and at once threw upon the shelf behind him. His personality withdrew, folded itself softly and silently out of my sight, became cold, and my spirit shivered as that icy wind passed.[9]

To Houston, at the time of their encounter, Yates remarked, "Our own contact with him after the concert was a waste of time. When he learned that Frances had not studied with anyone of his group he lost interest. What she had done for or with his music seemed of no interest."[10]

Yates's devotion was not easily shaken. In 1943, unable to find a local violinist willing to tackle Bartók's Second Violin Sonata (after Orline Burrow's success with the work and subsequent departure for a Texan marriage), Yates wrote Joseph Szigeti, who had toured and recorded with Bartók since the late 1920s. Szigeti replied that he could not imagine performing this difficult work with anyone but the composer. "Perhaps some day he may be brought to the Coast for some other assignment and we will be able to utilize *that* opportunity!" he wrote Yates.[11] In March 1945 Yates mulled over a plan (never realized) to raise money for Roof commissions to Bartók and Schoenberg.[12]

After the concert honoring Bartók's memory on 12 November 1945, he wrote Houston,

> Bartók in my opinion, next to Schoenberg, is the greatest composer of his time. But to compare Bartók with Schoenberg or anyone is like comparing Couperin with Bach. . . . Bartók was one of those creative personalities that are beholden to no one. They neither begin nor end an epoch; they are not transitional. What they make is in every way their own, unique, a single star in no constellation.[13]

Yates watched with irony the rise in popular esteem of Bartók's music, and musicians' and critics' changes of heart, after Bartók's tragic death in September 1945.[14] By 1949 he felt that this change caused greater acceptance of Schoenberg's music as well.[15] He ended the Bartók chapter in his *Twentieth Century Music* (1967) with a prophesy: "In perhaps fifty or a hundred years composers of a new order may return to him for renewal, as he himself and Schoenberg and Charles Ives did not imitate Beethoven but renewed their art in his."[16]

On 4 April 1977 Monday Evening Concerts presented an all-Bartók program dedicated to the memory of Peter Yates, who had died the previous year in Buffalo of a sudden heart attack at the age of sixty-seven. The program note reproduced the Roof's announcement of its first season and included Lawrence Morton's "Remembrance of Peter Yates," in which he spoke of the Roof's first all-Bartók program:

> On 23 April 1939 Peter Yates opened a door to let music in. Other doors had been opened before this, but only sporadically and temporarily. . . . Tonight's concert is not so much a memorial as an expression of gratitude for his idealism, his leadership, and his selfless labor. Bartók is by no means the only composer who might have been chosen as a symbol of Peter's work. But Bartók was "in the beginning". . .[17]

Schoenberg and Ives followed soon after Bartók. Yates's passionate commitment to Schoenberg grew as he took advantage of opportunities for direct contact with the composer in Los Angeles' rich gathering of émigré artists. From the spring of 1939 until Schoenberg's illnesses made communication difficult, Mullen and Yates had frequent meetings with the composer, whom Yates came to revere and understand, in spite of—perhaps because of—the obstacles the composer raised. Evenings on the Roof mounted nine all-Schoenberg programs between 1939 and 1954—more than any other composer received.[18]

Yates's and Mullen's study of Schoenberg began in 1933 and gathered impetus the following year with Schoenberg's arrival in Los Angeles. While Mullen tackled Schoenberg's Six Little Piano Pieces, Op. 19, for Houston's benefit Yates compared Schoenberg's aesthetic of the emancipation of dissonance to the attitude, particularly in modern poetry, that "to be good poetry, a combination of words need not necessarily make sense."[19] In the spring of 1935, after reading excerpts from Schoenberg's *Harmonielehre* in an English translation of Egon Wellesz's *Arnold Schönberg* (1925), he regretted that he could not afford to hear the complete series of lectures Schoenberg was offering in Hollywood. When he managed to hear the composer analyze J. S. Bach's *Art of Fugue* he reported to Houston Schoenberg's thesis that "nothing is admissible that is not related to the germ idea."[20] The Yateses heard Schoenberg conduct the Los Angeles Philharmonic on 27 December 1935 at USC in a program of his own works. "The sight of our rabidly modern-hating Philharmonic playing Schoenberg was damned comical," Yates wrote Houston.[21] (He later remembered that the orchestra sabotaged the works by "horsing around.")[22] In spite of a rough performance of the Chamber Symphony, Op. 9a (arranged by the composer for full orchestra), Yates wrote, "it is like nothing ever heard before. . . . This is tremendous compact music. . . . I hope to hear soon a sympathetic performance. It is perhaps our greatest music."[23]

In 1938, practicing the art of developing program notes for his prospective audience, Yates sent a short essay on Schoenberg to Houston, in which he maintained that

> Schoenberg's art is integral experience. . . . As a composer Schoenberg has been damned for everything from congenital madness to icy-minded mathematics. The laziest ruse is to dismiss him for a belated, soured Romantic. In reality he is ingenuous and passionate as Berlioz, and his Harmony Book a monument of musical thought to be compared with the treatise on orchestration. The most disturbing genius is profoundly naive; it is not convinced that there are bounds and regulations. "An artist," Schoenberg wrote of Gershwin, "is to me like an apple tree: when his time comes, whether he wants it or not, he bursts into bloom and starts to produce apples." . . . The music of Schoenberg is all character. It may be that Schoenberg will be more famous than performed; that is no reason to avoid or fear his music. It is uncomprehending fear which causes men to torment the naive revolutionary.[24]

As he began to prepare himself seriously for the art of criticism, Yates developed an idea to which he adhered for the rest of his life: that "true criticism is of those whom we are trying to love, not of those we detest or hate. A statement of hate or detestation is not yet criticism; like an axe blow it cuts out rank or precious growth; criticism is culling or pruning what we love."[25]

His affection was sorely tried in unproductive conferences in 1939 with Schoenberg about performances of *Pierrot lunaire* and the "fabulously difficult" Violin Concerto, Op. 36. Yates wondered "whether [Schoenberg] the professional artist is not professionally crazed."[26] Having been in his presence Yates noted, "It is easy to find him fallible and human."[27] At his "miniature estate" in Brentwood, outside Beverly Hills, Schoenberg showed Yates his paintings but would not allow him to exhibit them. Yates observed, "He is quick to act on the assumption that he is the greatest living composer and not to be classed as contemporary music," but little was known of his work, and Yates's efforts met many obstacles, chief among them Schoenberg's demand that musicians be paid for rehearsals beyond the financial capacity of the Roof's shoestring budget.[28] When the Schoenbergs, Adolph Weiss, and Joseph Achron attended the first all-Schoenberg program in the Roof studio in late January 1940, the composer, ever superstitious about the number thirteen, tried to evade having the thirteenth of the song cycle *The Book of the Hanging Gardens* (Op. 15) sung. During the performance, Gertrud Schoenberg whispered to Yates that it was just as well the German words of this song cycle could not be understood.[29] Yates himself had difficulty with *Pierrot* and found that while he was "always interested in [the] prophetic side of contemporary art," he cared least for the expressionist side of Schoenberg's music: "It is rather the abstract and classical side of his art, his great rhythmical and linear structures, electric with multiple voices or through silences, that I most enjoy. . . . Schoenberg's music is not likely to be worn out through too frequent hearing because it is of the sort which makes performances of it a special occasion."[30]

Yates's articles on Schoenberg took great care to address the average person who "is slow to abandon what he has learned to love, slow to incorporate into his affection new ways of thinking and feeling that are at first difficult." He ended the substance of his first Schoenberg article with the remark, "It is certain that before long the development of American musical taste will find out and learn to enjoy the vital personality embodied in his music. Artists of integrity may take new roads: the goal of excellence they seek is still the enduring love of average men."[31]

Yates saw to it that Schoenberg's works, or those of his pupils Gerald Strang, Adolph Weiss, George Tremblay, Lou Harrison, Leon Kirchner, Alban Berg, or (with some reluctance) Anton Webern were represented on programs every year of Evenings on the Roof. By the time of the all-Schoenberg program, on 10 May 1948, which included the West Coast premiere of the String Trio, Op. 45 (1946), and celebrated the tenth anniversary of Evenings on the Roof, Schoenberg had become more irascible, following his near-fatal illness. Yates reported to Houston on 5 March 1948:

> The other evening the hysterical voice of Schoenberg called me from supper to the phone. He wanted the negatives of his string trio, which we photostated for performance in May. He is quite convinced that all mankind is trying to steal copies of his music.

> I asked him whether he would come to our program of his music. The answer was not clear, but he made a statement to the effect that he will never again be seen at a concert in Los Angeles. . . . "After I am dead," cried Schoenberg, "they can honor my dead body, if they please." So I said that if he would not come to the music, we would bring the music to him. "Yes! Yes!" he shouted. I love the old man's warped and ropy guts.[32]

Yates described the large audience for this concert as "very cosmopolitan, able to sit through 35 exhausting minutes of the Wind Quintet, which Mrs. Schoenberg agrees is the most difficult piece to hear ever written, without wriggling more than a little." The String Trio was played "with the utmost accuracy and marvelous tone," and Yates privately claimed "a first performance, because the original performance at Harvard had, according to Jeno Lener [Eugene Lehner], formerly of the Kolisch Quartet, who followed it with the score, scarcely two right notes in sequence."[33]

Yates was asked by both the *Saturday Review* and the *New York Times* Sunday magazine for articles celebrating Schoenberg's seventy-fifth birthday. He visited Brentwood to obtain a photograph in August 1949 and observed to Houston:

> No one can be more gracious, more humble, more like oneself without thought of age than Schoenberg when he is interested in anything outside himself. Even himself he regards nowadays more dispassionately, from the outside, than formerly. . . . S. is like Ives less art-conscious, less the deliberate aesthete than Stravinsky. He has never reminded me of my amateur status, as so many lesser musicians find occasion to do, including some of his circle.[34]

In his *New York Times* article, "Arnold Schoenberg: Apostle of Atonality," Yates described the qualities that attracted him to the composer: "His art is infused with emotion. The force of his experience bears upon the listener with an urgency that will not be disregarded. . . . Technique and form are for him the outward expression of spiritual substance. . . . This overlying spirituality of his art should be kept in mind when talk runs too much on his technique or dissonance."[35] Schoenberg sent Yates a note of gratitude for his "really excellent" articles, adding, "This is what my affair needs: to state the true facts without apologies or attacks. I am really glad about all you wrote."[36] Yates continued his services for Schoenberg's cause, writing the liner notes for the first public issue, in 1950, of the Kolisch Quartet's 1937 recording of Schoenberg's four string quartets.[37]

After Schoenberg's death in January 1951, during the planning for the retrospective all-Schoenberg programs, Yates wrote Houston:

> I loved that difficult man, and now that I have well overcome the difficulties of hearing it I am convinced that until now the general reception accorded his music has been almost entirely uncomprehending, perhaps most uncomprehending on the part of the self-constituted disciples and dogmatic advocates of that primitive 12-tone method which Schoenberg himself had long since penetrated and outgrown. Far from being morbid, his music is fundamentally humorous, as he himself was, under the protective barbs of a sensibility raised erect like porcupine's quills against the virulence of public incomprehension, misrepresentation and unwillingness to listen to his art with simple common sense.[38]

The four all-Schoenberg programs were a great success, as the Roof's musicians and audience had become by then well accustomed to Schoenberg's music: "Even crusty conservatives go away admitting they are beginning to enjoy the stuff. These performances have none of the neurotic strain which mars performances by players who are not at home in the music. There is a wonderful serenity, humor, flow of multi-rhythmed motion in well-played Schoenberg which can be known only when have heard it played like this."[39] Yates reported the audience response to Schoenberg's Serenade, Op. 24, as "dewy-eyed between sheer delight in sound and admiration of both the work and the performance. Never has such beauty come from the humble mandolin, continually rising through the translucent instrumentation like spring water bubbling to the mouth along a little brook."[40]

Knowing Schoenberg was a precious experience to Yates. His article in *Arts and Architecture* immediately following Schoenberg's death recalled Schoenberg's vigor: "We had known him, behind the often querulous and eccentric mannerism, as a mind ceaselessly inquiring and maturing, a restless creative spirit that would not age. He was contemptuous of his own physical limitations as of other impediments, whatever stood in the way of his energy, that blending of emotion and intellect with action which was like a consummation of love."[41] In 1952, writing in *Arts and Architecture* about the Schoenberg retrospective, Yates continued ruminating on Schoenberg's composing as an act of love. He concluded, "The message of his art, from first to last, is love."[42] On 16 February 1961 he wrote Houston, "Schoenberg several times tried to compose a popular work, for example his concertos for violin and for piano, but could not escape the authority that prevented him. I know well how he suffered over this, because he could not understand how the gesture of love he had made, almost the sacrifice, should not be received. We are far too mundane in estimating the need of the artist."[43]

Yates's and Mullen's discovery of the music of Charles Ives in 1936, and Mullen's gradual mastery of the *Concord* Sonata, gave a strong impetus to the founding of Evenings on the Roof. Here was a true *American* modernist; Yates was elated. His first letter to Ives, 27 March 1938, fairly burst with excitement about the *Essays* (and begins to echo Ives's unique literary style):

> Thank you for your magnificent, religious, and gloriously musical book of essays [*Before a Sonata*]. There is a quality of thought which is not neo-European, which is vast, of the open air, mystical, harsh and often crude, the quality of Emerson's journals after he had begun to insist on his own way of expression, the quality of . . . Whitman, of Frank Lloyd Wright; this is our own way of speech and the speech of your music. We cannot learn that way of speech; it comes up in us through roots.[44]

He asked for a list of Ives's works for voice (for Radiana Pazmor, who was already well known to Ives), for piano, and for violin and piano; he inquired whether Ives had written a piano concerto. Ives replied—through Harmony Ives—that "there is nothing which is really a piano concerto—there was one but it is now buried." He will send the Second Orchestral Set ("almost a concerto") and the First Orchestral Set (*Three Places in New England*); he suggests the piano solos in the second movement of the Fourth Symphony and the Set for Chamber Orchestra, both published in Henry Cowell's *New Music Quarterly.* He will send the violin sonatas in photostat copies ("three are quite legible—but the good copy of the second was lost and only the one in my bad handwriting is left").[45] He suggests contacting Gerald Strang, who will be glad to let the Yateses have the nine volumes of chamber music belonging to the New Music Society.[46] He will have copies and parts of any pieces Yates asks for sent. Ives's letter continued, "You ask me to let you know the price of the music—I won't—I am not going to let your wife and Miss Pasmore do all the work—playing & singing and facing the 'guns' in the front row and taking so much time and trouble—and not do at least one thing that I can do—furnish the music copies."[47]

In early spring 1938 Yates was nervous about the reception Mullen would have for the *Concord* Sonata, when she was pressed to perform "The Alcotts" and "Thoreau" for the fading Los Angeles chapter of Pro Musica, which had degenerated into a social affair; he wrote Houston that the *Concord* "will be too near home and too near greatness for those stifled patrons of little new notions." Radiana Pazmor and Mullen read through Ives's Thirty-Four Songs (published by the *New Music Quarterly*), and Yates exclaimed to Houston, "This man stands with Melville, Whitman, and Wright. . . . I don't often feel myself explode with emotion that way."[48] A new recording by New Music Quarterly Recordings of six Ives songs gave him "more solid pleasure than any other song writer." Pazmor's recording of "General William Booth" "sets my hair straight up."[49] The Yateses obtained *New Music Quarterly*'s edition of the songs in September 1938. Yates reported his reaction to Houston: "This man is mad occasionally and makes accompaniments no human creature could play, reductions from extraordinary orchestral groupings. The literature he uses for songs is enormous and stops at nothing."[50]

As Mullen's performance of the *Concord* Sonata developed, Yates told Houston it "makes most other modern music sound thin."[51] To him "it is a tragedy giants like Ives and Ruggles, lame and craggy, should go to death unheard."[52] Having looked over the music Ives sent him, Yates asked Houston to visit the composer in New York City with a request for instrumental parts and more music; he was introducing Ives's works to other musicians, among them the choral conductor Hall Johnson, orchestral conductor Oskar Seiling, violinist Sol Babitz, and baritone John Charles Thomas (who sang two Ives songs at Town Hall through Yates's influence).[53] Houston's visit to Ives took place in February 1939. He recorded his description of the composer in his poem titled "Concord: A Recollection":

> Standing in the hallway, greeting a stranger,
> Reserved, kindly, a yankee deacon with your space around you.
> It was an errand I had with you for some friends,
> And you—who then knew of you?—
> Except some of us who were involved in odd matters
> Such as music with a truth in it.[54]

For Radiana Pazmor's performance of the song "The Indians," Yates borrowed from the pioneer choreographer Lester Horton's dance studio a drum made of a gasoline can. After the successful concert (which Klemperer attended), Yates reported to Houston an audience responsive to everything in Ives: "One is scarcely conscious of it as new or different, the appeal is so direct that almost immediately you get it. In this as I have believed for some time he surpasses Schoenberg. Indeed I can find no modern composer to compare with him in range."[55] Yates's very first article on music for *California Arts and Architecture,* "Charles Ives," compared Schoenberg's world fame with the long delay in recognition of Ives: "Schoenberg lived in a center of musical activity: sympathy might be lacking, but he could usually hear his music performed soon after he had written it. Ives composed in a provincial backwater—as far as music was concerned—which could not conceivably have any use for him or for his art." He predicted that Ives's music would be studied as poets study Walt Whitman: "But the secret of Ives's art is not simply its method. Through him New England and New York become vocal as communities. . . . The determination to find out the musical idiom of his own life has made Charles Ives's music a recognizable language, a continental reality, like the skyshape of its buildings and the wind-sound of its trees."[56] As he researched and wrote the article on Ives in the fall of 1940, Yates composed a poem, "For Charles Ives":

If there is left, men's God, in the world one single man
To speak of you and be friend, too many words
Cannot hide you or deny you for that man.
He will be like a history when it is lived,
Not yet made faith, and in him you in him;
The greens of leaves, the blues of seas will be no more tangible, no more real.
He will come up like spring; in winter men will live in memory of him;
And death shall be forgetting, even as some man has forgotten spring:
This God who inhabits words and works in men
And who is real in the person, real and final as the speech
Of one who, feigning, cannot feign to feign;
This real enduring stout truth's counterchange:
Death does not affirm and cannot fail
Him in whom living is a part in being.[57]

In early 1941 Houston sent this, with others of Yates's poems, to Dorothy Norman, founder and editor of *Twice a Year,* a new journal of the arts and civil liberties. She rejected the poems, with the comment, "If only the communication would be more direct, always more direct."[58] Several years later, Yates sent *A Smaller Poem Book* (1946), containing the poem on Ives, to the composer, who replied, "Most of your poems are strong works of art." Harmony Ives added,

"I like the Charles Ives. I take it to mean he is God-Possessed—and he is. . . . We are both so glad you are writing poetry."[59]

Yates was naturally interested to meet Ives's supporters, Henry Cowell and Lou Harrison. In 1941 Gerald Strang brought Cowell, in Los Angeles for the first time since his release from prison, to play the piano for the Yateses. Yates described him to Houston:

> Cowell is a little round man preceded by a long thin red Dickensian nose; his hair is thin, his manner furtive; he is shy when congratulated for anything except his music, for that he reddens and glows; he is hard to talk to. The old forwardness he must have had to drive himself and his purposes before unfriendly and amused audiences has been replaced by a fearfulness and suspicion. He is unlikely ever to lose the prison mark, the expression of something said or felt behind his back, the uncertain secrecy. But when he plays his extraordinary compositions with their so ordinary content everything changes: he is certain. The piano responds to him. His technical feats with strings, thumbs, nails, fists, elbows, forearms are their own justification. . . . He is here, the first time since his release, for ten days to record four of his pieces with Stokowski in orchestral arrangements.[60]

In 1943 Yates met Lou Harrison, who in 1936 had given to Cowell his collection of Ives chamber music (which Cowell had published in the *New Music Quarterly,* and Strang had then passed on to Yates).[61] This same year (1943) Harrison moved to New York, where he sustained himself writing music criticism, copying music, and writing dance music. In New York he worked as a copyist for Ives, conducted Ives's Third Symphony (which earned Ives the 1947 Pulitzer Prize), and—as he wrote Yates—was actively "bound up with the idea of the 'great tradition' in American music, i.e., Ives, Ruggles, Cowell, [Ruth] Crawford, etc."[62] He wrote Yates that he believed "the West is the coming cultural center of America," for "Music in N.Y. is a distinct disappointment & very commercial-minded & very flooded with 'parisian society.' I think that largely due to your efforts L.A. is the center of art music at this point. You had all ought to be very proud of yourselves & realize what an important thing it is that you are [doing]."[63] When Harrison learned of Yates's plans for Ives and Schoenberg seventieth-anniversary concerts in 1944, he suggested that the Roof attempt the world premiere of Ives's Second String Quartet, which he had been hired to proofread and correct.[64] Ives sent the music to Yates, along with a check for $50, specifically to help in the provision of instrumental parts for performance of *Schoenberg's* works. Ives insisted on anonymity but, Yates told Houston,

> This time I have written to tell [Ives] that I certainly will mention it: he must not always remain the anonymous giver, especially when knowledge of the gift is an inspiration to the performers, as it has been in this instance. I shall also tell Schoenberg, but later. I think he should know it. Ives was emphatic that he should not. . . . I must try to release the information in such a way that Ives will not be inundated with begging pleas.[65]

Yates may well have told Schoenberg of Ives's gesture. For the Schoenberg family 1944 was a difficult year. It was the last year of Schoenberg's salaried teaching at UCLA, to be followed by the frighteningly slim pension that the University of California's seniority system allowed the composer after only eight years of employment. In February 1944, as Schoenberg finished his classes, his entire family was ill and he himself was in very poor health. His biographer, H. H. Stuckenschmidt, reported that Schoenberg heard Ingolf Dahl conduct the Roof performance of *Pierrot* for his seventieth birthday on a radio broadcast and probably also heard music by Ives that year in broadcasts of Roof programs.[66]

In this period, Yates himself talked with Schoenberg about Ives and his music and later wrote,

> It is not generally known that in 1933, when Arnold Schoenberg and his family, refugees from Nazi Germany, arrived in New York, Ives, although unwell, went to a reception for them and gave Schoenberg a check. . . . Schoenberg told me of it, in the autumn when our Evenings on the Roof concerts in Los Angeles

celebrated the seventieth birthdays of the two composers by concerts of their music. . . . Schoenberg said that he clearly remembered Ives's appearance. In that same season (1944) Schoenberg wrote his celebrated tribute to Ives, which [after Schoenberg's death in 1951] Mrs. Schoenberg found among his papers for that year and sent to Mrs. Ives.[67]

Schoenberg's 1944 tribute reads:

> There is a great Man living in this Country—a composer.
> He has solved the problem how to preserve one's self-esteem and to learn.
> He responds to negligence by contempt.
> He is not forced to accept praise or blame.
> His name is Ives.[68]

Upon receiving it (probably in November 1951), Harmony Ives responded to Gertrud Schoenberg: "Mr. Ives thanks you so much for sending him the notation about him written by your distinguished husband. Mr. Ives is not well and I am writing for him. He was deeply moved in reading it and will put the paper among his treasures." She added that to her knowledge Ives and Schoenberg never met.[69]

In his last years, Ives continued to express his gratitude to the Yateses. He praised a 1946 *Arts and Architecture* article on his music, saying Yates "gets down to the roots of things."[70] As more of his works were recorded and published, Ives thanked the Yateses for their "muscle" in being his champions and creating interest in the music. Harmony Ives wrote for her husband, "The music has won its way for itself finally with practically nothing but itself—its honesty and excellence. As one of the few to speak emphatically for it, and for your wife as one of the foremost interpreters, this will interest you."[71]

Yates did not at first program chamber works by Stravinsky because his music was not neglected, and Yates was "always subject to prejudice in favor of not too well accepted causes."[72] Yates's impressions of Stravinsky and his music were generally negative until he came to know the composer. In 1933 he wrote to Houston, "Stravinsky deliberately astonishes and shocks. Delays the progress of music. . . . How weary, stale, flat, and unprofitable is the *Firebird!*"[73] But Yates was always open to discovery. In 1934 he reported, "Despite my general weariness of Stravinsky . . . his [*Symphony of Psalms*] impressed me as tremendously powerful and original."[74] In October 1940 he heard Stravinsky rehearse Sol Babitz in his Violin Concerto with a reading orchestra organized by studio musicians. To Houston he described the composer's manner as "withering." He thought of Stravinsky as "corroded by popularity," and therefore not of the top rank of Ives, Schoenberg, and Bartók.[75] He continued in his negative view of Stravinsky through most of thc 1940s. Thc violinist Sol Babitz and thc pianist Ingolf Dahl performed Stravinsky's works on the Roof concerts beginning in 1942. In 1943, in *California Arts and Architecture,* Yates wrote unsympathetically about neoclassicism as "a collapse or a weakening of creative energies. . . . Undoubted slackening in creative intensity of [Stravinsky's] later works leads on to the innocuously mature craftsmanship of the Symphony in C."[76] On 6 March 1944 Stravinsky was drawn to a Roof concert by Babitz and Dahl and professed his delight, particularly in early English keyboard pieces played by Wesley Kuhnle.[77] This softened Yates's attitude toward the composer, but in a 1946 letter to Houston he called *The Rite of Spring* "an insufferable noise."[78]

In 1947 Yates was invited to Stravinsky's house after a concert of works by the émigré film composer Hanns Eisler and warmed in the presence of Stravinsky's charm. "I enjoy Stravinsky and like him personally so much I regret I cannot share the general top rating of his music," Yates reported to Houston.[79] But from then on, Stravinsky and his music took a steadily growing place in Yates's respect and affection. Soulima Stravinsky's special recital program for the Roof (Soulima's second in this country) in September 1948 was the occasion for another party the Stravinskys gave for twenty-seven individuals afterward. These postconcert gatherings hosted by the Stravinskys soon became a delight and stimulation to musicians involved with Stravinsky performances in Evenings on the Roof and Monday Evening Concerts.

Robert Craft appeared in 1948, to become part of the Stravinsky household, and Yates invited him to conduct a program of local composers on 4 December 1951 for Evenings on the Roof. Craft was also received cordially in the Schoenberg household, as he was ambitious to conduct Schoenberg's works. Schoenberg's death, an event that deeply stirred Stravinsky, and Craft's performance and recording of Schoenberg's Suite for Septet, Op. 29, in the fall of 1952, were strongly influential in Stravinsky's conversion to the twelve-tone method.

Yates commented to Houston on Stravinsky's interest in Schoenberg's music, on 17 May 1952: "Nowadays artists work in closed boxes. . . . Our artistic life is typified by Stravinsky, who lived here more than fifteen years without ever meeting Schoenberg in public or private, but now attends performance of the old man's work like a devotee. He's been coming to a good many of our concerts."[80] There are eyewitness reports about times when Stravinsky and Schoenberg *were* present at the same public occasion: once at a dinner for their mutual acquaintance, Alma Mahler-Werfel, given by Eugene Ormandy on 7 July 1948 in the Crystal Ballroom of the Beverly Hills Hotel (Vera Stravinsky thought it was very boring; it might not have been if the two had spoken);[81] and in 1945 at the dress rehearsal of the *Genesis Suite,* a project of the music publisher Nathaniel Shilkret, who commissioned this collective work from a number of émigré composers, including Schoenberg and Stravinsky (Leonard Stein, who was present, remembered that they chose to remain on opposite sides of the hall, and not a word was exchanged).[82]

On 21 July 1953 a reading of Stravinsky's new Septet, conducted by Craft, took place in the Yateses' Roof studio. After the final movement, a Gigue built on an eight-note row, Stravinsky, influenced by Schoenberg's septet suite Op. 29 to venture into serialism in this work, leaped to his feet and exclaimed, "It is tonal! Fiercely tonal!"[83] Yates told Houston that, with this work, Stravinsky had "returned to his top form"[84] and confessed that Stravinsky "has completely won me over to admiration, of himself and of his later music. His Septet is one of the great works, written in honor of Schoenberg's, which he helped us to record, sitting in on [Craft's] recording session—but Schoenberg's is by far the greater—comment not for quotation."[85] As the Stravinsky programs of the 1953–1954 season were being arranged, Yates remarked to Houston that the composer was providing his jazz pieces and the Septet without fee, "proving how much Stravinsky loves us."[86] By then the "us" was Lawrence Morton and Robert Craft, who had taken on programming and performing decisions.

In January 1954, as his era as director of the concerts came to an end, Yates expressed his sense of the change in contemporary music in his letters to Houston:

> I hold that we have ended one of the supreme periods of musical creation. . . . The few younger creators are experimentalists or professors: John Cage or Ingolf Dahl. To say this in no way alters my opinion that Stravinsky is at the height of his form, a rise that began with the Symphony in Three Movements [1942–1945] after a depression which began around *Apollo Musagetes* [1927–1928]. Stravinsky's Mass or the new Septet are unqualified masterpieces, regardless of Berlioz or Beethoven. If a comparative rating be tried: Stravinsky belongs with Haydn; he is a matured Rossini, a more varied Verdi, a Handel, a Tchaikovsky who has lost crowd appeal by controlling his emotions. Therefore in no way to be disdained.

Continuing this way of drawing Houston's waning interest and engagement in contemporary music, Yates turned to Bartók, who was "linked by so many ties of structural continuity and emotional darkness with Brahms; a master of the keyboard as great as Couperin; and short of Schoenberg the supreme creator of chamber music since Beethoven and Schubert." As for Schoenberg:

> You have not heard enough of his music well performed to offer judgement. No one anywhere can say with more authority than I do that an entire evening of Schoenberg's music well performed is

> irresistible by any audience capable of enjoying, bodily and mentally enjoying late Beethoven or Bach. . . . I set Schoenberg as creator in the company of Beethoven and Byrd, a melodist equal to Schubert but with a more profound awareness of structure.

And about "my dear Ives," who interested Houston most of all, Yates continued:

> He is a Bach born out of context, potentially the master of them all but a mastery never fully realized or matured. To see him by comparison one must have him dead before 45 and prepare to wait a half-century until his music has been all edited and performed. You will see that I do not take the composers of our century at a low estimate. But for me the present became the past and forever when we buried Schoenberg.[87]

Five

DISCOVERIES IN EARLY MUSIC 1939–1954

In 1952, as he began summing up the accomplishments of Evenings on the Roof, Peter Yates wrote, "Our work in new music may be more spectacular and productive of good gossip in various parts of the musical world . . . but the old music studies are the most significant and enduring work we have accomplished."[1] Fewer musicians were involved in the Roof concerts' adventures in early music, and their fight for acceptance of new theories (many of which have since been proven) was if anything more difficult than the fight for acceptance of modern music. The concerts encountered not only audience resistance but tangles with the American musicological establishment, which was not always friendly to exploration of past performance practice by nonacademics.

Yates's own investigations into music of the past were inspired in the 1930s by reading Arnold Dolmetsch and hearing Wanda Landowska. He sought out the few fine performers in the Los Angeles area interested in the theories and practice of early music. The first was John Smallman, who founded the First Congregational Church's Johann Sebastian Bach festival in 1924. Born and trained in England, professionally active in Boston, and engaged by the Los Angeles Oratorio Society in 1912, Smallman gained national recognition for his choral performances. Yates particularly admired his a cappella choir of thirty-two voices and was an enthusiastic devotee of the annual Bach festivals. Smallman served the First Congregational Church for nineteen years as director of the choir but dropped dead of a heart attack in 1937 while conducting a festive pre-Christmas performance of Handel's *Messiah* before an audience of twelve hundred.[2] With his small choir, Smallman presented Bach's *St. Matthew Passion* in 1933, a year before it was presented in New York City for the first time. The vivacity of Smallman's performance of Bach's dance rhythms taught Yates this new perception of Baroque music.[3]

Richard Buhlig's famous performances (with his colleague Wesley Kuhnle) in his own two-piano arrangement of Bach's last work, *Art of Fugue;* Wanda Landowska's harpsichord recording of the *Goldberg* Variations; and Landowska's pupil Alice Ehlers's harpsichord performance of the *Italian Concerto* all inspired Yates, for whom Bach had long been his favorite composer. "Bach is the Plato of music, the simple speaker, who as he becomes more subtle is the more simple," he wrote Houston in 1938.[4] He felt the Los Angeles Bach festival was badly handled after Smallman's death, so he planned (as "fringe" festivals at the First Congregational Church) two intensive Roof-sponsored Bach series in 1942 and 1943. These presented a comprehensive view of Bach's works for keyboard, including performances of *The Well-Tempered Clavier* Book I, the first three volumes of the *Clavier-Übung,* the complete *Orgelbüchlein* in a transcription for two pianos by Wesley Kuhnle, the six French Suites, seven partitas, seven toccatas, the two-part inventions, and the fifteen sinfonias. To prepare for these concerts he embarked on a lengthy study of Bach's keyboard idiom but reported to Houston after the first series that the audience was at a loss hearing full sets of keyboard music.[5] The second Bach series in 1943 allowed more variety by including trio sonatas and violin sonatas as well as keyboard works. It was performed in the church's chapel, which provided better acoustics, and was "a big success."[6]

Yates's was inspired by reading Arnold Dolmetsch's pioneering book, *The Interpretation of the Music of the 17th and 18th Centuries* (published in 1915), to search for a copy of the *Fitzwilliam Virginal*

Book in 1933. He shared with Wesley Kuhnle discoveries in early keyboard music, which he enjoyed playing himself. He obtained pre-Elizabethan music from the New York Public Library, ordered *My Ladye Nevells Booke* from England, purchased most of the complete keyboard works of William Byrd, and talked the Los Angeles Central Library into buying the complete works of Orlando Gibbons and *Cosyn's Virginal Book.* He delighted in his study of Elizabethan ornamentation and in 1943 wrote Houston, "I have a new world to live in almost unknown to performing musicians. The Byrd Pavans and Galliards and the Gibbons fantasies stand with Bach, Mozart, Beethoven, and Bartók."[7] He was particularly proud that Stravinsky (on his first visit in 1944 to the Roof concerts) gave high praise to Wesley Kuhnle's performance of Gibbons, Byrd, and Purcell. Yates was one of the very few who endorsed and encouraged Kuhnle's researches.[8]

Wesley Krehbiel Kuhnle (1898–1962) was born in Detroit to a German Methodist minister and his musician wife, sister of the well-known American music critic Henry Edward Krehbiel, who wrote for the *New York Tribune* from 1880 to 1923. Kuhnle's family moved to California in 1902 and in 1913 settled in Glendale, on the outskirts of Los Angeles. Because Kuhnle seemed sickly as a child, he never went to school but studied academic subjects and piano with his mother. At age fifteen he went to USC for organ lessons, at which he excelled. When he was twenty-one he became the youngest associate of the American Guild of Organists. In 1920 he met and began piano study with Richard Buhlig, who had come to Los Angeles at the invitation of the Philharmonic to perform and remained to lecture and teach. In the summer of 1923, as Germany's economy was collapsing, Kuhnle and his fellow piano student Henry Cowell accompanied Buhlig to Berlin. They encountered the general social chaos caused by starvation and the wild inflation that boosted the value of the dollar from one million marks to four million in two weeks' time. In June Kuhnle attended the Leipzig Bach Festival, where hearing a harpsichord and viola da gamba for the first time gave him his lifelong ambition to work with old music and its own instruments. While Cowell and Buhlig settled in Vienna for the winter, Kuhnle returned to California. Kuhnle was shy and retiring, not cut out to shake up international musical establishments as Cowell did in the early 1920s. Upon Cowell's return to California in 1925 Kuhnle performed as a pianist in concerts of "Ultramoderns" put on in Los Angeles by Cowell's New Music Society. Kuhnle's 1927 New York Town Hall debut, in which he played Schoenberg, Scriabin, and rarely heard Bach and Mozart, produced lukewarm reviews. The *New York Times* noted "the stiff correctness of his style,"[9] while the *Telegram* complained of a "paucity of imagination" and sniffed that Schoenberg's Six Little Piano Pieces, Op. 19, would have elicited from his late uncle the critic Krehbiel "a fine flight of measured and orotund invective."[10] Thereafter Kuhnle confined his musical activities to California. He established a music studio, organized a chamber symphony, played celesta (at the time a novel instrument) and tympani with the Glendale Symphony, and presented an educational radio series on music. In the 1930s and 1940s he conducted extensive research into early keyboard instruments and their tuning, performed early music frequently for Roof concerts, and in the late 1940s began building his own harpsichords, virginals, and clavichords. His many performances in Roof concerts, beginning in 1939, were devoted to Baroque and Renaissance keyboard music.

From 1932 to 1944 Kuhnle made arrangements of Baroque keyboard works. Performing editions were not easily available; only one copy of the collected works of J. S. Bach existed in southern California, and that was in La Jolla, two hours' drive down the coast.[11] A unique aspect of Kuhnle's arrangements was his attempt to reproduce the sound of various organ registrations on two pianos by doubling octaves as well as depressing certain keys—without sounding them—in order to obtain overtones. Kuhnle often performed these arrangements with Frances Mullen. They played his version of Bach's *Goldberg* Variations twice in 1945–1946. Much to Peter Yates's agitation, that same season Buhlig planned to play the same work in his Roof concerts, and Alice Ehlers insisted on also performing it for the Roof series, but on harpsichord. (Her teacher, Wanda Landowska, had called it "the most difficult work ever written for the keyboard.")[12] In this unique battle of three concepts, Buhlig (who played Bach on the piano in the Busoni style) withdrew but performed his two-piano arrangement of *Art of Fugue* twice with Kuhnle instead. Yates found Kuhnle's version of the *Goldberg* Variations the more varied and expansive, Ehlers's ornamentation in the work the more authentic. Ehlers, who in May 1944 had presented the first Roof program with period instruments, clearly disapproved of Kuhnle's version on pianos, and Kuhnle was soon building his own clavichord.

In 1948 Kuhnle and the violinist Sol Babitz formed the New Friends of Old Music, as a part of Evenings on the Roof, to function as a public forum for their experiments in the performance practice of early music. Sol Babitz (1911–1982) was born in Brooklyn. As a violinist he was at first self-taught but in 1931 went to Berlin, where he studied violin with Carl Flesch and musicology with Curt Sachs. Like Yates's, his interest in early performance practice was aroused by the writings of Arnold Dolmetsch. He played in the Los Angeles Philharmonic from 1933–1937 (under Klemperer), and in the film studios until 1959, when he resigned in order not to have to mix modern and Baroque violin techniques. In 1940 he became closely acquainted with Stravinsky and interested him in theories on Baroque performance practice. (From 1941–1947 he assisted Stravinsky with the notation of the composer's string parts and published a treatise on modernization of fingering to facilitate performance of new works.)[13] After 1948 (except for occasional performances of Stravinsky, Ives, and Hindemith) Babitz specialized on eighteenth-century literature in his Roof performances.

Babitz later claimed he was "the first to give concerts using early violins played in strict accordance with the technical instructions in the sources" of seventeenth- and eighteenth-century performance practice.[14] In the book *Reprise: the Extraordinary Revival of Early Music,* published in 1985, Joel Cohen, music director of the Boston Camerata, wrote, "The courageous Sol Babitz experimented with Baroque violin techniques back in the 1950s: his ideas seemed outlandish to many at the time, but most of his positions have since been vindicated."[15] At the Yale Music School, Paul Hindemith was teaching performers techniques gleaned from early sources and making use of the collection of early instruments at the Metropolitan Museum of Art in New York City, but his focus in instrumental practice was primarily on Renaissance and medieval music. Babitz seems to have been alone in his field.

When Lawrence Morton reviewed the first series of four programs by the New Friends of Old Music in 1948, he noted that it was mostly avant-garde musicians who complained about the domination of concert halls by music of the nineteenth century. He pointed out to his readers that rediscovery of earlier musical tradition had been in process for a long time: Brahms had prepared [with Chrysander] the first complete edition of François Couperin's harpsichord music; Malipiero was presently working on an authoritative edition of Vivaldi; Nadia Boulanger's teaching was based on the study of such composers as Buxtehude and Monteverdi. He hinted at Stravinsky's debt to Monteverdi during the composition of his recent ballet, *Orpheus.* He could see that musical art was given refreshing impetus by Babitz and Kuhnle's New Friends of Old Music:

> Both have made an intensive study of the old music, but you will find nothing less pedantic than their approach to it. On the contrary, their first program was almost what one could call sensational. . . . I am not qualified to quibble about the scholarship. But my ears told me that what I was hearing was musically valid, consistently interesting, and far more beautiful than the mere luxuriousness of the current box-office style.[16]

By 1949 Kuhnle had built his own clavichord and had begun his research into mean-tone temperament in the Baroque—a topic still considered radical in Europe.[17] In April 1952 he demonstrated various temperaments, using several instruments tuned differently. He and Babitz also investigated what Arnold Dolmetsch had called "rhythmic alteration" in Baroque music. Babitz, "using the old light [bow] grip between thumb and forefinger with the [violin] on the chest,"[18] developed the application of *notes inégales* (unequal notes, which, in contradiction to notated rhythm, permitted an expressive freedom akin to that of swing in jazz). In his 1952 performance of Bach's Sonata in A Minor for Unaccompanied Violin, Babitz's approach to ornamentation was to appropriate for the violin the florid style of

Bach's clavier version of the same work. Kuhnle's taste was also for a great deal of ornamentation. Morton, reviewing the concert, deplored the loss of rhythmic impulse to lavish ornament. The same year Babitz's article, "A Problem of Rhythm in Baroque Music," dealing with the fingering practices and limitations in old instruments that affected the performer's physical movement, was published in *The Musical Quarterly*.[19] Although as editor of the *Musical Quarterly* Paul Henry Lang accepted the article, he joined other musicologists in reacting vehemently against these ideas. In Los Angeles the "local professional elite," Peter Yates wrote Virgil Thomson in 1950, "found the experimental projects in the playing of sixteenth-, seventeenth-, and eighteenth-century instrumental music unacceptable."[20] Babitz retreated from New Friends of Old Music concerts to found his Early Music Laboratory and began issuing polemics and articles.

Where Kuhnle was reticent, Babitz was belligerent, even—by his own admission—flamboyant and arrogant.[21] As Yates put it, "Sol himself, though golden-hearted, can be rough as a horse-brush without meaning to hurt anyone's feelings."[22] Babitz felt that his suggestion of adopting the physical limitations of past instruments was greeted as if he had made an obscene proposal. As he published articles, attended professional meetings and conventions of the American Musicological Society, and gave performance demonstrations, he insulted "establishment professors," and stirred up much resistance. He quarreled with musicologists about the national limitations of *notes inégales*. Doggedly, he pursued his crusade to "de-Wagnerize" the practice of music before 1850, proselytizing against the long legato "singing" line, and for "speaking" articulation, in Baroque phrasing. His ideas gradually gained acceptance in academic circles, and he was invited to give lecture-demonstrations in important institutions. Ford Foundation and Fulbright grants enabled him to pursue research in Europe in 1961–1963.[23] There he lectured on "Violin Style from the Middle Ages to Mozart" and recorded with the eminent harpsichordist Gustav Leonhardt, as well as for the highly respected *Archiv* historical anthology of music put out by Deutsche Grammophon.[24] But when back in the United States he remained truculent. "My articles transgressed the bounds of decorum when I pointed out that those of my colleagues who teach the sewing machine Bach style in the face of massive evidence to the contrary are doing something morally reprehensible," he wrote. "I have been punished by being excluded from academic employment."[25] Morton, who had endorsed Babitz's "very acute judgement as to styles" in *Script*,[26] wrote him a suggestion: "Why don't you try to 'sell' your idea more positively? . . . I'm not sure that you have presented your best arguments for a 'revival.' "[27] Yates continued to support Babitz, writing to him in 1970, "I believe that, despite all resistance, musicians are moving in your direction, although how much credit you personally will receive for what you have done is, sadly, problematical."[28] Like many other groundbreakers, Sol Babitz felt that "Unless I shout they will not listen."[29] By the 1970s an impressive international list of musicologists, performers, and institutions had become subscriber members of Babitz's Early Music Laboratory, including the scholar-performers Noah Greenberg, Jaap Schröder, Anthony Newman, Gustav Leonhardt, Putnam Aldrich, Robert Craft, and Ingolf Dahl; the musicologists Karl Geiringer, Barry S. Brook, Edward Lowinsky, Curt Sachs, Carl Parrish, Neal Zaslaw, and Walter Kolneder; the critic Donal Henahan and the composer Aaron Copland, to name just a few.

Other local musicians became increasingly involved in the Roof's presentation of early music according to their talents. The soprano Alice Mock, accompanied by Shibley Boyes, gave programs exploring lute songs of John Dowland in 1944, 1945, 1946, and 1950. Frances Mullen explored works of Johann Christian Bach in the 1940s and played a suite of François Couperin, with complete ornamentation, in 1943. Kuhnle and the harpsichordist Carol Rosenstiel continued performing Baroque repertoire in the fifties. Yates encouraged the exploration of works by Carl Philipp Emanuel Bach on the part of the cellist Kurt Reher, the flutist Doriot Anthony, the Coriolan Quartet, and the pianists Boyes, Mildred Portney, Helen Lipetz, Elizabeth Reames Spires, and Rosenstiel. Alice Ehlers's performance of Hindemith's continuo realization of the Biblical Sonatas of Heinrich Biber with violinist Adolf Koldofsky was a revelation in 1947. Roger Wagner's performances of sixteenth-century madrigals and masses were important concert high points in 1950–1952.

The 1949–1950 remembrance of the two-hundredth anniversary of the death of J. S. Bach culminated in the performance by Joseph Szigeti of the three sonatas for unaccompanied violin in 1950. Szigeti had offered them to the New Friends of Music in New York, Yates recalled, "and they were so scared of such an unconventional program that they would let him play only two of them," separated by Mozart's *Eine kleine Nachtmusik.*[30] The concerts' exploration of Bach cantatas began in 1946 but did not become intense until Craft's extended series began in 1953.

As he retired from the concerts in 1954, Yates regretted not riding further on the new wave of early music revival. He took immense private pleasure in early music—particularly in Elizabethan keyboard works and their ornamentation. But when he and Mullen founded Evenings on the Roof, even Mozart and Beethoven presented untapped areas for discovery. In 1938 Yates noticed the beginning of a reaction against nineteenth-century "thickness" and predicted a "rush to Mozart and moderns." At the same time he felt that Beethoven was misunderstood. "I believe the great day for Beethoven will come when he is rediscovered as a composer, not the writer of a few sure-fire pieces."[31] He began a study of Mozart's variations and the "psychological artistry" of the variation technique;[32] he hoped to program Mozart's complete violin sonatas and piano works in his concert series. He discussed in letters to Houston "the appalling question" of how melody differs from ornament; what was "muscular melody," what was decoration? The differences between Beethoven's and Mozart's treatment of the violin sonata, Mozart's emotional range, and the role of content in Beethoven's music were topics he wrote about in many versions of program notes he was developing for intensive programs. The Beethoven festival of 1940–1941, Buhlig's two cycles of the Beethoven piano sonatas, Beethoven's fifteen sonatas for violin and cello with piano, Mullen's series of Mozart's complete solo works for piano, and the series presenting Mozart string quartets and quintets in juxtaposition with twentieth-century quartets, were major efforts that fulfilled some of Yates's many wishes. These were unique in their time.

In 1984 Lawrence Morton asked Frances Mullen Yates why she and her husband had started the Roof. She replied in a letter:

> Peter was hungry to hear music he wanted to hear. I wanted to make him happy! We had to do something to get me out of the women's clubs engagements. I shared Peter's curiosity about *rarely* performed (never heard on the West Coast) classics and . . . contemporary composers. We had already found that there were a handful or so of L.A. musicians who felt as I did. Peter produced the potent glue which held us together.[33]

A glimpse of Peter Yates's private response (in 1940, two years before she performed it in public) to Mullen's developing performance of Beethoven's *Diabelli* Variations shows his relationship to her playing and gives a view of the character of their musical partnership:

> [Hearing her play the *Diabelli*], there were moments when I thought I would explode, when my body began rotating as in only the most agonizing concentration. . . . Everything that for years I have been demanding: the measured, sustained tone, never merely percussive, the pianissimo filling the room or creeping in the farthest corners of delicacy without thinness, the fortissimo that need not be noisy because it is rightly placed, the counterpoint responding in all parts but riding upon the massive sonorous assurance of the bass; . . . the pace so well controlled. . . . eliminating the smudging of a brilliant performance; . . . nothing anywhere was lost. . . . For me it was miraculous.[34]

Six

"WHAT IS NEWS IN THE MUSICAL WORLD"
1954–1959

In the spring of 1954 Vera Stravinsky wrote to her husband, who was in Portugal, "Imagine, Evenings on the Roof no longer exists! Morton is forming another organization, which Mr. Moss has promised to support. It will probably be called Monday Evening Concerts, and Morton and Bob are already working on the programs."[1] Lawrence Morton himself emphasized the continuity of aims in spite of the change in name from Evenings on the Roof to Monday Evening Concerts. He was profoundly irritated that Peter Yates had insisted on taking the name with him into retirement—a stipulation Yates had laid down in 1948, when attempting to turn the organization over to the musicians. Ever since the second season the concerts had taken place on Monday evenings, hence the practical new name. But Evenings on the Roof were widely known and respected; as late as November 1958 Morton wrote a colleague: "Evenings on the Roof was such a good title that we shall probably never succeed in living it down; 'Monday Evening Concerts' is hard to establish."[2]

In his oral history (taped in 1966), Morton remembered that Evenings on the Roof "were really vital to my own musical existence. . . . Practically everything I was learning about new music was going on at those concerts."[3] The catholicity of taste, the fact that the repertoire had always been "way ahead of what had been going on anywhere in the city and ahead of what was going on any place else in the country,"[4] was a tradition he vigorously embraced. Morton's new acquaintance, through these performances, with the music of Ives, the revelations he found in "rare and wonderful" experiences of the music of Bartók; the music of Schoenberg; the English Renaissance master John Dowland; Alice Ehlers's harpsichord performance of the *Goldberg* Variations; and the Philharmonic players' performance of the Beethoven Septet[5]—all were important experiences for him. In a country primarily accustomed to diets of symphonic and operatic repertoire, he was consistently hearing more chamber music than he had ever heard. He was determined that this legacy of exploration in chamber music would be carried on in the Monday Evening Concerts (MEC) and was proud to claim, after a dozen years directing the series, that "What is news in the musical world is to be found out at these concerts."[6]

Although they were opposites in most ways and often disagreed strenuously, Morton held many principles in common with Peter Yates. One was the attitude that "art is part of the morality of any civilization."[7] Morton was even more outspokenly opposed than Yates to impresarios like L. E. Behymer, who treated music as a commercial commodity. He attacked the control of music in Los Angeles by the "vested interests" of commercialism.[8] He campaigned vigorously against anti-intellectualism, which seemed to him "the smog of local nonculture" in Los Angeles.[9] In his articles in *Script,* he occasionally strayed from music criticism to embroil himself in politics that affected the musician. In the mid-1940s he took on a leadership position in the idealistic Musicians' Congress and urged musicians to involve themselves in a fight for freedom of ideas. The intent of the congress was "to mobilize the resources of music and musicians to serve humanity in war and in the peace to follow."[10] (This organization was subsequently hounded by the Un-American Activities Committee of the California legislature in the notorious Communist witch-hunts of the late 1940s in Hollywood.) He adopted Yates's policy of informing audiences through the discovery of unheard old and new music. Like Yates, whose interest was in "music which is always contemporary," he defended the continuum of modernism throughout music history, pointing out in the 1940s to readers of *Script* that in their time Mozart, Beethoven, Richard Strauss, and Debussy were considered modernists. He had the ability Yates had to divest himself of stylistic prejudices and preferences, and to listen to music with acuity and understanding. He was also able to sustain the concert seasons on absurdly modest budgets.

Lawrence Morton was born in 1904 in Duluth, Minnesota, and surmised that the chill of his native climate generated his natural "preference for the 'coolth' of classicism in the arts to the excessive warmth of romanticism."[11] His mother, a conservatory-trained pianist, introduced her children to music; an older brother (Jerry) played the violin, Lawrence the piano, and Arthur the cello. (He later became a Hollywood film composer and orchestrator.) Their sister, Beatrice, was not trained but was so musical that when she became an intimate of Stravinsky and Copland in California, she could whistle their melodies by ear. By the age of seventeen Lawrence had developed his sight-reading, improvising, and transposing skills to a high level and became a theater organist for silent movies when his parents' divorce brought financial difficulties to the family. In 1986 he remarked in a letter to Marni Nixon:

> What do you mean by "We are all in the wrong end of the music business"? Only if you are thinking about money. Poor as I am, I wouldn't change my past, so long as I have Stravinsky and Boulez as friends. When I was only 24 years old I was earning $10,000 a year as a theater organist—worth maybe 50 grand today—but it was a lousy job.[12]

Morton never completed his college education but attended the University of Minnesota, where he abandoned medical studies in favor of an English major, with supplementary studies in music history and theory. The advent of talking movies compelled him to leave his theater job to seek work in 1929 (at age twenty-five) in Chicago as a church and temple organist—but, as an agnostic, he hated this occupation. In Chicago he was inspired by conductor Frederick Stock and discovered contemporary music when he heard Copland's Piano Variations and Stravinsky's *Symphony of Psalms.* During the composer's American tour in 1935 he heard Stravinsky conduct in Chicago and thought him "the image of modernism."[13] After the death of his mother, Morton supported two of his younger siblings in the Chicago years. He suffered severely from hay fever and, when the younger Mortons were grown, in 1939 he escaped to Los Angeles, where he joined his brother Arthur, who was established in Hollywood.

Press clippings Morton kept reveal that he introduced himself to Los Angeles in the early 1940s as a composer. His setting of Psalm 150 was performed at the third annual festival of modern music at the First Congregational Church; the Los Angeles chapter of Pro Musica introduced his Three Psalms for mezzo-soprano and string quartet; the W.P.A. (Works Progress Administration) Symphony Orchestra in Chicago performed his *Suite for Dancing;* and his biblical opera, *Ruth,* scored for children's voices, was published and reviewed in the press. These forays produced no ripple of public enthusiasm; Morton later described himself as a composer of no significance, employing more craft than invention or originality.[14] The last press reference to Morton as "composer and critic" was in 1945, as he took part in a UCLA conference on American-Russian cultural exchange.

While working occasionally in the film studios as an orchestrator, Morton met the composers Aaron Copland, David Raksin, and Hugo Friedhofer, who became his lifelong friends. His reviews for *Script* initiated a long writing career, mainly devoted to reports on musical activity in film studios and Los Angeles' concert world, and book and music reviews (for *Modern Music* and *The Musical Quarterly,* among other periodicals), record liner notes, and program notes.[15] From 1945 until 1953 the role of film music critic was an important part of his work. Like George Antheil before him, Morton contributed a decidedly highbrow approach to the criticism of film music; in an example from his foreword to Clifford McCarty's *Film Composers in America,* he relates the tradition of "paste-pot-and-scissors" film scoring, and the earlier practice of theater organists (such as himself) stringing together "bleeding chunks" of Grieg, Tchaikovsky, Beethoven, and Schubert, with Borch, Becce, Rapee, and Zamecnik, to the precedent of eighteenth-century pasticcio opera.[16] McCarty considered Morton the James Agee of film music criticism, but Morton withdrew from this field as he became more deeply involved with concert music through his activities with Evenings on the Roof. The critic Peter Yates admired the critic Lawrence Morton's columns and reviews, and, when *Script* threatened to close in the late 1940s, wrote, "An independent and forceful critic, who in both the local and the national field has worked for the intelligent development of serious music as a way of thought, Lawrence Morton will be greatly missed by many readers who have found in him a voice for their own discontent with the safely commercialized product."[17] In 1954, when much rancor over control of the concerts had passed between the two men, Yates's admiration for Morton's carefully prepared program notes for the Ojai Festivals was tempered with only the slightest hint of bite: "Morton's program notes are a salad, crisp and a little curly with endive, a trifle sharp with the provincial herbs and a superior vinegar."[18]

Morton brought a sense of urgency to his criticisms of concert music. On the way he made enemies, whose criticisms he saved and relished in a file he titled "Fan Mail." In his *Los Angeles Times* obituary he was remembered as "sometimes churlish."[19] After ripping into Peter Yates for an article that he furiously resented, Morton only slightly apologetically confessed, "I am often told by my family that there is almost always a touch of acidity in my disagreements, whether spoken or written. I just count on the excessive understanding of others."[20] Marilyn Horne's nickname for Lawrence Morton was "Si," for Simon Legree. When asked why, Robert Craft remembered that she intended it affectionately but explained, "In the early years, LM could be very crotchety and nagging. He had to beg people to come to [unpaid] rehearsals, and in some cases as many as ten of them. He was on the telephone most of the day, which meant that his study of scores had to be relegated to the middle of the night. I often went to his house at midnight for two to three hours of discussing programs."[21]

Michael Tilson Thomas, who became a close friend of Morton in his later years, remembered his impression of Morton's sternness when he first met him: he was sharp; he would speak quickly, interrupt others, and go to a book to prove his point. Having been one himself, he had his lance out constantly for critics.[22] Igor Stravinsky described Morton as a "rugged Minnesotan,"[23] doubtless for the muscle of his mind rather than his physique, which was never robust. Pierre Boulez found him initially very austere, a man of northern inhibitions: "At first he was like an oyster which is completely closed. Nobody could guess that he was so witty. In his letters he was even wittier. I found his letters really very funny. Because he took time to think, he had pleasure in writing letters. Very, very funny." Boulez enjoyed Morton's company on two extended trips in California and Mexico in 1967 and 1970 ("complete holidays from music") and found him very likable, amusing when loosened by good Scotch, ever a good sport, and always dressed impeccably (which could be hilarious in adventuresome, muddy, and stormy conditions they encountered).[24] Friendships in music were deeply important to Morton, and there are many testimonies—inscribed in composers' scores and expressed in correspondence—to the strength and steadfastness of these reciprocal bonds. He spoke in public or wrote often in later life about the value of friendships to him: "I have enjoyed the friendship of Aaron Copland, Igor Stravinsky, Pierre Boulez, and a host of Southern California composers. . . . My closest musical friend, however, was Ingolf Dahl."[25] Loyalty was equally important to him. When his close colleague-in-arms on the Musicians' Board of Monday Evening Concerts, Leonard Stein, set up a competing concert series at UCLA, Morton felt betrayed and complained bitterly to others, trying at the same time to see Stein's side of the matter.

Arthur Morton describes his brother as a scholar. He approached all his tasks with a responsible erudition and attention to detail. His program notes for Ojai Festivals (beginning in their second season, 1948) were an important contribution to these concerts that led in 1953—just as he was assuming responsibility for Evenings on the Roof—to his appointment to succeed the festival's founder, John Bauer, as artistic director. From the 1954 season until his death, Lawrence Morton was a formative influence upon the Ojai Festivals. The programs he devised for the annual spring weekend of concerts at

Ojai were similar in aim to those of Evenings on the Roof and Monday Evening Concerts in their intent to be adventuresome, to present lesser known works of great composers of the past juxtaposed with new works, conducted and performed by their composers and other important musicians of the time.

Michael Tilson Thomas characterized the audiences who came to the Monday Evening Concerts as interested in widening their musical horizons "in the same way that they were interested in new literature, articles on new science, art history, or other things. It was fundamentally a very well-read, intelligent, knowing audience, which also had a certain element of people interested in the avant-garde." For this discerning audience, Morton developed the programming technique of "a connoisseur, a musical patrician."

> He always said, "For my audience I must have something very new, something different, something surprising from the past, but every program must have an absolute masterpiece on it someplace. It doesn't make any difference whether the masterpiece is a new or old one. Somewhere there must be a masterpiece, because you intuitively, instinctively sense that this is the center of the program, and this will make any of the musical combinations work out well." He made these programs in a way that took your mind on a journey, a stream of consciousness; it wasn't just a historical connection, but something perhaps about sonority, or the combinations of the instruments, or the use of contrapuntal procedures. . . . There was always some interesting thread: use of a certain text, certain literary inspiration . . . something that carried you thematically through the program, and gave you very strong places to rest, and to relish great music.[26]

The final years of Evenings on the Roof had been artistically successful, chiefly because of the efforts of Mary-Jeannette Brown. Morton, who had been brought into the organization in the mid-1940s by Ingolf Dahl and Edward Rebner,[27] had been closely involved with programming from about 1952, as Yates's fatigue forced him to withdraw. Morton gave Brown much credit for increasing season attendance to an all-time high through such fine programs as the choral concert with Palestrina's *Pope Marcellus* Mass and Stravinsky's *The Wedding,* the Messiaen *Quartet for the End of Time,* the series combining works of Mozart with contemporary works (all in the thirteenth season), and the Schoenberg retrospective (in the fifteenth season). When he took over her files, Morton realized how much research and correspondence Brown had undertaken to find new and interesting repertoire. (The critic Isabel Morse Jones had retired to Europe, from where she sent answers to Brown's inquiries about new European music. She died in Rome in 1951.)

In the period of transition there were "some very stormy times . . . some very rough meetings."[28] Yates at first found Morton's contribution hopelessly inadequate.[29] During Morton's initial year as coordinator, the musicians tried to run their organization and Morton withdrew, announcing that if they had complete control the musicians should do all the work. But, he recalled later, "Immediately, when they found out that they had to do all the work, they were through," and sent a delegation to Morton to resume his title. After Mary-Jeannette Brown left for New York and her successor, William Hume, subsequently withdrew in early 1954, Morton took over, running the concerts "from the top," while consulting Robert Craft, Ingolf Dahl, and Leonard Stein for program ideas.[30] When Peter Yates agreed to formally retire from the concerts there were some nasty exchanges of letters between Oscar Moss and Yates concerning income from the out-of-town concerts Yates had arranged. Moss accused Yates of "possessiveness" toward the concerts;[31] on 13 July 1954 he requested that Yates sign a formal resignation as trustee of the concerts.[32] Morton himself was less than gracious.[33] He made clear his opposition to Yates's idea of the musicians' autonomy and quarreled with Yates's "illusion of cooperation" with the musicians, who were no longer upholding the cooperative idea, and in any case had "very few notions about new repertoire."[34] Nevertheless, Yates made a friendly announcement in the press about the change in management, continued to support and show interest in the concerts, and, as Morton achieved success and confidence in his role as executive director, the animosity eventually passed—particularly after Yates left Los Angeles in 1968.

SEVENTEENTH SEASON: 1954–1955

The concerts continued, with the help of Los Angeles County Supervisor John Anson Ford, in the Los Angeles County Auditorium in West Hollywood Park. The ticket prices remained as low as previously ($1.50 for a ticket, and student tickets at $0.75 each), but the series was now reduced from as many as thirty to twelve concerts a season and remained thereafter at that number. For the first Monday Evening Concert there was a large crowd in anticipation of the world premiere of Stravinsky's *In Memoriam Dylan Thomas,* recently completed after the poet's death as he was on his way to Stravinsky's home in Hollywood to collaborate on an opera commissioned by Boston University.

Morton's relationship with Stravinsky dominated the first decade of MEC—and provided countless benefits for all. Morton had met Stravinsky in 1941 and, at a reception following the premiere of Stravinsky's arrangement of "The Star-Spangled Banner" by Los Angeles' W.P.A. Orchestra, had complimented the composer on his alteration of the national anthem's bass line.[35] Stravinsky's affection for the Roof concerts afforded many more contacts between the two men, and in the early fifties Morton became a member of the Stravinskys' inner circle in Hollywood. As Robert Craft wrote, "Stravinsky's proximity to these Los Angeles concerts has resulted in a major association. On the one hand it has given him an opportunity to study the works of Webern, to encounter the music of Boulez and Stockhausen, and to hear dozens of masterpieces of Renaissance and Baroque music. On the other, it has stimulated him to write many works for performance at these concerts."[36]

Following the gift of the *Shakespeare Songs* to Evenings on the Roof, *In Memoriam Dylan Thomas* was the second work clearly influenced by the concerts, and this first program of the seventeenth season was designated a memorial to the poet, whose death had shocked the intellectual world.

Earlier, on 9 November 1953, Evenings on the Roof had programmed Heinrich Schütz's *Symphonia sacra* for bass voice and four trombones, *Fili mi, Absalon.* Morton later recalled, "This was our four-trombone period, and I remember that I . . . arranged a number of pieces for that combination of instruments."[37] In the 20 September 1954 Dylan Thomas memorial, the somber sound of four trombones opened the concert with *ricercari* by the Venetian composers Andrea Gabrieli and Adrian Willaert, *Funeral Music for Queen Mary* by Henry Purcell, and Schütz's *Fili mi, Absalon.* Stravinsky, attracted to the sound by his earlier experience of the Schütz work, had framed his setting (for tenor and string quartet) of Thomas's own memorial text for his father, "Do not go gentle into that good night," with Dirge-Canons for four trombones. Before the performance of *In Memoriam,* Stravinsky's close friend Aldous Huxley read a short essay, the message of which was "God help the generation which does not read its poets,"[38] and Thomas's recorded voice was heard in readings of three of his poems. After the intermission the Stravinsky work was repeated. The program concluded with a funeral cantata of J. S. Bach, *Gottes Zeit ist die allerbeste Zeit.*

The funereal mood of this memorable concert was altered midprogram with six madrigals by Carlo Gesualdo, until then rarely performed. The five singers who developed an extensive repertoire of Gesualdo's madrigals and sacred motets and recorded them under the leadership of Robert Craft included Marilyn Horne in her first performance for Monday Evening Concerts. (Grace-Lynne Martin, soprano, Cora Lauridsen, contralto, Richard Robinson, tenor, and Charles Scharbach, bass, were others in the group. Paul Salamunovich, tenor, and Howard Chitjian, baritone, joined for larger ensembles. Several of the singers were associated with Roger Wagner's chorale.) Craft and Morton, in their enthusiasm for this "new," shockingly dissonant early music, sent for photostats of madrigals from a sixteenth-century manuscript in the Library of Congress and transcribed them.[39] The singers' rehearsals took place at Stravinsky's house in Hollywood, and his interest in the dramatic and individualistic harmonic practices of this late Renaissance prince subsequently resulted in his "recomposition" and arrangements of Gesualdo works.

The *Los Angeles Times* critic wrote that Stravinsky's tribute to Dylan Thomas was "touching . . . music of concentrated and tense poignancy."[40] The *Herald Examiner* reviewer wrote, "If the remaining concerts maintain the high standard of performance and intellectual stimulation this one did, Los Angeles will have a long awaited musical renascence."[41] Stravinsky was very happy with the program, as he "liked very much having his own works performed in the context of old music rather than other new music."[42] Many poets and literary people were in the audience, including Huxley's friends Christopher Isherwood and Gerald Heard. The great success of the evening initiated Lawrence Morton's "premiere fever." There were fifteen premieres amongst the twelve concerts of this 1954–1955 season alone, and premieres were thereafter an important component of Morton's programming.

Marilyn Horne—then age twenty—sang in four programs this season, which was also the season of her operatic debut with Los Angeles' Guild Opera, under the great émigré stage director Carl Ebert. Ensemble performances such as the Gesualdo madrigals were a joy to her. She later remembered, "I think quite truthfully that the musical thrills that I've had in my life in music have *not* been singing by myself. They have been singing with other people. . . . From the time I was a little girl, about seven years old, I sang with my sister, Gloria. . . . I was used to teamwork, blending, the thrills and excitement of what that can be, and it's never left me."[43] In her first year in Europe she was asked by Hindemith to sing Gesualdo madrigals at the 1957 Vienna Festival. The ensemble consisted of such renowned opera singers as Christa Ludwig, Murray Dickie, and Walter Berry. She wrote to her friend Morton, "Can't you just hear all our vibrati swinging against each other when we should be singing a heavenly well-tuned Gesualdo chord?"[44] She told Hindemith his choices were the "pop" Gesualdo madrigals, and—when he expressed surprise at her sophistication in these unknown works—retorted that she had recorded sixty or seventy Gesualdo madrigals in Los Angeles. For the same festival Hindemith, knowing her connection with Stravinsky's music, asked her to sing Stravinsky's Cantata on a program featuring Monteverdi's *Lagrime d'amante al sepolcro dell'amata,* a piece Horne had performed in her student days in Los Angeles. She expressed her enthusiasm for the Monteverdi work, and Hindemith exclaimed, "Don't tell me you know this too?" She replied, "Maestro, there's a lot more in Hollywood than just making films!"[45]

The second MEC program on which she sang (11 October 1954) was significant in Horne's memory. It was the first time she sang a work of Stravinsky's: the premiere of his revised version of the Four Russian Peasant Songs (called Four Russian Choruses by Craft, to distinguish them from other, similarly named works). Stravinsky not only helped her musically with this work but taught her to sing Russian, patiently encouraging guttural Russian pronunciation with his low voice. (The work was recorded in 1956 by Craft with the Monday Evening Concert performers.) The conductor Henry Lewis—whom Horne married in 1960—appeared on the same program, playing the double bass in the world premiere of *Sonatina giocosa* for double bass and piano, written especially for Lawrence Morton and the Monday Evening Concerts by Halsey Stevens. (Stevens's in-jokes in this work included a carefully hidden allusion to the name of the critic C. Sharpless Hickman, who had jabbed him with a bad review the year before.)[46] Henry Lewis was a "fairly fresh member of the Los Angeles Philharmonic Orchestra and already indicating the talent that subsequently brought him into the conducting business," Morton remembered.[47]

The third program of the season (25 October 1954) was "choppy," Morton thought, and included a disappointing premiere of a work Morton picked out from a catalogue, by the conductor Igor Markevitch. But André Previn (appearing "courtesy of MGM Studios") played Bartók's Second Rhapsody for violin and piano with the violinist Dorothy Wade, and Craft conducted the first performance of Arnold Schoenberg's propaganda cantata against the neoclassical movement, *The New Classicism,* Op. 28, No. 3 (1926). Stravinsky—at whom this satirical composition was originally aimed—did not attend this concert, though he frequently attended when Robert Craft conducted. He most often came with Aldous Huxley; Marilyn Horne remembered their contrasting physiognomies, enhanced by winter overcoats, presenting an amusing study in tall and short opposites. They always sat in the front row, because of Huxley's poor eyesight.

This program provided more exploration into Renaissance and Baroque realms: Telemann fugues for harpsichord, a Bach solo cantata for tenor, two of Heinrich Schütz's *Symphoniae sacrae* on texts from the "Song of Songs"; two short pieces for tenor by Heinrich Isaac and Bartolomeo Tromboncino, and Monteverdi's solo madrigal for two tenors and continuo, "Zefiro torna." The composer Mario Castelnuovo-Tedesco was in the audience and took Morton to task for printing the translation of the wrong Petrarch sonnet for the Monteverdi piece. Morton and Craft were particularly fond of Monteverdi's "Zefiro torna." In 1956 Lawrence Morton traveled to Europe by boat with the Stravinskys and Craft. In the Mediterranean, standing on deck, Morton saw dolphins for the first time. At the sight, he and Craft burst into song with "Zefiro torna," to Stravinsky's amusement.[48]

Works of Heinrich Schütz reappeared for the third consecutive program on 15 November 1954, when the mezzo-soprano Margery MacKay sang three of his *Symphoniae sacrae.* She also sang the first Los Angeles performance of Arnold Schoenberg's Three Songs, Op. 48 (1933), accompanied by Leonard Stein. Stein played in the first Los Angeles performance of Anton Webern's 1907 Quintet for Piano and Strings as well. In addition, twelve of Bartók's violin duos, played by Joachim Chassman and Myron Sandler, were "a big hit."[49]

Since the early forties Peter Yates had cultivated connections for the concerts with the League of Composers. In 1948 there had been a cosponsored Roof program, which honored the league's twenty-fifth anniversary, and a reciprocal New York program to honor the Roof's tenth season. Now the Los Angeles Chapter of the International Society for Contemporary Music (ISCM) was reactivated at USC, and an important concert of contemporary music was arranged (29 November 1954) in collaboration with this organization. There were four premieres on the program, including a world premiere of Stravinsky's new instrumentation of his two early Balmont songs and the American premiere of his instrumental versions of *Three Souvenirs of Childhood.* The similarly orchestrated *Three Japanese Lyrics* (1912–1913) by Stravinsky and *Trois poèmes de Stéphane Mallarmé* (1913) by Maurice Ravel were also performed. A String Quartet (1950) by the young German Giselher Klebe and Variations in C Minor for piano (1947) by Harold Shapero were premiered, and Schoenberg's Chamber Symphony, Op. 9 (1906), concluded the program. The Musart Quartet (Ralph Schaeffer and Leonard Atkins, violins; Albert Falkove, viola; Emmet Sargeant—brother of the *New Yorker*'s music critic, Winthrop Sargeant—cello) and the Los Angeles Woodwinds were featured. Robert Craft, who was to conduct, came down with a bad case of the flu and was replaced on the afternoon of the concert by the conductors Ingolf Dahl and John Barnett (at that time assistant conductor of the Philharmonic).

Marilyn Horne, who sang the *Three Souvenirs of Childhood,* remembered working with Stravinsky: "He'd have three pairs of glasses on, all on the top of his head, and he'd pick the one he needed at the moment. Those were pretty heady moments for a young person, to be around those incredible giants" of the émigré community she worked with. Others were Lotte Lehmann, who had established master classes in Santa Barbara, the vocal coach Fritz Zweig (the cousin of writer Stefan Zweig), the conductor Richard Lert, and the opera director Carl Ebert. "Not only did I learn a lot from them musically, I think I must have picked up a lot of cultural things too. That's all somewhere back in what I call that great tape recorder in the brain. We were really lucky." Morton tried to convince her in those days that she was a mezzo-soprano, but she had an easy high range: "I felt better singing soprano. I stuck with the thing I knew. Had I started lessons at sixteen, a teacher might have said, 'You're a mezzo,' but I didn't. I started lessons at five—I don't recommend it. But maybe I was lucky, because I sang soprano for so long, that maybe the upper extension on my voice was a lot more secure."[50]

On 6 December 1954 there were two choral works on the program: the *Missa pange lingua* of Josquin des Prés and Schütz's *Christmas Story,* sung by the Pomona College Glee Club, William F. Russell, director. Morton remembered the Schütz performance as:

> one of the most exciting events in our whole history of concerts. . . . Immediately after that performance, Craft [who had conducted], the Stravinskys, and I got on an airplane and flew to San Francisco. I remember that as we got on the plane and sat down, Stravinsky began to sing the final chorus; and the three of us, Craft and Stravinsky and I, just had a marvelous time all the way up to San Francisco singing that final chorus, faking it, of course, but having a marvelous time.[51]

On 24 January 1954, Marilyn Horne returned, with Marjorie MacKay and Paul Salamunovich,[52] as a soloist for Alice Ehlers's Baroque Ensemble in a program of Baroque choral and instrumental works, conducted by Ehlers's student Hans Lampl. Paul Hindemith's Sixth String Quartet (1945) was given a first Los Angeles performance by the Coriolan String Quartet.

Stravinsky's instrumentation of Four Russian Songs for voice, flute, harp, and guitar (1953–1954) were given their first performance by soprano Marni Nixon on 21 February 1955—"absolutely marvelous and a big hit," Morton remembered.[53] Nixon had made her concert debut in 1947 at age seventeen as a soloist in the Mozart Requiem, with the Los Angeles Philharmonic under Wallenstein, and the same year began working as a message girl at MGM in order to support her vocal career. In 1948 she found herself dubbing a Hindu lullaby for Margaret O'Brien in the film *Secret Garden* and later went on to important dubbing duties for Deborah Kerr in *The King and I* and *Affair to Remember* (in five different languages), for Natalie Wood in *West Side Story,* and for Audrey Hepburn in *My Fair Lady.* (She eventually dubbed over fifty films.) In the early fifties she was also appearing in the Guild Opera under Carl Ebert with Marilyn Horne, with whom she had sung in a trio when they were both teenagers. Nixon had been persuaded to try contemporary music by Leonard Stein, her teacher at Los Angeles City College. With her excellent musicianship, absolute pitch, and high coloratura voice she was able to sing so many adventurous works and premieres at Evenings on the Roof and Monday Evening Concerts that she gained a sense of "being a part of the musical intelligentsia of the world—something unlike anything else." She enjoyed rehearsals at the Stravinsky home. At lunch Stravinsky would talk about wines—of which she had no knowledge—and ask about her children. She felt Stravinsky was shy and needed Robert Craft to rehearse for him. She found Craft's cerebral, analytical approach to conducting useful, but his manner of dividing and subdividing the beat made it difficult to sustain a singing line. Craft seemed to have complete authority to do whatever he wanted with Stravinsky's music.[54]

On the same program, Nixon sang the first Los Angeles performance of Luigi Dallapiccola's *Goethe-Lieder* for soprano and three clarinets (1953), with, among others, the master clarinetist Mitchell Lurie. Dallapiccola seemed to Morton to be the answer to Virgil Thomson's prophesy that if the twelve-tone system ever took on any charm or grace it would come out of Italy.[55] His introduction to Dallapiccola, like many others to European composers, came through Craft's travels with the Stravinskys. Dallapiccola wrote Morton of his gratitude for the Los Angeles premiere of his *Goethe-Lieder,* which he regarded as having considerable importance in his development. He also congratulated him on his courage to program old and new works together.[56] A twelve-tone work for string trio by Ernst Krenek, *Parvula corona musicalis* (Little musical wreath; 1950), with musical citations from Bach, Beethoven, and Wagner's *Tristan,* all accomplished with skill, craft, and ease but "perhaps too long," Morton thought, also received a Los Angeles premiere on this occasion.[57] The program was framed by three works of Mozart, including the Adagio, K. 411, played by five clarinets, as no basset horns were to be found in Los Angeles.

This stimulating seventeenth season ended (28 March 1955) with another ISCM concert of contemporary music. René Leibowitz, the French advocate of twelve-tone music, was visiting and received a performance; and Leon Kirchner, at that time teaching at Mills College, came to perform his Piano Trio, commissioned in 1954 by Elizabeth Sprague Coolidge for the Coleman Chamber Music Concerts. Kirchner's composing career was soon to catch the interest of many of the national magazines, because of "the uncanny power of his music deeply to stir large audiences without the least sacrifice of artistic integrity and technical complexity."[58]

On the back page of the season's final program Morton printed a report summarizing in statistics the works performed and announced that in the coming season he planned to continue "our participation in the world-wide movement toward the revival of music from the 15th, 16th, and 17th centuries," while remaining in the vanguard of groups presenting music by living composers. To pursue these aims without compromise, in expectation of continued deficit financing, the Southern California Chamber Music Society proposed (for the first time) to offer memberships in the society.

EIGHTEENTH SEASON: 1955–1956

In the summer of 1955 Oscar Moss died, unexpectedly. He had come forward to support the concerts in 1946, when Peter Yates asked for financial help to keep the enterprise going. Aldous Huxley had been primarily a source of moral and intellectual—rather than monetary—support. Max Laemmle and Albert Rothenberg had offered financial backing, had served with Moss on the Board of the Southern California Chamber Music Society but had eventually lost interest, leaving only Oscar Moss to guarantee the concerts financially. As other fund-raising schemes failed to come to fruition, Moss steadfastly made up the deficits,[59] promising no interference in programming policies. "Don't overload the concerts with any one kind of thing," was the only programming admonition he ever gave Morton, who praised Moss as "the ideal patron of music. While he gave much in terms of energy, time, and resources, he asked for nothing in return but that the concerts maintain the highest possible standards without courting failure by reaching for impossible ones."[60]

Only a few hours after the news of his death had reached Morton, the Moss family sent word that the concerts were to go on as usual; their financial backing would continue. Morton must have felt a sense of danger, nevertheless, for in August, shortly after Moss's death, he formed an emergency committee of many important musical figures from both the concert and film-music worlds, to assure the continuation of the concerts. Stravinsky was named honorary chairman, and a letter sent out over his signature stated,

> In my opinion, Monday Evening Concerts are presenting the most valuable selection of music of any concert organization that I know of today. They give Los Angeles international prestige of a kind you would know about only if you traveled abroad as much as I do.[61]

Sadye Moss, an artist, continued to fill her husband's role for Monday Evening Concerts as president of the Southern California Chamber Music Society until 1984, when the support organization was dissolved and the concerts were taken over by the Los Angeles County Museum of Art.[62]

For the Ojai Festival, in the summer of 1955, Morton had mounted the Monteverdi *Vespers* of 1610 as a full evening's program. It seemed appropriate to repeat this performance as a Monday Evening Concert memorial to Oscar Moss. Robert Craft conducted, and the madrigal singers (Grace-Lynne Martin and Marilyn Horne, sopranos, Cora Lauridsen, contralto, Richard Robinson and Paul Salamunovich, tenors, Howard Chitjian, baritone, and Charles Scharbach, bass) were soloists. The remainder of the 1955–1956 season, Morton remembered, was "influenced by the availability of Robert Craft and the interest of Mr. Stravinsky and his group of friends, especially Aldous Huxley."[63]

Huxley (1894–1963) had spent two years in the early 1920s as music critic of the weekly *Westminster Gazette* in London. His musical interests, then and later, centered on late Beethoven, new works by Stravinsky, Bartók, and their contemporaries, and repertoire of the late Renaissance. During a severe (but temporary) blindness in his late teens, he had taught himself the piano, Braille, and Braille music, and was fascinated by syncopation and jazz in his university days. His spirit seemed to both Leonard Woolf and Yehudi Menuhin genuinely musical in nature.[64] Music played an important role in his books. In 1929 he wrote, "The most perfect statements and human solutions of the great metaphysical problems are all artistic, especially, it seems to me, musical."[65] One October day during 1946 he and his wife, Maria, spotted Stravinsky under the pleasant shade of the pepper trees at the Town and Country Market at Fairfax and Third, in Los Angeles. Huxley introduced himself and their great friendship began.[66] Igor Stravinsky said Huxley was "a guiding spirit to me."[67] It was Huxley who recommended W. H. Auden as the poet who should write the libretto for *The Rake's Progress*.[68]

Huxley attended the 1954 rehearsals of Gesualdo madrigals at Stravinsky's house and became very interested in the historical background of the music and the court of Ferrara. He helped translate the madrigals and prepared a talk—relishing the gory details of Gesualdo's murder of his first wife, her lover, and the son Gesualdo suspected of being illegitimate—to accompany the performance of ten more Gesualdo madrigals Craft and Morton transcribed and prepared for the 17 October 1955 concert. During Huxley's talk, Marilyn Horne and Robert Craft, sitting backstage in rising hilarity, counted the repetitions of Huxley's favorite word, "extrrraaawwdn'ry!"[69] The critic Albert Goldberg (after reporting that there were not enough seats for the crowd) found himself blushing: the famous author "spiced the dry bones of history with wit and even a shade of malice. . . . [Gesualdo was described as] a masochist to a degree that one does not dare even quote Mr. Huxley on the subject in this family newspaper."[70] Maria Huxley's diary recorded,

> The audience tittered, then laughed out loud. Aldous went on and on with story after story about the composer-flagellator . . . increasing laughter sweeping through the auditorium. [On the way home afterwards, he confessed] "I have done the most dreadful thing—and I'll be caught. . . . I was carried away and invented all those stories except the first one. Never have I done anything so preposterous. Oh dear!"[71]

The difficulties of intonation in Gesualdo's chromatic textures were eased by the fact that two of the madrigal singers had absolute pitch (though they did not absolutely agree on whose pitch was the correct one),[72] and by Craft pointing a finger up or down in anticipation of pitch difficulties during his conducting.[73] The singers remember recording the madrigals for eight hours at a stretch, performing the concert in the midst of recording, and receiving only $25 for the concert performance.[74] But the Gesualdo show, with Huxley, traveled to Santa Barbara, and a *Time* magazine article about the recording, titled "The Mad Madrigalist," focused a national spotlight on the twenty-eight-year-old conductor, Robert Craft.[75]

To celebrate the two hundredth anniversary of Mozart's birth, ten works of his were performed this season. The first was a Sonata for Piano four-hands, K. 521, played by André Previn and Lukas Foss. This four-hand sonata was a late substitution for another work, and Previn recalled:

> [I] accepted with enthusiasm which was tempered by the fact that I had not played those Sonatas before. However, I was perfectly sure that my friend Lukas knew them inside out and would guide me through them with expert hands. . . . We had some difficulty setting up a rehearsal . . . and we got together the day before the scheduled performance. When we eventually sat down at the pianos in his house, Lukas mentioned with total innocence that he hoped I knew the work in question thoroughly, because he had never played it before! Well, we read it through, decided on basic tempos and tried to play with all our fingers crossed. On the night, five minutes into the first movement, I heard a hissing noise on my right, emanating from my partner. I tried to disregard it but it persisted. At last I caught on; Lukas was trying desperately to find out whether we were making the repeats or not. I nodded frantically and we went back to the beginning. . . . I've played the Mozart Sonatas many times since then, but I doubt whether I've ever had a better time.[76]

In the *Times,* Albert Goldberg noted that "while a shade more rehearsal might have helped, it was a pleasure to hear such rarely lovely music played with so much spontaneity and professional skill,"[77] and C. Sharpless Hickman wrote that the work was "hastily-rehearsed but splendidly played."[78] The concert concluded with Renaissance and

Baroque music arranged by Morton for his favored instrumental combination of four trombones.

Ingolf Dahl stirred interest by conducting Mozart's Divertimento in B-flat, K. 287, from the piano, "a procedure," the *Times* stated, "which is rarely followed nowadays."[79] Dahl had also become interested in Donald Tovey's method of resuscitating Haydn's piano trios, making them more interesting for performers by transferring passages from the dominating piano part to the violin and cello. Several of Dahl's rearrangements of Haydn trios appeared on Monday Evening Concerts, the first on the 31 October 1955 program, which also included a performance of Stravinsky's *Elegy in Memory of Alphonse Onnou* (1946), played by Milton Thomas, solo violist.

Dallapiccola's keyboard work, *Quaderno musicale di Annalibera* (1952–1953), "a rather dry piece," Morton thought, received its first Los Angeles performance (by pianist Daniel Eller) on this program. Leonard Stein and Marni Nixon performed songs from four of Webern's works for voice and piano on 14 November 1955—and recorded them at about the same time, for Robert Craft's historic complete recording (Columbia) of the works of Webern. Stein recalls making "a crazy little speech before [the concert performance] . . . which didn't make any difference. Stravinsky was in the audience."[80] Stravinsky also attended the rehearsals and recording sessions for this landmark recording, which influenced an entire generation of young composers.

On 28 November 1955 Craft and Morton reached further back in music history to introduce to Los Angeles one of the earliest polyphonic settings of the Mass Ordinary, the *Messe de Nôtre Dame* (probably written around 1350) by Guillaume de Machaut. Morton remembered that the mass "was a stunning piece for those of us who are interested in the older music . . . but I must admit that many people found it dull."[81] Marilyn Horne sang two arias by Monteverdi, "Lasciatemi morire" and "Partenza amoroso." She also sang J. S. Bach's Cantata No. 84 for soprano, oboe, strings, and continuo, *Ich bin vergnügt.* Three out of the Six Pieces for Male Chorus, Op. 35, by Schoenberg were scheduled, but because these were so difficult, in the event only two were performed.

The South African composer Priaulx Rainier was the first of only three women composers whose work appeared on Morton's series; her Sonata for Viola and Piano (1945) was given its first Los Angeles performance on 5 December 1955, along with a Los Angeles premieres of Benjamin Britten's Canticle II: *Abraham and Isaac,* and Darius Milhaud's *Dreams of Jacob.* Morton found all three works disappointing but often programmed works he felt were interesting and should be heard, even if he was not convinced of their quality.[82] Elliott Carter's Eight Etudes and a Fantasy for Woodwind Quartet was performed by members of the Los Angeles Woodwinds on 9 January 1956, in a program of American music that included works by Billy Layton, Quincy Porter, Vincent Persichetti, Arthur Berger, and Theodore Norman, a Los Angeles classical guitarist.

Monday Evening Concerts introduced Luigi Nono, Karlheinz Stockhausen, and Luciano Berio—along with Pierre Boulez the central figures of the postwar generation—to America and the West Coast when they were at their most outspoken and critical toward their antecedents. The American premiere of Luigi Nono's *Canti per 13,* conducted by Robert Craft, provided something of a scandal at the 23 January 1956 concert. It was the first time Nono's music had been heard in this country.[83] Albert Goldberg pontificated, "The composer's name is pronounced 'No! No!' and if you give it the right emphasis you may consider yourself something of a critic. . . . We plainly heard the grunts of frogs, the hum of mosquitos and the screech of night birds, with possibly a jackal and a hyena in the near distance. Certainly the atmosphere was malarial and it would do no harm to take a dose of quinine as a precaution." He reported that half the audience left at intermission so they would not have to hear the work repeated.[84] At the following concert Morton made a speech claiming Goldberg had misrepresented the facts, for half the audience had remained. Craft remembers that the work was loudly hissed. Gertrud Schoenberg, Nono's mother-in-law, gathered signatures from the more illustrious members of the audience, including Stravinsky, to send to Nono in Venice.[85] Performances of Boccherini, Mozart, and another Bach solo cantata graced this event.

Karlheinz Stockhausen's *Kontra-Punkte No. 1* (1952) provided the next excitement, in its American premiere on 20 February 1956. This was also the first performance in America of any music by Stockhausen. Natalie Limonick, the pianist in the work, remembered slaving over it, and feeling

> absolutely panicked when the rehearsals were here. The rehearsal day came and one by one the musicians trekked in with these long, long faces and I was beginning to feel a little bit better. . . . What we played and what [Craft] had in that score, I don't know how he ever conducted, because it was chaos. There was not enough time, not all the notes were right. But the funny part was that some years later [1958] . . . this "seasoned orchestra" had to refurbish it! Only this time Stockhausen was conducting. . . . We met this very amiable gentleman, this sweet-smiling fellow. And two seconds in he would stop and say, "Can you do that harmonic, Miss Remsen [harpist], an octave higher, please? And Mrs. Limonick, is there not a thirty-second rest in the left hand? Would you please release the pedal?" I mean he really *heard*. . . . There was one place which I absolutely couldn't play. It was all over the keyboard, four staves of manuscript measures very compressed on the page, with all these millions of ledger-lines. You had to look at the keyboard to do it. He got this sardonic grin on his face and said, "You know, in the premiere I played the piano. I couldn't do those two measures either. I had another pianist come in." So Leonard Stein stepped over and did those two measures with me.

When asked how she felt about such music, Limonick replied, "I loved it. Because the ego was involved, the sheer doing of it, getting into and having the fun of making it. You loved every piece you played as a performer—maybe not as a listener."[86] The newspaper reviews for the first performance in 1956 were very unfavorable, but "we all believed that Stockhausen was a composer who was on the way up," stated Morton.[87] Goldberg had heard it bruited about that the piece was going to be "even worse" than Nono's but found it "not even irritating, it was just boring."[88] On the same program Marni Nixon sang Dallapiccola's *Goethe-Lieder* again, and Stravinsky's *Berceuses du chat,* which were low for her voice but were accompanied, like the Dallapiccola, with three clarinets. Craft conducted, and Brahms and Mozart sonatas framed the program.

After a program of Mozart, Bach, and Copland choral music, combined with Stravinsky's two piano arrangements of his Septet and *Scherzo à la russe,* the final program of the eighteenth season was "a good old solid classical program," Morton remembered: Bach's Brandenburg Concerto No. 3, Marilyn Horne singing Schubert songs, and Mozart's great Serenade in B-flat, K. 361, which became a particular favorite of the Los Angeles Woodwinds.

On the back page of many of the programs of this season, Morton printed congratulatory responses from Europe and the East Coast to the programs he had sent out as publicity. Now, in the summer of 1956, he set off with the Stravinskys, Craft, and—as it turned out—Marilyn Horne, for Europe. Stravinsky's *Canticum sacrum* was to be premiered in St. Mark's in Venice, and Horne was to be a soloist, as she embarked on the first European phase of her career. It was Morton's first trip to Europe as well. Morton, Craft, and the Stravinskys went by boat to Naples and were driven across Italy to the town of Gesualdo, where they explored the palazzo of the Gesualdo family. They traveled on to Greece and Istanbul then back to Venice. Stravinsky was not feeling well, so Morton explored Italy further by himself and traveled to Vienna. In October, after Morton had returned to Los Angeles, Stravinsky suffered a near-fatal stroke while conducting a concert in Berlin. He rejected medical advice to stop conducting; in fact he recovered sufficiently to conduct a concert in Rome on 29 November and to continue a hectic schedule of concerts and world travel in subsequent years. In early November, while Stravinsky was undergoing treatment in a Munich hospital, Pierre Boulez visited Craft, bringing a recording of his latest work, *Le Marteau sans maître.* Craft conducted works of Stravinsky and Webern for Boulez's two-year-old Paris concert series, the Domaine Musical, on 10 November 1956. By December Stravinsky was well enough to lunch with Boulez.[89] (Boulez later called Stravinsky his "bridge" to Los Angeles.)[90] The connections between Boulez, Craft, and Stravinsky were to be important in the coming Monday Evening Concert season. Morton returned to Los Angeles with the news that Monday Evening

Concerts were relatively better known in Venice and in Vienna than in Los Angeles. "Europe has an impression that Los Angeles is a fountain of culture," he told the music critic of the *Los Angeles Herald Examiner.* European composers and publishers had approached him with scores; Universal Edition, the Viennese publishing house, had called together all its executives to meet him.[91] Monday Evening Concerts now began to turn more and more toward Europe for its repertoire.

NINETEENTH SEASON: 1956–1957

For the first concert of the season André Previn conducted a long work by Boris Blacher, a distinguished German composer who had visited Los Angeles the year before and was eager to have a premiere at Monday Evening Concerts.[92] The concert performance of his scenic oratorio, *Romeo and Juliet,* took up most of the program, and was accompanied by one of Mozart's sonatas for two pianos, in continuation of the Mozart bicentennial. Previn reappeared as pianist on the second program, playing Maurice Ravel's Sonata for Violin and Piano and Beethoven's "Kreutzer" Sonata with Eudice Shapiro. Samuel Barber and Leoš Janáček received their first Los Angeles performances by a wind group, in which clarinetist Kalman Bloch returned to the concerts.

Now that the group of local performing musicians was no longer constant as it had been in the days of the Roof group, there was less cohesive development and promotion of new ensembles. While Morton tried to encourage those that did form, he took less responsibility for their continuance than had Peter Yates. Morton's hopes for permanence for a new piano quartet formed in the mid-fifties—which called itself The American Chamber Players—were disappointed after only a few seasons. The players were Dorothy Wade, violin, Milton Thomas, viola, William Van den Burg, cello, and Ingolf Dahl, piano—all longstanding performers for Monday Evening Concerts. In the 19 November 1956 program, this ensemble played one of the Dahl's reconstructed Haydn piano trios, Aaron Copland's Piano

Quartet (1950), and Brahms's Piano Quartet in C Minor, Op. 60. Musing about the breakup of this promising group, Morton remarked,

> I suppose the pressure of the commercial [engagements] makes it quite impossible to get along with [whatever] personal and musical disagreements [may have come up]. . . . Unless a group becomes internationally famous and has regular tours like the Juilliard Quartet and the Budapest Quartet, there is not a chance. But our people couldn't afford to take time out to go on tour, even if they could get the dates.[93]

On 3 December 1956, Pierre Boulez's *Sonatine* for flute and piano (1946) was given its first Los Angeles performance by Arthur Hoberman, flute, and Leonard Stein, piano. Its performance began a long association between Morton and Boulez, which, in 1966, Morton felt was "the closest relationship that [Boulez] has in the United States."[94] On the same program Lukas Foss conducted his own Concerto for Oboe and Chamber Orchestra. Foss had been appointed to teach composition at UCLA; he was in Los Angeles from 1952–1962, following years in Boston (where he had been pianist of the Boston Symphony), and Rome, on a Fulbright fellowship. He was well launched in a brilliant concert and composing career and frequently conducted the Philharmonic during his decade in Los Angeles (he had made his conducting debut at the age of seventeen with the Pittsburgh Symphony). Both Yates and Morton had written about his music as critics. Morton was impressed with his pianism, and eager to have him play Beethoven's "Hammerklavier" Sonata, but never got Foss to practice it. Foss was named to the Musicians' Board of Monday Evening Concerts but was usually too busy to attend meetings.[95]

The violist Milton Thomas took on conducting duties on 7 January 1957, presenting Bach's Brandenburg Concerto No. 6 and a Serenade by Heinrich Biber, which Morton found very interesting. On 21 January 1957 the baritone Heinz Blankenburg, a promising young artist studying at USC, presented Robert Schumann's *Dichterliebe,* with

Gwendolyn Williams Koldofsky, a Canadian pianist who had come to Los Angeles with her husband, the violinist Adolf Koldofsky. She was a distinguished accompanist and teacher whose pupils included Marilyn Horne and such well-known accompanists as Martin Katz. Other noted USC faculty members, the pianist John Crown and the cellist Gabor Rejto, played Copland's Piano Variations and Beethoven's Sonata in D Major for cello and piano, Op. 102 No. 2, and a premiere of Ernest Kanitz's Sonata for Violoncello Alone (1955). William O. Smith, a composer finishing a degree at USC, enjoyed the Los Angeles premiere of his 1952 String Quartet. The Monday Evening Concerts' association with USC's School of Music was very important in these years, and many USC music students, particularly from Ingolf Dahl's classes, came to the concerts.

The soprano Grace-Lynne Martin and the bass Robert Oliver were soloists under Robert Craft's direction in the 4 February 1957 program, which offered Bach's Cantata No. 152, *Tritt auf die Glaubensbahn,* and François Couperin's Third Lesson from the *Tenebrae* (the Couperin works that had influenced Stravinsky while composing his Cantata in 1952). The mezzo-soprano Nell Tangeman, who had sung Mother Goose in the Venice premiere and subsequent Metropolitan Opera production of Stravinsky's *Rake's Progress,* gave a special song recital with Gwendolyn Koldofsky on 8 February.

On 18 February Robert Craft conducted performances of Schoenberg's Serenade, Op. 24, and Monteverdi's *Il Ballo dell'ingrate,* in which the bass Robert Oliver sang Pluto, and the soprano Catherine Gayer appeared as An Ungrateful Soul. Gregg Smith, a UCLA graduate student at the time, prepared a small chorus. In his program notes Morton described for the audience the original "ducal extravaganza—a huge stage, with raging fires and flames, monsters and horrors stretching back into the distance as far as the eye could see. Contemporaries [of the 1608 production] wrote that the music moved the listeners to tears and transported the audience to an emotional state bordering on hysteria."[96]

A program the following month provided Gregg Smith with his conducting debut at these concerts. In a concert in collaboration with the Los Angeles chapter of the American-Scandinavian Foundation, he conducted an early group of the Gregg Smith Singers in a Los Angeles premiere of an a cappella work, *Laudi,* by Ingvar Lidholm. Smith remembered:

> It wasn't a great performance; we struggled through and got it out. I can't say the audience applauded vociferously, but I went off stage and Lawrence was back there with a towel. He immediately grabbed me and wiped my head. He was counting "1, 2, 3," and the minute he finished, even as the applause was dying out, he shoved me back on stage. To this day I count "1, 2, 3," and go right back on stage. He taught me right then and there that you don't wait for applause. You generate their applause. I never forgot that.[97]

The Gregg Smith Singers at that time were semi-amateur; Smith was a teaching assistant at UCLA and gathered willing students. By this time Roger Wagner's world-famous chorale had become professional. They had recorded widely and had been invited to perform for Queen Elizabeth II's coronation in 1953. The chorale singers received union scale wages, which were financially beyond the reach of Monday Evening Concerts.[98] The Gregg Smith Singers filled a need for MEC. Gregg Smith remembered, "Monday Evening Concerts were my growing up, my gestation, my career. It nurtured me and the Gregg Smith Singers, no doubt about it. . . . I was only 25. What was I doing up there? I had the good ears, and a group that was willing to do these things. Other directors weren't interested [in twentieth-century music], whereas it was my passion, my love, all this music."[99]

Since 1954 Morton had been in correspondence with Pierre Boulez to have the American premiere of his *Le Marteau sans maître* at Monday Evening Concerts. But the European premiere of *Marteau* at Donaueschingen was postponed from 1954 to 1955 because of the work's complexity. An American premiere was scheduled for Monday Evening Concerts on 18 March 1957, to be conducted by Craft, who would open the program with the five-voice a cappella Lamentations I and II of Thomas Tallis. Rounding up the seven musicians who could play Boulez's music was a challenge. The soprano Catherine

Gayer (who later developed a distinguished European career in contemporary music) was chosen. She had absolute pitch but little experience with contemporary music, and felt the experience was "like diving off the highboard while you're still learning to swim."[100] Her voice was wide-ranging, but the work was written for alto. The classical guitarist and composer Theodore Norman had had experience playing twelve-tone string quartets as a violinist, but he had to memorize much of his guitar part because of the extremely fast tempo called for in the first movement. The violist Milton Thomas had to cope with totally new technical challenges for his instrument. Arthur Gleghorn, a leading member of the Los Angeles Woodwinds, played alto flute. Morton was desperate to find three percussionists who could read the music and pressed the harpist Dorothy Remsen into service on the xylorimba; she had had early training on the marimba and had developed excellent technique. Her husband, the trumpeter Lester Remsen, another top-notch musician, played cowbells and nonpitched percussion. For the composer-percussionist William Kraft, who had joined the Philharmonic in 1955, this was the first appearance at Monday Evening Concerts—and, he remembered, the most difficult. He played vibraphone and remembered the occasion as "a cataclysmic revelation: Obviously here was a major compositional voice coming onto the scene; but, because the music was so staggeringly difficult, we doubted that it could be performed. (In my recollection, of several prominent composers who attended rehearsals, Stravinsky was the only one to turn the score pages at the right time.)"[101] After about fifty hours of rehearsal, Kraft remembers, "We couldn't get anywhere with it. . . . [Robert] Craft threw up his hands and said he'd call Boulez."[102] Boulez, who was touring the United States as pit conductor with Jean-Louis Barrault's theater troupe at the time, happened to be visiting a friend (an important backer of his Domaine Musical concerts) in San Francisco and was able to come to Los Angeles for ten days, during which he rehearsed *Marteau* strenuously and conducted it for Monday Evening Concerts on 11 March. This was Boulez's first concert appearance as a conductor in America. William Kraft found rehearsals with Boulez unforgettable:

> We assumed that *Marteau* had been mathematically conceived and mechanically notated. Certainly, it was not the product of the human mind and ear. When [Boulez] began the first movement with the count-off, "Un-deux-trois," so rapidly as to sound like one word (perhaps the name of a new French perfume or liqueur), we simply froze—and said, "What did you say?" . . . He has since reduced the tempo marking of that movement from a quarter-note equals 208 to a quarter equals 168. But it was when he sang our parts that the true shock hit us. The man *knew* what he had written. Furthermore, if it could be sung, albeit with the registral adjustment for the voice, it could be played. . . . My ears became so finely tuned that I could (and had to) hear what everyone else was doing. After that, rehearsing Debussy's *Iberia* with [Eduard] van Beinum and the Philharmonic was duck soup.[103]

Morton asked Pierre Boulez, when he came off stage after the performance, how the performance went. *Pas mal,* was the reply. In 1989 Boulez remembered, "I was not a very experienced conductor in '57. I had my own difficulties. Everybody had his own difficulties. So I cannot say that the performance was a virtuoso one, but it certainly was an honest one, therefore, *pas mal.*"[104]

The third work on this exceptional program was Karlheinz Stockhausen's germinal electronic work, *Gesang der Jünglinge* (1956), for vocal and synthesized sounds on tape. Genuine dissension in the community followed the concert, much of it fought out in a number of *Los Angeles Times* columns entitled "The Battle of Boulez."[105] His piece, using "normal" instruments, was the one that upset the audience, more than Stockhausen's electronic work. Albert Goldberg began his review with what Morton called "a salute to his betters" and went on to cavil:[106]

> What Virgil Thomson used to call the intellectual audience turned out en masse. . . . This sort of thing pretty well beggars description. . . . Three short poems by René Char . . . are sung, if that is the word, by a soprano. . . . Stockhausen's *Gesang der Jünglinge* was a collection of assorted sounds assembled on tape, with a boy's voice the only recognizable ingredient. There were noises like the

> croak of frogs, the plash of water, the rattle of sheet metal, gastric disturbances, or what have you?—and if this is music it's time to drop the H-bomb.[107]

Morton had won a promise from Stravinsky for the American premiere of *Canticum sacrum* at the final concert of the 1956–1957 season, but the expense of the large orchestra was daunting for MEC, and instead the program was cosponsored as part of a Los Angeles Music Festival celebration of Stravinsky's seventy-fifth birthday, given in Royce Hall at UCLA under the direction of the film composer Franz Waxman. Morton's earlier plan to combine Stravinsky with Bach and Obrecht evolved into a gala all-Stravinsky program, with Waxman conducting Stravinsky's *Greeting Prelude for the 80th Birthday of Pierre Monteux* (1955), and Craft conducting the Symphonies of Wind Instruments (1920), *Canticum sacrum* (1956), and the world premiere of *Agon* (1954–1957). Aldous Huxley spoke at intermission, and Stravinsky himself ended the concert, conducting his *Chorale and Canonic Variations on Vom Himmel hoch* by J.S. Bach (which had been premiered at the Ojai Festival in 1956) and the *Symphony of Psalms* (1930), sung by the Roger Wagner Chorale. A "glorious concert," Morton remembered.[108] He wrote in *The Musical Quarterly,*

> *Agon* is a complex score. It is "learned" music in the sense that it is full of highly organized and carefully worked-out details of polyphony and harmony and sonority, some of them very difficult for the ear to catch because of the lively tempo in which they happen. It will doubtless be a more popular work than the *Canticum,* but that is only because most people (not excluding conductors) would rather dance than pray.[109]

TWENTIETH SEASON: 1957–1958

Early music again reasserted itself this season. (The newspaper critics had little or nothing to say about early music—for or against.) Cantatas of Dietrich Buxtehude were a fresh contribution on two programs; Robert Craft conducted a program of vocal and instrumental works—predominantly composed for mourning—by Orlando di Lasso and Josquin des Prés, sacred music by Gesualdo, and Bach's *Trauer-Ode,* with its original text. On another program Craft repeated the Tallis Lamentations, along with instrumental works of Purcell and Vivaldi, and Bach's Cantata No. 60, *O Ewigkeit, du Donnerwort.* On 10 March 1958 Robert Oliver, bass, sang the often repeated *Fili mi, Absalon,* with another of Schütz's *Symphoniae sacrae* for the same combination of instruments (four trombones and continuo), *Attendite, popule meus.*

Morton (with the help of Ingolf Dahl) was "looking through the nineteenth century to see if we missed anything."[110] He came up with some out-of-the-way works, including a song cycle, *Haugtussa,* Op. 67, by Edvard Grieg, sung by the mezzo-soprano Eva Gustavson. "One of the most enjoyable things that we presented" was four sets of vocal quartets by Johannes Brahms, Opp. 31, 64, 92, and 112. Anita Priest (who was organist and second pianist to Shibley Boyes for the Philharmonic) accompanied and conducted these neglected works on 28 October 1957.

On this same program Ernst Krenek conducted his Capriccio for Cello and Chamber Orchestra (1955); Morton remembered that "the musicians had to pay very, very close attention because [Krenek] is erratic as a conductor."[111] A work by Milton Babbitt appeared on these concerts for the first time on 11 November 1957:[112] his Two Sonnets to poems by Gerard Manley Hopkins, for baritone, were conducted in their first Los Angeles performance by Leonard Stein, who also played a Concerto for Piano and Woodwind Quintet, Op. 53 (1953), by Wallingford Riegger. On 13 January 1958 the "big event" was the Los Angeles premiere of Aaron Copland's Piano Fantasy, played by his frequent interpreter, Leo Smit, who had recently joined the music faculty at UCLA. "It plays 30 minutes without a pause; is rather 'problematic' in content, and ought to be surrounded by nice music that is easy to digest," Copland wrote to his close friend Morton,[113] who responded after the performance to Copland, "I congratulate you with all my heart for this, your 'late Beethoven,' and I rejoice that you have been able to deliver yourself of a work so tragic as this."[114] Morton chose as companion pieces a Quintet for Piano and Winds by a friend of Brahms, Heinrich von Herzogenberg, and a Quintet for Winds (1955) by Karl Kohn, a versatile musician teaching on the music faculty at Pomona College in Claremont, who was soon to become very active with MEC. The Herzogenberg and Kohn works, respectively, were played by Ingolf Dahl and the Los Angeles Wind Quintet (members of the Los Angeles Woodwinds).

On 27 January 1958 the center of interest was Elliott Carter's "new and rather difficult" Sonata for Flute, Oboe, Cello, and Harpsichord.[115] On the same program Gregg Smith, "plunging into the new repertoire for which he has become rather well known,"[116] performed with his singers three choruses by Schoenberg, Op. 50a, Op. 27, Nos. 1 and 2, as well as J. S. Bach's motet, *Lobet den Herrn.* Smith remembered, "We hoped to do more [of Schoenberg's Op. 27] but it was an effort, and we worked liked the devil to get two done."[117]

At this time William Kraft formed the Los Angeles Percussion Ensemble, which was to become an importance force in these concerts in the sixties. William Kraft, born in Chicago in 1923, was raised in San Diego, California. After war service in the Air Force he studied timpani and composition in New York. While playing percussion for the Metropolitan Opera, he earned his master's degree in composition at Columbia University (1954), where he studied with Luening, Ussachevsky, Beeson, Brant, and Cowell. He later served as assistant conductor of the Los Angeles Philharmonic, then composer-in-residence to the orchestra, and director of the Philharmonic's New Music Group. On 10 March 1958, Kraft's Theme and Variations for Percussion Quartet, Bo Nilsson's *Doppelspiel,* and Edgard Varèse's *Ionisation* were played by the ensemble, conducted—except for the Kraft work, which needed no conductor—by Robert Craft. Robert Craft subsequently made a recording of the Varèse; it was a work Morton considered the classical masterpiece of percussion music and chose for his final program with Monday Evening Concerts. The work had a checkered history in Los Angeles, as it was one of Nicolas Slonimsky's offerings to the 1933 season at the Hollywood Bowl, and the particular target for indignant Angelenos, who brought pressure to have Slonimsky removed before the end of his contract and thus ended his—until then—brilliant conducting career.[118]

Ingolf Dahl performed Stravinsky's *Perséphone* (1934), which had never been performed on the West Coast, with students and faculty from the USC School of Music, 25 November 1957, to honor Stravinsky's seventy-fifth birthday. A chamber orchestra of MEC performers—many of them USC faculty—played the *Dumbarton Oaks* Concerto (1938), and the student orchestra played J. S. Bach's Overture No. 3 in D Major. Another Stravinsky performance, on 24 March 1958, was the Concertino for twelve instruments, a 1952 reinstrumentation of a 1920 string quartet piece. About this program Morton commented, "A kind of program that I particularly like: the first half, Stravinsky, Schoenberg, Stockhausen, Dallapiccola; and the second half, Bach." On it Leonard Stein gave "an incandescent performance" of Schoenberg's Three Piano Pieces, Op. 11,[119] and Stockhausen's Piano Pieces, Op. 2 (1953–1956), in which the composer allowed the performer his choice of the number and order of the pieces to play. Robert Craft conducted the Gregg Smith Singers in Dallapiccola's *Cinque canti* (1957) and Bach's Cantata No. 4, *Christ lag in Todesbanden.*

In the summer of 1958 Oxford University Press approached Morton (on the recommendations of Ingolf Dahl and Halsey Stevens) with a commission to write a biographical-critical book on Stravinsky, designed to parallel the appeal and success of Stevens's *Life and Music of Béla Bartók* (published in 1953). Stravinsky gave the project his blessing and allowed Morton access to his studio and files. Morton applied for a Guggenheim fellowship. Aldous Huxley recommended him; so did Joseph Kerman (with whom Morton had been in correspondence since 1950), Paul Henry Lang (who had recruited Morton to write reviews for *The Musical Quarterly*), and his longtime friends Ingolf Dahl and Aaron Copland. On 17 October 1958 he wrote Copland,

> This is the first time that the machinery has worked to enable me to write at all. And if I am successful with this task, and I am confident that I will be, then I mean to settle down (maybe in Ojai)

and spend the rest of my life writing, which I really ought to do, and want to do. I have had enough of the impresario's life.[120]

TWENTY-FIRST SEASON: 1958–1959

Because Yates had started the concerts with two six-month seasons, the season count was out of sync with the years; the twenty-first season was also the twentieth anniversary of the founding of the concerts. The first program (13 October 1958) proved yet again the strength of the half-new music, half-old music formula that had been a unique feature during those twenty years. Another strength—perhaps by this time taken for granted, but worth remembering—was the high quality of performances by purely local performers. The violist Milton Thomas, who had been inspired by Joseph Szigeti's all-Bach program for the Roof in 1950 and was now a steady performer at Pablo Casals's annual festivals, directed the complete *Musical Offering* of Bach, "with great polish, great intensity, and great expressiveness," remarked Morton, adding, "To me, [his interpretation is] rather romantic and too expressive, but he does it expertly."[121] (Goldberg—who never liked Bach—felt the hour-long work was unduly academic and diminished the large audience by the time it was over.)[122] On the same program a new group, the Los Angeles Brass Ensemble (led by the trumpeter Lester Remsen), played works of Giovanni Gabrieli and the later Baroque composer Johann Christoph Petzold, then joined with William Kraft's Los Angeles Percussion Ensemble to premiere Kraft's Nonet for Brass and Percussion, written for Monday Evening Concerts, and conducted by the composer.[123] Natalie Limonick, who had tackled many contemporary piano works in the concerts since 1950 and was now beginning to specialize in working with singers, accompanied and directed the *Spanisches Liederspiel,* Op. 74, vocal quartets of Robert Schumann, on 27 October.

The major events of the season in new music centered on Karlheinz Stockhausen and Luigi Nono. Leonard Stein had been in correspondence with Stockhausen, who was traveling in America that year but demanded a fee for conducting higher than MEC could pay; the Stockhausen program was planned therefore as a collaboration with UCLA's music department, under Lukas Foss's direction. Morton wrote Stein that program decisions were "protracted, difficult, complicated, delayed, and revised beyond all reason. . . . One would think we were planning the musical setting for the second coming of Christ. I think now we should remind ourselves that it is only His vicar, Stockhausen, who is coming."[124] When the composer arrived, Stein worked with him on further sections of the Piano Pieces, Op. 2, from which he had played in the previous season. He now successfully performed two interpretations of the longest and most difficult, *Klavierstück XI* (1956), printed on a sheet of paper "about the size of a pillowslip. . . . There are various little sections printed in various positions on the page, and you go from one to another as you choose."[125] Goldberg could see little difference in the interpretations. "If Mr. Stein does his practicing at home we are not sorry he is not our next-door neighbor. . . . It is going to take the world at large a long time to catch up with [Stockhausen]."[126] The American premiere of Stockhausen's quintet for winds, *Zeitmasse* (1956), was prepared for this concert by the Los Angeles Woodwinds, under Robert Craft, who had recorded this difficult work with these players the previous February. (Krenek, writing to Craft after witnessing the recording, remarked, "I've never believed that outrageous difficulty is a token of superior quality, as some people seem to do.")[127] Unfortunately, before the concert the flutist, Arthur Gleghorn, fell ill. A satisfactory substitution for this outstanding performer in such a difficult work could not be made, and the premiere—with Stockhausen conducting—had to be canceled. Morton, making the announcement, remarked that only three-quarters of the quintet had been able to rehearse—and was disappointed when the audience (cramming the hall to capacity, and evidently very serious) didn't catch his joke.[128] Stockhausen, however, conducted his hastily reassembled *Kontra-Punkte No. 1* and presented a taped work. Stravinsky's Cantata (1951) was prepared for this concert by Richard Dufallo, then a student of Foss's at UCLA.

The American premiere of Luigi Nono's *Coro di Didone* (1958), composed for Darmstadt, was performed by the Gregg Smith Singers and Los Angeles Percussion Ensemble, conducted by Leonard Stein, on 19 January 1959. Stein, through his long-standing connection with the Schoenberg family and Nuria Schoenberg Nono, was closely in contact with Nono and felt, "This is the kind of project for which Monday Evening Concerts exists."[129] Goldberg, struggling to understand what was going on in this music, had written an article titled, "The New Music: What is it About, What does it Mean?" previous to the Nono performance. Goldberg warned his readers, "Boulez, Stockhausen, and Nono . . . use mathematical phraseology like 'parameter' and 'vector' to describe their music, and performers must be calculators as well as musicians to play it. Their experiments have rendered conventional musical terminology vague and somewhat meaningless, as Mr. Craft has shrewdly pointed out."[130] In his review of the concert, Goldberg announced that "the intellectual audience turned out to the last beard." He heard nothing but the achievement of "complete linguistic unintelligibility" in Nono's work. "To our ears, although the audience applauded heartily, this accomplished only infinite boredom."[131] Morton, as a recompense to the Gregg Smith Singers (who had sung the disconnected syllables of Nono's choral parts to an accompaniment of suspended cymbals, tam-tams, and a set of chimes), and "also to the audience," had the singers, under Gregg Smith, then perform Lassus, a Brahms motet, and Charles Ives's Psalm 67,[132] an early essay into the Ives repertoire in which Gregg Smith has since become a specialist. To end the program (which had begun with early Baroque arias), Leonard Stein directed and played the piano in Schoenberg's *Ode to Napoleon Buonaparte,* Op. 41 (1942).

On 2 February 1959 the Fromm Music Foundation collaborated in sponsoring a concert in which new pieces, commissioned from Gunther Schuller and Ingolf Dahl by the foundation, were performed, along with Stravinsky's Octet for Wind Instruments, and three works—*Hyperprism* (1923), *Octandre* (1923), and *Intégrales* (1925)—by Edgard Varèse, conducted by Craft. Walter Arlen (just now emerging with his full name as a music critic in the *Los Angeles Times* from behind the initials W.A.) reported that the largest and most distinguished crowd of the season attended this "rambunctious affair."[133] The connection with Paul Fromm—a successful Chicago wine and liquor importer and merchant, who was born in Germany and had a passion for contemporary music—had been made through Stravinsky, "as many of our good connections have been," Morton acknowledged,[134] and this was the first in a series of Fromm sponsorships that lasted until April 1981. Fromm funding enabled MEC to expand ensembles, such as required by Varèse's *Intégrales,* which called for eleven wind and seven percussion players.[135]

Ernst Krenek, who for a decade had interested himself in all the explorations in Monday Evening concerts, wrote to Robert Craft in November, 1957, inquiring about the availability of Marni Nixon to sing the premiere of his second Fromm commission, *Sestina,* for soprano and nine instruments, in New York the following February. He had carried the idea of "total determination" into the text of his new work, which he had written himself, according to a highly organized poetic form used by Petrarch and Dante. For it he needed a singer with the range required in Schoenberg's *Herzgewächse.*[136] Paul Fromm had meanwhile engaged Bethany Beardslee to sing the New York premiere, but Marni Nixon sang the Los Angeles premiere, conducted by the composer, on 16 February 1959, as well as some fifteenth-century chansons by Johannes Ockeghem, to whom Krenek felt a special kinship, as he had written a book on this music. Theodore Norman played the world premiere of Krenek's Suite for Guitar Solo. Peter Yates wrote John Cage about increasing conflicts in the musicians' schedules: "We are drastically reduced in rehearsal time, as Krenek found out when he could scarcely bring together two players at a time to rehearse his Sestina. The effect was pretty confusing."[137]

Boulez's completed version of Claude Debussy's incidental music to recited poems by Pierre Louÿs, *Les Chansons de Bilitis,* was combined with Debussy's *Danses* and works for winds by Mozart in a program on 2 March 1959. A week later the Parrenin Quartet, from Paris, played string quartets of Bruno Maderna, Elliott Carter, and Jean Martinon with the cooperation of the Coleman Chamber Concerts and extra sponsorship by Paco Lagerstrom, a professor at the

California Institute of Technology. The pianist David Bar-Illan came as guest artist on 8 December 1958 to play Roy Travis's First Piano Sonata. Travis had recently been appointed to the composition faculty at UCLA. On the same program Mel Powell, introduced in the *Times* as "a noted jazz pianist" (though he was by then chairman of composition and director of the electronic studio at the Yale University School of Music), had his first performance at these concerts with his Divertimento for Violin and Harp (1954).

The final concert of the season combined a Handel oboe sonata, Bach's Cantata No. 51, *Jauchzet Gott in allen Landen,* sung by Marni Nixon, and Schoenberg's *Pierrot lunaire,* again performed in the Beier-Dahl English translation. Robert Craft conducted. Marni Nixon remembered that Craft had her sing the pitches of the *Sprechstimme* in *Pierrot.*[138] Albert Goldberg noticed that "the decadent quality did not invariably come through; it did not always sound lurid enough."[139]

At intermission, to celebrate the twentieth anniversary of the concerts, Morton invited Peter Yates (who had been a member of the Board of Directors of the Southern California Chamber Music Society since 1955) to blow out the candles on a large birthday cake and asked Sadye Moss to cut the cake.

> [Slices of cake] were ceremoniously presented to such prominent sponsors of the concerts as Igor Stravinsky, Mrs. Arnold Schoenberg, Lowndes Maury [representative of the musicians' union, Local 47], Mr. and Mrs. Yates, Mrs. Oscar Moss, and Mrs. Artie Mason Carter. The audience was then invited to partake of what was left of the cake, with a hint from Mr. Morton that birthday gifts in the form of contributions would be acceptable.[140]

Morton's Guggenheim Fellowship had been granted for 1959–1960, and he intended to spend at least one year in Europe. He named an executive secretary to take on administrative and financial tasks and parceled the programming tasks out among Ingolf Dahl, Leonard Stein, Leo Smit, Lukas Foss, Peter Yates, and Karl Kohn (all members of the Board of Directors; Kohn—who had assisted Ingolf Dahl at

Tanglewood—was the newest), as well as to the film composer David Raksin, Robert Craft, and Henry Holt (who was later to become an opera conductor). He wrote detailed instructions, among them the admonition that "Musicians' fees must average [a total of] $240 per concert."[141] Before leaving he worked at gathering memberships in the Southern California Chamber Music Society, so that 75 percent of the season's money had been garnered in advance. He discussed programming with the program directors and left with "a perfectly good conscience."[142] The tasks he now set for himself were to learn Russian, to investigate the sources of many of Stravinsky's compositions, and to write his "own" book, without any distractions from his Los Angeles relationship with the complex Stravinsky entourage.

Seven

"SWIMMING AGAINST THE STREAM" 1959–1963

TWENTY-SECOND SEASON: 1959–1960

The West Hollywood Park auditorium underwent remodeling during the summer of 1959 to accommodate basketball and other gymnasium uses. Just outside, "They added a pool, and the whole atmosphere of the place just became sort of nonmusical," Morton said.[1] The solution County Supervisor John Anson Ford found for MEC was another West Hollywood auditorium, Fiesta Hall in Plummer Park, at 7377 Santa Monica Boulevard, between Fairfax and LaBrea Avenues. The park was the site of the oldest house in Hollywood and a small Audubon Society bird sanctuary. The auditorium was another all-purpose hall, but gracious and intimate. Somewhat smaller than the West Hollywood Park hall, it seated four hundred. Albert Goldberg called it "a better mousetrap" in his review of the season's first program. He noted that "seats were at a premium, and the indispensable place the Monday Evening Concerts occupy in the city's musical and intellectual life was never more firmly demonstrated. . . . If succeeding ones maintain the same standard there is going to be nothing to worry about."[2]

Ingolf Dahl was in charge of this opening program and presented ensembles the size of which horrified Morton ("No one was being quite as economical about these things as I was"),[3] in works of Bach, Toch, Haydn, and Hindemith. Alice Ehlers was to have played the Bach Concerto for Harpsichord and Strings in D Major but canceled, and Dahl played it from memory, conducting from the harpsichord. He conducted the premiere of Ernst Toch's Music for Winds and Percussion (1959) and Paul Hindemith's Concert Music for piano, brass, and two harps (1930), and he accompanied Joseph Haydn's solo cantata for soprano and piano, *Arianna a Naxos.*

David Raksin, best known as composer for the film *Laura* yet deeply interested in serious music, directed the second program, a hodgepodge of works from various countries (Prokofiev, Louis Saguer, Bengt Hambraeus, George Tremblay, and Dallapiccola), and dedicated the program to the United Nations on the fourteenth anniversary of its founding. Goldberg praised the imperturbable aplomb and accuracy of Marni Nixon, singing (with Natalie Limonick, piano) Dallapiccola's *Quattro liriche di Antonio Machado,* "a comparative ray of sunshine amidst the encircling gloom."[4]

Two weeks later, to honor the rare delegation of Russian composers (Shostakovich, Kabalevsky, Dankevich, Khrennikov, Amirov, and the musicologist Yarustovsky) visiting Los Angeles, the program director Henry Holt presented a special concert of works by Leonard Bernstein, Halsey Stevens, Dahl, and Haydn, in cooperation with USC's School of Music and the Young Musicians Foundation. Ingolf Dahl's piece was his *Concerto a Tré* (1947; earlier called *Concertino a Tré*),[5] composed for—and premiered by—Eudice Shapiro, Victor Gottlieb, and the jazz clarinetist Benny Goodman in 1948, at the time when Goodman was changing his technique and becoming more involved in classical music. In this performance it was played by Mitchell Lurie, Dorothy Wade, and Emmet Sargeant.

In November the pianist-composer Karl Kohn, in his first appearance as a performer on these concerts, presented a program in which he played his own Three Pieces for Flute and Piano (1958), and with his pianist wife, Margaret Kohn, Bartók's Sonata for Two Pianos and Percussion and Boulez's *Structures I* (1952). Walter Arlen, in the *Los Angeles Times,* found the Bartók "arresting," the Kohn flute pieces "charming vignettes," and said of the Boulez, "Karl and Margaret

Kohn produced the cold and glassy sounds with astonishing sureness on two pianos which, as one wag remarked, surely must have been wired for agony."[6]

At this time Morton was in Paris. He wrote that he was being cagey and circumspect yet was persona grata everywhere in his efforts to gather information among Stravinsky's colleagues and friends, still maintaining his freedom to write his own book. "I haven't yet slipped on a banana peel," he wrote Paul Henry Lang.[7] He reported to Peter Yates, who was arranging a January MEC concert of American music,

> Encourage them all that concert life in Los Angeles is far better than it is here in Paris. . . . Everywhere the repertoire is dull. . . . Only Domaine Musical is exciting, stimulating, adventurous, and I must say I am jealous when I see 2,000 people crowded into the Odéon to hear (and see) Boulez, Stockhausen, Berio, and the rest of the avant-garde. Of course a flutist like [Severino] Gazzelloni helps! But there are only four such concerts a season. And so I like MEC better: 12 concerts of *mixed* repertoire. And tell our performers that the Paris musicians are *also* underpaid. And tell them finally that I miss them and love them all.[8]

To Leonard Stein, Morton wrote fuller reports of the avant-garde programs and personalities. In the 8 December 1959 program, Gazzelloni, playing a premiere of *Musica su due dimensione* by Bruno Maderna, had his music spread across seven music stands and was "A glorious sight as he moved across the stage!" Messiaen's *Le Merle noir* was "very pretty, a good piece for MEC, to lighten the heavy load of the avant-garde music." Morton thought Alexander Goehr's *The Deluge,* though a major work, also a bit dull. Luciano Berio's *Sequenza* for flute solo was the most interesting piece on the program. Boulez's *Sonatine* for flute and piano (played at MEC in 1956) seemed to Morton on a second hearing "too long and now a little obvious." Schoenberg's Suite for Septet, Op. 29, was played with the finesse of a Beethoven quartet. Gazzelloni—such a great flutist, with his golden flute, that all the avant-garde composers were writing for him, and he played only this repertoire—was "a great showman, a ham, an Italian operatic tenor, and he really 'stars' in [the Berio]. Get him when he comes to L.A. . . . I think [he] should be a sensational success. The problem is to get the audience there first."[9] In January there was again a full house for the Domaine concert, with Francis Poulenc in the audience. After the concert there was "a grand party *chez* Mme. [Suzanne] Tézenas [president and important benefactor of Domaine Musical] which must have cost enough to support MEC for a season." Stockhausen's *Zyklus* (1959), for percussion solo, was premiered: "You hear the cycle of sounds—skins, metals, woods, each group 'decorated' with elements of the others. Applause was terrific, from the gallery cries of 'Bis!' [There was] a hubbub of talk-back until Boulez restored quiet by his Napoleonic remarks: 'You are badly brought-up. . . . This is not genteel.' " The management made a mistake in playing it again; the piece was not difficult enough to be heard twice, Morton opined. But "Stockhausen is a doll: he came out to bow but didn't bow: instead, he merely surveys his subjects, as though he were examining every face in the audience; then, because he knows he is only acting, he breaks down in a big smile, lifts one arm from the elbow, and wiggles his fingers in a kind of 'toodle-doo' gesture. Thus his enemies become bewitched into adoration."[10]

Leonard Stein reported to Morton that in Los Angeles plans were getting under way for a new county museum of art. From the earliest stages of this idea, Morton had angled for a home in the museum for Monday Evening Concerts. Now the planners announced they would consult MEC's management when the time came to design the auditorium. Morton was determined to get an idea of the Domaine budget, how well the musicians were paid, and what the free theater meant to them in terms of money. "Twelve stagehands last night pushing the piano around! Activities of Domaine should be cited to the Museum people as an example of proper sponsorship."[11]

Meanwhile Morton met Luciano Berio in Paris: "I'm not yet ready to make judgements of the *quality* of this kind of music," he wrote Stein.[12] Boulez was too busy to be friendly, and Stockhausen was not cordial. Stockhausen, it turned out, had spread the word about in Europe that Monday Evening Concerts were poverty-stricken, that all the Los Angeles musicians cared about was money, and that the

United States was a cultural desert.[13] Stein wrote Morton, "I think [Stockhausen's] attitude toward you is disappointment that you are not a wealthy impresario—then you could be of use!"[14] Stockhausen expanded on his view of Monday Evening Concerts in an article, "Amerikareise 1958," in *Melos,* which did not appear until the summer of 1960. Morton, at that time still in Europe, demanded an apology and received it: "I am a bad boy, I know, and I have a complete lack of diplomacy," Stockhausen wrote to Morton. He had hoped to help Morton "find more support for your concerts or your unique activity—which, as I wrote—seemed to me to be the simple one 'swimming against the stream' as far as I could see."[15] Leonard Stein made a visit himself to Europe in spring 1961, and, when in Cologne to play a concert, told Stockhausen he had "succeeded in stabbing his only friends in America in the back, and [I] got over the idea that he was far from popular in the US (he seemed shocked by the idea); he became quite apologetic and regretted having written the article at all."[16]

Stein busied himself corresponding with Berio in the hope of "getting" him, his mezzo-soprano wife, Cathy Berberian, and the fabulous Gazzelloni for a Monday Evening Concert on their spring tour in the United States. "What they represent is just what our audience (MEC) needs," he wrote Morton.[17] He was thrilled at the prospect of playing with Gazzelloni ("the world's best flutist") on a concert.[18] One difficulty was to find extra lectures for Berio—who would receive, as Boulez and Stockhausen had, the same level of pay for a Monday Evening Concert the performers earned: $10 per piece performed, and no pay for the numerous rehearsals necessary for these difficult new works. (Stein, embarrassed by this policy, suggested to Morton that the fees be raised to $15 per unit.) Another difficulty was to find adequate equipment for the taped works that would comprise part of the program. Sadye Moss agreed to put up an extra $250 for the postseason concert.

In January 1960 Peter Yates mounted a program of works of Lou Harrison. Yates's musical preoccupations had turned increasingly toward American experimentalists in sound, now "the only field of contemporary music which interests me," he wrote John Cage.[19] Between 1953 and 1959 he gathered much information, wrote articles, and broadcast programs on this music in a series (which he called "Evenings on the Roof") on the new Pacifica radio station in Los Angeles, KPFK-FM. It was his feeling that Berio and Boulez were "essentially academic and conventional,"[20] whereas, in a proposal to propagandize for the experimental tradition, he wrote Cage, "As I see it, the Experimental tradition stems from Ives, draws strength from Cowell and Varèse and proceeds through yourself. We should be prepared to digress into the younger Europeans enough to show them as followers instead of the initiators they declare themselves. And as I believe, we should include the influence of Schoenberg, directly, and of Satie, remotely."[21] Yates had suggested to Harrison in the forties that he write a concerto for violin and percussion. He wrote in his program notes for the 18 January 1960 MEC concert, "All four of the compositions were composed originally around twenty years ago . . . during the period when Lou Harrison was working with John Cage in propagating percussion concerts." In the draft for his notes, Yates struck out his criticism of MEC for "acting as a showcase for the most advanced European music, while New York has jumped ahead of us in the performance and recognition of American music." Instead he remarked, "There's only one thing wrong with the best American music—most of us have not taken the trouble to find out about it. This evening you are being given one opportunity." Yates persuaded William Kraft to take on his first assignment conducting another composer's works for this concert. (Upon hearing the special skills of Kraft and his dauntless Los Angeles Percussion Ensemble performing his works, Lou Harrison gratefully said, "They play better than I write.")[22] The evening included a film (a dance to Harrison's *Canticle III* for percussion), his *Song of Quetzalcoatl* for percussion orchestra, and his Mass for mixed chorus, trumpet, harp, and strings. Eudice Shapiro gave the West Coast premiere of Harrison's Concerto for Violin and Percussion Orchestra. (Its premiere in New York had been played at half-tempo.)[23] Albert Goldberg admired its long, intensive and expressive violin melodies and the "fetching fabrics of sound in tightly organized forms." He reported the unconventional array of percussion instruments—a washtub, coffee cans, brandy snifters, flower pots, lengths of iron pipe, clock chimes, brake drums (sounding surprisingly pleasant), and exotica such as sistra, guiro, dragon mouths, and Japanese wind bells—which harked back to the depression-poor practices Cage and Harrison had developed separately and together on the West Coast in the 1930s and 1940s.

On 15 February Leonard Stein enjoyed the combination of conducting Stockhausen's *Kreuzspiel* (1951) and Gunther Schuller's Wind Quintet (1958), along with four of Monteverdi's *Scherzi musicali.* On the same program, Gregg Smith's Singers presented five settings, from William Byrd to Schoenberg, of Psalm 130, "Out of the depths I cry unto Thee." For Robert Craft's program on 29 February, Sol Babitz returned to the concerts to play in a Bach cantata, Stravinsky's double canon: *Raoul Dufy in Memoriam* (1959), and *L'Histoire du soldat,* with Stravinsky present. Stein reported to Morton, "Babitz is still the Soldat incarnate. . . . [Stravinsky's] sprightliness seems to be wearing away, so you notice his lack of height more. . . . I know he is 78, but it is still a little distressing to see him showing some of the signs of age."[24]

Albert Goldberg was delighted when, on 7 March, Leo Smit programmed Robert Schumann's Piano Quartet, Op. 47: "If the Monday Evening Concerts are not careful that shameful old nineteenth century, in which composers wrote nothing but beautiful music, is going to come to life again";[25] but he suffered abysmally in the final concert, for which Robert Craft conducted a program sponsored by the Fromm Foundation, featuring composers of interest to founder Paul Fromm: Arthur Berger, Milton Babbitt, Kazuo Fukushima, and Ernst Krenek. Goldberg found the concert "An utterly dismal collection of contemporary so-called music. . . . Every piece on the program sounded alike."[26]

As for the postseason Berio-Berberian-Gazzelloni special, Goldberg's headline howled: MONDAY CONCERTS GO MAD ON TUESDAY,[27] while Stein mailed off an ecstatic report to Morton, and in a letter to Peyton Houston Peter Yates described the scene:

> Cathy [Berberian] Berio, wife, a marvelously gifted reader and singer, for whom John [Cage] wrote this version of his *Fontana*

> *Mix* [1959] in five languages, innumerable noises, eleven vocal styles, and electronic accompaniment of rhythmically organized silence and noise, told me that she is unhappy performing this piece unless the audience fights back with laughter and responsive noises. Ours did. . . . Next November I shall present Cage and his pianist friend David Tudor for the Monday Evenings. Last year when I proposed some of his music, everybody laughed and dismissed the subject. This year they want him in person. . . . His fame is rebounding to us from Europe.[28]

The program (10 May 1960) featured Severino Gazzelloni in works for flute alone: *Density 21.5* (1935) by Varèse, Debussy's *Syrinx* (1912), Berio's *Sequenza* (1958); in Bruno Maderna's *Musica su due dimensione* for flute and tape (1958) (the work requiring seven music stands); and in Messiaen's *Le Merle noir* and Boulez's *Sonatine* (1953), both accompanied by pianist Leonard Stein. Cathy Berberian and Leonard Stein performed Sylvano Bussotti's *Voix de femme* (1959); Berberian performed Cage's *Aria for Mezzo Soprano* and *Fontana Mix* (1959) and Berio's *Omaggio a Joyce* (1958) with tape, and the only purely electronic work was Maderna's *Continuo* (1958). Stein wrote to Morton,

> On the whole I think it was one of the most successful ventures of MEC, and regardless of financial outcome will do more to create international goodwill and reputation than any other event this year and, for that matter, more than makes up for whatever slander Stockhausen cast in your direction. In addition it may help pull MEC out of the ever-lurking dangerous morass of mediocrity and polite acceptance of the new. The S[travinsky]s attended the concert (the first time I remember without Craft participating) and seemed to enjoy it tremendously. . . . The tape works were played over a four-speaker system situated around the hall, with Berio at the controls handling the distribution and intensity of sound. It all held the attention as the sound kept changing. . . . The first half passed without incident, but the Cage—which Cathy sang or spoke in five different languages and in ten different styles ranging from blues to coloratura and with a few vocal noises thrown in for good measure—began to get a rise out of the audi-

> ence. . . . Then a real, almost unbelievable, reaction to the Bussotti: Cathy and I had very little time to work on this more or less chance piece and it was really my first excursion into the bowels of the piano—plucking, muting, striking the strings with fingers, flat of the hand, drumstick, as well as making noses on the sounding board, slamming the lid, and other outlandish cageish activities—but somehow we both got into the spirit of the thing and really lived it up. The result: immediate and spontaneous audience reaction—half bravos, half boos—lively and tumultuous, which caught Cathy by surprise but delighted me thoroughly. . . . MEC had a real "scene" on its hands which they will be talking about for some time to come. . . . The work itself I consider a lot of tomfoolery and if I am asked to do anything like this in the future I shall insist in making it up myself without reference to the composers' "suggestions"; after all I now possess a promising repertoire of tricks and could add a few new ones as well with little encouragement (let's say just one belt of Scotch straight).[29]

The decade of the sixties, with its struggle between compositional control and happenstance, and its emphasis on new means of producing musical sound, was well under way.

TWENTY-THIRD SEASON: 1960–1961

Morton applied for a renewal of his Guggenheim fellowship, and it was granted for 1960–1961. He planned to remain in Europe and hoped to make a trip to the Soviet Union. Meanwhile a financial and managerial disaster had been brewing for the concerts, and Stein finally reported it fully to Morton in the summer of 1960. The executive secretary, although he had demanded a larger salary than was offered, had taken money from MEC, and had kept very disorderly financial records, and performers and printers remained unpaid. The Board had not been aware of what was going on. Morton was horrified; he feared the musicians' union would rescind its permissive stance toward the concerts if it discovered the mismanagement. Paul Fromm withdrew his financial commitment in disgust. Morton contacted the Mosses' lawyer son and wrote Stein to get all the financial records.

> I can't think, at this moment of shock, how to proceed for next season. Peter would know most about the mechanics, but there is great danger for the organization in letting him get hold of the reins. . . . This disaster has driven me right into the ground. I see all my labors of many years completely canceled.[30]

Sadye Moss worked tirelessly to untangle the financial records, discovered that $1,800 was missing, and wrote numerous letters to assuage anxieties and clear up the problems. Dahl recommended a dependable USC graduate student, Douglas Talney, to take on the duties of executive secretary. But the union was pressing to raise the musicians' fees, and Craft was demanding larger ensembles for works he planned to record (such as Schoenberg's opera *Von Heute auf Morgen* and Bach's *St. John Passion*). A symbiotic relationship had grown up between Craft's performing at the concerts and his ambitious recording plans. Columbia Records would not pay for his rehearsals, and the only way Craft could rehearse adequately was to perform at Monday Evening Concerts. Morton replied to Stein in regard to Craft:

> The problem with Craft is a tough one. Of course he wants to do the bigger works, and surely he is entitled to them in return for past efforts. But whatever he does, it must be in the framework of *our* possibilities vis-a-vis the Union. I think this is a crucial point with MEC. If we branch out into orchestral music, then we are in competition with the Philharmonic, [Franz] Waxman [who presented a festival of larger contemporary works each spring] etc., and not entitled to a special rate. Also, if we raise "special funds" for such big works and pay regular scale, then the musicians who get those jobs are favored above those who play for $10 per unit. Come what may, we have got to retain our uniqueness simultaneously in all departments: repertoire, fees, equality amongst performers (including conductors!)[31]

This policy was rooted in Yates's original ideas of equality and fairness amongst the performers and steadied the ship among the rocks of ego. It was also necessary because the union had always made a large across-the-board exception for the concerts, in recognition of their importance to the musicians and to Los Angeles: as long as the concerts remained in the chamber-music category, musicians did not have to be paid for rehearsals.[32] (The union's definition of chamber music allowed no more than one string player on a string part.) But now the union was in doubt about the concerts' management and resented Craft's playing "double strings" with his recording arrangements. The union demanded that the unit fee for performers be raised to $15 and with difficulty was talked down to a compromise: $12.50 per unit. Stein recommended that Craft be cut down to one concert. Each music director began sending out appeals for funds to keep the concerts going. The Fromm Foundation agreed to make plans to return to its sponsorship after a season's hiatus.[33]

For the 1960–1961 season, KPFK-FM broadcast Sunday evening discussions by the program directors about the music to be heard on the Monday concerts. Again Ingolf Dahl took on the first concert, showcasing USC performing faculty in works of Bach, Schubert, and Los Angeles composers Joseph Achron and Ramiro Cortés (a graduate of USC)—and pleasing the critic Goldberg. On 7 November Peter Yates produced a concert of American works: Carl Ruggles's *Evocations* and Ives's Sonata No. 1 for piano (1902–1909) played by Peter Hewitt (one of Buhlig's last pupils), along with Gerald Strang's Percussion Music (1935) and Lou Harrison's *Fifth Simfony* (1939), both played by the Los Angeles Percussion Ensemble conducted by William Kraft, and a trio by John Antes, an American Moravian composer (his trios, written circa 1790, the earliest known chamber music by a native American composer, had only recently been uncovered).[34] Stein reported to Morton that Yates's concert "went much better than I expected. . . . We will make it [financially] this season."[35] André Previn was responsible for an unusually large turnout for his performance of Hindemith's Third Piano Sonata on 21 November. He had recently recorded all of Hindemith's piano sonatas. Critic

Walter Arlen found his performance meticulous, musicianly, and beautifully proportioned.[36]

The 16 January 1961 program was a concert performance of Handel's *Acis and Galatea,* conducted by Henry Lewis. Lewis had founded The String Society of Los Angeles, with which he now performed frequently as a conductor, often featuring Marilyn Horne as soloist. She had had great success in Europe in the role of Galatea and was eager to sing it in Los Angeles.[37] When Lewis proposed the work as a Monday Evening Concert, he agreed to provide the orchestra, chorus, and soloists, all under the $300 budgetary limit posed by MEC. Marni Nixon sang Damon, the tenor John Guarnieri sang Acis, and the bass Roderick Ristow sang Polyphemus. The Camerata Chorale provided the chorus. Shibley Boyes, regular harpsichordist for the String Society, returned to the concerts for this performance. Goldberg was ecstatic. The performance was "quite likely the first one hereabouts." His praise was eloquent:

> One of the peaks of [MEC's] invaluable existence. . . . Fiesta Hall was jammed to capacity for an experience that was sheer delight from beginning to end. . . .[It was] Henry Lewis's . . . biggest assignment to date, and it disclosed a major talent. . . . The hall rang with "Bravos" for him at the conclusion, and they were well earned. The soloists were splendid, too. Marilyn Horne sang like an angel. The voice was luscious, with a silvery sheen and a starry glint that enchants the ear, and it had the fluency of a coloratura and the power and eloquence of a dramatic soprano.[38]

In this same month a complex situation at the Los Angeles Philharmonic necessitated several substitutions for the conductor Georg Solti, and Henry Lewis—who had studied with Eduard van Beinum both in Los Angeles and in Holland—was the first native of Los Angeles chosen to conduct the Philharmonic. Substituting for Lewis in his role as conductor of the Young Musician's Foundation orchestra was nineteen-year-old Lawrence Foster. His assurance and genuine talent were soon noticed by Stein and Dahl, who engaged him for the following MEC season.

The Cuban composer Aurelio de la Vega, who had studied in Los Angeles with Ernst Toch in the late 1940s, returned to the city in 1959 to teach at San Fernando State College. On 30 January 1961 he presented a program of contemporary Latin American music that offered samples from various countries and stylistic attitudes by Silvestre Revueltas (Mexico), Juan Carlos Paz (Argentina), de la Vega, Juan Orrego Salas (Chile), and Alberto Ginastera (Argentina). On 20 February William Kraft introduced Stockhausen's *Zyklus* for percussion solo, a work influenced by John Cage's ideas of indeterminacy. Kraft passed out copies of the first page of the score to the audience and explained the choices the performer could make. He later remembered performing it:

> There is this primary line that must be played. It's obligatory, it goes through the center of the page. Then above and below are several other groups of notes and patterns and various events, and the idea is to take your choice, as you're playing, as to which you're going to do. They have to fit into either certain places, or into an area, and you have to be finished with it at a certain time. . . . A very strong part of the aesthetic of the piece is the idea of choice. This was a period of the input of the performer, and changing from the general stream. It was a piece that was open-ended. You could start anywhere, end anywhere. You could even turn it upside down and play it. Time was a controlling factor. [Stockhausen] tells you the timing for each page. . . . You have a lot of instruments [in a circle], and you have to know where they are, because if you take choices, you don't have time to look. . . . You might be tempted, if you're centered on the marimba (which is a large instrument), not to go too far. But if you want to be theatrical about it, and think you can make it, you might whip around and take a choice that would take you to the other side—to the drums, for instance. I think that was the first time [choreography] was really a conscious part of the composition.[39]

But to Goldberg, unaccustomed to aleatoric principles, "it was still as clear as mud."

> Kraft displayed the dexterity of a grasshopper . . . frequently breaking and losing his sticks and mallets in the excitement of the chase. It was a one-man circus, but aside from watching Mr. Kraft do his calisthenics it made no musical sense whatever; it was just twenty-five minutes of infinitely boring monotony. . . . [On the same program, Ernst Krenek's *Santa Fe Time Table,* for mixed chorus a cappella] was a tedious and joyless ride on a local that made all stops—for some reason the audience laughed when Pasadena was reached—and it was a great advertisement for the superior advantages of air travel.

The suffering critic found the other works on the program (Mahler, Brahms, and Johann Zelenka, a Czech contemporary of J. S. Bach) a balm to his "bruised ears."[40]

Leonard Stein had made a deal with Marilyn Horne that if she and Henry Lewis put on *Acis and Galatea,* she should also sing Schoenberg's Eight Songs, Op. 6 (1905), with Stein accompanying. She performed them on 6 March 1961, and Goldberg found her performance "most absorbing," although the total event, including an early sixteenth-century Mass by Jean Mouton, instrumental pieces from the *Glogauer Liederbuch,* and two piano works by Debussy and Stravinsky (played by the Kohns) struck him as "scarcely an example of well-balanced program construction."[41] The West Coast premiere of Varèse's *Deserts* (1954) was Robert Craft's contribution on 20 March.

Lukas Foss produced a program (3 April 1961) introducing his newly formed Improvisation Chamber Ensemble, along with Morton Feldman's *Durations* (1960), two works by Gunther Schuller, and Boulez's *Improvisation sur Mallarmé* No. 1 (1958). Having done some homework, Goldberg now summoned an exposition on the aleatoric concept of music in his column. He found the Foss improvisations, "if not precisely beautiful . . . quite astonishing in their interplay and ingenious freedom." The Boulez struck him as "harrowing and meaningless."[42] Since meeting Boulez in 1957, Lukas Foss had moved from relative conservatism into the avant-garde with his ideas of improvisation.[43] He had started the Improvisational Chamber Ensemble with his students at UCLA "to change them, but it turned out to change me much more. . . . It was a big departure; an early attempt at chance music before the word aleatoric had even permeated the jargon. . . . Music that was . . . born out of a jealousy of jazz."[44] Morton's personal opinion, from having done a good deal of improvising as a theater organist, was that Foss's ensemble work was not improvisation, as it required too much planning and was too dominated by Foss's concepts.[45]

On 17 April students and faculty of USC's School of Music presented Luigi Dallapiccola's *Canti di prigionia,* written in Mussolini's Italy between 1938–1941 to protest persecution through texts of the martyrs Mary Stuart, Boethius, and Savonarola. Critic Walter Arlen mentioned the fitting coincidence that it should be performed while the world's attention was focused on the Eichmann trial in Jerusalem. Arlen was moved by the deeply felt expressiveness and grandiose sweep of the work. Copland's *Nonet for Strings* (1960) was given its West Coast premiere the following month, with Leo Smit conducting. Copland (who was now sixty) wrote Smit, asking for a color of "*moyen âge* gloom, but not dull," at the beginning of the piece.[46]

TWENTY-FOURTH SEASON: 1961–1962

When Lawrence Morton returned from Europe in the spring of 1961, he was appalled at the concerts' financial situation; he felt money had been spent unwisely, and there was much fence-mending to do. Sadye Moss's contributions had been larger in those two years, "because economy had not been practiced as I had practiced it."[47] Moreover, he himself was out of money and facing a September 1961 deadline on his book. He told Sadye Moss he could not continue to be available for MEC. Mrs. Moss consulted with others and suggested he apply to the Los Angeles County Music Commission for funds. He prepared a budget, taking into account the rise in musicians' fees and $1,000 for secretarial help, and requested a $5,000 salary—over double what he had received in the past. "If I can't maintain a roof over my head and eat, then I can't take the job at all," he wrote Stein.[48] He estimated $10,000 income in ticket sales and contributions from members of the support group. He forecast a $5,000 deficit, and he applied to the county for $6,000—but was turned down, albeit with sympathy, because the deadline was long past. Morton clearly wanted to continue running the concerts. He often referred to himself as "the only fool around who would accept a job like that—all work and hardly any pay."[49] He asked Fromm for an increased grant for the reinstated Fromm Foundation program and suggested a return of the Berios for this event. He found that some subscribers had left in anger over the new music. He wrote Leonard Stein, "I think it would be a tactical mistake to limit contemporary music to what Darmstadt-Donaueschingen-Baden Baden are doing. . . . Can you agree?"[50] He spent August "madly juggling figures" and deciding that there should be a maximum of ten performers per program, those ten to provide the whole concert. There should not be more than two works on a program played by any single player, and each program should be built on one large ensemble piece, with the rest of the repertoire determined by that instrumentation.[51] At the end of August he and Sadye Moss sent out a letter to friends of the concerts announcing that financial problems were desperate and that income from contributions must be doubled. The results enabled him to print an impressive list of contributors, a list of only twenty-eight subscribers, and the planned roster of artists and works for the coming season, which promised many premieres. Although he spent much of the summer isolated in Ojai, trying to write his book on Stravinsky as migraine headaches plagued him, his publisher's contract deadline passed, unfulfilled.[52]

The first concert of the season offered Beethoven's forty-minute Piano Sonata ("Hammerklavier"), Op. 106, played by a USC faculty member, Lillian Steuber; Lukas Foss's *Time Cycle* in its chamber version, played by the Improvisation Ensemble with the soprano Grace-Lynne Martin, with the composer at the piano; and Hindemith's Sonata for Violoncello Solo, Op. 25, No. 3, played by Howard Colf, Jr., the cellist of Foss's Improvisation Ensemble. Goldberg headlined his review, "Monday Concerts Off to Fine Start," and made his usual friendly season-opening remarks with perhaps more warmth—and welcome to Lawrence Morton—than usual. Fiesta

Hall was crowded with adventure-seekers. Goldberg found that Beethoven still seemed to belong among the moderns. The Foss work gained in coherence without interpolated improvisations and was fascinating for its imaginative spareness. The soloist Grace-Lynne Martin showed a fine intelligence.[53] (She went on to perform the *Time Cycle* at Lincoln Center, and recorded it with Foss.) Morton himself remembered this as "one of the best concerts we ever put on. . . . a really stunning program, and the performances were first class. I immediately pointed out to everybody that here was a program that was done with six players, a very elegant program, and I brought it in well within the budget."[54]

The same was true of the next concert, which, Walter Arlen noted, presented "youth and good music": first performances of works by Leonard Rosenman and Dorrance Stalvey—as well as two Mozart piano trios. Morton felt Stalvey's piece was notationally problematical and therefore difficult to perform,[55] but Arlen admired its "airy texture, some interesting tone colors and sound combinations, and a sense of logic and purpose." Arlen found Rosenman's work "heavy-textured and rather opaque in sound,"[56] while Morton opined that his was "one of the most important clarinet pieces written in our time."[57] Rosenman, whose film scores included *East of Eden, Rebel Without a Cause,* and *The Savage Eye,* was at this time a twelve-tone composer in his "serious" music. His *Music for Fifteen Instruments* had been premiered the previous MEC season by his colleague David Raksin.

Lawrence Foster made his first appearance at MEC on a program in collaboration with the Los Angeles Chapter of the International Society for Contemporary Music, 4 December 1961, conducting the American premiere of Alexander Goehr's *The Deluge,* a cantata derived by the composer from a script prepared by the Soviet film director Sergei Eisenstein from notes by Leonardo da Vinci. Subsequently Foster met Goehr in London, where they became good friends, and Goehr introduced him to the BBC, which engaged him for a number of concerts.[58] Foster was brought up in Los Angeles and had studied conducting with Fritz Zweig. (Fritz Zweig had a brilliant conducting career as head of the Prague Opera and the Deutsche

Oper in Berlin, and after emigrating to California became Klemperer's assistant conductor at the Los Angeles Philharmonic. He was known as the finest teacher of conducting in the city.) The ISCM-MEC concert, the *Los Angeles Examiner* critic wrote, brought the audience to a point of impatience and restlessness seldom witnessed in the concert hall.[59] Goldberg found it "a real dilly of concentrated nothingness."[60] The program also included works of Messiaen, Roman Haubenstock-Ramati, and George Rochberg.

Stravinsky's eightieth birthday year occurred in 1962, and Morton again scheduled his compositions on each program. On 15 January 1962 Bach, Handel, and Mozart framed six works by Stravinsky: the Shakespeare songs, the Septet, the Four Russian Songs for voice and piano (1919), Two Early Piano Pieces (1922 and 1915) that Morton had dug up in his researches, Three Easy Pieces for Piano Duet (1915), and Five Easy Pieces for Piano Duet (1917). Leo Smit and Grace-Lynne Martin were featured, and Eudice Shapiro and Victor Gottlieb played a Mozart piano trio with Smit. Morton was disappointed in one aspect of this program:

> When I programmed the [easy piano] pieces, I said, "Leo, I'm going to play them with you." You see, in one set of pieces, the left-hand part is very easy, for amateurs, and in the other set, the right-hand part. I said, "That's my style of piano playing and I want to play them." But Leo did not go for that. He wanted to bring in this young girl student who had a very short skirt and looked very childish.[61]

The Polka of the 1915 pieces was written for Diaghilev, who could play the easy part, but as Stravinsky's image was of a circus master with a whip in his hand—a reference to Diaghilev—Diaghilev didn't know if he should be flattered or not.[62] During this 1962 season many of Stravinsky's lighter pieces were performed.

On 5 February Leonard Stein gave the first American performance of Boulez's Third Piano Sonata (1957), another aleatoric work that Goldberg found "mercilessly boring despite Mr. Stein's comprehensive mastery."[63] Stein wrote an article in this period, titled "The

Performer's Point of View," on the relationship of the performer to new notations used by Boulez, Stockhausen, Cage, Krenek, and others. He described the challenges and contradictions a specialist in the newest music faced but also pointed out the advantages, now that a performer's work was collaborative in nature: "Few periods in recent music history have granted him so great an opportunity to participate in the creation of new musical idioms."[64]

On 19 February Robert Craft conducted a complete program that included the world premiere of Stravinsky's short a cappella anthem, "The Dove Descending Breaks the Air" (completed only a month before), sung by the Gregg Smith Singers to a text from T. S. Eliot's *Four Quartets.* A special grant from Paul Fromm also enabled Craft to give the first Los Angeles performance of Elliott Carter's Double Concerto for Harpsichord and Piano with Two Chamber Orchestras (with Leonard Stein playing harpsichord, and Pearl Kaufman, piano), along with Schoenberg's *Kammersymphonie,* Op. 9, and Bach's Wedding Cantata *O holder Tag* (with Grace-Lynne Martin, soprano).

Carter visited Los Angeles for the performance. Morton's invitation gives a rare glimpse into his lifestyle:

> I invite you to stay with me during your visit. There are definite disadvantages: mine is a bachelor set-up, hence wanting in certain refinements. Clean, but sometimes a bit disorderly. Living-dining room, bedroom, kitchen, bath, hence no real privacy—but do you require it? The bed available for you is hard as a rock—I'm a sacro-iliac sufferer. I'm a bear in the mornings. . . . 5 minutes to the Stravinsky-Craft menage (about $1.20 by cab). I'm that anomalous Californian who has no car. . . . If you can remain here for Tuesday evening, I'll ask my sister [Beatrice Cunningham] to make a small dinner party for Craft, the Stravinskys, and ourselves—no more than that. Vera Arturovna, Igor Feodorovitch, and Robert Lawsonovitch will all tell you that my sister is a superb cook, and we can have a pleasant evening.[65]

Carter's thank-you note after the visit did not mention a stay with Morton but did say he was "impressed with the work you do and its efficiency." Apparently the performance was not all that Carter had hoped:

> The writing of such a piece as the one of mine Monday Evening Concerts performed implies—as I was well aware—so many different kinds of ministrations for its publication & performance that it takes a great deal of nerve—or folly—to embark on its composition at all—and naturally its many problems can seldom be expected to be solved at every performance. The story of Bartók's two piano & percussion sonata which was played—in early days—so badly and so unintelligibly—and now to such good effect—gives me hope.[66]

Peter Yates's efforts on behalf of John Cage in MEC board meetings met with enthusiasm, now that Cage's influence upon European composers was becoming more evident.[67] Yates wrote to Cage, "I'd advise you not to use this as an endorsement [although there is] a big change from the blank incomprehension I met with when I proposed last year that we might try one of your compositions. . . . The program budget for performers is $240. . . . Can you spin your wheel of chance and come up with an agreeable disposition?"[68]

The event was planned to be coordinated with a Los Angeles exhibition of paintings by Robert Rauschenberg, who wanted to use Cage's orchestral work *Atlas eclipticalis* (1961–1962) as an ancillary theatrical event. However, financial backing for this venture fell through, and Cage offered *Atlas* to Monday Evening Concerts, with the services of David Tudor playing *Winter Music* (1957), a piano work that could be performed simultaneously with the orchestral work. Peter Yates personally offered to guarantee $100 toward the extra cost for orchestral players and made arrangements with Gerald Strang to provide necessary electronic equipment. Cage himself agreed to pay other expenses above MEC's budget for musicians but wrote Morton, "Please, keep our financial arrangements *sotto voce.* I will be conducting and should have a fee, and instead will possibly be underwriting a part of the expenses. If anyone questions you about this, say that I was born in the Good Samaritan Hospital [in Los Angeles], and have a soft place in my heart for Los Angeles."[69]

Because of the plan to perform Stravinsky at every concert this season, Morton wrote Cage that it was not obligatory that he and David Tudor follow this plan in their performance: "We are well aware of how much time and space separated Stravinsky from your and the youngest generation."[70] Cage responded, "If you wish to open the program with some work by Stravinsky, do so; but do not involve Mr. Tudor or myself in its performance. On the other hand, I am willing to make a present to Mr. Stravinsky of a special realization of my *Imaginary Landscape No. 5* [a recording on tape, using any forty-two phonograph records, chosen by methods from the *I-Ching*], one that would use his music exclusively as material."[71] After considering this potentially hilarious and certainly irreverent idea, Morton replied that he appreciated the suggestion but, with Leonard Stein, had decided that a program with Marni Nixon singing Stravinsky's *Pastorale* (1908), *Two Poems of Balmont* (1911), and *Three Stories for Children* (1915–1917) "would be more appropriate for the kind of celebration we are having this season."[72] The Cage half of the concert began with works by Christian Wolff, one of Cage's close associates. *Atlas eclipticalis* (inspired by an astronomical atlas) with *Winter Music* was played with instruments equipped with contact microphones with amplifiers and loudspeakers operated by Gerald Strang. For Goldberg the performance was excruciating:

> a cesspool dredging operation. . . . Sometimes [Cage] beat time to dead silence for as long as two minutes; that was the best part of it. This went on for a full half hour, while the audience snickered, called out "Good!" when David Tudor whacked the keyboard with his flat forearm . . . a few brave souls walked out. . . . Stravinsky's bonbons sounded like masterpieces in this environment.[73]

Morton reported that the racket was too loud for many listeners but that the calligraphy of Cage's score was absolutely beautiful.[74]

On the 19 March program, Leo Smit played Beethoven's *Diabelli*

Variations, a work last played on these concerts by Frances Mullen. Goldberg wrote:

> You must take your hat off to an organization that is broad-minded and flexible enough to risk having its pet avant-garde inanities [works on the same program by Roberto Gerhard, Morton Subotnick, and Niccolò Castiglioni] overwhelmed by such a colossal work as this. . . . Smit played it so superbly that the audience broke into prolonged cheers. The Stravinsky pieces [transcriptions for violin and piano from *Mavra* and *Baiser de la fée*] would hardly have been likely to find their way onto the program had they been written by anyone else.[75]

Before the end of the season, a special benefit for the concerts was mounted with the help of the dancer-actress Vera Zorina (at this time the wife of Goddard Lieberson, president of Columbia Records), with whom Robert Craft planned to record Debussy's melodrama, *Chansons de Bilitis,* and Hindemith's *Hérodiade,* with chamber orchestra. As the concert was outside the normal season, a special ticket price of $3.50 was set—and, Morton recalled, the project "backfired terribly. We had a marvelous program, a perfectly beautiful program, and practically no audience." Morton speculated that the MEC audience did not attend because of the "exorbitant" price; "Monday Evening concerts is stuck with its policy of inexpensive concerts."[76] Four of the *Eight Instrumental Miniatures* Stravinsky had recomposed for fifteen players from his piano suite *The Five Fingers* were premiered on this program, Craft conducting. Mozart's Adagio and Rondo, K. 617, for flute, oboe, viola, cello, and celesta (originally for glass harmonica), and instrumental movements from Bach cantatas filled out the program, which also featured the first Los Angeles performance of Schoenberg's Three Pieces for Chamber Orchestra (1910, unfinished). The subsequent Columbia recording of the Debussy and Hindemith gave no credit to Monday Evening Concerts. This practice repeatedly angered Morton, as the concerts were subsidizing Craft's projects for Columbia Records.[77]

Fiesta Hall was, however, packed to capacity for the season's final concert, cosponsored by the Fromm Music Foundation and including three new works: Berio's *Circles* (1960) with Cathy Berberian, Leon Kirchner's Concerto for Violin, Cello, Ten Winds and Percussion (1960), and excerpts from Foss's work in progress, *Echoi* (1961–1963), for the Improvisation Ensemble. The Berio and Foss works were Fromm commissions. Berio was teaching that year at Mills College and came from San Francisco. His program notes for *Circles,* for mezzo-soprano, harp, and percussion, to texts of e. e. cummings, announced another developing trend in music:

> Music is never pure: it is attitude: it is theater.
> It is indivisible from its gestures. . . .
> The theatrical aspects of the performance are inherent in the structure of the work itself which is, most of all, a structure of actions: to be listened to as theater and to be viewed as music.

Berberian's performance, with the use of finger cymbals and other small percussion, was "really a smash. I don't think that piece can ever be performed by anyone with anything near her style," Morton remembered. She sang Stravinsky's *Berceuses du chat* delightfully and theatrically as well. Foss conducted Stravinsky's Octet, but his *Echoi* was a disappointment; he was having compositional problems and hadn't yet worked them out, so the excerpts were "far from the [completed] work," Morton thought. Kirchner had recently been appointed to the music faculty at Harvard University but came to conduct his concerto, with his two close friends Eudice Shapiro and Victor Gottlieb as solo violin and cello. It was a commission from the Baltimore Chamber Society and had earned the interest of—and several performances sponsored by—Paul Fromm. Albert Goldberg called the work "a tough nut to crack" (one of his favorite phrases for use when puzzled) but could not deny its "certain inescapable emotional force."[78]

The 1961–1962 season was one Morton was very proud of. Once again the series had pulled out of a financial hole and gone on to greater strengths. In this case a midseason contribution from Stravinsky of $1,500 (to offset the tax consequences of his large performance royalty check from ASCAP) enabled MEC to produce a number of large works in the second half of the season. Peter Yates reported this to Peyton Houston, adding, "Only strong love and real financial desperation could have persuaded him to part with money. He is no longer able to come to the concerts, but he told me when I last saw him how much they had meant to him during the years he has been here—the only music worth hearing."[79] In fact Stravinsky was still able to come to a few concerts, but because he was increasingly frail and too often besieged by fans in the audience, he began to attend performances backstage.[80]

Morton himself was losing his battle to write his overdue book on Stravinsky. His review of Eric Walter White's 1966 work on Stravinsky shows his approach to the subject: he felt White lacked skepticism, took too much on faith, was too grateful to his informants, and did not dig deeply enough. "This is particularly true in respect to Stravinsky himself. . . . Every Stravinsky statement depending on memory has to be checked and doublechecked."[81] Morton had concentrated on uncovering materials from Stravinsky's early periods and translated long-buried accounts, such as the following firsthand observation from the diary of Romain Rolland (25 July 1916):

> [Stravinsky] is superficial and violent, both in his opinions and in his music. Intelligent and lively in his way, but only within the light coming from his own beacon: a single sharp shaft, but all about it total darkness. In these times of intellectual unilateralism he is the ultimate unilateralist.[82]

In July 1961, as his deadline for Oxford University Press approached, Morton wrote to Sheldon Meyer, at that time senior vice-president of the press, about his "conflict between love and the requirements of rigorous criticism."[83] Now, in August 1962, he informed Meyer that he had to undergo surgery for a duodenal ulcer. Infection set in, and in September and October he had further small surgeries. In November he applied—unsuccessfully—for a Ford Foundation grant.

Meanwhile Morton prepared a short history of the concerts for an article by Raymond Kendall that appeared in the *Los Angeles Times,* Sunday, 4 November 1962. "Before anything else, Monday Evening Concerts is its repertoire," Morton wrote in his memo. "It remains unique in its coverage of music literature from the late middle ages to tomorrow."[84] The brochure for the new season included the highest of praise in quotes from Stravinsky, Copland, Carter, Colin Mason of the *Manchester Guardian,* Berio, Boulez, Stockhausen, Roman Vlad, and Dallapiccola. Morton also used the brochure to publicize the many premieres in the program repertoire, and to list the performers for the season, the subscribers, and contributors. Laurence Lesser (later appointed president of the New England Conservatory), in 1962 a fine cellist who had returned to his native Los Angeles (after graduating from Harvard and enjoying a Fulbright fellowship), testified to the "cachet" associated with Monday Evening Concerts.

> It was tremendously important even far beyond what it did for Los Angeles as a cultural community. I think the Monday Evening Concerts have as important a place in the history of *music,* period, as [had] Diaghilev and the *Ballets Russes* in his day, or all of Mitropoulos's golden years with the New York Philharmonic, or Koussevitsky in Boston. I think the Monday Evening Concerts—starting with Evenings on the Roof—really fits into that category of a place where, first of all, there was a filtering process that went on in terms of compositions picked and performers picked that lent a kind of aura; that if something was happening there it was important. There was a tremendous sense of importance around those concerts.[85]

TWENTY-FIFTH SEASON: 1962–1963

The Los Angeles Percussion Ensemble had now become the William Kraft Percussion Ensemble, and Kraft, conducting frequent performances, filled an important role in the exploration of the volumes of new music now being written for percussion. In 1957 it had been impossible to find regular percussion players other than himself to play Boulez's *Marteau.*

> The training for percussionists up until the fifties—and even past the fifties in most places—was rudimental. There are thirteen basic rudiments which go way back to revolutionary days. They are military exercises . . . there was never any reference to . . phrasing, ensemble, all these things that other musicians know. . . . Percussionists couldn't do quintuplets. . . . *Marteau* was a whole change of basic technique for all the instruments.[86]

To solve these problems, Kraft had begun composing pedagogical works for percussion. He and the violist Milton Thomas shared leadership in the first program of the twenty-fifth season. Thomas opened with an unaccompanied Bach cello sonata (played on the viola), three of his own transcriptions of fourteenth- and fifteenth-century dances, and the premiere of Henri Lazarof's Inventions for Viola and Piano (1962). Kraft played and conducted percussion works by Arthur Cohn, Alan Hovhaness, Earle Brown, and Lou Harrison. "Put this one down as OK," wrote Goldberg, who noted the large audience of devotees. Milton Thomas, "one of the best violists around," played enchanting music exquisitely. The audience laughed at Brown's *Hodograph I,* for flute, piano, celesta, bells, vibraphone, and marimba, but Eudice Shapiro played Lou Harrison's *Concerto in Slendro,* based on a gamelan scale, and scored for violin, celesta, two tackpianos (pianos with tacks in the strings), and percussion, with "silken charm."[87] Morton felt the Earle Brown piece was the most successful of the percussion pieces. Hovhaness struck him as "really not the kind of composer that belongs on our program."[88]

On 15 October 1962 Beethoven, Schubert, and Bach were programmed. Eudice Shapiro played an unaccompanied Bach sonata for violin. Schubert's songs for soprano, piano, and obbligato instruments "Der Hirt auf dem Felsen" and "Auf dem Strom" were performed, and the new discovery on the program was Beethoven's arrangement for four-hand piano of his *Grosse Fuge* for string quartet, played by Ingolf Dahl and Pearl Kaufman. Morton had obtained a photostat of the work from the Library of Congress. Beethoven had altered the work to make it more suitable for piano. Morton made a bet with his brother that the review would say, "It doesn't sound like a string quartet"—and won the bet.[89]

Karl Kohn had been granted a Guggenheim Fellowship in 1961–1962, and upon his return two new works of his from that year were featured on the 5 November program: Serenade for wind quintet and piano and *Capriccios* for harp, cello, flute, clarinet, and piano, both with Kohn at the piano. Baroque music of Frescobaldi (it turned out this was a musicological error; composer Ellis Kohs pointed out to Morton that the pieces were not by Frescobaldi), Bach, and Boismortier, along with Debussy's Sonata for Cello and Piano (Kohn playing), completed the program. Walter Arlen reported that Kohn had joined the serialist avant-garde; he commented on a lack of contrast in his compositions but heard "an interesting mind at work."[90] Lawrence Morton, on the other hand, found the difference between Kohn's two pieces "astounding," the *Capriccios* quite modern, with passages of indeterminate music. These were both substantial pieces, and Morton felt they established Kohn as a composer.[91]

The highlight of the 12 November 1962 program was Peter Hewitt's performance of Ives's *Concord* Sonata, which had not been heard at the concerts since Frances Mullen had last played it in 1949. Arlen commented favorably on Hewitt's "big, imposingly substantial tone, modulated by dynamic and expressive requirements, his clear articulation, unflagging technical fluency and sensitive pedalling. . . . [The performance] amounted to a definitive statement of Ives's music worthy to be preserved."[92] The second half of the program was devoted to Polish composers: songs by Chopin and by Kazimierz Serocki and a larger work for soprano, reciter, and ten instruments, *Strofy* (1959), by Krzysztof Penderecki. Leonard Stein conducted this American premiere of an important composer who was as yet unknown in this country. Arlen found Penderecki "untalented."

Ernst Toch's seventy-fifth birthday was celebrated by MEC on 3 December. He had taught himself composing as a child in Vienna by studying Mozart's scores, and the program was a graceful alternation of two works by Mozart with three by Toch: his *Sonatinetta* for flute, clarinet, and bassoon, Op. 84, *Tanz-Suite,* Op. 30, and Piano Quintet, Op. 64. The Screen Composers' Association, represented by David Raksin, Elmer Bernstein, and Arthur Morton, contributed funds for the performers and distributed many tickets to their members. Toch was surprised, delighted, and grateful. Morton felt "we had outgrown [his music] largely. He represented a period in music that Monday Evening Concerts was not particularly eager to promote anymore. But he had been a very important figure in music in this city."[93]

Ernst Krenek, a close friend of Paul Fromm, was featured on a Fromm Music Foundation concert, 21 January 1963. His *Alpbach* Quintet (1962), Flute Piece in Nine Phases (1959), and a Fromm commission, *Quaestio temporis* (1958–1959; a large serial work for twenty instruments), were complemented by a suite Krenek had adapted in 1936 from Monteverdi's *Incoronazione di Poppea.* The first issue of *Perspectives of New Music,* sponsored by the Fromm Foundation and published by the Princeton University Press, was announced in the program.

The New York composer Netty Simons received a first performance of her *Facets II* (1962) for flute, clarinet, and string bass on 18 February, and the audience reaction, Morton remembered, was very good.[94] In March Leo Smit, whom Goldberg described as "an ornament to any occasion and it is regrettable that this was presumably his farewell appearance at these events," performed in all the pieces presented: a Mozart cantata, K. 619; Schumann's *Faschingsschwank aus Wien,* Op. 26; his own witty *Academic Graffiti* on texts by W. H. Auden; Variations by Irving Fine (who had died prematurely the previous year); and a Beethoven piano trio. He had been appointed pianist-in-residence at the University of Buffalo and was to leave the area. The Gregg Smith Singers carried the 18 March program, "in better shape than ever," Walter Arlen reported. They sang works of Irving Fine, Arnold Schoenberg's Three Pieces for Male Chorus, from Op. 35, and the first American performance of *Ha venido,* by Luigi Nono—which Arlen claimed was "a harder nut for the singers than for the listeners." In comparison, he found the Schoenberg pieces sounded like child's play.[95]

In December 1961 Morton heard that Boulez was invited to Harvard to give the Lamb lectures in the early months of 1963 and immediately wrote to invite him to conduct a Monday Evening Concert during that visit. Boulez accepted, on condition airfare be paid, and negotiations about repertoire began. Apologies from Morton for Goldberg's criticism of Boulez's Third Piano Sonata met with Boulez's response that Goldberg was certainly not a gold-mouth. "I have been especially favored by your organization, and I am very grateful to you for that. . . . It is fortunate there is a group like yours in the United States!" he wrote.[96] Boulez hoped to conduct Schoenberg's *Pierrot,* if a reciter capable of a good German accent could be found. Morton replied there was a tradition in the concerts to give *Pierrot* in English, and the idea was dropped. It was decided that settings of Mallarmé by Debussy and Ravel would be combined with Boulez's *Improvisations sur Mallarmé;* Morton proposed "Igorissimo's" *Three Japanese Lyrics* as well, and Webern's Concerto, Op. 24, to be conducted by Boulez. Boulez's *Structures II* (1962) for two pianos would be the American premiere on the program, played by the Kohns.

In October 1962 Morton urgently requested the score of *Structures* from Boulez but, having not received it by February 1963, decided to drop it from the 3 April program. Karl and Margaret Kohn were very busy. Having experienced the preparation of *Structures I* in 1959, and having heard Boulez and Yvonne Loriod perform a version of *Structures II* in 1961 at Donaueschingen, they felt they would not have time to do justice to the difficulties in the new work. Boulez replied that the piece must be played; the Kohns would have time; he himself preferred not to play it as it was easier to see others suffer; and sent off the parts—green for the first piano, blue for the second. By March, "in spite of discussions [with the Kohns] over Scotch," it was decided that Boulez would have to play with Karl Kohn, and Morton sent the blue part back to Boulez for his own "herculean struggle." He soon reported that Karl Kohn "works on the music with greatest enthusiasm and joy, and would be rapturous if he had the still-missing six pages. Please send them by airmail . . . so that Karl might pass into ecstasy. I remain in frenzy. . . ." To assuage Boulez for having to practice the piano, and as he was planning to stay in Los Angeles ten days, Morton proposed trips to the Pasadena Art Museum to see the paintings of Klee and the *Blaue Reiter,* to Marineland to see the dolphins that had ravished "les Berio," and perhaps a little visit to Mexico.[97] Several lectures—sufficient to pay thc airfare—were also planned; one of them, titled "poésie—centre et absence—musique" (Boulez was in his lowercase–e.e. cummings period), took place at Pomona College. Leonard Stein drove Boulez and Morton to the lecture—which seems to have been a stiff affair, as Boulez's English was not easy for the audience to understand, and his thought was lively. On the way back, probably well fortified with wine or Scotch, Morton remarked that there was not enough "haha" in new music. The three began to laugh, and the hilarity continued on another trip when Stein got lost driving the three of them on a freeway that went nowhere. Thereafter, for years Boulez's letters and communications with Morton remained filled with every possible notation of laughter. This joke saw Boulez through many a journey in his burgeoning conducting career, as he sent Morton, from locations all over the world, pages and postcards covered, in all colors of inks, with convulsive diaphragmatic syllables separated by exclamation marks. Morton kept up his part of the giggle and stimulated it further with his wit.

Prior to Boulez's arrival, Stein and Dahl rehearsed the works Boulez would conduct. It was his second concert as a conductor in the United States—the first having been the 1957 *Marteau* performance for MEC. (After a 1962 performance of that same work on a Domaine Musical program, Boulez wrote Morton, "I believe I have had enormous progress as a conductor. Like the good wines, one gets better upon aging!")[98] The 3 April 1963 concert was cosponsored by the USC School of Music, and given in Bovard Auditorium on the university campus, where many more than usual could attend. Goldberg, who had never had a good word to say about Boulez, reported that the hall was packed. To his surprise, he found Boulez

> an extremely sensitive and discerning musician, not at all the intellectual cold fish one might have expected from a composer of such advanced tendencies . . . a conductor with a remarkably keen ear for tonal refinements. . . . *Structures* does not sound like serial music . . . more like free improvisation, rhythmically complex and

> relentlessly dissonant at times. . . . It rivets the attention with a sense of arresting drama.

He commended Natalie Limonick's beautiful piano accompaniment to Marie Gibson's soprano in Debussy's *Trois poèmes de Stéphane Mallarmé* and found Webern "more comprehensible with exposure."[99]

Morton felt Boulez's and Kohn's playing of *Structures II* was "just a bang-up, marvelous performance." The concert "was one of the all-time exciting programs that we have ever put on. . . . [Boulez] made a hit with everybody." It was a hectic ten days of rehearsing and rushing Boulez off to lecture engagements, good eating, drinking, and parties. Morton put Boulez on his plane back to Harvard and a day or so later collapsed with a heart attack. "Well," he reflected in 1966, "if one had to go out, to go out after that Boulez concert would be about as good a way as I can think of, because that was a marvelous, marvelous concert."[100]

(Top) Lawrence Morton and Igor Stravinsky in Stravinsky's home, 1955. Photo courtesy of Ojai Festivals, Ltd., Ojai, California.

(Bottom) Pierre Boulez rehearsing. Department of Special Collections, University Research Library, University of California, Los Angeles.

Lukas Foss's Improvisation Chamber Ensemble in Foss's studio, 1960; left to right, Howard D. Colf, Jr., Foss, Charles DeLancey (standing), Richard Dufallo (sitting). Department of Special Collections, University Research Library, University of California, Los Angeles.

Leonard Stein in 1961. Photo by permission of the photographer, Lütfi Özkök, Stockholm.

Karlheinz Stockhausen in 1958, Los Angeles. Photo by Don Christlieb.

Mitchell Lurie in 1955. Photo by Toplitt Studio, Beverly Hills. Department of Special Collections, University Research Library, University of California, Los Angeles.

Marvin Hayes, bass, winner (with Marjorie Low, soprano) of the 1952 Evenings on the Roof Competition in the Performance of the Art Song. Photo by Toyo Miyatake, Los Angeles. Department of Special Collections, University Research Library, University of California, Los Angeles.

Karl and Margaret Kohn, 1966. Department of Special Collections, University Research Library, University of California, Los Angeles.

William Kraft in the late 1960s. Courtesy of William Kraft.

Monday Evening Concerts tour group, Hunter College, New York City, December 1968; left to right, (standing) Sheridan Stokes, flute, Don Christlieb, bassoon, John Ellis, oboe, Stuart Fox, guitar, Barry Silverman, percussion, (sitting) Gloria Grace Prosper, soprano, Phillip Lehrman, percussion, Christie Lundquist, clarinet, Mary Jo Ahlborn, viola, (front) Michael Tilson Thomas, conductor and pianist. Department of Special Collections, University Research Library, University of California, Los Angeles.

Lawrence Morton receiving the Laurel Leaf Award of the American Composers' Alliance, for distinguished service to American Music, from Quincy Porter, president of ACA, New York, May 1966. Department of Special Collections, University Research Library, University of California, Los Angeles.

Eight

"FROM THE MIDDLE AGES TO TOMORROW" 1963–1971

TWENTY-SIXTH SEASON: 1963–1964

Morton recovered and was back in shape at the 30 September opening of the season, in which Stravinsky's newly completed *Eight Instrumental Miniatures* were conducted by Robert Craft in their entirety. This was not the premiere, which took place in Toronto, but Stravinsky dedicated these pieces to Lawrence Morton—a gesture Morton claimed as his "passport to immortality"—and gave Morton the manuscript. Stravinsky had received the 1956 Jan Sibelius Gold Medal and in 1963 orchestrated a small Sibelius piece, *Canzonetta,* for four horns, clarinet, bass clarinet, harp, and double bass. He gave Monday Evening Concerts the premiere of this arrangement, which now brought the count of Stravinsky world premieres to eleven.

Morton had long felt that Joseph Haydn was a neglected composer, and on this program Craft conducted Los Angeles premieres of two rarely heard works of his, a *Cassatio* and a *Notturno,* along with Schoenberg's Suite, Op. 29, and Richard Wagner's *Siegfried Idyll.* Morton admitted disregarding his normal budgetary constraints for this concert, which demanded twenty-three instrumentalists but meant a lot to him.

Ingolf Dahl directed and appeared as composer-pianist-conductor of a program on 21 October 1963, which Goldberg called "one of the best programs of the series . . . handsomely performed."[1] Along with works by Handel, Domenico Scarlatti, Schubert, and Manuel de Falla, Dahl's own Trio for Piano, Violin, and Cello (1962, commissioned by the Koussevitsky Foundation) was performed. Malcolm Hamilton, who had studied at USC with Alice Ehlers, was the harpsichord soloist in Scarlatti sonatas and de Falla's Concerto for Harpsichord, Flute, Oboe, Clarinet, Violin, and Cello. "Every time we have Malcolm we have a very good audience; he has a large following," Morton commented.[2] Another outstanding performer was Laurence Lesser, at the time a cello pupil of Gregor Piatigorsky. Lesser had received much of his training from Los Angeles' finest musicians (Gregory Aller, grandfather of Leonard Slatkin, Gabor Rejto, and Peter Meremblum, founder of the California Junior Symphony), and Piatigorsky encouraged him to play contemporary music.

A string trio (Howard Colf, Sr., violin, Myra Kestenbaum, viola, and Vance Beach, cello) formed and worked through the summer to perform Schoenberg's String Trio, Op. 45, and one by Goffredo Petrassi, on 4 November 1963. Walter Arlen felt that Schoenberg's trio represented "imagination at its most fertile and ingenious."[3] On the same program the original version of Hector Berlioz's *Nuits d'êté,* for soprano and piano, was performed by Grace-Lynne Martin and Pearl Kaufman. Schütz's *Symphoniae sacrae* were back on the 18 November program, with Bach's Cantata No. 78. Morton enlisted the services of the choir of All Saints Church, Beverly Hills, the first step in a plan to mount all of Bach's cantatas over a period of four or five years, with various local church choirs. By the end of the season, after hearing three such choirs, Morton gave up this idea. "[The choirs] were large, always twice as many singers as Bach had, but they were not professional singers and a certain tone quality was missing," he said.[4]

Karl Kohn had been given the duties of presenting concerts previously taken by Leonard Stein, who was now involved with a new concert series at UCLA that was in direct competition with Monday Evening Concerts. Kohn presented a newly discovered Divertimento in C by Joseph Haydn on 2 December. He and Margaret Kohn played works by Stravinsky, Berger, and Schubert for two pianos and piano duet, and he conducted and played in Webern's Quartet, Op. 22, for violin, clarinet, tenor saxophone, and piano. The saxophonist William Ulyate, who was busy playing with the Elliott Brothers' Band, rehearsed strenuously with the ensemble but—a week before the concert—was summoned for a lucrative twelve-evening television series, beginning the Monday evening of the concert. Morton called David Raksin, who contacted the series' producer. Bill Ulyate was allowed to pay a substitute $150 for that first night, so he could play the Webern—for which he was paid the grand sum of $28 (MEC's special union rate at the time). Karl Kohn recalled the event:

> Lawrence dealt with these things in a very gentlemanly fashion. He did not lose Bill Ulyate. He knew you could not get just anyone off the street to play that kind of music, and to be the musician that Bill Ulyate was. There were devoted characters around, and he knew who they were. He didn't tear his hair. The players subsidized the concerts. One didn't feel that it was a commercial venture. Studio players were making a substantial contribution. Sometimes they did forfeit other engagements. It kept them *artistically alive.* There were some regulars who taught in the schools, and there was a substantial cadre of people Lawrence depended on from the studios, who made big money and didn't teach. Their rehearsal schedules had to conform to the most complicated daytime studio schedules. Rehearsals for larger works could take place from 8 p.m.–12 midnight. Lawrence held it all together. He had a remarkable way of inspiring high effort in other people.[5]

Morton remembered that "that was as good a performance of Webern as we have ever had."[6]

Morton was completing ten years at the helm of Monday Evening Concerts and enjoyed recording the achievements. The twenty-fifth anniversary of the American Composers Alliance (ACA) coincided with MEC's twenty-fifth anniversary. Morton took the occasion to point this out, in a letter to the ACA bulletin's anniversary issue:

> Monday Evening Concerts (once known as Evenings on the Roof) has surely played more music—new, old, American, and European—than all the other groups together. . . . Your [correspondent] ought to get out into the great world and learn that Monday Evening Concerts are about a generation ahead of the little outfits now a-borning in New York and elsewhere.[7]

A few months later Morton wrote his old friend Aaron Copland:

> I think MEC ought to have a Laurel Leaf Award [given by ACA] "for distinguished achievement in fostering and encouraging American music." Can you propose this to ACA? Or can you get some satellite, hanger-on or debtor to do it for you? It would be very valuable to us now. Because: we hope to have a new home next season in the new Los Angeles County Art Museum, now building. . . . In order to get this as our official residence, we need prestige of the kind that our repertoire certainly does not bring us! And surely we get the world's worst reviews from Albert Goldberg and his second stringer, both of whom have just no interest and no knowledge of anything newer than, say, "The Cat and the Mouse." We have a continual uphill fight, against the kind of thing that prompted my letter to the ACA bulletin. Can you do anything for us in this department? If you can, thanks. If you can't, we love you anyway.[8]

Copland replied: "It would be pushy for me to suggest recipients at this point. But don't get me wrong: I'm sure the MEC deserves an accolade."[9]

In celebration of Walter Piston's seventieth birthday, Kurt and Sven Reher returned to the concerts on 20 January 1964 to play the Duo for Viola and Cello they had commissioned from him in 1949. Laurence Lesser, having won a fourth place in the recent Tchaikovsky competition in Moscow, played Elliott Carter's Sonata for Cello and Piano (1947), as well as a Beethoven cello sonata, with his partner, Ellen Mack, on 17 February 1964.

A Stravinsky premiere, "cooked up in two days" because the composer was eager to hear his new work, was added to the 6 April 1964 program. It was the *Elegy for J.F.K.,* which Stravinsky had just composed to a haiku by Auden, for baritone, two clarinets, and an alto clarinet. The tenor Richard Robinson, who had a low range and had performed many Stravinsky works, jumped in, although he had another singing engagement in the early part of the evening and had to rehearse more when he got to the concert. Morton recalled,

> While they were rehearsing on the evening of the performance [the concert was going on] Stravinsky made some changes in the music. It was a nerve-racking evening. But, of course, it's a very short [serial] piece, a couple of minutes, and with Stravinsky present we could be sure of getting it done the way he wanted it.[10]

Goldberg found the work expressive because of its reticence.[11] The clarinetists were Mitchell Lurie and his students Mitchell Weiss and John Neufeld. The alto clarinet had been hard to find for Neufeld on such short notice. Lurie reminisced about rehearsing the work with the ink barely dry. "We were afterwards walking to the hall to perform it. I walked with Stravinsky, and I couldn't help remarking, as he walked with such difficulty to the hall just a few yards away, that he still traveled all over the world, conducting orchestras almost beyond his endurance. How did he do it? His answer: 'It is my revenge.' I remember so well the wicked flash in his eyes."[12]

Morton frequently asked Boulez to recommend works and composers scheduled on the Domaine Musical programs. Heinz Holliger, the Swiss oboist and composer, interested him, and on 20 April 1964 Holliger's *Mobile* for oboe and harp was played in two versions, separated by his *Séquences on St. John* for harp. Lawrence Moss, the composer son of Oscar and Sadye Moss, received a first performance that evening of his *Remembrances* for Eight Instruments, conducted by Karl Kohn, who also played the piano part in Schubert's "Trout" Quintet with true Viennese flare.

In the summer of 1964 Morton was in Ojai, still working on his Stravinsky book. He had not yet abandoned the project, although his approach had changed. It was not until 1973 that he wrote Sheldon Meyer at Oxford University Press, "There will be no book." He explained that his strength was in serious decline.[13] A later (1983) explanation was contained in a footnote to his article, "Stravinsky at Home," in the collection of essays edited by Jann Pasler, *Confronting Stravinsky: Man, Musician, and Modernist:*

> One of the things that unnerved me, and that still disconcerts me, was a remark Stravinsky made to me in the fall of 1960, on the last evening we spent together in Venice just before I returned to the United States. At the entrance to his hotel, Stravinsky paused and, after the usual goodby embraces, said, "If you are really writing a book about me, say what you have to say—but please be kind."[14]

Morton's main concern in this summer and the coming season was about Monday Evening Concerts' move to a new, prestigious hall. A painter herself, Sadye Moss had connections with the art community in Los Angeles. From 1958 to 1966 she was the main financial backer of the successful Ferus Gallery, which, under the direction of Walter Hopps and Irving Blum, focused wide attention upon the Los Angeles artists John Altoon, Billy Al Bengston, Robert Irwin, Craig Kauffman, Ed Kienholz, Ed Moses, Ken Price, Ed Ruscha, and others. From the beginning of the plan to build a new museum of art, Sadye Moss talked with Richard F. Brown, director of the new museum, about it being a new home for the concerts. A case was made that Monday Evening Concerts was performing a museum function in that it "exhibited" music from the earliest times to the present. Brown and Morton reached an assumption that the concerts would be housed at the museum and would maintain their own organization and attitudes about music, with the Southern California Chamber Music Society as the support group. There was no formal agreement or arrangement, and no announcement, for Brown did not want public debate on the question. The concerts would take up residence in the new auditorium the museum was planning for its own lectures, films, and meetings. The museum's board of trustees was satisfied with the reputation of the concerts as the oldest concert-giving organization in southern California with the exception of the Philharmonic and the Coleman Chamber Concerts in Pasadena. The Los Angeles County Music Commission had been granting MEC one thousand dollars a year since 1961. Morton claimed that Monday Evening Concerts, rather than the Los Angeles Philharmonic, most frequently represented Los Angeles in international music magazines and the European press, because the programs were unique. There was no comparable organization anywhere in the world, he declared. Other organizations, like Domaine Musical or university groups, gave only four or five concerts a year in comparison to MEC's twelve; furthermore, they did not mix the old and the new in music. (Domaine concerts had done so in the first two seasons but abandoned the concept in favor of propagandizing for new music.)

The new Los Angeles County Museum of Art would provide a new piano and ask no rent for use of the auditorium, which would seat six hundred. The location was central in terms of the city's population growth in the mid-1960s. Concerts would remain Monday evening affairs, and parking would not be difficult because the museum was closed on Mondays. Gerald Strang, by then a well-known expert on acoustics, was pleased with the prospects in the blueprint stage. But Morton commented that there were no backstage facilities for performers: no places to hang up coats, put instruments, no toilet facilities or drinking fountain. Green room and restrooms had to be added to the plans and were inconveniently located up three flights of stairs behind the stage. The hall would be ready in the spring of 1965, so in the twenty-seventh season eight concerts were planned for Plummer Park, and the last four for the museum. Concert planning was difficult, because completion dates were never certain, and Morton had much distraction, worry, and concern.

Since Boulez's successful visit in 1962, he and Morton had hopes for a return. Morton wrote Boulez that he would give a concert the *eighth* day of the week if necessary to accommodate Boulez's schedule.

He hoped to present a Boulez concert in the new museum. Karl and Margaret Kohn would play both books of *Structures.* Would Boulez consider conducting Machaut's Mass? and would he have a new piece to contribute?[15] Boulez's conducting career was going into international orbit, but he replied that he would be conducting in Toronto and Pittsburgh in the spring of 1965 and would save nine days for a trip to Los Angeles. The two continued negotiations about the program, and the instrumentation for the Machaut Mass. Morton scheduled the concert to coincide with the opening ceremonies at the museum, at the end of March.

On the first of October 1964 Ernst Toch died, and Morton opened the first program, 5 October, with a memorial performance of the slow movement from Toch's *Sonatinetta,* Op. 84, for flute, clarinet, and bassoon. The program itself juxtaposed Beethoven's arrangement for piano, clarinet, and cello of his popular Septet, Op. 20, with works by "Third Stream" film composer Lalo Schifrin. Schifrin brought in and conducted numerous jazz celebrities, such as trumpeter Don Ellis, drummer Shelley Manne, flutist Buddy Collette, tuba player Red Callender, and others. There was an overflow crowd. Goldberg noted that "while some musical audiences in town appear to remain stationary . . . the public for the Monday Evening Concerts . . . seems to be rejuvenated with young blood each year."[16]

The Los Angeles String Quartet (Paul Shure and Bonnie Douglas, violins, Myra Kestenbaum, viola, and Frederick Seykora, cello) presented Berg's Lyric Suite (1925) for the first time at MEC on 19 October 1964. On the same program Lawrence Foster, whose conducting impressed Albert Goldberg "for the ease and surety with which it negotiated . . . tricky rhythms and kept . . . complicated patterns securely in the groove,"[17] gave the first American performance of Hans Werner Henze's cantata, *Being Beauteous,* for soprano, harp, and four cellos, with Carole Bogard singing. She also performed Purcell, and Foster conducted Bach's Brandenburg Concerto No. 6. Martin Katz, who was later to have an international career as an accompanist, played in Halsey Stevens's *Sonatina giocosa* for double bass and piano (written for MEC in 1954).

Craft returned, to conduct a chamber version of Webern's Symphony, Op. 21, on 2 November. Rare works of Haydn and Biber were presented on the same program. Two days later a special program of canons Schoenberg wrote as gifts and acknowledgements to friends and professional colleagues, as well as for his own amusement, were performed by a quartet of singers and the Los Angeles String Quartet as an outreach concert at California State College, Long Beach. Just a few months previously a volume of thirty canons by Schoenberg had been published. Morton did not consider these right for the MEC concert programs but held the private performance, with Leonard Stein giving commentary on the canons, for the Southern California Chamber Music Society. The program was also "sold" to Pomona College and to the Pasadena Art Museum.[18] Morton had less success with these traveling concerts than had Peter Yates, although he did attempt them occasionally. The organization made little income—in fact, often lost money—on them but gained prestige.

Gilbert Amy and Wlodzimierz Kotonski, students of Boulez whose works had been performed at Domaine concerts, were given American premieres in a program on 16 November 1964 by Karl Kohn, who performed as pianist, conductor, and musicologist. Morton remembered Amy's Inventions I and II as "one of the most difficult pieces we have ever done."[19] Kohn had to memorize the score in order to conduct it. He also presented his own realizations of chansons of Machaut, Stravinsky's Four Russian Songs for voice, flute, harp, and guitar, and a piano trio by Mozart.

Laurence Lesser, with the pianist Ellen Mack, the clarinetist John Neufeld, and the violinist Grisha Goluboff (who had been a child prodigy of Isaac Stern's generation), played works of Schubert, Ives, Copland, Charles Wuorinen, and William O. Smith—a clarinetist-composer originally from Los Angeles—on 30 November. Morton remembered Neufeld's performance, with tape, of Smith's work as "one of the wonders of the world;"[20] Walter Arlen found the clarinetist superb.[21]

In his recollection of playing in the concerts, Lesser described a young oboist, who had studied in the preparatory division of USC as a thirteen- or fourteen-year-old and then entered the college "as much interested in paleontology, anthropology, and god-knows-what as music. An absolute polymath." This young musician studied piano with John Crown and composition and conducting with Ingolf Dahl. Lesser, who was playing cello sonatas with the young pianist, brought him into Piatigorsky's master class. "They hit it off immediately. Piatigorsky was tremendously fascinated by interesting people. Michael, of course, *is that*. . . . He wasn't Michael Tilson Thomas in those days; he was Michael Thomas."[22] The pianist-teacher John Crown was scheduled to perform Charles Ives's *Over the Pavements,* along with works by Leoš Janáček and Jan Ladislav Dussek, on 1 February 1965. Crown grumbled to Tilson Thomas about having too many works to learn quickly and about the extraordinary difficulties of the Ives part. Tilson Thomas had heard the work often but had never played it. He offered to perform it and was assigned the piece, although Morton did not know him. "So I practiced like mad," Tilson Thomas remembered. Dahl was to conduct, and the performers met for the first rehearsal in his studio in the attic of Clark House at USC. Tilson Thomas described the occasion:

> That's actually when I met Lawrence for the first time, upstairs in Clark House. He was very trim, wearing a dark suit with a very thin tie, very precisely clipped with a tie pin. His hair was in a rather severe crewcut. He introduced himself very properly, sat with a score, and noted everything that was going on. I was really playing up a storm. I had practiced very hard, and I whipped this thing off, with great aplomb and panache. Ingolf really appreciated that, because he and I had rehearsed separately; especially the cadenza, which is very tricky. Then, after the concert, I was very pleased with the way the performance had gone, and Lawrence came up to me and he shook my hand and said, "Good. Thank you." I was nonplussed by that, because I really thought it was *terrific*. People told me that was typical of Lawrence. He later himself told me, "You must understand, when I really like something, I say it is good."[23]

Monday Evening Concerts' last program in Fiesta Hall at Plummer Park on 15 February ended with choruses by Schubert, performed by the Pomona College Glee Clubs, directed by William F. Russell. Lucy Shelton was a mezzo-soprano soloist. The pianist Lincoln Mayorga, with Don Christlieb, played a forty-minute *Sonata concertante* for bassoon and piano by Nikos Skalkottas on the first half of the same program.

Morton remembered the next six weeks as one of the most hectic periods he ever went through.

> Boulez was supposed to bring with [him] or send to us a new piece. He didn't finish it. He didn't answer my letters. I didn't know where he was; I heard that he was in Rome. (I'm talking about maybe two weeks before the concert.) We didn't know what the program was going to be yet [except for the Machaut Mass, and *Structures* I and II played by Karl and Margaret Kohn].

Boulez finally telephoned from his conducting assignment in Cleveland and said the new piece might be ten minutes long. This was not enough music. *Equivalences,* for eighteen instruments by Jean-Claude Eloy, one of Boulez's students, was in Morton's collection, but the parts were in Europe, and only a few days were available to ready the work for performance. Meanwhile it was discovered that because Boulez had to leave the country to conduct in Toronto, he had no valid visa to reenter the United States. Morton, who was again recovering from recent surgery, went to the Department of Immigrations and asked them to negotiate with Canada by telephone and charge it to his telephone bill. When Boulez arrived, the new piece was not finished. Morton made three xerox copies, and after a drink and dinner they cut and pasted the parts onto cardboards. The concert was on Friday, to accommodate Boulez's schedule and the opening ceremonies at the museum. Morton recounted the trials (which his damaged heart somehow withstood):

> On Thursday at one o'clock the last page of Boulez' piece, *Éclat,* was completed. It was pasted up on the cardboard and brought to rehearsal Thursday afternoon (I think it was at four or four-thirty) to get ready for the performance on Friday night. The stage at the

museum was not yet ready, so we rehearsed in the foyer. We carted percussion instruments back and forth, chairs, music stands and whatnot, and I think that we brought this concert off was a miracle. I must say that Boulez' patience was inexhaustible. He's a man who gets sixty rehearsals if he wants them and would never think of lifting a music stand when he is on his own home grounds, but he just pitched in here and was marvelous. . . . In the midst of rehearsal [with workmen walking through], our mandolin player became temperamental and decided that what Boulez wrote was not music and he would not play. So he dropped out and we had great difficulty in finding another mandolin player who could read music. We ended up with Sol Babitz, a violinist, but since the fingering of the mandolin and the violin are identical he managed the part which was not terribly difficult. This sort of crisis happening in the midst of other crises was almost unendurable. Well, in the midst of all this commotion Boulez had his fortieth birthday.

Morton gave the birthday party. He invited the Stravinskys, the Kohns, Sadye Moss, Ingolf and Etta Dahl. He got his sister-in-law to cook a turkey and Sadye Moss to contribute wild rice and a birthday cake that she also decorated. The Stravinskys came with a jeroboam of champagne. Everyone had a wonderful time, and a year later, on his forty-first birthday, Boulez remembered it with a long distance call to Morton from Baden-Baden.

Meanwhile the opening concert in the new hall, attended by a large crowd, came off marvelously: "Boulez was great. Karl and Margaret played the *Structures* so that Boulez was beside himself with joy. He said that Karl Kohn is the best performer in the world of any of his piano music. . . . It was an electric evening; everybody was excited."[24] Boulez dedicated *Éclat* to Lawrence Morton. Eloy, who had flown from Paris, was very happy with the American premiere of his *Equivalences.* The new program featured on its front page a picture of an ear, commissioned by Sadye Moss from the Los Angeles artist Ed Ruscha. (Oddly enough, Ruscha's musical taste began with Spike Jones, Bing Crosby, and Bix Beiderbecke and even now tends "to evoke a rather romantic notion of the America of the past.")[25] Albert Goldberg found the new Leo S. Bing Theater "a beauty. The comfortable seats are upholstered in gold, and the wide cross-aisles [on the Bayreuth model] are generously spaced." The juxtaposition of Machaut and Boulez convinced him "there is nothing new under the sun"; the clashing harmonies of Machaut's contrapuntal lines, the sparseness and angularity sounded "rather up-to-date." The audience received *Structures I* and *II* "so enthusiastically that perhaps others found it less problematical." Eloy's music seemed "robust and energetic" and held the attention.[26]

Leonard Stein returned again to perform in a program of works commissioned by the Fromm Foundation on 26 April 1965. He conducted Donald Martino's Concerto for Wind Quintet but was unable to prepare Harvey Sollberger's Chamber Variations for Twelve Players and Conductor in time and instead substituted Elliott Carter's Sonata for Flute, Oboe, Cello, and Harpsichord. Claudio Spies conducted his *Tempi* for fourteen instruments. Morton considered Mario Davidovsky's *Synchronisms No. 2,* with tape recorder and four instruments, a strong piece, and Davidovsky the most successful composer in the combination of tape and live instruments.[27] The final program (10 May 1965) presented Schoenberg's *Verklärte Nacht,* Op. 4 (1899), felicitously combined with Brahms's Sextet, Op. 18, played by the Lyrica String Sextet, comprising members of the Los Angeles Philharmonic (Harold Dicterow and Jeanne Aiken, violins, Myra Kestenbaum and Joseph Reilich, violas, and Vance Beach and Raymond Kelley, cellos).

TWENTY-EIGHTH SEASON: 1965–1966

In September 1965 Albert Goldberg retired as music editor of the *Los Angeles Times* but continued, as critic emeritus, to review concerts until shortly before his death in 1990 at age ninety-one. He had come to Los Angeles as a former pianist and conductor from Chicago. He had served as Illinois state director of the Federal Music Project, a WPA program. He and Izler Solomon had been co-conductors of the

Illinois Symphony. His replacement as music editor was Martin Bernheimer, age twenty-nine, most recently assistant music editor on the *Saturday Review,* and managing editor of programs for Philharmonic Hall in New York City. He was born in Munich, came to America at age three, but returned for music studies at Munich's Hochschule für Musik. He was not a performer but had taught the history of music at New York University and had served on the *New York Herald Tribune* as a music critic. His master's thesis was on Richard Strauss, his greatest interest was opera, and he seemed for a long while totally at sea reviewing Monday Evening Concerts. Goldberg and Arlen were frequently assigned to cover these events.

William Kraft (with his Los Angeles Percussion Ensemble reverting to its original name) presented world premieres of works by Aurelio de la Vega (*Exametron,* 1965) and Carlos Chávez (*Tambuco,* 1965) on the first program, which included Ravel's *Chansons madécasses* for contrast. On 25 October Robert Craft returned with Schoenberg's Serenade, Op. 24 (1923)—which he was about to record—in a program of Mozart, Haydn, and Brahms. On 29 November the Los Angeles String Quartet, with Leonard Stein, performed five works of Webern—one of them the newly published 1905 string quartet—and Harold Kjellberg, choral conductor, presented four Schütz motets and Hindemith's a cappella Mass (1963), his last completed work.

Morton worked out a sponsorship from the Elizabeth Sprague Coolidge Foundation in the Library of Congress for a program of new works requiring many performers on 13 December; Lawrence Foster conducted, Michael Tilson Thomas appeared as pianist in Dallapiccola's *Parole di san Paolo* (1964), and the Lyrica String Sextet played Walter Piston's Sextet for Strings (1964) and assisted in works of William Schuman, Riccardo Malipiero, and Juan Orrego-Salas. All five works were commissioned by the Coolidge Foundation, in celebration of Mrs. Coolidge's one-hundredth birthday. Walter Arlen found it "the dreariest program of the year."[28]

Harvey Sollberger, flutist-conductor, and Charles Wuorinen, pianist-conductor, came to Los Angeles from Columbia University in January 1966 and presented their works on a Fromm Foundation program. The complexities of Sollberger's Chamber Variations for

Twelve Players and Conductor (1964) and Wuorinen's Chamber Concerto for Flute and Ten Players (1964) were offset by the pianist Peter Hewitt's performance of Debussy's two books of *Études.* "COMPOSERS TALENTED BUT LACK FLAIR," claimed Bernheimer's headline; he had little of substance further to say but noticed that Sollberger disclosed special virtuosity in subdividing beats with his elbows and shoulders.[29]

By this time, graphic scores had become so prevalent that Morton displayed them on a music stand at the front of the auditorium or sometimes reproduced segments in his program notes. George Crumb's *Night Music I* (1963), to texts of Lorca, was one score displayed. Leonard Stein was the pianist in the work, and Morton felt it was "one of the best pieces we've had by an American composer."[30]

The next two programs were "avant-garde concerts of the kind we could not produce ourselves," Morton reported.[31] The guest pianist Jocy de Oliveira, assisted by a percussionist from the St. Louis Symphony (of which Oliveira's husband, Eleazar Carvalho, was conductor), came on 14 March 1966 to present Berio's new *Sequenza IV* (1966), two suites by Erik Satie, and Four Preludes for piano (1963) by the Brazilian Claudio Santoro, along with Lejaren Hiller's *Machine Music* (1964) and Ben Johnston's *Knocking Piece* (1962). Goldberg wrote, "Words are ineffectual tools to describe what took place." The pianist was on her hands and knees, in a shocking pink evening gown, doing "Lord knows what under the piano. She blew up a balloon until it exploded, and ran about the stage propelling a musical push-toy." The percussionist, in black turtleneck and trousers, set off an alarm clock. The inscrutable Lawrence Morton, in a tuxedo, worked the controls of a two-channel electronic tape machine. The audience "marched out" when one phrase of the Satie work was repeated 267 times.[32] Morton reported his version: "We weren't going through [playing] that, nor did she want to; so we had that passage on tape and after she played it a couple of times it was repeated on the tape. . . . She simply got up from the piano, left the stage, and I left . . . the tape machine, and we just let the tape run. That was the end of the concert and people could get up and go whenever they wanted. A rather amusing effect."[33]

Further works involving tapes, slides, film, and other visual projections were brought on 21 March by Morton Subotnick, composer-conductor, and Anthony Martin, composer of visual projections from the San Francisco Tape Music Center, along with instrumentalists from Mills College. Works of Gerald Shapiro, Ramon Sender, Davidovsky, Martin, and Subotnick were offset by a cantata by Jean-Philippe Rameau.

John Doe (alias Lawrence Morton) appeared as continuo harpsichordist, and program annotator, on 4 April, in which works by Johann Joseph Fux ("a very intellectual composer," wrote Doe), Alessandro Stradella, and Ferruccio Busoni contrasted with Krenek's *Fibonacci Mobile* (1965) and *Polyphonies* (1962–1963) by Jacques Guyonnet, one of Boulez's pupils. The critic Martin Bernheimer announced that the season "ended in a blaze of glory" on 18 April 1966, with the return of Robert Craft to conduct the Gregg Smith Singers in Bach's Cantatas No. 82, *Ich habe genug,* and No. 51, *Jauchzet Gott in allen Landen,* and Gregg Smith conducted ten Ives pieces he was about to record, among them four psalms (100, 150, 54, and 90) that MEC claimed had never before been performed. The scheduled soprano, Karan Armstrong, who had recently won the Metropolitan auditions on the air, became ill, and at the last moment Gloria Grace Prosper, one of the Gregg Smith Singers, substituted for her to sing Bach's virtuosic Cantata No. 51. Harold Enns sang Cantata No. 82. Bernheimer noticed John Doe, "who realized the continuo in rather primitive terms."[34]

In May Lawrence Morton received the Laurel Leaf Award of the American Composers Alliance, presented to him by the American composer Quincy Porter, president of the Alliance, "for distinguished achievement in fostering and encouraging American music." Porter's talk began:

> Most musicians who live near New York, may easily become, or already are, pretty smug. They are likely to think that a very high proportion of all important musical activities originate in that metropolis. For this very reason we felt very strongly that we should get out our telescope, and try to find out what is happening in the

> outlying districts of the U.S.A., and most important, *who* was responsible for anything especially good that was happening in some other metropolis.[35]

Morton wrote to Boulez, "the Laurel Leaf is pretty—prettier than American music!"[36]

TWENTY-NINTH SEASON: 1966–1967

During the summer Lawrence Foster won the Serge Koussevitsky Memorial conducting prize at Tanglewood. In Los Angeles, Goldberg began the season of reviews with a summary:

> [MEC's] remarkable record of courage and persistence and, not incidentally, of genuine achievement. The concerts have been, and you may be fairly sure will continue to be, often abrasive and irritating, but at the same time they have also been never less than provocative and instructive and have enlarged everyone's horizon immeasurably in the special field of contemporary and unfamiliar music. They have also acquired a special audience of intelligentsia, a public not to be observed in toto anywhere else, and this segment of the body politic again turned out in full force for the inaugural program under the direction of Ingolf Dahl . . . one of the most versatile musicians to be found anywhere.[37]

Lawrence Lesser's piano partner, Ellen Mack, had moved to the Peabody Conservatory to teach, and on 17 October, with pianist Peter Hewitt, Lesser and John Neufeld presented a program particularly distinguished by Lesser's performance of Luigi Dallapiccola's *Ciaconna, intermezzo e adagio* (1945) for cello solo.

Stravinsky's twelfth world premiere at these concerts was hastily readied for 31 October 1966. The piece was *The Owl and the Pussycat.* Gloria Grace Prosper was to sing this twelve-tone love song to Vera Stravinsky but became ill, and a late substitution was made. Ingolf Dahl coached the substitute singer and took her to 1218 Wetherly

Drive, Stravinsky's last home in Hollywood. Stravinsky, now eighty-four, frail, shrunken, dressed in pajamas and negotiating the stairs to the basement rehearsal room with a cane, seems by his mere presence to have unnerved the singer, who—in a "Fellini-ish scene"—went to pieces and couldn't sing the pitches. Dahl and Stravinsky debated whether to cancel but went ahead. After the performance Dahl saw Stravinsky backstage:

> The old strength, flash, conviction, straightness of uncompromising, unpopular purpose arises as he stops me to talk (with speech difficulties) about the song performance. IS: "Everything is always too loud, too loud for me. More delicate—it should be like threads and it is like macaroni. On my piano upstairs, it is muted, you know, I can hear it right. It is like spiderwebs. One must speak *softly* in order to be understood *clearly.* The softer you sing, the clearer the syllables, syllables, syllables." ID: "And the softer you sing, the clearer the pitches." IS: "Yes, the pitches!"[38]

On the same program Michael Tilson Thomas played Beethoven's Piano Sonata, Op. 111, and Stravinsky, sitting backstage, leaned closer and closer to the curtain, becoming totally absorbed in the performance. Tilson Thomas had a photostat of Beethoven's original manuscript, which he gave Stravinsky to follow. Afterwards they sat together backstage and drank tea, while Stravinsky talked about the sonata.[39] William Kraft's Double Trio (1966) for piano, tuba, percussion, prepared piano, and electric guitar was given its first performance on the same program. Kraft conducted and recalled Stravinsky,

> sitting in the wings, watching me. It made me a bit nervous. In the fourth movement I had a solo section for the percussionist. I had said, "just improvise for twenty seconds on previously given material." Kenny Watson didn't play his improvisation for me during the dress rehearsal. I said, "Aren't you going to play your solo cadenza for me?" He said, "No, I want to surprise you." Well, what he surprised me with was not a twenty second improvisation but a prepared cadenza, of about two or three minutes. It

> was *long,* and I was helpless. I looked up after that and saw that Stravinsky was gone. The next night [at a rehearsal Robert Craft was conducting] Stravinsky stopped to tell me how much he liked the piece. . . . Then he said, "I'm sorry I had to leave. I don't have the energy to sign the autographs. And also, I must tell you, I don't like drum solos." Little did he know that everything I've done for multiple percussion is patterned after *L'Histoire du soldat!*[40]

Walter Arlen congratulated the singer for learning Stravinsky's score in two days, "very well indeed," and reported that Kraft "has the true composer's gift for convincing the listener of the rightness of his ideas."[41]

On 16 January the program was entirely taken by Monteverdi's *Vespers* of 1610, with the Gregg Smith Singers and the Texas Boys Choir, conducted by Robert Craft. This performance was about to be recorded by Columbia. Michael Tilson Thomas played the harpsichord continuo and remembered:

> Schütz, Monteverdi, these composers I discovered through Lawrence and through the series, were *revelations* to me. The first time I ever heard a piece of Monteverdi was when I was playing a continuo rehearsal of the *Vespers.* I was absolutely astounded that the chord changes were so simple, and so beautiful. There was a kind of noise, and I realized someone was looking over my shoulder. It was Stravinsky. He was following his own score and looking over my shoulder as I was playing. I was trying to sight-read this piece, barely able to concentrate, because the changes of chords were so beautiful—swept away—I'd lose my place because they were so wonderful! Then I really was totally nervous because Stravinsky was reading over my shoulder. I really had to try to keep my mind together. Bob Craft was wonderful in presenting that music. We loved that music for its freshness and its sincerity.[42]

This performance celebrated the four-hundredth birthday of Claudio Monteverdi, and in the program a plea was made for contributions to the reclamation and restoration of Italian art damaged by recent floods in Venice. Music by Monteverdi appeared on every program for the remainder of 1967.

The University of Chicago had recently celebrated its seventy-fifth anniversary by commissioning pieces from two composers on its music faculty, Ralph Shapey and Easley Blackwood. The Fromm concert on 6 March 1967 brought them to Los Angeles, together with enough players to perform Mario Davidovsky's *Inflexions for Fourteen Players,* Blackwood's *Un Voyage à Cythère,* Op. 20, and Shapey's *Incantations,* both for soprano and ten players. Shapey conducted. Bernheimer called him "the Toscanini of the coherent far-out" and found the program intelligently planned as well as splendidly executed.[43]

On 27 March Eudice Shapiro masterfully took the stage alone to play Bartók's Sonata for Unaccompanied Violin (1944) and Bach's second Partita for Unaccompanied Violin, with its famous Chaconne. There was a large audience, and Goldberg wrote that her "invariably confident and secure" performance was "not only painless but an obvious pleasure to the audience."[44]

THIRTIETH SEASON: 1967–1968

Michael Tilson Thomas took on more and more of the difficult piano assignments and now began conducting for MEC. Walter Arlen had noted on 2 November 1966 that "Thomas' interest in and ability to perform new music should soon propel him into the front rank of young American pianists in this field."[45] On 6 November 1967 he and Ralph Grierson played Stravinsky's reduction of *Le Sacre du printemps* for four hands, a performance that was later recorded. On the same program Tilson Thomas played a Webern piece for piano from 1925 (posthumously published) and conducted Stockhausen's *Adieu* (1966) for wind quintet.

Peter Yates had established contact with Robert Ashley and Gordon Mumma, founders of the Cage-influenced ONCE Group (1961–1968) and members of the Sonic Arts Group (1966–1973), which performed live electronic music. They presented a program of electronic music on 11 December 1967. Robert Ashley's *Frogs* (1967), a section of a larger work for voices and dancers, opened the program. Gordon Mumma's *Mesa* (1966) was a commission for the Merce Cunningham Dance Company, Ashley's *The Wolfman* (1964) a theater piece for amplified improvised voice (Ashley performing) modified electronically. Peter Yates wrote to Peyton Houston after the performance:

> You may be interested to learn that, as of now, my slightly middle-aged friends who have until lately thought of themselves as the forward edge of advancing musical discovery, who marched stoutly with me in the name of Bartók, the causes of Ives and Schoenberg, the discovery of Webern, who would not entirely abandon me to Cage, are unanimously furious against me for having arranged the local appearance of my friends Mumma & Ashley from ONCE. Men and composers who believed themselves prepared to fight to the death in the cause of aesthetic freedom and modern music were stalking out in the first 15–25 minutes, enraged, outraged, glaring, uncompromising, just like the fathers, grandfathers, & g-g-fathers of musical integrity before 'em. . . . The sound is produced "live" on the stage, then whistled, groaned, burped, bleated, blasted through circuits, filters, loops, oscillators, ring modulators, a mere toot becoming in the process an extended symphonic utterance continuing and continuing to the detriment of imagination. (P.S. A letter from Bob [Ashley] today tells me our conversations opened up ideas previously tentative and will cause much change in *Frogs* [a lecture accompanied by ninety-two various frog calls from a record]).[46]

Dahl, who had not involved himself in the new musical fashions flowing through MEC, gave a contrasting all-Haydn concert on 8 January 1968, for a bigger than usual crowd. He had become a Haydn expert and offered one of the piano trios he himself had revoiced, the solo cantata *Arianna a Naxos,* and two nocturnes Haydn wrote for the king of Naples and rescored in his late London period for ten instruments.

György Ligeti's *Aventures* (1962), "five enmeshed chains of musical happenings" for three singers "expressing the text by a non-semantic, imaginary language, a phonetic composition emanating from the musical one" played by seven instrumentalists,[47] caused a bit of a stir on 22 January 1968, reported Albert Goldberg,

> though virtually nothing happened. The curtain went up to reveal a shabbily dressed man, a woman in an Oriental kimono . . . and a woman in gauzy draperies . . . with a small orchestra off to one side conducted by Leonard Stein. The three characters moved around aimlessly, like refugees from a play by Beckett or Pinter, all the while emitting wordless sounds like gibberish. . . . Every so often . . . the orchestra put in a few plunks and groans to justify union scale. That was it, and the Monday nighters were stirred to their depths. They cheered and whistled and recalled the performers repeatedly.

Goldberg's ears were then cleansed by the "delicious" forty-five-minute Mozart Divertimento for string trio, K. 563.[48] Ligeti wrote to Morton from Vienna, "Be not disturbed that the review was uncomprehending. I like bad criticism, it gives inspiration."[49] Looking back the following year, Ingolf Dahl wrote, "many of us felt that [*Aventures*] was one of the most significant and provocative events of the Los Angeles music season that year. . . . One can't deny Ligeti's remarkable ability to shape in each of his major works a unique vision."[50]

Martin Bernheimer was discomfited by the prospect of two programs surveying the six quartets of Bartók, in performance by the Los Angeles String Quartet, 5 and 12 February. He wrote that he would prefer less concentration.[51] The Bartók expert Halsey Stevens led a discussion of the quartets for members of the Southern California Chamber Music Society, at Sadye Moss's house.

Lawrence Foster conducted the first American performance of Peter Maxwell Davies's *Leopardi Fragments* (1961) on 13 March 1968, and on 25 March Monday Evening Concerts, "stronghold of anti-Romanticism, closed its season . . . with Brahms!" as well as with works of Schoenberg, Bernard Rands, and Henri Pousseur (who was present, having flown from a teaching stint in Buffalo). Walter Arlen found that the Schoenberg String Trio (Op. 45), in comparison to Rands's *Espressione IV* (1964, for two pianos), and Pousseur's *Mobile pour deux pianos* (1957–1958)—played by Karl and Margaret Kohn—"appeared about as tame as Brahms compared to Schoenberg. Schoenberg not only continuously shaped technical ideas, but also never gave up the belief in the emotional roots of music."[52]

THIRTY-FIRST SEASON: 1968–1969

This season Lawrence Morton, suffering from further heart trouble and perhaps still agonizing over his Stravinsky book, announced that he would take a leave of absence from the concerts. He arranged the programs and engaged an assistant to administer them. Yet things did not proceed as he wished, and he continued to function as "artistic director," while assigning detailed negotiations to a personnel director. Much of the programming repeated earlier adventures. However, Natalie Limonick's performance with the mezzo-soprano Margery MacKay and the baritone Edward Crafts of Hugo Wolf's entire *Italienisches Liederbuch* was "a distinct occasion in this song-recital-poor community," Walter Arlen reported.[53]

In 1962 Peter and Frances Yates had suffered the loss of their youngest son, John, who—since 1954—had been paralyzed with polio and confined in an iron lung. The year of John's death Yates retired from his job in the California Employment Service, after twenty-five years' service, and devoted himself to lectures and writing. His second published book on music, *Twentieth Century Music* (1967), met with considerable success. In the fall of 1968 he took a post as chair of the Department of Music at Buffalo State College and left Los Angeles. As a going-away gift to the concerts they had founded, and in anticipation of the thirtieth anniversary of the first program in their home on 23 April 1939, he and Frances Mullen Yates invited the harpsichordist Margaret Fabrizio, from San Francisco, to present a half-program of works by François Couperin and C. P. E. Bach, unique composers for the keyboard who had long interested them. The date was 11 November 1968, three hundred years and a day from the birth of Couperin. It may be interesting to note that Cage and his adherents were not featured on the Yateses' final concert. Yates commented to Houston in 1967 on his view of Cage's development and influence:

> Nothing in the book [Yates's *Twentieth Century Music*] says that the lines to the future, as you put it, will go through Cage. The entire thesis is that music will go through Ives to occupy the entire field of sound. But Cage has done more than any other composer to open up areas of sound and modes of dealing with them not previously exploited and leading directly to the computer. . . . I'm not convinced that John hasn't reached a dead end, but he writes me that he has several new compositions, a second book, and a collection of pieces for the harpsichord.[54]

Gerhard Samuel, music director of the Oakland Symphony, made a "conscientious and adroit" impression on Walter Arlen, conducting works of Alden Ashforth and Edward Applebaum in November.[55] Michael Tilson Thomas, now twenty-four, conducted a Monday Evening Concerts group touring to St. Louis and New York City in December, Schoenberg's Five Pieces for Orchestra in its chamber version back in Los Angeles in January, and Boulez's *Le Marteau sans maître* in February. On the January program he played Debussy's late sonatas for cello and for violin with Laurence Lesser and Eudice Shapiro. "The performances were uniformly polished and played with style and flair," Goldberg wrote, "but [in Debussy's music] there was not much substance for concentration."[56]

Robert Craft conducted Schoenberg's *Pierrot lunaire* and Olivier Messiaen's *Couleurs de la cité céleste* for a capacity crowd on 9 December 1968. On the same program, Lesser performed J. S. Bach's Suite No. 2 for solo cello. Goldberg found his playing "an island of classical calm. He is one of the smoothest of cellists—no rasping, no frenetic sawing, just creamy, mellow tone, objective control, and a meditative insight into the ways and thought of Bach."[57] On 13 January 1969 the German pianist Alois Kontarsky, the first pianist to perform Stockhausen's *Klavierstücke I–XI* in its entirety, presented these works as a complete program. Bernheimer lamented,

> Monday's exposure left me bored. Bored. BORED. . . . I found myself longing for the emotionalism of Hindemith, the cheer of Webern, the charm of late-Schoenberg, the expansiveness of John Cage, the variety of Carl Orff. Mea culpa. . . . Alois Kontarsky sustained the monstrous challenge with obvious devotion and heroic strength. For the evening's finale, the tenth and most violent of the pieces, Kontarsky braced his wrists with bandages and proceeded to attack the piano with terrifying gusto. The keys fell victim to elbows and arms as well as the usual digits.[58]

At this time Boulez began what became a long-term relationship with the Los Angeles Philharmonic, by conducting the orchestra in ten stimulating concerts during January and February 1969. Morton invited him to be music director of the Ojai Festival in 1970. His reappearances with both these organizations continued through the 1980s and 1990s to be peaks of Los Angeles' musical seasons.

The pianist Charles Fierro's February performance of (Boulez's student) Gilbert Amy's *Cahiers d'épigrammes* "demonstrated involvement with the avant-garde beyond the notes, beyond the gimmicks, and beyond the special techniques," wrote Walter Arlen.[59] In March Ingolf Dahl presented a program of Purcell and Byrd string fantasias, with Stravinsky's *Duo concertant,* Copland's *Nonet for Strings,* and Bartók's *Contrasts,* with his long-esteemed colleagues the clarinetist Mitchell Lurie and the violinist Eudice Shapiro. Leonard Stein gave the first Los Angeles performance of Boulez's First Piano Sonata in February and with Marni Nixon performed Webern's complete songs with piano on the final concert, 14 April 1969. This Monday evening also happened to be the night of the Academy Award presentations, where Marni Nixon was scheduled to sing. Henry Mancini introduced her to a new song of his that very morning. She sang it, gowned elaborately in white, for the glittering award ceremony at 8:15 P.M., Arlen reported, and walked onto the stage of the Bing theater in blue at 8:55 to sing the Webern for Monday Evening Concerts; "the shift from Mancini to Webern evidently posed no problems."[60]

Although April 1969 was the thirtieth year of the concerts' existence, there was no celebration of this anniversary beyond the Yateses' farewell concert. Nor was there a celebration in the thirtieth season. The origins of the concerts were slipping easily from Los Angeles' memory.

THIRTY-SECOND SEASON: 1969–1970

For this and the next season Morton, in response to what he called "mistaken criticism" of the concerts in the newspapers, initiated critical reviews of the concerts by "Our Own Music Critic." The writers, mostly members of the Board "chosen from a group of composers and performing musicians, one for each concert, will assess the music and performances on a highly professional level and with complete independence and freedom of opinion."

These enlightened reviews would be available only to members of the Southern California Chamber Music Society and would be mailed shortly after each concert.[61] The chosen critics—among them Dahl, Kohn, Kraft, Stein, the composer Marshall Bialosky (a new member of MEC's Board of Directors, and a professor of fine arts at the new California State College at Dominguez Hills), the pianist Richard Grayson, the cellist Laurence Lesser, and Ramiro Cortés (a composer on the USC music faculty)—found themselves faced with a very difficult and dangerous task. (The first review was unsigned: subsequently the critics had to take responsibility for their opinions.) Getting to know the music well enough beforehand took work and time, and writing honestly about colleagues' work sometimes met with bitterest rancor. Laurence Lesser, in the hot seat, wrote: "Music criticism is an impossible job. . . . Because a music review can never be a news report anymore than any words can ever explain sounds, perhaps the only justification for the review is not to pass judgement, but to provoke reaction."[62] From his new home in Buffalo, Peter Yates sent Morton congratulations on the idea, with an experienced critic's point of view: "It isn't often that a professional critic has the opportunity to check his own written reports against reports of such high quality written by professional musicians."[63]

Karl Kohn returned from a sabbatical year in London with a program (6 October 1969) of his own works, his instrumentations of German Renaissance and Baroque songs and dances, and Stravinsky's Octet. Kohn's Rhapsodies for Marimba, Vibraphone, and Percussion (1968) was a work written for the percussionist Kenneth Watson. His Impromptu for Eight Wind Instruments (1969) was written to match the instrumentation of Stravinsky's Octet and was dedicated to Lawrence Morton. Walter Arlen reported that of the works for live instruments with electronic tape on 20 October, only Leon Kirchner's String Quartet No. 3 had "something to say and something real to play. . . . The gist of the work lies in its vitality."[64] (This work won Kirchner the Pulitzer Prize.) On 10 November two of Ligeti's works, *Aventures*—given a repeat performance—and *Nouvelles Aventures,* struck Arlen as theater of the absurd that worked.[65] A Handel trio sonata and Mozart's *Musical Joke* were companion works on this program.

On 24 November Ingolf Dahl's *Cycle of Sonnets* (1968) was performed by the baritone Robert Hasty and the pianist Charles Fierro. Dahl's increasing number of commissions, grants for composing, and duties in Washington, D.C., on the policy committee of the Contemporary Music Project, and in Los Angeles as director of the Young Musicians Foundation—along with his very successful teaching at USC—now allowed him little time to perform. He withdrew from the concert stage but prepared a full performance of Bach's *Musical Offering* for this program, which three hundred students attended. Morton paid tribute to his "formidable scholarship and highly cultivated taste," in what turned out to be Dahl's last direct involvement in Monday Evening Concerts.

William Kraft's *Triangles* (1965–1968), a concerto written for himself as a virtuoso solo percussionist, with ten other instruments, was premiered on 8 December. In it three groups of percussion instruments (membranophones, keyboard, and timpani) were arranged on the stage in triangles, as opposed to the circular arrangement of Stockhausen's *Zyklus* and Berio's *Circles.* The form of the work, in three large sections, resulted from the performer's movement through these groups of instruments.

A completely French program on 23 February 1970 presented Olivier Messiaen's hour-long *Quartet for the End of Time* (1941) with works of François and Louis Couperin (whose "modernist" attitudes Morton pointed out in his program note). John Rockwell, a fresh voice on the *Los Angeles Times* staff of music critics, found the Messiaen an extraordinary piece of music and commended the "stunning performance" of Charlotte Sax, violin, Michele Zukovsky (the daughter of Kalman Bloch), clarinet Vance Beach, cello, and Ralph Grierson, piano.[66]

The four Schoenberg string quartets were presented in consecutive programs in March 1970 by the Los Angeles String Quartet (with Peter Mark now the violist). This time Bernheimer announced that "the playing was a model of finesse, suavity, and understanding."[67] Schoenberg's own comments on the works, first published for a 1959–1960 quartet series given by the Pro Arte Quartet, were condensed by Morton for the program notes. Answering his self-imposed question, what made the composer take departures in formal organization, Schoenberg wrote,

> There are many causes, but only one answer: a composer must possess a full, unshakable confidence in the logic of his musical thinking. Such an artist will not be afraid of loose association of ideas. Profundity does not require methodical procedures. . . . Music is the emanation of the soul and its governing forces are the same that govern all manifestations of the soul.[68]

The final program of the season presented Alfred Schnittke's *Dialog* for cello and seven instruments, with Laurence Lesser as soloist, and Karl Kohn conducting. It was the first performance of this work outside the Soviet Union, and only the third Schnittke performance in the United States.[69] The *Los Angeles Times* critic John Rockwell commended the first-rate performances, especially Lesser's intense projection. About Schnittke's work, he wrote that it was "full of rhapsodic unbarred passages alternating with rapid tempo fluctuations, and a variety of delicate, sparingly employed atmospheric effects. Yet what is most striking about this music is its kinship with Russian romanticism."[70]

Michael Tilson Thomas was to have returned to Los Angeles from his new post as associate conductor of the Boston Symphony to conduct this program. But the previous October, in New York City with the Bostonians, Tilson Thomas had substituted in midconcert for the ailing conductor William Steinberg. His confidence and authority, and the vitality he elicited immediately from the orchestra, had catapulted him to international recognition. He was now conductor-designate of the Buffalo Philharmonic, still busy with the Boston Symphony, and was receiving invitations from the London Symphony, New York Philharmonic, Berlin Philharmonic, and Tokyo Philharmonic as well. In his absence, a documentary film about him was shown, and the recent arrival Rockwell caustically noted that it provided "insight into an in-crowd."[71]

THIRTY-THIRD SEASON: 1970–1971

This was Lawrence Morton's last season as director of the concerts. Many things had changed since the early 1950s, and he wrote increasingly to Peter Yates in a vein of sadness about the concerts. In September 1969 the Stravinskys and Craft had moved from Hollywood to New York, after a last dinner at Morton's, who loved above all things the challenge of preparing a fine meal for them on his very stringent budget. In February 1970 he wrote to Yates that he missed these occasions, "which honored me even more than it wore me down to spend a whole day cooking and another cleaning up the debris." He reported that Madame (Vera Stravinsky) could no longer cope in Hollywood with the household problems—servant, shopping, leaky roof, the stairs, the unreliability of Stravinsky's nurses, the confinement, the smog.[72]

On 10 August 1970 he wrote Yates that he had tried vainly to telephone him in Buffalo that "Ingolf died last Thursday [in Europe] of some kind of respiratory failure. I can't begin to tell you of the shock to his friends here—and after the shock the grief and sadness and sense of loss. Well, you will know this too."[73] In the spring of 1970 Dahl, suffering ill health from asthma, which had plagued him throughout his life, took a sabbatical and left for Frütingen, Switzerland. His wife, Etta, had battled cancer for years and died in Switzerland in June. He continued composing but died of heart failure barely a week after completing Five Duets for Clarinets, the last movement of which was dedicated to Mitchell Lurie. At the time of his death one of the compositions he had on his desk to finish was the *Elegy Concerto* for violin and small orchestra, originally conceived in 1963 as a memorial for the cellist Victor Gottlieb, to be played by Eudice Shapiro. (It was completed in 1971 by Dahl's friend and former student, the composer Donal Michalsky.) Morton described the music to Yates as "impassioned (less cool than *unser* Ingolf was wont to be in his late years)."[74]

No performer or composer had a more sustained or active history of involvement with the concerts than Dahl. In turn the concerts served as encouragement for his composing, a platform for his expert conducting, pianism, and skilled musicology, and a bridge to his successful academic career. It was Dahl (with his colleague Edward Rebner) who had brought Lawrence Morton onto the Board of Evenings on the Roof, and their relationship had been the closest of all Morton's relationships. His family called Lawrence "Lorny" (a name otherwise used only by closest relatives) and knew the telephone was of no use for an hour when Morton called Dahl. Now all Morton had was his memories, memos from "I.D." on scores, and a thick file of letters dating from as early as 1941 (which have unfortunately not been available for this study). "Ingolf remains constantly in my thoughts and I continue to want to telephone him for advice, gossip, and music talk. He has left a huge hole in my life," Morton wrote Yates a year after Dahl's death.[75]

In October 1970 Lawrence Morton decided to retire from the concerts. Bernheimer announced the news in the *Los Angeles Times* in November and at the end of the year mentioned this decision in his annual "Beckmesser Awards" as the "Year's most worrisome departure."[76] Bernheimer's article on Morton's retirement acknowledged that "Los Angeles may not be an international mecca for musical modernism, but it can boast at least one super-substantial distinction in that area: the Monday Evening Concerts." He described Morton:

> a seemingly tireless gentleman of tremendous knowledge, imagination, and wit. . . . He made the pursuit of musical esoterica, new and old, an overwhelming one-man crusade. A few might complain that some MEC performances were on the rough side or that occasional repertory combinations were problematic. . . . But no one can underestimate the value of Morton's contribution, the valor of his effort on a preposterously modest budget, or the vision of his artistic convictions.[77]

There were other indications in Morton's letters to Yates of his fatigue with the concerts. In 1965 he wrote, "What I'm critical of today is the vast outpouring of 'anonymous' composers, nobodies."[78] He felt the pieces were too long, the ensembles too large.

> Oh for the "good old days" when one could tell from a score what the music would sound like, when concerts could be arranged sans percussion ($26.35 for 1-way delivery), sans electronics, ("we must have both a 10-inch and a 16-inch speaker, and a tape recorder with 1½-second time lag"), when "ring-modulators" meant marriage brokers, when "trio" meant piano and two strings, when you could find two or three new pieces with identical instrumentation, and when one paid the musicians 10 bucks a unit![79]

He even lamented, "Oh for the simple life of Evenings on the Roof before we became part of the establishment!"[80]

The season opened with a musical memorial to Dahl, cosponsored by MEC and the USC School of Music. It was pointed out in the program that Dahl had been one of the most ardent champions of American composers and had given premiere performances of works by Halsey Stevens, Ellis Kohs, Ramiro Cortés, Gail Kubik, Walter Piston, David Diamond, Carl Ruggles, Lukas Foss, and many others.

For years he had taught a famous course on the music of Stravinsky. He had received two Guggenheims, Huntington Hartford Fellowships, a Ditson Foundation Award, and a National Endowment for the Arts award. His student Michael Tilson Thomas (who wrote a tribute to Dahl for the *Los Angeles Times* of 20 September 1970) conducted. The concert opened with Dahl's Music for Brass Instruments, which itself opened with a fantasy on the chorale, "Christ Lay in the Bonds of Death." The Adagio from Bach's Violin Concerto in D Minor—a score Dahl and Josef Szigeti had edited—was played by Dahl's close friend Eudice Shapiro. Works of Schütz and Purcell were followed by Stravinsky's Symphonies of Wind Instruments.

The season's programs were recorded for broadcast by The Voice of America. Beethoven's bicentenary was celebrated by the performance in the opening concert, 5 October 1970, of his Septet, Op. 20, a work that had excited many—including critic Morton—in its first Roof performance by Philharmonic players in 1942. The only other work on the program was *Domaines* (1968), Boulez's work for clarinet solo, in which Mitchell Lurie played from six different scores allied with six different instrumental groups. Gerhard Samuel, now associate conductor with the Los Angeles Philharmonic, conducted, and Lurie was "the ultra-virtuosic clarinet protagonist," wrote Bernheimer. He described the piece (having heard its American premiere a few months previously at the Ojai Festival) as a "marvelously intricate study in sonic relationships" and found Samuel "unfazed . . . extraordinarily poised [in a] lucid, even propulsive performance."[81] The film composer Hugo Friedhofer, long a friendly (personal) commentator on the concerts, wrote Morton that a flock of film and television composers attended and that he expected the *epigonoi* would soon be appropriating such Boulezian devices as might prove useful to them.

On 19 October Dorrance Stalvey, now a member of the MEC Board, was given a half-program. Two of his works (*Togethers II* and *Togethers III,* 1970) were for solo instruments and tape. Stalvey described his *Points—Lines—Circles* (1968) as "a sound-event stressing multi-colored vibrations as the object of attention. . . . Slide and film are obvious counterparts of the conception. . . . [The work] is a variable-form composition playable in four structural versions resulting from a re-ordering of the sections." Stalvey conducted an ensemble of players new to MEC, except for the percussionist Kenneth Watson. Walter Arlen commented that "in spite of a rather complicated ground plan, which leads one to suspect a case of mind over matter, the music comes out on top. . . . The variable-form composition has its longeurs, but its alfresco idiom and cohesive sonorities assure sustained attention."[82] The first half of the program featured Charles Fierro accompanying Hayden Blanchard, tenor, in songs of Robert Schumann and playing a sonata by C. P. E. Bach and Brahms Fantasies, Op. 116. Morton, thumbing his nose at those who called him an enemy of the nineteenth century, was presenting in his last season a survey of Brahms's last piano pieces, Opp. 116–119, "the swan songs of classical Romanticism," the remainder to be played on succeeding programs by Ralph Grierson, Adrian Ruiz, and Peter Hewitt.

Henri Lazarof (with J. S. and Wilhelm Friedemann Bach) was the featured composer on 16 November, and both his works played were written especially for Monday Evening Concerts in 1970: *Continuum,* for string trio (Lesser, Milton Thomas, and the violinist Stanley Plummer), and *Cadence III* for violin (Plummer) and two percussion players. John Rockwell found "intriguing aspects" in these world premieres. "Lazarof seems in both pieces to be looking for new formal answers, for a way to shape an eclectic musical language."[83]

Thea Musgrave, an English composer currently teaching at UC Santa Barbara, was one of only three female composers to be heard at Morton's Monday Evening Concerts. On 30 November her work for viola and tape, *From One to Another* (1970) was premiered by violist Peter Mark, in company with a premiere of Aurelio de la Vega's *Labdanum* (1970) for flute, viola, and vibraphone, and Harold Budd's *Black Flowers* (1968) for soprano, clarinet, chimes, and percussion.

Ernst Krenek's seventieth birthday was celebrated by MEC on 7 December, with five of his works, and the same three chansons by Ockeghem that Krenek had requested programmed in February 1959. In his notes, Morton summed up Krenek's history of performance at these concerts from 1947, when he moved to southern California. He mentioned his regret that it had not been in the chamber concerts' power to perform Krenek's operas. Leon Kirchner, another old friend of the concerts, returned on 11 January 1971 (during a year as visiting professor at UCLA) to play works of Mozart and his own Piano Trio (1954) and *Sonata concertante* (1952) with Eudice Shapiro. Bernheimer expressed a debt to MEC for the Krenek evening,[84] and "admiration for Kirchner-the-modern-romanticist" along with "affection for Kirchner-the-Mozartean. . . . The fickle audience," he reported, "which stayed away from the recent Krenek celebration in droves, packed the house for Kirchner (and Mozart)."[85]

Lawrence Moss had had a success at Bayreuth with his miniature opera, *The Brute,* and on 25 January MEC mounted it as a low-budget production (three characters, nine instrumentalists, a single set, modest costumes, and a duration of about twenty-three minutes), with Natalie Limonick and John Hall (both faculty members in UCLA's opera workshop) as music director and stage director. On 8 February Lukas Foss returned for a full program with *Echoi* (1961–1963)—incomplete when last heard at MEC—and two more reverberations from his earlier days with his Improvisation Ensemble: *Non-Improvisation* (1968), and *Paradigm* (1969), a four-movement work composed for the Center of the Creative and Performing Arts, SUNY Buffalo, dealing with themes of chance and control, safety and risk. To Martin Bernheimer, "much of the program was entertaining, some was baffling, and a little was nerve-frazzling."[86]

On 22 February 1971 John Rockwell, on the other hand, was "grateful for a chance to hear an extensive sampling of Webern's output" of instrumental songs, Opp. 8 (1910), 13 (1914–1918), 14 (1917–1921), 15 (1917–1922), 16 (1924), 17 (1924), and 18 (1925), performed by Marni Nixon, Leonard Stein, and others. Works of Bach provided contrast. Rockwell found the performances "scrupulously conscientious and precise," but he disliked Stein's nonsequential ordering of the songs and would have preferred immersion in Webern without the interruptions of Bach. "It all sounded a bit dry," he wrote. "It would be both refreshing and characteristic to see MEC sponsor Bach performance of similar quality which came closer to authentic Baroque performing style."[87]

Karl and Margaret Kohn provided two Stravinsky works for two pianos and one by Earle Brown on 8 March. Walter Arlen remarked on the scarcity of Stravinsky repertory this season and opined that in spite of "elbow, wrist and fist clusters, plucking, strumming, and wrapping . . . the protracted [Brown] piece remained curiously non-provocative and unexciting."[88]

The final program of Lawrence Morton's term was conducted on 3 May 1971 by Michael Tilson Thomas. In an intermission speech Karl Kohn announced the choice of Dorrance Stalvey to succeed Morton in the post of director. Kohn went on to pay tribute to Morton's "zeal, imagination, wisdom, patience, wit, and the high sense of taste and style with which he has faced and overcome the endless challenges—both artistic and administrative—in bringing to life some 240 concerts. Rarely has any organization been served with devotion so firm, loving, and selfless." For his choice of repertoire, Morton (harking back to the earliest principle of Evenings on the Roof) chose a program "for my own pleasure," he wrote in his "Very Personal Program Note." The repertoire spanned nine centuries, from a four-part twelfth-century organum, *Sederunt principes* by Pérotin, to Stravinsky's *Eight Instrumental Miniatures.* "I like to emphasize the continuity of the concerts," Morton wrote. Of course there must be Schütz, and of all the *Symphoniae sacrae* the most beloved by MEC performers, Morton, and Stravinsky, *Fili mi, Absalon* for bass voice, four trombones, and continuo. There must be the wonderful Bach Cantata No. 60 (*O Ewigkeit, du Donnerwort*). It was one of the first cantatas Craft and Morton explored in the 1950s. Morton recalled playing the harmonium to accompany the "Voice from Heaven" in the 1953 performance: "Unhappily, the Voice could not count beats correctly and he left me still on a tonic while he took off into foreign harmonic territory. I stumbled in making a recovery, and after the concert Madame Stravinsky chided me. 'It was not very pretty,' she said. Tonight I leave the playing to my betters."[89] From Monteverdi Morton chose his beloved jewel, the central "Sonata sopra Sancta Maria" from the *Vespers* of 1610. In his note he reminded the audience of Oscar Moss, in memory of whom the *Vespers* was first performed at MEC, and Sadye Moss, who had continued her husband's sponsorship and kept the concerts on a firm foundation. He wrote, "I program the Sonata for the Moss family, for without them I would have had no work to do." He chose Varèse's *Ionisation,* "now that percussion has won tenure on the faculty of instruments," as a reminder to younger composers "of the difference between invention and imitation." Schoenberg might seem an odd choice to those who knew Morton's long resistance to Schoenberg, and some of the resistance still showed. He wrote:

> Schoenberg, like Stravinsky, stood like a colossus astride this musical community. Their size was obscured by the smog of local non-culture. There are those who still reject Schoenberg's music even while acknowledging his "influence." But there are those of us who are mostly interested in the achievements that made him influential. The [Three Pieces for Chamber Orchestra (1910)] played tonight (they take about three minutes) are tiny gems, but they do show the fierce intensity and concentration of his thought. They remain incomplete, the third piece breaking off where Schoenberg, probably like Coleridge, was "called out by a person on business from Porlock."[90]

There was an undertone of mourning in the program, as there had been in Morton's remarkable first program, the Dylan Thomas memorial, in September 1954. Now Stravinsky had died in New York, only weeks before, on 6 April. Morton's recollection was spare and simple:

> In this time of mourning for our great friend Igor Stravinsky, it may seem trivial to remember him with such a small work as the *Miniatures.* In those days, when he gave us the gift of the premiere of four of the little pieces, he was in his prime—his prime lasted long, and I try to remember him that way. When the eight pieces were completed, he dedicated the set to me. That dedication is my passport to immortality (if there *is* any). Besides, I like the music.[91]

Nine

LAWRENCE MORTON AND CONTEMPORARY MUSIC

Lawrence Morton's attitudes toward new music are by no means as easy to report as Peter Yates's. In 1958 Morton wrote a forthright "No" to the question whether he liked all the music that was being played at Monday Evening Concerts. In his verbally playful way, he confessed to being "content to be discontented some of the time so long as a few paying customers keep me company." He went on to say that music did not have to be likable, beautiful, or pretty to be programmed, but it had to be interesting.[1] What he considered interesting changed considerably with his experience of the changing climate in music. Furthermore, his own changes reflected two contradictory aspects of his personality, the idealist and the pragmatist.

In the forties, writing in *Script,* he was the idealist, scorning the hackneyed or unimaginative and searching out performances or compositions that provided the kind of probing insight necessary to satisfy his (and what he assumed were his readers') needs. If a great artist didn't live up to Morton's hopes, he did not hesitate to exhort that artist—as he might have encouraged a debutante—to fulfill the audience's dreams. The war raised questions of great urgency, and Morton became caught up in a new cultural self-consciousness. He wrote in 1940:

> Music has extraordinary duties to perform in these crucial times. More than ever it is needed to remind us of the magnitude and beauty of man's creative impulse. It is one of the torches of civilization that must be kept burning even if its light is temporarily dimmed by the faraway flames of homes and wheatfields ignited by incendiary bombs. . . . It is well to consider this: that the very compositions you think are too old-fashioned for modern audiences or the pieces you think are just plain noise, with no melody, may be the very ones which have been banned from programs somewhere in war-torn Europe; that the composer whom you abhor above all others might be a refugee in a strange land, or a prisoner in a concentration camp or a young American who is struggling to get a hearing. Thoughtful audiences will remember that they, as well as the performing artists, are carrying a torch for the arts. They will realize that to carry a torch for music means first of all to go to concerts, and then to *work* at listening, not merely to bathe in beautiful sounds. They will be grateful that they still have time for listening, time for enjoying, time for studying. They will make the most of it, for they are perhaps the last free audiences listening to the last free artists.[2]

At the end of the war, when words like "demobilization" were in the air, music was to be "mobilized" in the coming peace. In 1944 Lawrence Morton took on the chairmanship of the Musicians' Congress and cochaired the Institute on Music in Contemporary Life that involved most of the musical leaders in Los Angeles in considerations of the ways in which music could and should serve humanity. Liberals, and leftism, were naturally deeply involved in this discontent with the status quo and desire for change and growth. In his leadership roles Morton spoke and wrote with a solid, comfortable authority, asking questions, not necessarily answering them, but challenging himself, artists, and audiences to deeper thought. His address for the institute's opening session at UCLA on 14 September 1944 stated that "musical life in America is at a very low level" and pointed to the profound disunity in American music due to conflicts and lack of integration between the worlds of folk music, art music, and jazz.[3] A talk he gave in 1945 (titled "Democracy and the Musician") centered on a quote from Walt Whitman: "No art can long afford to be out of touch with the people."[4]

In 1948 the Musicians' Congress with which he had been so deeply involved was listed as a Communist front organization in a report by the Joint Fact-Finding Committee to the California Legislature on Un-American Activities in California. The report accused this "front" of being "organized for the purpose of 'involving' non-Communist musicians in communist activities" and listed members of the general board of the Musicians' Congress, including Alfred Wallenstein, Aaron Copland, Lena Horne, Hanns Eisler, Johnny Green, Ira Gershwin, Manuel Compinsky, George Antheil, Ingolf Dahl, Hugo Friedhofer, Victor Gottlieb, Eudice Shapiro, Miklos Rozsa, David Raksin, Gerald Strang, and Franz Waxman. Among those the report listed as members of the advisory board were widely known celebrities, including Nadia Boulanger, Carlos Chávez, Henry Cowell, Benny Goodman, Eugene Goossens, Howard Hanson, Jascha Heifetz, Charles Ives, Otto Klemperer, Serge Koussevitsky, Paul Henry Lang, Lauritz Melchior, Yehudi Menuhin, and numerous other extraordinary artists. It labeled Artur Rubinstein, Alfred Newman, Morton Gould, Artie Shaw, and Miklos Rozsa as suspicious Hollywood figures who figured prominently in the Institute on Music and Contemporary Life, cosponsored by UCLA on 14 September 1944.[5] It named Lawrence Morton with these luminaries and listed him as a member of the southern California board of directors of the American Russian Institute, and a participant in a conference on Russian-American cultural exchange held at UCLA in December 1945.[6]

After this experience in 1948, the idealist in Morton let the pragmatist have the upper hand, as he confined his writing and public activities to unassailable topics. (After *Script* folded in 1948, he wrote musical analysis and criticism of film scores for the industry periodicals *Film Music Notes* and *The Score* and conducted radio interviews with prominent film composers.) In the strongly liberal magazine, *Frontier,* which published Morton's views on music from 1951 through 1958, he occasionally attacked James C. Petrillo, president of the American Federation of Musicians (the musicians' union), but mostly aimed his barbs at music critics, conductors, the opera composer Gian Carlo Menotti, and at virtuosity and the programming philosophies of the Hollywood Bowl and the Ojai Festival (before it summoned him to take on programming in 1954). By 1952 (he explained in his 1958 application for a Guggenheim fellowship) he had ended his connection with commercial music, except for assistance to David Raksin in scoring the 1953 MGM film, *The Bad and the Beautiful*, an occasional book review in trade publications, and the preface to Clifford McCarty's 1953 listing of film composers and orchestrators. His objective was to clear his desk for work in art music. "Music must not only be consumed; it must also make a difference to us; it must matter," he wrote in 1950. "It is idle, then, to ask *if* composers have contributed to our culture. It is idle to ask *what* they have contributed, or if it measures up to the masterpieces of Mozart and Beethoven. The important question is: Are we cultured enough to know what to do with the work our composers give us?"[7] With his increasing involvement in Evenings on the Roof, and his acceptance of the directorship of Monday Evening Concerts, the fostering of intellectual independence became his preoccupation.

His natural early predilection was for American music—in particular Aaron Copland's. Evenings on the Roof systematically programmed Copland's chamber music as it was published, and Monday Evening Concerts introduced all his later works to Los Angeles audiences. (Morton propelled Copland's conducting career by inviting him to conduct the 1957 Ojai Festival; Copland had never before conducted other than his own works.)[8] Morton liked the fact that Copland's was "music that most certainly is 'felt.' "[9] In 1954 he wrote about the Piano Variations (1930), the Piano Sonata (1941), and Copland's Third Symphony (1946): "This kind of music is the weightiest part of his whole *oeuvre.* It may not be the most beautiful part, and certainly it is not the most charming or most popular part. But it is the part that, in the end, makes a real difference to the art of music."[10] However, when Copland began a journey into serialism in his Piano Quartet (1950), Morton concluded his review of its Ojai Festival premiere with an anguished cry to his old friend: "Aaron, come home. All is forgiven."[11]

Morton struggled until the end of his life with his attitudes toward

Schoenberg's music. In 1941 he found it "incomprehensible."[12] As we have seen in chapter two, he found the 1944 groundbreaking performance of *Pierrot* in English translation "perverse music set to a perverse text." In 1947 he visited Schoenberg in Brentwood and, since the composer's eyes gave him difficulties, read aloud to him a thoughtful article about Schoenberg by Virgil Thomson, whom Morton had long admired. He then wrote to Thomson, introducing himself and reporting about his visit to Schoenberg that "the old gentleman was touched, very deeply moved; so much so that I did not dare look at him while I read, for fear of losing my own voice, in the emotion of seeing the tears well up in his eyes."[13] After that occasion Morton's writings on Schoenberg were truly ambivalent. In 1948 he wrote about Schoenberg at seventy-four: "If we were honest, we would admit that much of Schoenberg's music is far beyond our comprehension. It is an intellectual phenomenon of such magnitude that it has turned topsy-turvy the whole concept of music in our time." Unlike Yates, he could find no charm in it. His answer to the question, "How did you like the Schoenberg?" after a performance, "must be given with a gesture, an exclamation, or, best of all, silence and a stony stare." Yet he urged his readers to honor Schoenberg's music by listening to it, by trying to understand it, and by telling the composer "that, because we listened, our lives are a little different, perhaps better, than they were before."[14] In 1950 he wrote perceptively about Schoenberg's "verbal" rhythm in an article for *Arts and Architecture* and earned Schoenberg's compliments.[15]

In the days following Schoenberg's death Morton wondered whether Schoenberg's music would ever inspire love.[16] He found the Roof's 1952 retrospective programs of "unmitigated Schoenberg" severe and reiterated his dislike for the music on the grounds that Schoenberg's was "one of the most analytical and constructivist minds of the 20th century."[17] Robert Craft remarked that when he met Morton in the summer of 1950, Morton "deeply disliked Schoenberg's music. . . . He took the position that the whole atonal movement was a mistake, that musicians were dishonest to promote it since they could not 'hear all of the notes,' that the rigidity of the rhythms was a consequence of the system. I think he never changed his mind about this and was never greatly interested in 12-tone music before Stravinsky began to write his brand of it."[18] The bassoonist Don Christlieb corroborates this view in his *Remembrance of Lawrence Morton:*

> He once asked me point blank, "Do you really enjoy that 12-tone work you're doing?" I said, "Lawrence, I can't give you a straight yes or no answer. All I can say is: 'Why do I return year after year to rehearse the Schoenberg Woodwind Quintet, the bible of 12-tone? There has to be something [more] in it than we [the Los Angeles Woodwind Quintet] have achieved so far!' " . . . Much later when I saw Lawrence pouring over a submitted serial work I confronted him with his previous statement and attitude and he said, "Well, a man can change can't he?"[19]

On the other hand, Morton's early criticisms of Stravinsky's music turned to total acceptance as he became a close friend of the composer and a faithful member of the composer's inner circle. Although he respected Stravinsky's reharmonization of the national anthem in 1941, even after two hearings he was not won over by Stravinsky's *Piano-Rag-Music,* played by his close friend Ingolf Dahl in 1942.[20] In the forties—Stravinsky's period of low ebb, according to Robert Craft[21]—Morton wrote no further reviews on Stravinsky's music until January 1947, when he reviewed a performance by Klemperer of the Symphony in Three Movements (1945). He heard in the first movement of this work a logical sequel to President Roosevelt's invocation of humanity's inherent nobility of spirit in the great struggle between democracy and totalitarianism. The context of his interpretation was the president's State of the Union address to Congress, broadcast ten hours before Morton heard Stravinsky's new symphony. Morton admitted that if the order of his experiences had been different he would have heard the first movement of the work with different ears: "as a continuity of blocks or planes of sound," instead of as "a mighty affirmation of confidence and resolution . . . a lengthy discussion of disturbing collateral issues," and a restatement of high resolve, with a quiet but hopeful ending. But, he continued, "under no circumstances can the movement be heard as anything less than a work of high seriousness which compels earnest attention and contemplation. . . . I wish it could be said that the other two movements are as impressive."[22] In May 1948 Morton contemplated Stravinsky's fame in a caustic article titled, "From Billy Rose to God." The adoration, reverence, devotional literature, and publication of countless photographs of the composer in all his activities irritated Morton. He gibed at the solemnity of it all and pointed out what ultimately appealed to him the most about Stravinsky: his wit and humor. He wrote: "The gift is not common among composers. On the contrary, Stravinsky is probably its sole possessor. Let us not hide it under the grand sonorities of *Sacre, Oedipus,* and the symphonies. The special qualities of these large works are sufficiently appreciated. But in paying them homage, we are missing all the fun of hearing Stravinsky speak for the Comic Muse."[23]

Craft has written about his role in providing a path out of Stravinsky's depression;[24] Evenings on the Roof and Monday Evening Concerts widened and smoothed the path by offering an early forum and fine musicians for Craft's own talents as a conductor. As Craft prepared for the Roof's 1952 Schoenberg retrospective programs, the players noticed at rehearsals that Stravinsky could not resist leafing through Schoenberg's scores, which were all new to him. Craft wrote:

> He was so taken with the Serenade that he used a mandolin in *Agon* and a guitar in a new instrumentation of his Four Russian Songs. Yet the Septet-Suite [Schoenberg's Op. 29] with its serial language, had the more profound influence on him, its Gigue movement directly inspiring the one in his own Septet. . . . To some extent I "directed" and "controlled" Stravinsky. . . . In truth, every Stravinsky opus after and including the Septet and *In Memoriam Dylan Thomas* (1954) was undertaken as a result of discussions between us. . . . I sometimes went so far as to suggest forms that new pieces might take. . . . Without me Stravinsky would not have taken the path he did after *The Rake's Progress.*[25]

Morton admitted that "premieres of Stravinsky works would not have come to us without Bob Craft's interest in the concerts because it was he that would ask Stravinsky for them."[26] Craft wrote that "the chamber music format [of the concerts] had a considerable influence on Stravinsky; . . . [Morton] would tell him the instrumentation of a program months in advance."[27] In a 1957 article Craft listed works Stravinsky had written for performance at these concerts: the *Shakespeare Songs* and *In Memoriam Dylan Thomas,* as well as the arrangements of the Russian Choruses with four horns, the Four Songs for voice, flute, harp, and guitar, the *Balmont Songs,* the Tango, the *Praeludium* for chamber orchestra, and the version of *Renard* with piano replacing the difficult-to-find Hungarian cimbalom.[28] To this list later works should be added: *Eight Instrumental Miniatures* (1962), *Elegy for J.F.K.* (1964), and "The Owl and the Pussy-Cat" (1966). According to Craft, in the mid-fifties and early sixties Morton "knew Stravinsky better than anyone else outside of the household";[29] he helped garner such a wealth of premieres with his quiet persuasion and was justly proud of them. At the premiere of Stravinsky's setting of Edward Lear's poem "The Owl and the Pussy-Cat" (for which he privately presented the composer with a "runcible spoon"), Morton gave a speech summing up Stravinsky world premieres at Roof and MEC concerts; the list of twelve (below) exceeded the nine world premieres Diaghilev had presented of Stravinsky works. Larger, weightier works though Diaghilev's were, Morton enjoyed outdoing his list in number.

Praeludium (1953 version)	19 October 1953
Tango (1953 version)	19 October 1953
Three Songs from William Shakespeare (1953)	8 March 1954
In Memoriam Dylan Thomas (1954)	20 September 1954
Four Russian Peasant Songs (1954 version for equal voices and four horns)	11 October 1954
Two Poems of Balmont (1954 instrumentation)	29 November 1954
Four Songs for voice, flute, harp, and guitar (1953–1954 instrumentation)	21 February 1955

"The Dove Descending Breaks the Air" (anthem, 1962)	19 February 1962
Four Movements from *Eight Instrumental Miniatures* (1962 instrumentation)	26 March 1962
Canzonetta Op. 62a, by Jan Sibelius (1963 arrangement)	30 September 1963
Elegy for J.F.K. (1964)	6 April 1964
"The Owl and the Pussy-Cat" (1966)	31 October 1966[30]

The *Miniatures'* dedication by Stravinsky reads:

> to Lawrence Morton, the rugged Minnesotan musicologist and formidable musical director of the Monday Evening Concerts, which are for me the most interesting concert series in the U.S., having been (and still being) about five to ten years in advance of any New York group in the presentation of "new" music, and being unique in the world in the high standards of its selection of "old" music.[31]

Another important world premiere Morton did not list, because the concert was cosponsored with Franz Waxman's Los Angeles Music Festival, was the first performance of *Agon* in 1957. Craft conducted, in the gala seventy-fifth birthday tribute to Stravinsky at UCLA's Royce Hall, and a recording was made soon afterward. Michael Tilson Thomas commented:

> *Agon* is a portrait of a season at Monday Evening Concerts. It begins with fanfares, strongly influenced by the antique brass instrument music that was being played at Monday Evening Concerts. And then there's Stravinsky's impression of a piece of Boulez; a piece of Webern; of early Renaissance dances; of some music by Schütz; of some Schoenberg; the whole season of music at Monday Evening Concerts in these little gem-like pieces that form together the ballet of *Agon*.[32]

Morton and Craft both emphasized the importance to Stravinsky of Craft's commitment to the music of Anton Webern, and his project to record the complete works. "Through the rehearsals, concerts, and recording sessions he became intimately acquainted with the music of the one member of the Viennese triumvirate for whom he had complete sympathy," wrote Morton in 1981.[33]

Stravinsky's association with the concerts became a family affair many musicians enjoyed. "There was in Stravinsky something of Haydn and of Mozart, a kind of play function," Morton remembered.[34] The harpsichordist Carol Rosenstiel, rehearsing under Craft's direction Monteverdi's *Il Combattimento di Tancredi* in her home in 1953, was almost unnerved when the Stravinskys and Aldous Huxley turned up to listen, scores in hand. During the rehearsal break the maestro sat on the living-room floor next to a hastily swept-aside pile of the Rosenstiel children's playthings and carefully examined all the toys, asking how they worked when he couldn't figure it out himself. "I thought it quite wonderful that a man in his seventies, totally immersed in music, could find such pleasure in childlike things. He somewhat reluctantly tore himself away when we resumed the rehearsal," she said.[35] The pianist Charles Fierro remembered an incident at the premiere of the *Elegy for J.F.K.,* when a chorister who had sung a Renaissance work on the program strode boldly up to Stravinsky after the performance of the new work and said, "Very good, Mr. Stravinsky!" The maestro thanked him, unfazed.[36] The soprano Grace-Lynne Martin, who premiered the *Three Shakespeare Songs,* tells of Stravinsky saying to her before the performance, "Remember, with no fear there is no fire!"[37] Another soprano, Catherine Gayer, adds that Stravinsky put a shot of cognac in the hot tea Vera offered her when she arrived at their house for a rehearsal with a cold. She wasn't used to alcohol and later couldn't recall the rest of the rehearsal.[38]

Morton witnessed Stravinsky's struggle with serialism. Over a Scotch on the memorable day in 1954 when the composer finished *In Memoriam Dylan Thomas* and showed it to him, Stravinsky told Morton that it was still difficult to "unlearn" tonality and that he still felt the pull toward a tonal center. "I do resist the academic approach," he said, "except that I find it very interesting to 'experience' the serial method in my *Dylan Thomas* piece, so long as the harmony is correct. I must have the correct harmony!" Morton continued:

> In subsequent visits to Stravinsky's studio, I never paid much attention to the machinery of his serial practices. I am no Champollion of the tone row, and once I found out what he was doing with his alpha, beta, gamma, and delta rows, with his diagonals and verticals and all the other upholstery of his pieces, I was quite content with just listening to the fabulous and always fresh sounds he concocted.[39]

Stravinsky first heard Pierre Boulez's music in October 1951 at Baden-Baden. In the summer of 1952 Craft obtained from the publisher, Heugel, the score of *Polyphonie X,* and took it back to California, where he conducted its first American performance in an October Roof concert. Craft recalls that Don Christlieb persuaded the performers to come to rehearsals, "and to stick with the piece, which of course they derided. About an hour before the concert the trombonist dropped his instrument on the concrete floor and dented the slide, whereupon the program order was changed while another instrument was fetched. The audience was indifferently polite."[40] Morton's review of that piece—one that Boulez thereafter withdrew from his list of works—contrasts with his later endorsement of Boulez's music:

> The music does not lie sweetly in the ear. . . . Boulez succeeded in boring some of [the audience], amusing others, and making a few angry. But there was no demonstration of any strong feeling other than admiration for the performers, the Los Angeles Woodwinds and Brass, and for Robert Craft, the conductor. . . . Pierre Boulez is . . . rigorously intellectual, extremist, experimental. He may be musical, though I heard no convincing evidence of this. . . . It is as though he has sterilized his music so thoroughly that there isn't a

> familiar germ left. We can't "catch" anything from it. . . . His new kind of organization is clearly visible to the eye which scans the score. It is not, however, audible to the normal (i.e., my) ear. What I perceive . . . is a geometrically cultivated abnormality that ends up in a kind of eccentric pedestrianism. Or, a deadly *moderato* punctuated by stutterings. . . . His music must stand or fall, like everybody else's, on its expressive content and its power of communication. . . . I cannot pretend to have discovered what this music is about. I suspect that it is only about a system of organization. And if this is so, then it is not music at all but only a laboratory notebook for acoustical experiments.[41]

Stravinsky was "intrigued by the arrogance of the music," Craft observed. That same year Stravinsky and Boulez first met at a party in Virgil Thompson's apartment in New York.[42] In 1956, when Stravinsky was recovering in Munich from his serious stroke, Boulez, Luigi Nono, and Karlheinz Stockhausen all visited Stravinsky in the hospital. When Boulez came to Los Angeles to conduct *Le Marteau sans maître* in 1957 he spent considerable time with Stravinsky.[43] Morton wrote about that visit, and their relationship:

> This was . . . the first time they had an opportunity for a thorough exchange of views—though one can be quite sure that the Boulez view of music was more exchanged than the Stravinsky. In many ways, the relationship of Boulez to Stravinsky was similar to that of Stravinsky to Debussy nearly a half-century earlier. In both cases, the younger composer acknowledged indebtedness to the older master while rejecting major masterpieces. Stravinsky has expressed his esteem for his young colleague in his books of conversations, and it is much to his credit that his judgement of Boulez's music was unaffected by the anti-Stravinsky demonstrations that Boulez had engineered in Paris in the years just after the war. Their friendship was to be clouded several times in the future. Stravinsky was to say privately some harsh things about the man, but he was to remain objective about the music. Though he had a genuine sympathy for the work of the younger generation, he did not view it uncritically. After Boulez's departure, he said, for

> instance, that he could not accept the serialization of dynamics and rhythm (which Boulez had himself abandoned by this time), and still later he said (and demonstrated) that the 12-tone method was far from exhausted in spite of the noisy declarations of the Darmstadt group.[44]

The New Grove Dictionary of Music and Musicians' article on the Domaine Musical concerts states, "It was largely to correct the balance in the presentation of new music in Paris (Stravinsky and his epigones were still favored) that Boulez founded the *Domaine Musical*" in 1954.[45] The first three seasons of these concerts juxtaposed old masters (Dufay, Bach, Gabrieli, Dowland) with twentieth-century classics and young composers, in much the way the Roof and MEC had but abandoned this practice in the 1957–1958 season. Stravinsky's music appeared with Webern's in a program conducted by Craft in November 1956, but thereafter Boulez, Karlheinz Stockhausen, Luciano Berio, and Luigi Nono, central members of the Darmstadt group and leaders of the new generation in Europe, were more interested in sweeping their elders aside and promoting their own adherents. Morton was won over to this avant-garde, partly because of Stravinsky's interest. There were eleven premieres of Boulez's works between 1952 and 1970 at Evenings on the Roof and Monday Evening Concerts; the ten after *Polyphonie X* were presented by Morton, who asked Boulez to write *Éclat* for Monday Evening Concerts.

In the mid-1950s Robert Craft made regular visits to the Viennese music publisher of the avant-garde, Universal Edition, and obtained new scores he was interested in performing at Monday Evening Concerts. Stockhausen's 1958 visit upon the occasion of the American premiere of his *Zeitmasse* (prepared by Craft) made a strong impression in Los Angeles. Albert Goldberg took the trouble to interview him and reported that he was tall, fit, and athletic. "He does not have the 'beat' look, his clothes are not rumpled, his blond hair is neatly combed. He speaks idiomatic American English with very little accent and he has a sense of fun. But he is most characteristic when he talks of his work; then his wide, brown eyes flash, he becomes intensely serious, and a torrent of ideas pours from his agile mind with the conviction of a visionary." Stockhausen commented to Goldberg on the enmity he was encountering over his electronic music, which "refuses the dictatorship of material and the dictatorship of money." Goldberg quoted him further: "We must consider that we are all people of the same world and have to live together, participating in the eternal creative process. In the United States people have lost completely this sense of creativity. . . . If [critics] like you have any function it should be to fight against the resistance of society. . . . One word can destroy a whole life. Your position should be to save young life, not to kill babies when they are born."[46] Clearly Stockhausen had a chip on his shoulder in 1958. Craft wrote that same year that the musicians he rehearsed in *Zeitmasse* were "less than wildly enthusiastic about the music at first sight, and even at fifteenth sight they were inclined to invent 'lazy dogmas of impossibility'. . . . However, the performers now feel that [*Zeitmasse* and Boulez's *Marteau*] are perfectly imagined for their instruments. In fact the instruments have been used so well and to such an effect as to cause every player to regret not having more to play."[47]

The 1960 visit of Luciano Berio and Cathy Berberian, with the flutist Severino Gazzelloni, charmed everyone; of his generation it was Berio who developed the closest relationship with America in the 1960s. In his letters to Paris Leonard Stein described the three to Morton, focusing first on Luciano:

> quiet but enthusiastic, with a quick and generous response to people and nature; Cathy—a more extrovert American of Armenian extraction, warm-hearted, bound up in all her husband's interests but critical where it helped (speech, etc.); Gazzelloni—I only wish all musicians were as generous, with a quiet Roman distinction but loving every moment and simple things—children, pretty girls, automobiles, etc. The response to them was terrific . . . I feel I made some true and lasting friends. . . . For a climax a visit to Stravinsky the last evening, from whence we all departed really crocked.[48]

Berio felt that he and his generation had been robbed by fascism of much musical experience. His first hearing of works of Schoenberg,

Stravinsky, and Milhaud in 1945 (when he was twenty) had an incredible impact upon him. It was not until 1951–1952, the year he first came to the United States, that he began to understand his own position historically and socially.[49] Paul Fromm met Berio at Tanglewood the summer of 1960 and gave the composer his first commission, which resulted in the very successful e. e. cummings settings for Cathy Berberian, *Circles.* Although the couple was equally at home in America and Europe, Berberian wrote to Morton, whom she addressed as "Carissimo Lorenzo il Magnifico" after their MEC performance in 1962 of *Circles,* "the kind of music we do has a wide public in Europe, whereas in America it's regarded as a curiosity."[50]

American composers felt the strength (in many ways, the threat) of their European colleagues' determination to command their own musical position. In 1957, soon after Boulez's visit, Lukas Foss, who participated in the European revelations in MEC, became an adventurer in non-jazz improvisation to free himself and his students from the tyranny of the printed note, "long before the word aleatoric even existed." But, he admitted later, "you improvise what you know, you don't improvise what you don't know." The experiments in improvisation changed his vocabulary and resulted in *Time Cycle* (1960), but he rejected methods of chance to suffer for three years in the labyrinths of serialism while writing *Echoi* (a Fromm commission completed in 1962).[51]

During his ordeal with *Echoi,* Foss remembered John Cage remarking, "I don't suffer when I compose."[52] By 1959 Cage was recognized as "the one here and abroad who stirs up music most," in Yates's words.[53] Lawrence Morton considered Cage less important than the Europeans;[54] yet he realized that Cage's growing influence among the European composers, and Stockhausen's and Boulez's recognition of this, meant that MEC must program his work. He fiercely resisted Yates's suggestions to put Cage and his followers in the repertoire until 1961, when he wrote Cage that "We have always been first in this community in the presentation of new music."[55]

In this period competition became more and more bitter among composers in the United States for the small amount of funds for their work. The composer Seymour Shifrin, thanking Morton for his courteous help, wrote, "I regret sounding soupy but I am afraid you are a man who is strangely out of touch with the prevailing style of dealing with composers."[56] Leon Kirchner admitted about composers that "we Americans treat each other rather shabbily and therefore deserve the contempt of our European colleagues."[57] By 1960, as each composer developed his own language, the solidarity between the Europeans was unraveling as well, but because government subsidies promoted the performance of their music this was not so evident to Americans. While in Germany in 1959, Morton heard rumors that Stockhausen and Boulez had become rivals.[58] Luigi Nono, committed to socialism and not interested in his music being packaged, labeled, or sold, wrote to Morton in 1960 that the Stravinsky-Boulez-Stockhausen circle no longer interested him "because such supermarkets are entirely foreign to me."[59] In 1961 Morton shared his thoughts with Leonard Stein (who was at the time in Europe) on the European versus the American scenes in music:

> I go along with your observations about the difference between the dog-eat-dog attitude of American musicians and the let's-cooperate-for-God's-sake-or-we-all-go-down-the-drain attitude of the Europeans. I suppose one must make a choice since there is no alternative. But both, I think, are withering effects on The Art of Music. We had that European attitude here during the days of *Modern Music* magazine—the mutual back-scratching of, for example, such aesthetic opposites as Aaron Copland and Jerome Moross! Aaron, the professional do-gooder of American music, is responsible for the huge growth of professional composition—inevitably it turns out to be mediocre. Paul Rosenfeld made a career out of promoting second-raters and worse. Sure, Art needs fertilization (Encourage the Second-Rate, remember? [a reference to an article Arnold Schoenberg published in Los Angeles in 1940]) but I do wish there was something better than all this *merde* that is being spread around.[60]

At the same time, in a London interview, Stravinsky's close friend, and long-time devotee of Roof and Monday Evening Concerts, Aldous Huxley, expressed his concern about the turn of musical events:

> It seems to me that fully self-conscious and artistic music is [now] far remoter from popular music than Tallis was remote from "Greensleeves." It *was* remote from "Greensleeves," but not *nearly* as remote as Boulez, say, from *My Fair Lady,* and this doesn't seem to me to be at all a healthy situation—when you have an immense gap between the ordinary taste and the taste of the highly refined and educated. It is a fact: but is it a *desirable* fact? There just is *no communication.* . . . Now we have reached a point where we really don't accept any tradition without question and we run through an immense capital of artistic forms and are continually trying to amass new capital and exploit new forms, and so much of contemporary artistic effort is somehow *spent* in this *desperate* procedure of trying to find wholly novel methods of saying things. . . . This is particularly true of music I would say.[61]

In the later 1960s this separation widened. The early commissions by Paul Fromm (which Monday Evening Concerts programmed) had fostered the work of Ingolf Dahl, Irving Fine, Krenek, Berio, and Foss. In the mid-1960s Fromm's relationship with and help to the concerts intensified.[62] Annual Fromm concerts were high points of each season, as the extra funds allowed larger ensembles of performers to tackle premieres of newly commissioned, larger works. But looking back in 1975, Fromm reflected:

> Somehow in this century, communication between composers and audiences has broken down more than ever before. . . . For a while, especially around Princeton, there was an almost obsessive interest in the theoretical, scientific, and mathematical aspects of music. Many composers were writing highly cerebral music for a very small audience. . . . I have come to believe that music not meant to communicate some strong emotion is not viable and will not endure. . . . Too many composers in the recent past lost whatever audience they had because they concentrated too much on construction and too little on humanism. I'm afraid that the aridity of much of this music led to further alienation of listeners; . . . there was no emotion they could latch on to. I think this trend may have been associated with the fact that these days it's almost

> necessary for a young composer to start his career on the faculty of a college or university; that's the only way he can earn a steady income.[63]

William Kraft, an orchestral timpanist in his early career rather than an academic, had another way of viewing the audience's predicament:

> When total serialism began, you had a conscious effort to change the whole approach of composition. The total reaction against it was, of course, John Cage with his music of chance and indeterminacy. You have on one side total control, on the other side a relative lack of control. These were the extremes, and in between everything's up for grabs. . . . There are so many different ways of approaching music that the audience didn't have anything to hang onto—nothing to connect with. There was a time in the '50s and '60s when composers were even exploring one element at a time. A piece was made of nothing but crescendos; another of nothing but glissandos. Then you get the quotations: "Well, we'll put a little bit of Beethoven in here, a little Mahler—" A little of this and a little of that, and with all these things one eventually doesn't know what the hell music is about.[64]

Michael Tilson Thomas recalls the strain in the concerts when Morton, strongly influenced by Stravinsky's turn to serialism, became very involved with and frequently programmed the "totally serialized, hard-edged music" of the Darmstadt, Donaueschingen group of composers:

> That definitely caused a certain split in the musical community in Los Angeles. There were a lot of people who *did not* receive Boulez and Stockhausen with the same kind of open arms that Lawrence did, and felt that Lawrence was jumping on a certain kind of bandwagon, which was fashionable at that particular moment, but which didn't represent some of the deeper musical values that music should, or that American music should. . . . Stravinsky . . . used to say, "Nothing is as boring as the music of the recent past—or the assumptions of the recent past." So it was necessary,

I suppose, that some of the language of American neoclassicism, or free dissonant counterpoint of American music, was eclipsed for a while by this highly organized, systematized, and very well publicized music that came from Europe. It was a very strong propaganda movement. It advanced the cause of this music, that this was *the* serious direction in music. Now of course we've seen a lot of that music become itself the music of the recent past, and we know the cliches of that sort of music very well, and observe composers who were part of it trying to find their way out of it to something else. It's also much easier for us to look back and say, "Well the really good pieces were these three or four pieces, and the other ones were not so important." But I think that that was a tough thing for American music to live through, at that point, and it was very tough on the West Coast, because in a certain way it broke a tradition that had existed here. There was this tradition on the West Coast, and it was tied in with Stravinsky and neoclassicism, and with people like Lou Harrison, people like Bill Kraft; people who were just writing notes as they wanted to write them. Suddenly there was enormous pressure to write notes which were part of some vast complicated intellectual scheme, and which would take a very hard and tough position. It was considered retrogressive and not as serious—old-fashioned—to be writing music that worked well for the instrument, and that sounded mellifluous and that had a bit more heart to it, a bit more depth below the surface. I think it's sad that that happened, that that contact was broken.[65]

Tilson Thomas's teacher, Ingolf Dahl, was particularly resentful of the direction Morton and Monday Evening Concerts were taking. When Tilson Thomas himself became involved in performances of graphic music, Dahl sent his student "a bunch of squiggles and blotches" on a pieces of music paper, accompanied with a rubber eraser, a comb, and other objects. "It just arrived. He never spoke to me about it," remembers Tilson Thomas.[66] Dahl's stepson, Anthony Linick, corroborates Tilson Thomas's report of Dahl's anger but adds, "It wasn't just an unhappiness with European composers but with the attention paid to the trendy avant-garde of the time, regardless of nationality. . . . Rampaging avant-gardism brought him to the fury point. Some of this loathing succeeded in putting a strain on his friendship with Lawrence." Dahl exercised his right to boo at Monday Evening Concerts and congratulated Morton on his "public success." Linick cites further evidence of anger from Dahl's diaries:

> Ingolf was practicing his art in a world in which he felt out of place and uncomfortable. . . . "Anonymous soundwaves" from Poland were not among his favorite listening experiences. . . . [György] Ligeti was probably the avant garde composer he had the greatest praise for, but . . . [he described] a "godawful" happening by [Toshi] Ichiyanagi [thus]: . . . "all those barefoot mindless ones taking in anti-intellectual waves of bedlam." . . . In 1967 he chanced on an article in the *New York Times* that elicited his own opinion: . . . Boulez [was quoted as saying]: "I am not interested in how it sounds, I am only interested in how it was made." [Dahl responded in his diary:] "That should be *exactly* reversed! Who the hell cares how it was made? Except the 'non-musicians.' "[67]

Morton "was not content that music be just American" and had argued that point with Dahl since the 1940s. He quoted Stravinsky to make the point that "Modern music is what *interests* us." It was very important to Morton that "What is news in the musical world is to be found out at these concerts."[68] His philosophy in 1966, after many further adventures, was similar to his declaration of 1958:

> There's a lot of music going on that I don't happen to like; but I don't have to like it, I just have to see that it gets performed if it's representative of anything that is important in the world of music. I suppose if I were going to program only pieces I like I'd not be able to get more than two or three concerts a year.[69]

Lawrence Morton led Los Angeles' intelligentsia into the labyrinths of the newest developments in the world of concert music. But while doing so, in his pragmatic way he kept the welfare of the concerts high on his list of priorities:

I think it would be a loss . . . if we didn't continue to present the avant-garde music. This comes back to us as a great good in many ways. For instance, Boulez may be the most significant musician of this generation, among the people, say, around forty years old. . . . He had made three appearances for us before he had appeared anywhere else in the United States. It's very good for us to be in touch with composers of that sort because they propagandize for us in Europe and elsewhere in the United States, and if we have a certain prestige and importance, it is because of that. We presented for the first time in America such composers as Boulez, Stockhausen, Berio, and Nono—people of that sort. This is, I think, one of our unique contributions, together with the principle of associating them with the old music.[70]

Ten

MORE DISCOVERIES IN EARLY MUSIC 1954–1971

In 1953, propelled by new anthologies of musicological discoveries and more accessible collected works of early composers that stirred curiosity about music of the past, Robert Craft and Morton began investigations into music of the Renaissance and early Baroque periods. Their enterprising search further and further into the past became as important as the search for newest contemporary trends in Monday Evening Concerts. Morton excelled in the unique principle of associating newest discoveries in earlier music with those in twentieth-century music. His experience on the cutting edge into both the past and the future of music enabled him to keep his balance when criticism of the concerts grew turbulent. In the 1960s *Los Angeles Times* readers' responses to critic Albert Goldberg's opposition to MEC's programming of avant-garde serial music reached an overwhelming crescendo. The composers Eugene Zador, William Grant Still, David Tamkin, Alfred Sendrey, and Ivor Darreg; the cellist Gregor Piatigorsky; the violinist Joachim Chassman; the pianists Ethel Leginska and Gerhard Albersheim; the former critic (and Roof booster) Alfred Price Quinn—among others—sent their support for Goldberg's 16 June 1963 *Times* article, "The Music Critic Versus the Avant-Garde."[1] Lawrence Morton and Leonard Stein felt embattled, and Morton found it inspiring and heartening to read documents of the attack upon Claudio Monteverdi's modernity in the early 1600s. He wrote to Goldberg:

> Unfortunately, the partisanship of the rear-guard is a negative force—it wants to delay the future. The avant-garde characteristically pushes on, but it never seeks to exclude the past—Monteverdi called his new music "the second practice," intending it not to supplant the "first" but to exist alongside it, and Schoenberg taught his students not serial techniques but the forms and structures of Beethoven sonatas and quartets. . . . I would hate to contemplate a world without an avant-garde—a radical avant-garde. How dull it would be! Our world, happily, is not dull. As I contemplate, I can see very clearly from my minority view point what are the monuments of our time—and who are the pigeons.[2]

Peter Yates had maintained a proportion in programming of roughly one-third contemporary to two-thirds earlier music, with the year 1900 as an arbitrary dividing line between the categories. For Monday Evening Concerts, Morton kept this dividing line and proportion at first but, as a wider repertoire from the eighteenth and nineteenth centuries was programmed elsewhere in Los Angeles, he changed the proportion to half new, half old music. Then, as audiences' assimilation of contemporary styles accelerated, he changed his dividing line between old and new to 1914, and later to 1945. (With one exception: in 1966, when Monday Evening Concerts' dividing line had become 1945, the year of Webern's death, this composer's music was still considered "new" and unperformed elsewhere though it had become standard repertoire at MEC, and so Morton programmed Webern as a "new"—rather than "old"—composer.)[3]

While Morton had a strong affection for early music, his relationship to musicology was distant prior to 1954. As musicologist Otto Gombosi wrote in 1952, "Musical performance is still the most uncertain, the most controversial field of historical research."[4] Reviewing the work of Sol Babitz and Wesley Kuhnle in May 1952, Morton remarked that, in the general view of the time, musicology was seen as "an esoteric activity of queer persons who are moved more deeply by the appearance of a neume on vellum than by the sound of an orchestral tutti," and that the "dried up musicologist" had become a recognizable type. Remarks by J. A. Westrup, a scholar from Oxford University visiting the USC School of Music that spring, alerted him to the fact that musicologists were now advocating performance as a principal vindication of scholarly research; he nevertheless wrote of his shock at hearing Babitz's and Kuhnle's stylistic discoveries:

> Until you get used to it, mean-tone sounds out-of-tune. I am not yet used to it. . . .[Babitz's] short bow makes impossible the long sustained phrases of modern music, and a constant vibrato is impractical when the [eighteenth-century] instrument is supported by the collar-bone and the left hand without the help of chin pressure. Thus equipped, Messrs. Babitz and Kuhnle proceeded to play in a manner suited to their instruments and their repertoire, and to stir up, as they have before, some fairly violent arguments over their practices. . . . I still maintain, according to my nature, some skepticism.[5]

Morton confessed that he "became a musicologist through a stroke of fortune."[6] The stroke of fortune was his accession to the directorship of the concerts. As Los Angeles' growing concert activity in the 1950s made it necessary for MEC to abandon the classical and romantic periods, Morton became a musicologist looking for works of the early Baroque, then the Renaissance, and finally the Middle Ages. In many ways Morton was continuing in early music what Yates and Mullen had done by founding the concerts in the first place: he was filling a vacuum. Aldous Huxley, who had developed expertise in music of the late Renaissance, remarked in a 1956 article in *Esquire* that although space, time, all corners of every continent, and prehistoric civilizations had been explored, there had been a great failure to explore the history of music:

> Practically everybody likes music; but practically nobody has heard any music composed before 1680. Renaissance poetry, painting

> and sculpture have been studied in minutest detail, and the labors of five generations of scholars have been made available to the general public in hundreds of monographs, general histories, critical appreciations and guidebooks. But Renaissance music—an art which was fully the equal of Renaissance poetry, painting, and sculpture—has received relatively little attention from scholars and is almost unknown to the concert-going public. . . . How few people have heard, or even heard of, the music of Dufay and Josquin, of Ockeghem and Obrecht, of Ysaac and Wert and Marenzio, of Dunstable, Byrd and Victoria![7]

This statement had particular force in Los Angeles, Huxley's home at the time. When music prior to the eighteenth century was performed, Los Angeles music critics had little to say. Albert Goldberg's aversion to J.S. Bach is a case in point. When Morton and Craft began programming early Baroque music in the November 1953, Goldberg grumbled that "the Josquin, Isaac, and Gabrieli for four trombones was elementary contrapuntal lessons, interesting only to musicologists."[8] In 1955 at the Ojai Festival when he first heard Monteverdi's *Vespers* of 1610 and *Magnificat,* Goldberg was surprised at the public's "wholehearted response," for he found the music difficult to listen to and rated its "rigorous modal style . . . as nearly esoteric as Schoenberg."[9] Morton noted in the 1960s that young musicians were not generally accustomed to playing early music, and were often as reluctant to venture into this unknown territory as their predecessors had been to play contemporary music.[10]

Morton became convinced enough by his own studies and reading (and, perhaps, by listening to the New Friends of Old Music) to quarrel with the performance style of such stalwart performers as the violinist Eudice Shapiro and the violist Milton Thomas, both of whom offered important MEC programs of Baroque music. He realized they did not favor the new ideas about phrasing, embellishments, and other stylistic matters. "Our whole school of string playing descends from teachers such as Leopold Auer, and we'd like the violin always to sound the way Heifetz's sounds, for instance, and this is not the proper sound for music of the late baroque period," he said in 1966. He continued:

> This is one of the great performance problems all over the world in our time. Musicology has discovered much about the performance of Baroque music, but its application to performance is extremely difficult. . . . To get an old instrument [for example, the harpsichord] played authentically means that everyone in the ensemble has to have an old instrument played authentically; and, of course, we don't know exactly what authenticity is.[11]

On 24 Jan 1955 Alice Ehlers brought a chorus and her Baroque Ensemble of advanced student instrumentalists from USC to play a Carissimi oratorio and a Handel solo cantata. Ehlers's student Hans Lampl conducted and made the instrumental arrangements. On the same program Marilyn Horne sang a choral aria, "Wachet auf," by Franz Tunder. Authentic instruments—which most of her students did not own—were not so much Ehlers's concern as was the desire to unearth early music and get it played and heard. She brought to her students her early experience of study with the harpsichordist Wanda Landowska and the musicologist Curt Sachs in Berlin, her shared love for Bach with her close friend Albert Schweitzer, and her famous ability to achieve a singing legato on the harpsichord. The Biber violin sonatas she played for the Roof in 1947 were ones she had also performed in Europe with Paul Hindemith.[12] Morton later commented that the style of her students' performances of Biber was, to his mind, all wrong:

> The trombone played with vibrato, the strings all played with a vibrato; and you cannot get them to play a nonromantic kind of expressiveness. They think of expressiveness as being communicated by tone quality, whereas we, the people who are most active in preparing concerts, conceive of expressiveness as concerning such things as not only quality of tone but tempo, accentuation, articulation, and a drier kind of tone.[13]

In 1962 Malcolm Hamilton came to Los Angeles from the state of Washington to study with Madame Ehlers, bringing his own harpsichord. He soon became a strong and popular performer for Monday Evening Concerts, often playing with the cellist Laurence Lesser. He remembered that Morton, rather than retire to his impresario role, insisted upon points of style in early music with malleable young performers. By the late 1960s Hamilton objected to being told where to put his fingers, and for several years Morton stopped inviting him to perform.[14]

With his wealth of energy, ambition, and brilliance Robert Craft supplied many of the ideas for and performances of early music in the fifties. Morton commented,

> He had what I suppose I must now view as an inordinate number of appearances per season. But he did have repertoire ideas that were far more interesting than anyone else's, and there was no point in holding any of these ideas in reserve. . . . Bob Craft and I were having a sort of holiday with the music of Schütz, Bach, Monteverdi, some Gabrieli and other early Baroque, late Renaissance composers.[15]

Stravinsky's excitement upon hearing Monteverdi's *Il Combattimento di Tancredi e Clorinda* in 1953 must have spurred their enthusiasm. Morton remembered the inspiration of seeing Klemperer come to Roof concerts that featured the music of Beethoven, always with scores to study to satisfy his endless curiosity about Beethoven.[16] Stravinsky's similar—even broader—curiosity about early works demanded that he hear all Craft's rehearsals of early works (many of which took place at his home) as well as performances. His interest in early music, and his preference for having his works performed in combination with old, rather than new, music, must have been a spur to Craft's and Morton's explorations into the musical past.

One of Craft's projects was a series of sixteen Bach cantatas; another was the exploration of *Symphoniae sacrae* and the *Christmas Story* of Heinrich Schütz; he conducted and eventually recorded some sixty-five Gesualdo madrigals and motets. Other projects were groups of late Renaissance and early Baroque music for brass, the large Monteverdi works, Guillaume de Machaut's early fourteenth-century *Messe de Nôtre Dame,* performances with chorus of works by Thomas Tallis and François Couperin, and newly discovered works for winds by Haydn and Mozart. Of the many concerts he conducted, Craft's favorite programs were performances of the Schütz *Christmas Story* in December 1954, and the Monteverdi *Vespers* in October 1955. He felt the most successful of his and Morton's programs was the first MEC concert in September 1954, the memorial to Dylan Thomas that combined four trombones in music of Andrea Gabrieli, Purcell, Willaert, and Schütz with the first performance (possibly in three hundred years, Aldous Huxley surmised in a January 1956 article in *Esquire*) of Gesualdo madrigals, Bach's Cantata No. 106, and Stravinsky's *In Memoriam Dylan Thomas.*[17]

Craft and Morton worked closely together to find and edit for performance music not yet available in performing editions. In his Guggenheim application (1959), Morton said he was proud of "editing" old music; for him, editing did not mean preparation of scores from original manuscripts but rather prescription of performance styles appropriate to the period. He told the Guggenheim committee that while he claimed no academic background or standing, he had kept abreast of musicological studies.[18]

Because very few of Carlo Gesualdo's madrigals existed in modern reprints, Morton carried out a search for unsullied material through the mail with the help of the Music Division of the Library of Congress. From the library's copy of the Pavoni edition (1613) of Gesualdo's madrigals (actually published in score, rather than in the customary part-books), Assistant Reference Librarian William Lichtenwanger sent photostats, which Morton and Craft then transcribed for the singers from the original clefs. Aldous and Laura Huxley translated the texts for three of the four recordings Craft and the madrigal singers made of Gesualdo's works. The strangeness of the music, and the stir caused by Gesualdo's life history, were noted in an article in *Time* magazine (10 September 1956) that followed Huxley's brilliant article on Gesualdo in *Esquire.* In it Huxley traced similar essays in musical expressionism by Gesualdo's "advanced" contemporaries

Giaches Wert and Luzzasco Luzzaschi, and their effect upon the musical revolution of Claudio Monteverdi. He discussed Gesualdo's indifference to the poetical quality of his texts, in spite of his personal friendship with the poet Torquato Tasso, and his manipulation of texts to serve exaggerated expressive purposes.[19] Much of this material, including Gesualdo's increasing insanity, his daily submission to flagellation, and his remorse for the violent crimes of his youth—was presented in Huxley's "extraordinary" talk during the 17 October 1955 MEC program. (Morton reported that Huxley was making a collection of stories about composers who had killed their wives.)[20]

The following summer Morton traveled to Europe with the Stravinskys and Craft. It was Morton's first trip to Europe. When their boat landed in Naples, Eugene Berman and other friends of the Stravinskys met them and drove them to Gesualdo, where they explored the castle of the Gesualdo family. In the chapel they found a picture of Gesualdo with his uncle Carlo Borromeo (who became a cardinal and was canonized as a saint) appealing to the Virgin Mary for mercy for Gesualdo's crimes.

In November 1957 the Gesualdo Singers and Craft performed some Gesualdo motets found in Rome and transcribed by Ruth Adams, a Los Angeles early music performer and scholar.[21] Stravinsky became so interested in the music that he composed two voice parts for the lost ones in a Gesualdo seven-voice motet ("Illumina nos," from *Tres sacrae cantiones*). Subsequently he did the same for the bass line in two of Gesualdo's other motets from the same collection ("Da pacem Domine" and "Assumpta est Maria") and published the three in 1960 to celebrate the four hundredth anniversary of Gesualdo's birth. He celebrated the same anniversary by "recomposing" for instruments three of Gesualdo's madrigals and published them as his *Monumentum pro Gesualdo di Venosa ad CD annum,* which Balanchine subsequently choreographed. In the Stravinsky-Craft conversation book *Expositions and Developments,* Stravinsky calls Gesualdo "one of the most personal, and most original musicians ever born to my art (for Gesualdo is a natural, an involuntary composer)."[22]

The fusion of German and Italian, Renaissance and Baroque styles and attitudes in the music of the great seventeenth-century German composer Heinrich Schütz clearly fascinated Craft and Morton. The performance on 9 November 1953 of *Fili mi, Absalon,* with four trombones, was the beginning not only of Morton's "four-trombone period" but of an extended period of exploration of the works of Schütz. This investigation was given added impetus by Robert Craft's desire to record for Columbia Records an overview of Schütz's sacred works for voices and instruments: two of the *Cantiones sacrae* (1625), *Symphoniae sacrae* from the three volumes of these pieces (1629, 1647, 1650), and the last motet in the collection of Schütz's old age, *Geistliche Chormusik* (1648). The performers for this recording were all Monday Evening Concerts personnel, including (among others) Grace-Lynne Martin, soprano, Marilyn Horne, mezzo-soprano, Richard Robinson, tenor, Robert Oliver, bass; Sol Babitz, violin, Milton Thomas, viola, and Lloyd Ulyate, trombone. Morton himself played the harpsichord continuo part (and was haunted by a note he omitted in an exposed spot).[23]

Morton must have particularly enjoyed Schütz's writing for brass choir, an influence from Venetian antiphonal music, and mentioned in his liner notes for Craft's recording how Schütz deplored the tendency of the younger generation to bypass old contrapuntal techniques in haste to achieve quick and easy success with the newer Italian style.[24] He set about transcribing for trombones works of Andrea Gabrieli, Josquin, Isaac, and Willaert, which he found in such collections as Archibald T. Davison and Willi Apel's *Harvard Anthology of Music* (1947) and Arnold Schering's *Geschichte der Musik in Beispielen* (1931). He used these brass works in many programs.

In the matter of string performance of works by Schütz, Morton attempted to achieve the tension in sound on modern instruments that he imagined to have been intended on viols (of much less range), by substituting violas for violins so that there might be effort in bringing forth high notes. He found that this sound was good in Schütz's *Symphoniae sacrae,* but the color was not bright enough. "We never make the pretense that we are giving authentic performances," he said in 1966, "but we do try to make these performances *not* sound as though the music had been composed just a century ago."[25]

As Craft moved on to other interests, Morton continued exploring Schütz's works, prevailing upon other conductors (Michael Tilson Thomas, Harold Kjellberg, Owen Brady) and performers to present a very comprehensive Schütz repertoire to audiences between 1953 and 1971.

An enterprising soprano, Olive Mae Beach, had introduced arias of Claudio Monteverdi in Roof concerts in 1950 and 1951; Roger Wagner's madrigal group performed Monteverdi in 1951 and 1952; the full Wagner chorale performed Monteverdi's *Magnificat* for double chorus in 1952; Charles Hirt, with the USC Madrigal Singers, and Howard Swan with the Occidental College Alumni Chorus performed Monteverdi for Roof concerts in 1953. Monteverdi was a going concern in these concerts by 21 September 1953, when Stravinsky was inspired by Craft's performance of the dramatic madrigal *Il Combattimento di Tancredi e Clorinda* to compose and dedicate his *Shakespeare Songs* to Evenings on the Roof. This was not a staged performance. Lawrence Morton and Carol Rosenstiel played harpsichords; there was a string quartet plus double bass, and three singers.

The 1955 presentation of Monteverdi's *Vespers* of 1610 posed many challenges and problems. There was no satisfactory performing edition, so Morton and Craft made their own, based on the 1932 publication in the collected edition (not intended for performance use) by Gian Francesco Malipiero and the 1935 edition by Hans F. Redlich (published by Universal Edition in 1949) and with reference to two separate recordings made under Redlich's and Leo Schrade's direction. Morton never felt entirely secure about his arrangement of the work. "The moment you hear it in a performance you think of other ways that might possibly be better," he said in 1966.[26] He continued to follow scholarship on Monteverdi's *Vespers* and corresponded with the Monteverdi scholar Denis Stevens, who argued that only half of the total is liturgical music. Stevens paid Morton and Monday Evening Concerts a compliment when he wrote from England, 25 September 1961, that in his view California was way ahead of Europe as regards accuracy in performance.[27] The *Vespers* remained close to Morton's heart, and he picked its central jewel, the "Sonata sopra Sancta Maria," to grace his farewell MEC concert, conducted by

Michael Tilson Thomas in 1971. When Tilson Thomas returned in 1987 to conduct this piece again for Monday Evening Concerts' memorial to Morton, the carefully copied full score was still available, but Morton had discarded the individual parts, feeling that his work, which he considered questionable, should be superseded.

For Robert Craft's performance of Monteverdi's *Il Ballo dell' ingrate,* Morton simply used Malipiero's text. He remembered the bass Robert Oliver's performance in the role of Pluto as very exciting: "The voice is a real bass and it has gravel in it; it's not at all a voice for sentimental music, but for a very virile, muscular sort of music, and he sang this really magnificently." Both Oliver and Catherine Gayer (who sang the part of the Ungrateful Soul) moved away from Los Angeles to continue their careers, because while USC, UCLA, and Los Angeles City College had renowned opera workshops, and Lotte Lehmann held master classes each summer at the Music Academy of the West in nearby Santa Barbara, there was no full-scale opera company in Los Angeles to receive the extraordinary vocal talent the area produced.

When Ernst Krenek was given a complete program by the Fromm Music Foundation in January 1963, Morton asked him to combine his own works with selections from his 1936 adaptation of Monteverdi's *L'Incoronazione di Poppea.* Krenek conducted three instrumental sections and two dramatic scenes. Morton recalled, "It made a very good suite. I must say that all of us were rather surprised at how Viennese it sounded. . . . But . . . he is one of the great musical scholars; his work and his devotion to people like Monteverdi and some of the older composers is really profound."[28]

In 1955, when Craft and Morton presented Guillaume de Machaut's *Messe de Nôtre Dame,* they used the Machaut edition by Jacques Chailley, which transposed the work down so that it could be sung by mens'—instead of boys'—voices. Craft and Morton had doubts about this but swallowed them and used their imaginations in choosing instruments—English horn, bassoon, bass trumpet, and trombone—to double the voices. Pauline Alderman, head of the department of musicology at USC, gave a preview lecture on Machaut, his poetry, and his friendship with Chaucer. When, ten years later,

Pierre Boulez conducted a second performance of this Mass, for MEC's opening concert at the new Los Angeles County Art Museum, Morton reported,

> He was not really terribly eager to do the piece but he had done it in Europe in an unpublished edition by [Leo] Schrade, and there the original key was kept. . . . I don't know what instrumentation he used over there, but Boulez was quite content to do it with whatever arrangements we wanted to set up, so we did do it here with a different instrumentation altogether and returned it to the original key. I'm not sure that it was any better than our first performance in the wrong key and with different instruments. As a matter of fact, I don't suppose that one can say that there is any correct way of doing this music at all.[29]

The same could be said for the earliest of the early music Morton presented, Pérotin's *Sederunt principes,* a four-voice organum written at the end of the twelfth century. The work opened Morton's farewell concert on 3 May 1971 and was conducted by Michael Tilson Thomas, who had rather fancifully doubled the four male vocal parts with strings, woodwinds, brass, celeste, chimes, and organ. He took liberties with tempo and obtained great orchestral variety and color in the long melismas on single syllables by occasionally dropping the instruments and letting vocal timbre dominate, occasionally even omitting the voices and letting instruments take over. Morton proudly noted that "though none of us knows how it sounded in the twelfth century, it submits to several kinds of performance without any loss of greatness. This performance belongs entirely to Michael Tilson Thomas. My only part in it was to have copies xeroxed."[30]

For musicians like Tilson Thomas, Karl Kohn (who performed his instrumental arrangements of secular vocal works of Machaut, as well as little-known German works of the Renaissance and Baroque periods), Ernst Krenek, Leonard Stein, Craft, and others who performed pre-Classical music in Monday Evening Concerts, the purist authenticities of the early music revival that gained foothold in the 1970s acted as a deprivation. Since Peter Yates's time, the enchantment of these concerts for musicians had been the opportunity to be adventurous in many aspects of music, not merely in specialized corners. The continuum of music had been their playground, and in the 1970s that was to change. With recording companies dominating the field, early music became specialized. With specialization came specialized audiences, and the intellectual ambience of the concerts was drastically altered.

But Lawrence Morton had perhaps his greatest enjoyments as a musicologist. In this field he was a true amateur—with all the positive meaning of that word—as Peter Yates had been. Worldwide tours of such influential performer-musicologists as Gustav Leonhardt, David Munrow, Frans Brüggen, Jaap Schröder, Nikolaus Harnoncourt, Anner Bylsma, Ton Koopman, and others were yet to come when Morton retired from Monday Evening Concerts. Puzzling over the available musicologists' disagreements, transcribing photostats and microfilms, trying to obtain satisfactory antique colors from modern instruments, brooding over difficulties of balance, endlessly copying parts, were all activities of great joy for him. He had caught the wave Peter Yates—at *his* retirement from the concerts—had yearned to meet, the revival of "the older music," and felt that this aspect of Monday Evening Concerts was perhaps its most interesting.[31]

Eleven

MANAGEMENT STYLES IN THE "MECCA FOR MUSIC-MAKING"

THE FACT THAT (by rough count) over one thousand musicians performed in Monday Evening Concerts under Lawrence Morton, whereas about three hundred thirty took part in Evenings on the Roof under Peter Yates (and some fifty of those were new performers brought in by Morton and Craft in Yates's last years) speaks eloquently for the differences in philosophy between the two directors. It was the performers who provided the real energy of the concerts, and how to harness that energy was the question determining the styles of Yates and Morton in their roles as catalysts. Personality, influences, and background were important factors in their opposing styles of management. They were approximately the same age, but growth and changing times in Los Angeles thrust Yates and Morton into distinctly differing periods, requiring opposing attitudes toward management.

Yates's communal idea was to encourage risk and deviation through trust and confidence. He wrote in his first book, *An Amateur at the Keyboard,*

> A musician became a member [of Evenings on the Roof] by taking part in three concerts during two seasons, in any capacity,

> accompaniment, obbligato, as a member of a group, or solo. All were equal in duty and in opportunity; there were no exclusive soloists. As our membership increased to and beyond a hundred musicians, we had to give more concerts to fulfill our promises.[1]

Yates's defiance of box office considerations and uncompromising daring in programming was an idea related to Schoenberg's concept of the post–World War I Viennese Society for Private Performances. While Yates's concept, unlike Schoenberg's, did not prevent critics from examining the concerts, in other ways it did protect musicians and the music from potential hostility. "It was a musicians' performance for musicians, for musical people," said Sadye Moss about the Roof concerts.[2] Kurt Reher, one of the series' finest performers, recalled, "You didn't have to cater to the public. . . . That made it unique. I think that's why it succeeded."[3] His brother, Sven Reher, remembered "tremendous cooperation between management, composer, and performer . . . for the first 10 or 15 years."[4] At Yates's request the musicians learned repertoire they would not have otherwise tackled. They took on nonmusical responsibilities such as mailings and selling tickets. Mary-Jeannette Brown Selwyn testifies that musicians "were putting building blocks in their own careers. . . . Yes, [musicians] were involved in mailing and the chores that had to be done . . . because they believed in the thing itself."[5] "We really grew audiences," the violinist Eudice Shapiro remembers;

> From the very beginning they were all performances that were worthy, really worthy. . . . We were playing for ourselves. We wanted to grow, to try out different things. For studio musicians this was absolutely essential. We were in a darkened studio, playing "footballs"; here we had a chance to come out and be in front of the public, and to play music we loved playing. We knew we had a platform. [Los Angeles] was like a melting pot. So many composers came here to live. They were our friends. We played their music. We had the best of all worlds. We could try out a new piece with the composer coaching us. Then, if I wanted to play a Beethoven sonata, I knew I also had a platform for that. . . .

We were paid nothing. We did it because we loved doing it. It was the most prestigious group of concerts in the town. Everybody was clamoring to get on that. The Music Guild brought in visiting artists. This was *us*. This was *home*. We were playing for each other. . . . It was quite a different life. . . . Los Angeles was really a mecca for music-making.[6]

With the success of the concerts, and the long establishment of a sophisticated and expectant audience, Lawrence Morton faced a great personal challenge in the early fifties. There was, in his estimation, a turnover of 90 to 95 percent in the people involved in the concerts.[7] The change of name and altering loyalties among the musicians demanded all his courage and conviction—but he had developed these qualities in abundance. His aim at the end of the war (inspired by writers such as Dalton Trumbo and John Howard Lawson in the Fall 1943 Writers' Congress at UCLA) was to work with leaders of the musical community to question the basis of music, to find ways in which music could serve mankind for good, and to "seek unity of aim and effort . . . within the whole world of music."[8]

This grand concept was snuffed out in the McCarthy era. In 1949 Morton accompanied his friend the film composer David Raksin to the hearings of the House Un-American Activities Committee, by whom the film composer had been subpoenaed. Raksin recalls the ordeal:

I had been a member of the Communist Party for several years but had been asked to leave the Party because my questioning of their directives was considered disruptive. Tormented by the alternatives of remaining silent and thus terminating my employability, or "naming names," I had decided that the honorable course was to refuse to testify, and had sought reinforcement from friends whom I believed would support this position. To my surprise, I was asked several times why I was so determined to ruin my career, and even Lawrence advised me not to immolate myself. In desperation, I decided to pretend to cooperate with the Committee by naming people who had either been already named in the hearings or who were dead. I persisted in this course despite the counsel of my lawyer, who warned me the investigators would easily trip me up, and that for every refusal to identify a person known by the Committee to have been a member of the Party I would almost certainly get a year of jail time. After my testimony I was vilified by staunch leftists, but found some comfort in the statement of the writer Dalton Trumbo: "There were no villains, no heroes, only victims."[9]

Robert Craft remembers that Lawrence suffered and felt deeply involved with the terrible consequences of that time. "He wasn't questioned, but he did take sides among the musicians. It bothered him for many years. He was ostracized by some."[10]

After these searing experiences, Morton's work reflected the pragmatic in his character. In the early fifties, when he took over the concerts, his combative nature came to the fore and helped him establish himself. Raksin describes Morton as "self-invented." He had absolute conviction and was very opinionated. "Nobody can know as much as Lawrence pretended to know," said Raksin, "but it worked. He managed to navigate in very difficult waters."[11] Marilyn Stalvey, who worked for Stravinsky and Robert Craft from 1962 until the Stravinskys left Hollywood for New York in 1969, was a close friend of Morton's from 1958 and had worked for him as well. She knew the side of Morton that said, "I know what I want. So I'll do what I have to do to get it." And what Morton wanted was Stravinsky for Monday Evening Concerts. For that he was willing to weather difficulties with Craft, with whom he had a complex love-hate relationship. Vera Stravinsky was an important key to Stravinsky, and Marilyn Stalvey agrees with Craft that Morton found his way through her. "Lawrence was a man who loved a star," she remembered. "I don't mean movie stars, I mean musical stars. That impressed him, he loved it." Morton himself could be rude, but he could also be extraordinarily charming and showed great heart and kindness to those whom he cared about. Marilyn Stalvey once accused him of being a snob. He replied, with great emphasis, "I've worked all my *life* to become a snob!!"[12]

He was a difficult person to know well. He concealed much of himself, but it must be remembered that the prejudices of the time promoted concealment. His close friend Ingolf Dahl concealed for his lifetime the fact that his father was a prosperous German Jew and that his own name was Walter Ingolf Marcus. In accounts of his life he altered the date of his arrival in the United States to 1935, so that it would not appear that he was an émigré, like others, fleeing Hitler in 1939. He emphasized his Swedish heritage from his mother's family (the Dahls) and became a strong "Americanist" in his musical activities.

Lawrence Morton had many sides to his nature, and his friends agree that he was different with different people. Marilyn Stalvey says that he told her that he never liked contemporary music, a fact other friends and colleagues cannot agree to. Craft says Morton compartmentalized his life and relationships.[13] Colleagues who worked closely with him remember his ability to make each person seem to be the favorite, the only one; this naturally aroused jealousies as he gained the stature of a guru in music.

He was deeply sensitive yet "ashamed to be moved," in David Raksin's words. This is borne out in his undated speech against *espressivo* in music, to be found among the papers he saved. "Nowadays it is not the meek but the mathematical who have inherited the earth," he wrote. He favored the classical principles of restraint that "never demand that we, too, suffer with the composer." What he treasured about the art of Stravinsky was that it was "so civilized, so humane, so full of wit, and so profoundly touching in its avoidance of the merely domestic emotionalism of Central Europe."[14]

Although Anthony Linick, Ingolf Dahl's stepson, remembers Morton as an unknowable mandarin, perhaps his letters to Ingolf Dahl reveal the true Lawrence Morton. His affection and concern for both Ingolf ("Igu") and Etta ("Ettolf," when writing the two of them) is clear. He seeks advice from Dahl and confides to him his thoughts and opinions, many of them critical. Critical by nature, even when favorably impressed by a piece of music he mentions his "reservations." In a letter to Dahl dated 21 August 1964, he admits to cynicism since birth. His devotion to Monday Evening Concerts, the energy of his imagination in programming, and his desire for a "good show" for the audience—whether or not he liked the music, and particularly if he did not—are evident in his chronicles for Dahl's amusement and information. About Stravinsky's dedication to him of the *Eight Instrumental Miniatures* in April 1962, Morton immediately wrote Dahl that he was honored and grateful to be counted as a friend of Stravinsky's. But, he wondered, what made Stravinsky do this? He supposed the answer was that he had never asked Stravinsky for anything, not even a photo. Then he confessed to Dahl his embarrassment at being identified as Stravinsky's friend, which might condition the minds of reviewers of his unfinished book.[15]

As Peter Yates gradually withdrew himself from the concerts yet held on to his connection with them, Morton quarreled often with him. His devotion to the enterprise overcame his reluctance to work with Yates. The shadow lingered, however. He complained to the music historian Henry Leland Clarke as late as 1958, "I do wish E on the R would realize it is dead."[16] Yates established a series of radio programs in a loose format, called "Evenings on the Roof," on the new Los Angeles public station, KPFK-FM. In these he sometimes presented live keyboard music (often played by Mullen or Kuhnle) or held discussions with or about composers, along with recordings of their new works. His correspondnce with composers grew in depth and quantity. In June 1959 Elliott Carter wrote Yates (presumably for a broadcast) about his new Second String Quartet:

> Certainly my music has sought mainly two things—to deal with vertical and horizontal dimensions in a more varied way than is usually done. I try to find continuities that gain meaning, change and operate in time on a level of interest that is parallel to our present experience of living. . . . The other aspect is an attempt to use the performing situation, the instrument, its player and their combination of instruments as a means of individualization. . . . As I see it it is all about the problems, the pleasures, of human cooperation.[17]

Yates's continued activity in the name of Evenings on the Roof—after resigning from the concerts—irritated Lawrence Morton. His resentment resulted in a schism. Over the years, some adherents to the Roof versus others in the MEC camp prolonged a controversy that resembled the intellectual turf wars of Los Angeles disciples surrounding Stravinsky and Schoenberg in the forties. Morton's adherents looked down upon Yates for not being a certified professional musician, while his status as an amateur who had built a professional musical organization was Yates's great pride. On the other hand, Roof members saw the history of the original concerts being subsumed under the name of Monday Evening Concerts, with rare mention of Evenings on the Roof.

Yates's and Morton's attitudes toward the musicians' part in the organization was the major source of their divergence. Morton felt that

> The musicians themselves were withdrawing more and more from everything except their playing; of course to prepare a program is a lot of work and that's why they wouldn't show up at mailing sessions, for instance. They couldn't take time to sell tickets and so on; they were just busy getting the music ready. And this was proper; it was a normal development, I think. . . . The musicians themselves are not aware of, don't keep up with, new repertoire; they don't read catalogs, or magazines to see what's being played and what's being composed elsewhere. . . . The musicians were no longer operating, shall we say, as a cooperative; they *were* cooperative, but the organization was no longer a cooperative organization. The concerts were from this point managed entirely from the top; the musicians had no obligations whatsoever except to learn the pieces and perform them.[18]

Horn player James Decker remembered Morton being "way ahead of the time. . . . He had to talk to us like a Dutch uncle to convince us what we were looking at was music," he recalled.[19]

Morton frequently admitted that "at Monday Evenings and Ojai Festivals I played the part of a dictator!"[20] He spoke of Monday Evening Concerts somewhat as if he were chief of a Hollywood studio music department, where projects originated "in the front office."[21]

In his view, "Before anything else, Monday Evening Concerts is its repertoire."[22] It was no longer necessary to give performers a chance to play now that Los Angeles was burgeoning with musical activity.[23] If a performer canceled because of a studio commitment, Morton was very reluctant to hire him or her again.[24] Performers were still severely underpaid, as was Morton, yet continued their labor of love, for Morton earned their highest respect through the high level of quality in his programming and his ability to attract exciting new composers. The concerts remained the performers' strong priority. While by contract film musicians could not refuse calls from their studios and were on call any hour of the day and night the year around, many worked out special arrangements to honor their prior commitments to Monday Evening Concerts. (These were arranged far in advance of studio calls, which came at the last moment.) The pianist Ralph Grierson arranged never to play a studio call on the day of a concert, as the concert would be the culmination of a full day of rehearsal, and would demand his total concentration. The bassoonist Don Christlieb worked out a special arrangement with the 20th Century-Fox composer Alfred Newman (who liked to record at night because film producers would not be present): Christlieb was always let out of studio recordings for Monday Evening Concerts. This did not always work so well for other performers, and Robert Craft remembers,

> We were often obliged to find substitute players at the last minute and let them perform without rehearsal, and once or twice a program had to be changed because of a studio call. Why did the city's best players agree to work hard for a pittance? Because performance in the concerts carried prestige in a highly competitive scene, and because the players performed real music, as distinguished from film scores.[25]

"A whole coterie of people involved in the movie business made Monday Evening Concerts possible. It's really the foundation of Los Angeles musical life. It should never be underestimated," says the cellist Laurence Lesser.[26] Eudice Shapiro remembers the extraordinary opportunities Monday Evening Concerts presented:

> One of my big triumphs here was doing the whole D minor Bach unaccompanied Partita with the Chaconne—the whole thing—and the Bartók Solo Sonata in one program [27 March 1967]. Everyone went crazy! But where can you do a program like that, unless you do it in a place where you know the audience is there to receive what you have to give them, and they've come, not to criticize but to enjoy?[27]

Gregg Smith adds,

> Very famous composers came to these concerts, because they wanted to hear the music. You'd have some pretty high-powered audiences. They weren't enormous, but they were the crème de la crème. The music wasn't being played anywhere else in the United States, not even in New York, for that matter. Nothing like this. We really got our ears trained.[28]

Michael Tilson Thomas remembers the exuberance in the atmosphere:

> You had the feeling that this was an extension of the Society for Private Musical Performances that Schoenberg had run in Vienna, or evenings that one princess or another had put on when Stravinsky and Diaghilev were involved in their activities in Paris. . . . You felt, ah, *here* were people who were stretching the boundaries of music. . . . It was fascinating to hear a piece performed and then go out at intermission and have a chance to discuss it with Ingolf Dahl and Leonard Stein, Lawrence himself, and Boulez, if he were in town, and Bob Craft. Just terrific times. . . . Stravinsky was so alive, interested in the process of music-making, and so intrigued with both the old and the new music; every piece was a new adventure for him, and I think that spirit of being an explorer—even someone who was a master, as he was, having that

spirit, saying "I want to explore music, I want to know more about music"—I think that affected us all.[29]

Sadye Moss described seeing Stravinsky with Huxley at the concerts:

> Stravinsky would come almost to [Huxley's] waist. . . . It was very moving at intermission to see [Stravinsky] standing there, completely surrounded by students who would be asking him questions. He was very kind and disposed to talk with them and answer their questions. I don't think [Los Angeles], other than the awe in which we held him, was ever mindful of the great genius.[30]

Lawrence Morton had often criticized, in print and in speeches, Los Angeles' ignorance of the great who had lived and worked there. After Joseph Szigeti's death in 1973, he wrote a tribute in which he remembered the Los Angeles Philharmonic playing badly and being insolent in a rehearsal of the Berg Violin Concerto (January 1946) that Szigeti played under Klemperer, who had to chastise the orchestra.[31] In Monday Evening Concerts Morton worked hard to keep the great in mind. As he gathered accolades for the concerts from Stravinsky, Dallapiccola, Copland, Stockhausen, Carter, Berio, Boulez, and others he must have felt great satisfaction. The eloquent paragraph with which he concluded his entry in the 1984–85 edition of *Who's Who in America* might speak not only for him, but for hundreds of musicians who took part in both Yates's and Mullen's Evenings on the Roof and Morton's Monday Evening Concerts:

> To have lived one's life in music, and, through music, with the other arts and literature, is to have enjoyed the companionship of the best minds and noblest spirits that have justified mankind's existence on this earth.[32]

But the concerts could not survive on accolades alone. In his reorganization of the management of the concerts, Morton amalgamated what had formerly been the Musicians' Board (which, prior to 1954, had worked with Yates or Brown on programming and management policies) with the board of the Southern California Chamber Music Society (SCCMS) and relegated it to the background. While membership continued to consist of mostly musicians, a few non-musician members were brought onto the board in the 1960s as a means of broadening audience interest. Sadye Moss continued to provide an average of around two thousand dollars a year to make up the deficits of the concerts—except in emergencies, when this sum was increased—but she was not avid about fundraising, other than to write a yearly letter to the membership of SCCMS. In fact, the board was not organized to attract donors, long-time members Karl Kohn and Leonard Stein remember. Another board member (and a composer), Marshall Bialosky, felt that it was not a functioning board; matters of policy were not discussed openly and were a mystery to him. He remembered meeting once or twice a year to make suggestions about money problems.[33] Karl Kohn says that Morton consulted with individuals on the board and passed scores around among the musician members (most of whom were composers) for their opinions, but the last word was always Morton's.[34] Stein felt that the MEC series "fell behind in the sixties because it was a one-man organization, with devotion to particular people."[35]

This fundamental change to a one-man management continued after Lawrence Morton retired and Dorrance Stalvey became executive director of Monday Evening Concerts. Stalvey made important changes in two basic policies of the concerts, the programming of a combination of old and new music, and the predominant use of local performers. He writes,

> I attempted to continue the philosophies and policies of the concerts as they had been developed by Morton. The Board was emphatic that I not change a thing. Therefore, the first decade of my tenure was pretty much business as usual, regarding programming. As the eighties approached it became clear to me that musical life in Los Angeles was changing, and that these programming precepts were becoming increasingly less defensible. Concerts of

> early music were becoming more abundant and more focused on unbending concern for purity of reproduction; aficionados of this music became less tolerant of performances on anything other than replicas of period instruments. Therefore early music (pre-twentieth-century) claimed its niche on other museum series, and program repertoire became almost exclusively twentieth-century. As we approach the end of this millennium, the "classics" of this century have become the concerts' "early music" repertoire. Another change was the increased inclusion of touring ensembles, both foreign and U.S., as they are often more affordable than local musicians individually contracted for ensemble performance. Our audiences are now privileged to experience contemporary-music practices world-wide, without leaving Los Angeles, and at world-class performance levels.[36]

The Southern California Chamber Music Society, and its board under Sadye Moss, continued as the sponsoring organization. The board, now with Morton on it, continued to meet irregularly. While Stalvey found new sources of foundation grants, expenses for larger and larger ensembles—and particularly for theater works presented in the early 1980s—raised the concert deficits to alarming heights. Suddenly, when in 1984 the California Arts Council denied MEC a grant, the season was jeopardized by lack of funds and MEC incurred a $12,000 debt. This was more of a subsidy than Mrs. Moss would bear, and the board discussed ending the concerts.[37] The museum's proposed solution was to assume the debt and take the Monday Evening Concerts into its music department, which would mean the end of the Southern California Chamber Music Society and the independence of the concerts. The board felt it had not been informed about the extent or handling of the debt. Further, members were disgruntled that they had not been consulted about programming and the concentration on new music. In a bitter echo of past history, Lawrence Morton proposed that the museum, or any other organization, be enjoined from appropriating the name Monday Evening Concerts. Alternatively, the board attempted, unsuccessfully, to maintain its status as a governing entity for Monday Evening Concerts within a museum music council. One of the musician members of the board, not informed of an important meeting between the board and museum administration, resigned during the altercations, protesting that matters were proceeding on a unilateral basis, and relations between Stalvey and the board deteriorated. In February 1985 the board was sent a purchase agreement (which would assume the $12,000 debt) and dissolution papers from the museum's attorneys. On behalf of the board, Mrs. Moss wrote a letter to Earl A. Powell, III, director of the Los Angeles County Museum of Art, pointing out that a unique and critical feature of the organization of MEC was the board, the functions of which were to advise, consult with, and support the concerts' director in artistic goals and purposes, and that no move had been made by the museum to propose an advisory MEC committee within a music council.[38] Powell replied with dismay at the misunderstandings that had arisen, for the museum had taken on the debt, continued the concerts under their name, but had never mentioned any intention of establishing a music council. Rather he had left it to Dorrance Stalvey to call together any such advisory group. Since the board had not yet signed the documents, the only alternative for the museum would be to recover the funds it had paid to cover the debt.[39] By now the board members were in deeply painful despair. The title had already been appropriated, and so by 31 July 1985 the papers (with certain phrases regarding the Southern California Chamber Music Society stricken out by the board in resentment) were signed, and the name, Monday Evening Concerts, belonged to the Los Angeles County Museum of Art.

The fact that there was deep acrimony in each of the changes of hand governing these concerts, accompanied by an abiding bitterness and sense of loss, testifies to the positive values of what was established by Evenings on the Roof and Monday Evening Concerts: the importance of the concerts in Los Angeles' cultural life; their contribution to the national and international reputation of the city; and the strongest evidence of Angelenos' passionate desires to aspire, to achieve, and to have these unique aspirations and achievements valued by the world. A lasting legacy still lives in distinctive concert program-building that links the past with the present in enlightening ways, spread worldwide by successful alumni of Yates's and Morton's phases in the directorship of the concerts.

In its third phase the concert series continues to present contemporary music, but what has been lost is a sense of community. Though a local group is presented as ensemble in residence in Monday Evening Concerts' seasonal offerings and from time to time other local performers appear, the series and its repertoire are no longer built on local talent. Instead there is a reversion to reliance on visiting groups—a principle Peter Yates abhorred and Lawrence Morton allowed only when it seemed financially or politically advantageous to do so. Now Dorrance Stalvey finds that the practice is financially necessary. But audience pride in the home-grown product has gathered elsewhere, around new music concerts played by members of the Los Angeles Philharmonic and the artist faculty and advanced student performers from the local California Institute of the Arts. Belief in the city's own rich and varied musical resources is still—as in Albert Goldberg's remarks from the mid-1950s quoted in the introduction to this book—the key to the building and maintenance of a living musical culture.

NOTES

INTRODUCTION

1. Susan Sontag, "Pilgrimage," *The New Yorker,* 21 December 1978, 39, 54.
2. Lawrence Weschler, *Seeing Is Forgetting the Name of What One Sees: A Life of Contemporary Artist Robert Irwin* (Berkeley: University of California Press, 1982), 12. See also Irving Blum, "At the Ferus Gallery," transcript of oral history, 1984; interviews by Joann Phillips and Lawrence Weschler, 1976–1979, Department of Special Collections, UCLA.
3. Leonard Stein, interview with the author, 7 July 1988, Santa Monica, Calif.
4. See Catherine Parsons Smith and Cynthia S. Richardson, *Mary Carr Moore, American Composer* (Ann Arbor: University of Michigan Press, 1987), 175–85.
5. Newspaper review by Carl Bronson, no date [23 October 1925], in the Wesley Kuhnle repository, Special Collections, California State University, Long Beach (hereafter, Kuhnle repository, CSLB).
6. Patterson Greene, "Music Masters Give Modern Hearing," no date [22 October 1925], clipping in Kuhnle repository, CSLB.
7. Isabel Morse Jones, *Los Angeles Times,* 24 October 1925.
8. Gilbert Brown, *Los Angeles Record,* 23 October 1925.
9. Gottfried Reinhardt, "It Was No Paradise," in *Exiles in Paradise,* ed. Carol Merrill-Mirsky (Los Angeles: Los Angeles Philharmonic Association, 1991), 71.
10. On the Hollywood Front, *Modern Music* 14, no. 1 (1936): 48.
11. On the Hollywood Front, *Modern Music* 14, no. 2 (1937): 105–8.

12. On the Hollywood Front, *Modern Music* 14, no. 1 (1936): 47–48.
13. "Breaking into the Movies," *Modern Music* 14, no. 2 (1937): 84–86.
14. "Schoenberg, Mahler, and Others in Los Angeles," *Modern Music* 14, no. 4 (1937): 223–24.
15. On the Hollywood Front, *Modern Music* 15, no. 1 (1937): 48.
16. On the Hollywood Front, *Modern Music* 15, no. 3 (1938): 187–88.
17. Arnold Schoenberg, letter to Bessie Bartlett Fraenkel, 26 November 1935, quoted in Erwin Stein, ed., *Arnold Schoenberg Letters,* trans. Eithne Wilkins and Ernst Kaiser (Berkeley: University of California Press, 1987), 195–96.
18. The Sounding Board, *Los Angeles Times,* Sunday 31 May 1953. Italics added.

CHAPTER ONE

1. Lawrence Morton, "A Remembrance of Peter Yates," Monday Evening Concert Program Note, 4 April 1977, from the Morton collection in the Arnold Schoenberg Institute, University of Southern California. I am grateful to Leonard Stein, Director Emeritus of the Schoenberg Institute, for calling my attention to this collection.
2. During the 1930s Peter Yates wrote two plays, many philosophical essays, much poetry, and several children's stories; in the late 1940s and 1950s he worked on a novel. After the concert series began, most of his writing was channeled into program notes and magazine articles on music. In his lifetime he published two books on music, *An Amateur at the Keyboard* (New York: Pantheon, 1964) and *Twentieth Century Music* (New York: Pantheon, 1967), as well as a privately printed collection of poems, *A Smaller Poem Book* (Los Angeles: A Roof Publication, 1946). He became widely known as a music critic through his column and feature articles on music in the magazine *Arts and Architecture* (until January 1944, named *California Arts and Architecture*), which appeared monthly between 1940 and 1967; other articles on music appeared in the *New York Times Magazine, Saturday Review, Musical Digest, Arts in Society,* and *The Piano Quarterly.* His poems appeared in *Open Places, Arts in Society, Poetry Los Angeles I, Coastlines,* and *Prairie Schooner.* A posthumous collection of his poems, *The Garden Prospect,* edited by Peyton Houston, was privately printed by the Jargon Society in 1980.
3. Peter Yates, letter to Peyton Houston, 30 January 1934. I am deeply indebted to Frances Mullen Yates for her permission to quote from Yates's correspondence, articles, and oral history, and to Peyton Houston for releasing to me his rich correspondence from Yates. This correspondence can be found in mss. 14 of the Peter Yates collection, Mandeville Department of Special Collections, University Library, University of California, San Diego (hereafter Yates collection, UCSD). Since many letters from Yates to Houston were

very long, often written over a period of months, when necessary I include a postmark or second referential date if one is available.

4. Yates, letter to Houston, 14 September 1938.
5. Morton, "A Remembrance of Peter Yates," 4 April 1977.
6. Yates, excerpt from a poem sent in letter to Houston, n.d.; postmarked 29 October 1934.
7. Yates, Music, *Arts and Architecture,* April 1952.
8. Ibid., March 1946.
9. Yates, "The Los Angeles Musical Community Before 1930," unpublished article in Yates collection, UCSD.
10. Mullen's primary teacher in Los Angeles was Olga Steeb, an admired performer and principal teacher of two generations of southern California pianists.
11. Much material on Frances Mullen Yates (hereafter Mullen Yates) comes from a four-hour taped interview with the author, held in Buffalo, N.Y., 2 January 1988; a continuing correspondence provided many other details.
12. Dean Christian Gauss was overseeing a "rigorous procedure of intellectual and scholastic tightening," combined with "pushing a program of a lot of independent work" at Princeton, when Yates applied as a transfer student from Union College. He was accepted by Dean Gauss on the basis of a long poem he submitted (Houston, "Recollections of Peter Yates and the Genesis of 'Evenings on the Roof,' " letter to the author, 26 April 1988).
13. Yates, "A Column and a Roof," *Arts and Architecture,* December 1952.
14. Houston recalls: "It was as if each of us was an anvil [onto which] the other beat ideas into form, tested them, worked out the definition and expression" ("Recollections").
15. Mullen Yates, interview, 2 January 1988.
16. Houston, "Recollections." Houston adds, "He was always an excellent listener, and not merely to music."
17. Yates, letter to Houston, 22 October 1932.
18. Mullen Yates, interview, 2 January 1988; and Yates, letter to Houston, postmarked 15 April 1934.
19. Yates, letter to Houston, 6 November 1932.
20. Yates, letter to Houston, 3 January 1933.
21. Yates, letter to Houston, 30 January 1934.
22. Review by Bertha McCord Knisely in *Saturday Night,* n.d., copied in Yates, letter to Houston, 20 February–3 March 1934.
23. Yates, "Evenings on the Roof, 1939–1954," transcript of 1967 oral history interview by Adelaide Tusler, Department of Special Collections, University of California, Los Angeles, 1972:26. Permission to quote from this source is granted by the Department of Special Collections, University Research Library, University of California, Los Angeles.
24. Yates, letter to Houston, 10 March 1933.

25. Yates, letter to Houston, n.d., postmarked 15 April 1934.
26. Yates, letter to Houston, n.d., postmarked 29 April 1934.
27. Yates, letter to Houston, n.d., postmarked 27 December 1933.
28. Yates, letter to Houston, n.d., October 1933. A drawing of "monumental" Klemperer, surrounded by adoring females, tops the letter, with the note, "One's first impression of Klemperer, out of scale."
29. See Peter Heyworth, "Klemperer and the L.A. Philharmonic," in *Festival of Music Made in Los Angeles,* ed. Orrin Howard (Los Angeles: Los Angeles Philharmonic Association, 1981), 58–64.
30. Yates, letter to Houston, 18 September 1933.
31. Catherine Parsons Smith, talk on L. E. Behymer for the Music Library Association, 18 October 1991, Los Angeles, Calif. See also Howard Swan, *Music in the Southwest: 1825–1950* (San Marino, Calif.: Huntington Library, 1952).
32. See Swan, *Music in the Southwest,* 202, 211, 251–56.
33. Houston, interview with the author, 30 July 1988, Greenwich, Conn.
34. Swan, *Music in the Southwest,* 284.
35. Yates, letter to Houston, 1 October 1938.
36. Yates, letter to Houston, n.d., postmarked 9 January 1935.
37. Yates, letter to Houston, n.d., postmarked 11 June 1934.
38. Yates, letter to Houston, n.d., postmarked 21 July 1934.
39. Ibid.
40. Yates, letter to Houston, n.d., November 1933.
41. Yates, letter to Houston, n.d., postmarked 21 July 1934.
42. Yates eventually did meet Krishnamurti in the 1930s, spoke with him several times directly, went to his home, and continued to be inspired by him in the 1940s and 1950s.
43. Yates, letter to Houston, n.d., postmarked 21 July 1934.
44. Yates, letter to Houston, 9 January 1935.
45. Yates, letter to Houston, n.d., postmarked 16 April 1935.
46. Henry Cowell, letter to Wesley Kuhnle, 10 January 1924, Kuhnle repository, CSLB.
47. Information on Buhlig is not widely available. Most of these details are from Yates's column on the death of Richard Buhlig (*Arts and Architecture,* April 1952). Arnold Schoenberg kept the program of Buhlig's Berlin performance of his Three Piano Pieces, Op. 11, on 16 February 1912; it is in the Arnold Schoenberg Institute. Buhlig's interests were described in a letter from his friend Paul Sorel to Morton, 5 September 1986, in the Lawrence Morton collection, Department of Special Collections, University Research Library, University of California, Los Angeles (hereafter Morton collection, UCLA).
48. Yates, letter to Houston, n.d., postmarked 12 February 1935.
49. See Dorothy L. Crawford, "Peter Yates and the Performance of Schoenberg Chamber Music at 'Evenings on the Roof,'" *Journal of the Arnold Schoenberg Institute* 12, no. 2 (November 1989): 175–201.

50. Yates, oral history, 3, 6.
51. Swan, *Music in the Southwest,* 259.
52. Houston, "Recollections."
53. Eudice Shapiro, interview with the author, 28 June 1988, Studio City, Calif. This point of view was echoed in interviews with several musicians, among them Kalman Bloch, appointed principal clarinetist in the Los Angeles Philharmonic Orchestra by Klemperer in 1937.
54. Yates, letter to Houston, n.d., postmarked 2 January 1936.
55. Mullen Yates, letter to Houston, 26 March 1937.
56. Mullen Yates, letter to Houston, 26 March 1937.
57. Beyond Bartók's Sonata for Piano (1926), Schoenberg's Six Little Pieces for Piano, Op. 19, and Ives's *Concord* Sonata, she tackled Bartók's Sonata No. 2 for Violin and Piano, Franz Liszt's Legends, Beethoven's Bagatelles, Op. 126, and Piano Sonata, Op. 109, along with works by Busoni and Ernest Bloch.
58. Yates, letter to Houston, n.d., postmarked 8 December 1937.
59. Leonard Stein remembers that she later taught at the Eastman School of Music (Leonard Stein, interview with the author, 7 July 1988, Santa Monica, Calif.). Radiana Pazmor described her own voice as "a sort of mezzo-contralto but it is quite supple and I have a very good range, singing many songs in the mezzo-soprano tessitura" (Radiana Pazmor, letter to Charles Ives, 29 July 1933, Ives collection, Yale University). Her recording of Ives songs, on a CRI L.P. (S39OE), was still available in 1991.
60. Lou Harrison, interview with Vivian Perlis, 24 March 1970, Aptos, Calif., for oral history, American Music Project, School of Music, Yale University, New Haven.
61. Orline Burrow is remembered by both Leonard Stein and Mullen Yates as the most capable young Los Angeles violinist in the late 1930s.
62. Yates collection, UCSD.
63. Gerald Strang, interview with Vivian Perlis, March 1975, in oral history, American Music, Yale School of Music, Yale University. Rita Mead reports that Cowell sold the organization to Strang for one dollar (*Henry Cowell's New Music, 1925–1936* [Ann Arbor: UMI Research Press, 1981], 355). Radiana Pazmor, close to Cowell since childhood, reported to Yates in March 1938 that Cowell, when charged with a homosexual act with a minor, "confessed in detail against his lawyer's advice" (Yates, letter to Houston, n.d., postmarked 28 March 1938).
64. Yates, letter to Houston, n.d., February 1938.
65. Yates, letter to Houston, n.d., postmarked 4 March 1938.
66. Yates, "A Statement of Policy," *Arts and Architecture,* August 1950; emphasis added.
67. Carey McWilliams, *Southern California: An Island on the Land* (Santa Barbara: Peregrine Smith, 1973), 362.
68. Yates, oral history, 6.

69. Yates, ibid., 5–10.
70. In the summer of 1938 he began writing an antiwar play, titled *Invasion.*
71. Yates, letter to Houston, 7–28 August 1935.
72. Yates, letter to Houston, 17 November 1938.
73. Yates, letter to Houston, n.d., postmarked 21 July 1934. On 14 September 1938 Yates wrote to Houston, "I am too Communist for Mr. [Earl] Browder," head of the American Communist party.
74. Yates, letter to Houston, 1 October–3 November 1938.
75. Yates, letter to Houston, 14 September 1938.
76. Yates, letter to Houston, n.d., postmarked 28 March 1938.
77. Yates, letter to Houston, 14 September 1938.
78. Yates, letter to Houston, 4–13 March 1939.
79. Yates, letter to Houston, 26 January 1939.
80. Mullen Yates, interview, 2 January 1988.

CHAPTER TWO

1. Heyworth, "Klemperer and the Los Angeles Philharmonic," in *Music Made in Los Angeles,* 60.
2. Nicolas Slonimsky, *Perfect Pitch* (Oxford: Oxford University Press, 1989), 140–41.
3. Peter Yates copied his letter to Ives in a letter to Houston, 4 March 1938.
4. Yates, letter to Houston, 17–22 November 1938.
5. At the time Yates was the only member of the Busoni Society outside Philadelphia and New York. After a good deal of study, he opined that "Busoni seems never to have mastered the problem of a conclusion" (Yates, letter to Houston, 30 November–20 December 1938). He was also disappointed to find that Busoni's output of chamber music was small.
6. Yates, letter to Houston, 17–22 November 1938. Alice Ehlers taught at USC from 1941 to 1967.
7. Yates, letter to Houston, 1 October–3 November 1938. Throughout his fifteen years administering the concerts, Yates planned at least a year in advance and often, as in this case, further ahead.
8. Yates, letter to Houston, 26 January–14 February 1939. Gilman's quote is used, along with others from Olin Downes and Paul Rosenfeld, in the first announcement of the Roof concerts, sent in Yates's letter to Houston postmarked 3 March 1939. Yates was showing or suggesting Ives's music to orchestral conductors Oskar Seiling, Klemperer, Gastone Usigli (conductor of the local Federal Music Project Orchestra), choral conductor Hall Johnson, and alumnae of John Smallman's fine a cappella choir (Smallman, whose influence and national renown continued to reverberate in Los Angeles, had died tragically while conducting Handel's *Messiah* in 1937).

9. This relationship is more fully documented in Crawford, "Peter Yates and the Performance of Schoenberg Chamber Music at 'Evenings on the Roof.' "
10. Yates, letter to Houston, 14 September 1938.
11. Ibid.
12. Yates, letter to Houston, 4 March–13 March 1939.
13. Yates, letter to Houston, 28 May–23 June 1939.
14. Volya Cossack knew Prokofiev, who liked her performance of his works and wanted her to do his Fifth Piano Concerto in 1938 (Yates, letter to Houston, 4 March 1938).
15. Yates, "A Column and a Roof," *Arts and Architecture,* December 1952.
16. Yates, letter to Houston, 3 March 1939.
17. Yates, letter to Houston, 20 March–21 April 1939.
18. Houston, interview with the author, 30 July 1988, Greenwich, Conn.
19. Frances Mullen's practice in her performances in Roof concerts was to read from music (Yates, letter to Houston, 6 April 1939, sent after 23 July 1939).
20. Ibid.
21. Ibid.
22. Yates, letter to Houston, 28 August–6 September 1938.
23. Yates, oral history, 31.
24. The songs were an addition to the printed program announcement (which was sent out well in advance for the first six-month season). As in many of Yates's early programs, arrangements changed after programs were printed. For this all-Bartók program, "Radiana sang a book of songs that added to the pleasure and was repeated" (Yates, letter to Houston, n.d., postmarked 23 June 1939).
25. Ibid.
26. Yates, letter to Houston, 6 April 1939, sent after 23 July 1939.
27. Ibid.
28. Ibid.
29. Yates, oral history, 36.
30. Busoni program: Second Sonata for Violin and Piano in E Minor, Op. 36a; Sonatina for Piano No. 1; *Kultaselle* for violoncello and piano; Ten Variations on a Finnish Folksong; *Turandot's Frauengemach* (Intermezzo). The performers were Orline Burrow (violin), Frances Mullen and Volya Cossack (piano), and Annie Timmner (cello). The German pianist Michael Zador, founder of the Busoni Society, played as well, Yates said (Yates, oral history, 39).
31. Yates, letter to Houston, 7 August 1938, postmarked 17 August 1938. Houston was strongly opposed to Yates's pacifism. Perhaps through discussions with Krishnamurti on acceptance versus action—two values that Krishnamurti felt were opposed and could not be reconciled—and through his reading of Thoreau on civil disobedience, Yates eventually decided not to claim exemption from war duty as a conscientious objector (letters to Houston, 2 October 1939, 14 June 1940, 28 September 1940, and 6 February 1941).

32. Yates, letter to Houston, 24 August–2 October 1939.
33. Yates, letter to Houston, 2–8 March 1940.
34. Sven Reher, "We Must Go Farther Yet," transcript of oral history interview by Thomas Bertonneau, 1981, Department of Special Collections, University of California, Los Angeles, 180.
35. Ibid., 223, 367–68.
36. Kalman Bloch and Leonard Stein, interview with the author on "Backstage at Royce," broadcast for the University of California, Los Angeles, Center for the Performing Arts on KUSC-FM, Los Angeles, 8 July 1988.
37. Ibid.
38. Mullen Yates, interview, 2 January 1988, Buffalo, N.Y.
39. Yates, letter to Houston, 1–23 February 1940.
40. Dika Newlin, *Schoenberg Remembered: Diaries and Recollections 1938–76* (New York: Pendragon, 1980), 174–75.
41. Yates, letter to Houston, 8–20 October 1940.
42. Yates, letter to Houston, 18 June 1940, sent after 30 July 1940.
43. Paul Pisk remembered that Lucille Crews Marsh came as a divorcee from the Middle West to Redlands, had a fine home, and held regular chamber music sessions. She became friends with the music faculty of Redlands University and was on the Board of the Redlands Bowl (Pisk, letter to Lawrence Morton, 3 July 1986, Morton collection, UCLA). Yates knew her well and mentions her ventures as a Los Angeles playwright in his correspondence.
44. Yates, letter to Houston, 18 June 1940, sent after 30 July 1940.
45. Yates, oral history, 103.
46. Yates, letter to Houston, 30 November–20 December 1938.
47. 25 June 1939. In a letter to Morton, 10 July 1985, Anthony Linick (Dahl's stepson) reported references to Evenings on the Roof in Dahl's 1939–1940 diaries (Morton collection, UCLA).
48. Isabel Morse Jones, music critic, *Los Angeles Times,* 6 January 1942.
49. Yates, oral history, 56.
50. Yates, letter to Houston, 18 June 1940, sent after 30 July 1940.
51. Charles Ives, letter (dictated to his wife, Harmony) to Yates, 2 October 1939, in Yates collection, UCSD. Charles Ives's drafts of letters to Yates, in his own handwriting, are in the Ives collection, Yale University.
52. Ives, letter (dictated to Harmony) to Yates, 26 October, 1939, in Yates collection, UCSD.
53. Yates, letter to Houston, 8 October–10 November 1939.
54. Not the Fourth Violin Sonata, as printed in the program announcement. There were many changes between the printing of program announcements of Evenings on the Roof and the actual performances. Yates's contemporary correspondence with Houston is the most accurate record of what actually took place. Another source, contemporary newspaper announcements, has

also been consulted. I am grateful to William Russell, Professor Emeritus of Music, Pomona College, for his research in this field.

55. Yates, letter to Houston, 23 August–28 September 1940.
56. Yates, letter to Houston, 8 October–10 November 1940.
57. Ives, letter (dictated to Harmony) to Yates, 3 October 1940, Yates collection, UCSD.
58. *California Arts and Architecture,* November 1940.
59. Harmony Ives, letter to Yates, 29 November 1940, in Yates collection, UCSD.
60. *California Arts and Architecture,* November 1940; emphasis added.
61. The Iveses reported they had read the article wrong—or heard about the money wrong from a nephew (Harmony Ives, letter to Yates, 15 December 1940, in Yates collection, UCSD).
62. Yates, oral history, 76.
63. This radio performance in February 1940 preceded the first concert performance of the work by Louis Krasner and the Philadelphia Orchestra under Stokowski on 6 December 1940. A repeat of Swaby's and Mullen's performance of the second movement was scheduled for a Roof concert 8 June 1942 but was canceled by the violinist (Yates, letter to Houston, 15 January–18 February 1942). After this, family circumstances caused Helen Swaby to give up the violin.
64. See Crawford, "Peter Yates and the Performance of Schoenberg Chamber Music at 'Evenings on the Roof.' "
65. Helen Swaby Rice, interview with the author, 8 December 1988, Temple City, Calif.
66. Yates, letter to Houston, 8 October–10 November 1939.
67. *B'nai B'rith Messenger,* 12 September 1941.
68. *Los Angeles Times,* 24 November 1940.
69. Yates, letter to Houston, 27 November 1933.
70. Yates, letter to Houston, 23 August–23 September 1940.
71. Yates, letter to Houston, n.d., after 27 April 1941, postmarked 12 May 1941.
72. Publicity for the fourth season, January–June 1942.
73. Isabel Morse Jones, *Los Angeles Times,* 6 January 1942.
74. Bruno David Ussher, *Daily News,* 6 January 1942.
75. Yates, letter to Houston, 15 January–18 February 1942. As far as anyone knew, Kodály's cello sonata had had only one previous performance in America, in New York, by Raya Garbousova.
76. Ibid.
77. Yates, letter to Houston, 5 October–7 November 1941.
78. Lawrence Morton, "An Autobiographical Sketch," in *Tempo* 164 (March 1988): 29.
79. Morton, *Script,* 20 December 1941 and 31 January 1942. Morton's published articles may be found in the Morton collection, UCLA.

80. Morton, "Monday Evening Concerts," transcript of 1966 oral history interview by Adelaide Tusler, Department of Special Collections, University Research Library, University of California, Los Angeles, 1973, 14.
81. Yates, letter to Houston, 15 January, postmarked 18 February 1942.
82. Morton, *Script,* 29 August 1942.
83. Yates, letter to Houston, 5 August 1941.
84. Yates, letter to Houston, 16 February–4 May 1942.
85. Yates, letter to Houston, 27 January–18 May 1942.
86. Yates, letter to Houston, 8 May–17 July 1942.
87. Yates, letter to Houston, 5 October–7 November 1941.
88. Yates, letter to Houston, 9 February 1941.
89. Mullen Yates, interview with author, 2 January 1988.
90. Yates, letter to Houston, 23 November–10 December 1941.
91. Alan Citron, "S. California in WWI—Sleeping Giant Awakens," *Los Angeles Times,* 1 September 1989.
92. Yates, letter to Houston, 24 February–4 May 1942.
93. Yates, letter to Houston, 22 December 1941.
94. Yates, letter to Houston, 15 January–18 February 1942.
95. *Los Angeles Times,* 3 March 1942.
96. Morton, *Script,* 14 March 1942. The program: Roy Harris, Piano Sonata, Op. 1; Paul Creston, Viola Sonata; Busoni, Sonatina for Piano No. 1; Samuel Barber, Cello Sonata; Dahl's performances in Ives's Third Violin Sonata and a Beethoven trio were canceled.
97. Yates, letter to Houston, 24 February–4 May 1942.
98. Morton, *Script,* 28 March 1942.
99. Morton, *Script,* 6 June 1942.
100. Morton, *Script,* 20 June 1942.
101. Yates, letter to Houston, 11 April–1 June 1943.
102. Mullen Yates, interview, 2 January 1988.
103. Melissa Blake Levitzky, letter to Ann Yates, 24 February 1985, sent by Mullen Yates to Morton (Morton collection, UCLA).
104. Yates oral history, 81, and Wittgenstein ticket (Morton collection, UCLA).
105. Yates, from his poem, "The Squash," in *The Garden Prospect* (Charlotte, N.C.: The Jargon Society, 1980).
106. *B'nai B'rith Messenger,* 22 January 1943.
107. Ibid.
108. Yates, "Evenings on the Roof: Second Report," n.d., *California Arts and Architecture* before January 1943.
109. Isabel Morse Jones, *Los Angeles Times,* 20 January 1943.
110. Yates, letter to Houston, 11 October 1943–3 January 1944.
111. Virginia Majewski remembers always bringing a book to studio rehearsals, for the men resented "a girl" being principal violist, and no one but the

concertmaster and the contractor would speak to her on breaks (interview with the author, Los Angeles, February 1989).

112. After the war Gottlieb became principal cellist for RKO.

113. Yates, oral history, 107, and author's interview with Eudice Shapiro, 28 June 1988, Studio City, Calif.

114. Yates, letter to Houston, 15–22 February 1944.

115. Yates, letter to Houston, 27 January–18 March 1943.

116. Shibley Boyes, letter to the author, 2 June 1988.

117. Eula Beal began her musical education in her hometown, Riverside, Calif., and made her recital debut at age seventeen. Isabel Morse Jones compared her interpretations to those of Marian Anderson (*Los Angeles Times,* n.d., review of Roof program, 26 February 1946, which included Sibelius songs). Her New York debut with Shibley Boyes at Town Hall (in much of the repertoire they had performed at Roof programs) was acclaimed by the critics. Peter Yates reported that "she became a victim of too much touring for the Columbia Community Concerts. She decided that she would rather not be a professional musician than go on with that kind of thing" (Yates, oral history, 108).

118. Yates, oral history, 38.

119. Ibid., 124.

120. Yates, letter to Houston, 11 April–1 June 1943.

121. Yates, letter to Houston, 15–22 February 1944.

122. Yates, letters to Houston, 27 January–18 March 1943, and 11 April–1 June 1943.

123. Yates, oral history, 127.

124. Beethoven's complete piano sonatas had been presented in 1896 in Los Angeles, by a pianist from Boston named Carlyle Petersilea, in eleven recitals, according to Robert Stevenson, in "Los Angeles" *The New Grove Dictionary of American Music,* ed. H. Wiley Hitchcock and Stanley Sadie (New York: Macmillan, 1986), 3:109.

125. Yates, letters to Houston, 4–9 June 1944, and 12 January–2 February 1944.

126. Morton, *Script,* 22 January 1944, and oral history, 48–49.

127. Yates, letter to Houston, 12 January–2 February 1944.

128. With the brothers Alfred and Edgar Lustgarten, and Michael Perriere.

129. *Script,* 1 April 1944.

130. Yates, letter to Houston, 12 January–2 February 1944.

131. *Script,* 5 February 1944.

132. Yates, letter to Houston, 11–15 May 1944.

133. Quoted in Yates, *Evenings on the Roof: Fourth Report* (Los Angeles: Roof Publications, 1946), 15.

134. Ibid.

135. Yates, letter to Houston, 15–22 February 1944.

136. "The peculiarity of this disease is that while it is developing I cannot stop work," Yates wrote to Houston, 11–15 May 1944.
137. Yates, letter to Houston, 4–9 June 1944.
138. Ibid.
139. *Script,* 7 July 1945.
140. Yates, *Arts and Architecture,* May 1946.
141. *Script,* 6 January 1945.
142. Yates, oral history, 65–67.
143. *Script,* 6 January 1945.
144. Manuel Compinsky played weekly on the CBS radio network in Los Angeles with his pianist sister, Sara, and cellist brother, Alex, in the Compinsky Trio. Manuel became a steady member of the Roof group, performing frequently with Mullen. He conducted the Pacific Sinfonietta in *The Chinese Flute* by Ernst Toch, which was recorded and used in the film *Rashomon.* Alex Compinsky's recording company, named Alco, issued several Evenings on the Roof recordings.
145. In this season the following Ives and Schoenberg works were programmed:

Ives	Third and Fourth Sonatas for Violin and Piano; Twelve Songs; Piano Sonata No. 2 (*Concord*); two movements of the Second Sonata for Violin and Piano
Schoenberg	Six Little Piano Pieces, Op. 19; eight songs from *The Book of the Hanging Gardens,* Op. 15; the entire cycle *The Book of the Hanging Gardens;* Suite for Piano, Op. 25; *Pierrot lunaire;* Six Songs, Op. 6; four songs from Opp. 2 and 3.

146. Yates, oral history, 133.
147. Yates, letter to Houston, 12 January 1945.
148. Yates, letter to Houston, 5–7 October 1944.

CHAPTER THREE

1. A reader, who called himself "Old Timer" complained to *Script* when Morton "panned the pants off" of Stokowski's rule in the Hollywood Bowl (22 September 1945).
2. *Script,* 3 November 1945. Alfred Leonard, founder-manager of the Music Guild, took Morton to task in print over these remarks (*Script,* 1 December 1945).
3. Peter Yates, letter to Houston, 1–11 June 1945.
4. Yates, letters to Houston, 13–21 August 1945, and 20–30 November 1945.
5. This is Oscar Moss's first communication to Evenings on the Roof (Yates collection, UCSD).
6. Yates, letter to Houston, 9–15 May 1946.

7. *Script,* 3 November 1945. "The music is always clear and direct and communicative. . . . Given a chance to be heard, and honestly performed, it reaches out to all that is good in the human spirit. A comparable goodness is required of the performer, and Klemperer subscribes to that kind of musical morality."
8. Yates, letter to Houston, 4–8 February 1946.
9. Yates, letter to Houston, 26 June 1946.
10. Yates, letter to Houston, 9–15 May 1946.
11. *Script,* 6 July 1946.
12. Yates, letter to Houston, 9–15 May 1946. Dahl's *Allegro and Arioso* for wind quintet was written for bassoonist Adolph Weiss and his wind ensemble; *Six Variations on a Swedish Folk Tune* for unaccompanied flute was written for Leonard Posella. Both were prominent Philharmonic members who played for the Roof.
13. Yates, *Arts and Architecture,* February 1946.
14. Yates, letter to Houston, 1 January–27 March 1946.
15. Yates, oral history, 189.
16. Yates, letter to Houston, 21 January–18 March 1943.
17. Yates, letter to Houston, 27 May–12 June 1946.
18. Yates's *A Smaller Poem Book* was privately printed (as a Roof publication) and distributed in 1946.
19. Frances Mullen Yates, letter to Houston, 1–3 October 1945.
20. Yates, letter to Houston, 30–31 March 1947.
21. Yates, *Evenings on the Roof: Fourth Report* (Los Angeles: Roof Publications, 1946), 1.
22. Paul Henry Lang, *Saturday Review of Literature,* February 1947.
23. Lang, letter to Yates, 23 October 1947, Yates collection, UCSD.
24. Lawrence Morton, *Modern Music* 21, no. 4 (May–June 1944): 255.
25. *Los Angeles Times,* 1 June 1947.
26. Advertisement in the *Fourth Report* (1946).
27. Yates, oral history, 144.
28. See her autobiographical story, "Pilgrimage," *The New Yorker,* 21 December 1987, 38–54.
29. *Script,* 15 February 1947.
30. Doriot Anthony Dwyer, letter to the author, 18 January 1990.
31. Yates, letter to Houston, 11–17 June 1947.
32. Morton, oral history, 476.
33. Yates, oral history, 144.
34. *Los Angeles Times,* 1 June 1947.
35. Yates, letter to Houston, 21 September–6 October 1947.
36. Adolf Koldofsky (1905–1951), a chamber player, soloist, and conductor, came to Los Angeles from Vancouver in 1944. He commissioned Schoenberg's *Phantasy* for Violin and Piano, Op. 47 (1949), and premiered it on Schoen-

berg's seventy-fifth birthday, 13 September 1949, with Leonard Stein as pianist, for the Los Angeles chapter of the International Society for Contemporary Music. Gwendolyn Williams Koldofsky was a widely respected accompanist, who toured with Lotte Lehmann, among others, and became an important teacher on USC's music faculty.

37. Yates, letter to Houston, 3–5 December 1947.
38. Reher, interview with the author, 20 June 1988, Santa Barbara.
39. Yates, oral history, 149.
40. Strang, letter to Yates, 14 March 1948, Yates collection, UCSD.
41. Yates, oral history, 155–56. The exact date and program are not available.
42. Yates, letter to Houston, 25–26 May 1948.
43. Yates, oral history, 44–45.
44. Yates, letter to Houston, 21–25 November 1946.
45. Studio players could receive a guaranteed annual salary of $7,500, whereas Philharmonic players received only $2,000 for a twenty-week season (Morton, *Script,* 6 July 1946). Kurt and Sven Reher were among those who left the Philharmonic at this time.
46. *B'nai B'rith Messenger,* Friday, 25 April 1947.
47. Yates, oral history, 101–2.
48. *Musical Digest,* May 1948.
49. *Musical Digest,* August–September 1948.
50. The two articles in the *Saturday Review* were "Leverkühn and the Magician," 26 February 1949, and "Five Decades of Schönberg," 27 August 1949.
51. *Music of the West* 4, no. 2 (October 1948).
52. *Arts and Architecture,* May 1949.
53. Yates, letter to Houston, 19 November 1948.
54. Mary-Jeannette Brown Selwyn, "A Lapse of Musical Memory in Los Angeles," 5. This unpublished manuscript, written in February 1984 as a letter to the *Los Angeles Times* by the former executive secretary of Evenings on the Roof, was the document that jolted Lawrence Morton's conscience about neglecting the importance to Monday Evening Concerts of the heritage from Evenings on the Roof. In a sense, it began the process that led to the writing of this book.
55. Ibid., 4.
56. "Terms of Agreement Between Peter Yates and Members of Evenings on the Roof," March 1948, Yates collection, UCSD.
57. *Script,* October 1948.
58. Yates, oral history, 162.
59. Ibid., 163.
60. Ibid., 162.
61. Yates, letter to Houston, 21 June 1949. Her performance was broadcast and recorded. She now had domestic housekeeping help, and her youngest child had started school.

62. Yates, letter to Houston, 13 October 1948.
63. *Arts and Architecture,* December 1949.
64. Yates, letter to Serge Frank, 5 January 1950, Yates collection, UCSD.
65. Don Christlieb, letter to Morton, 6 March 1985, Morton collection, UCLA.
66. Some of the early members were (flute) Haakon Bergh, Arthur Gleghorn, Robert Armer; (oboe) Norman Benno, Gordon Pope, Ray Weaver; (clarinet) Gerald Caylor, Hugo Raimondi, Franklyn Stokes, Mitchell Lurie, William Ulyate; (bassoon) Don Christlieb, Ray Nowlin, Jack Marsh, Carl Jeschke; (horn) James Decker, Jack Cave, George Hyde, Wendell Hoss. Don Christlieb, Gerald Caylor, and Ray Nowlin first appeared on these concerts in 1946, to play Stravinsky's Octet.
67. Abraham Weiss, letter to Morton, 26 March 1985, Morton collection, UCLA.
68. Yates, letter to Charles and Harmony Ives, 20 Oct 49, Yates collection, UCSD.
69. Stein recalled that he broke company with Yates after the first two years of Evenings on the Roof. It seemed to him that Yates's attitude was that the program notes were uppermost, and that the music was programmed to prove his theories (interview with the author, 7 July 1988, Santa Monica). On another occasion, Stein admitted being envious of Yates's wide musical knowledge (broadcast interview with the author, "Backstage at Royce" KUSC-FM, 3 September 1988).
70. Roger Wagner, interview with the author, 5 January 1989, Santa Monica.
71. Marni Nixon, interview with the author, 30 December 1988, Santa Monica. She performed (and encored) the work again, with her husband, Ernest Gold, conducting, in the Schoenberg retrospective programs, 22 September 1952.
72. Yates, oral history, 180.
73. The Sounding Board, *Los Angeles Times,* 5 February 1951.
74. Morton, oral history, 132.
75. Prospectus for 1950–51 Roof season, Morton collection, UCLA.
76. *Time,* 8 October 1951, Morton collection, UCLA.
77. *The Music Review,* May 1951.
78. The transcribers were Ellis Kohs, Harold Byrns, Mario Castelnuovo-Tedesco, Edward Rebner, Lawrence Morton, Arthur Morton, Gilbert Grau, Don Christlieb, Adolph Weiss, George Hyde, Haakon Bergh, David Raksin, and Walter Sheets.
79. *Los Angeles Times,* 23 April 1952.
80. Yates, letter to Houston, 17 May 1952.
81. Yates, letter to Houston, 2–6 December, 1951.
82. Yates, letter to Houston, 18–25 January 1954.
83. Yates, letter to Houston, 15 July 1952.
84. Morton, letter to Ingolf Dahl, 21 August, 1952. I am indebted to Anthony Linick for a glimpse into these letters. Ingolf Dahl's letters to Morton were unfortunately unavailable for this study.

85. Yates, letter to Houston, 15 July 1952.
86. Musicians' Board to Yates, 12 July 1952, Yates collection, UCSD. The letter was signed by Victor Gottlieb, Doriot Anthony, Alexander Reisman, Shibley Boyes, Manuel Compinsky, Natalie Limonick, Kalman Bloch, Alice Mock, Zoltan Kurthy, and Muriel Maxwell.
87. Program prospectus for 1952–53 season, Evenings on the Roof, Morton collection, UCLA.
88. Morton, oral history, 140.
89. *Frontier,* January 1953. Lawrence Morton wrote for this monthly from April 1951 to March 1956, and occasionally thereafter until May 1958.
90. Yates, letter to Houston, 16 September 1952.
91. Yates, letter to Houston, 16 September 1952. See Crawford, "Peter Yates and the Performance of Schoenberg Chamber Music at 'Evenings on the Roof.' "
92. Robert Craft, letter to the author, 1 June 1989.
93. Yates, letter to Houston, 30 August 1952.
94. Yates, letter to Melissa Blake Levitzky, 4 November 1952, Yates collection, UCSD.
95. Yates oral history, 184, 189.
96. The serpent excited the interest of the film composer Bernard Herrmann, who used it in *The White Witch Doctor,* and Jerry Goldsmith, who used it in *Tora! Tora! Tora!,* both with Christlieb playing (Christlieb, *Remembrance of Lawrence Morton* [Los Angeles, 1988], 37–41).
97. Yates, letter to Houston, 17 May 1952.
98. Morton, letter to Dahl, 8 April 1953, in the possession of Anthony Linick.
99. Robert Craft, *Present Perspectives* (New York: Knopf, 1984), 252–53.
100. Albert Goldberg, The Sounding Board, *Los Angeles Times,* 31 May 1953.
101. Yates, letter to Albert Goldberg, 30 May 1953, Morton collection, UCLA.
102. Yates, letter to Melissa Blake Levitzky, 12 November 1953, Yates collection, UCSD.
103. Yates, oral history, 193–94.
104. Morton, oral history, 144. In his memoir Don Christlieb recounts the musicians' difficulty with Robert Craft, who insulted one of the most respected players in his first rehearsal with the woodwind group. When their tensions grew over time, the players went to Morton, who convinced them that the importance of Stravinsky's interest and involvement in the concerts outweighed their complaints (Christlieb, *Remembrance,* 13–14).
105. Yates, letter to Houston, 2–3 March 1954.
106. The Elliott Brothers' Band was organized by William Ulyate Elliott, one of the most talented and versatile of the fine wind players who played in the Roof and Monday Evening Concerts. He played clarinet and saxophone. His brother, Lloyd Ulyate Elliott, played trombone.
107. Craft, letter to the author, 1 June 1989.
108. Yates, letter to Cowell, n.d., Yates collection, UCSD.

109. Craft, letter to the author, 1 June 1989.
110. Yates, *Arts and Architecture,* April 1954.
111. Yates, letter to Houston, 3–5 February 1954.
112. Yates, letter to Houston, 24–25 January 1954.
113. Epic record, Fromm Foundation Composers Series.
114. Eudice Shapiro, interview with the author, 28 June 1988.
115. "History and Organizational Set-Up of 'Evenings on the Roof,' " outlined by Mary-Jeannette Brown in *Note* 4, no. 4 (1948), published for the Music Committee of the Los Angeles Junior Chamber of Commerce.
116. In the early years, particularly Ingolf Dahl, Adolf Weiss, Charles Wakefield Cadman, and Stravinsky. The list lengthened as years accumulated.
117. Dahl, letter to Yates, 14 August 1943, Yates collection, UCSD.
118. Wolfgang Edward Rebner, letter to Morton, 31 December 1983, Morton collection, UCLA.
119. Her emotional strength was again severely tested in December 1955, when her youngest son, John, was completely paralyzed by polio. Faced with his need, she gathered her steadfast courage, not flinching from her ministrations to John, who lived in an iron lung and died in 1962.
120. Yates, letter to Houston, 30–31 March 1955.
121. Yates, letter to Houston, 24–25 January 1954.
122. Yates, letter to Houston, 3–5 February 1954.

CHAPTER FOUR

1. Peter Yates, oral history, 42.
2. Ralph Hawkes, in *Béla Bartók: A Memorial Review* (New York: Boosey & Hawkes, 1950), 17.
3. Yates, *Evenings on the Roof: Fourth Report,* 3.
4. Yates, letter to Houston, 28 August 1938. The program is enclosed in Yates, letter to Houston, 1 October–3 November 1938.
5. Yates, letter to Houston, 20 March–15 April 1939.
6. Yates, letter to Houston, 29 May–14 June 1940.
7. Yates, letter to Houston, 12 November–9 December 1940.
8. Yates, pencil draft of "Bartók Plays," in letter to Houston, 23 November–10 December 1941. The article, only slightly altered, was published in the January 1942 issue.
9. Yates, *Arts and Architecture,* August 1953.
10. Yates, letter to Houston, 23 November–10 December 1941.
11. Joseph Szigeti, letter to Yates, (on tour) 28 January 1943, Yates collection, UCSD.
12. Yates, letter to Serge Frank, 1 March 1945, Yates collection, UCSD.
13. Yates, letter to Houston, 5 November 1945.

14. Yates, in his column Music, *Arts and Architecture,* April 1946.
15. Yates, letter to Houston, 20 August 1949.
16. Yates, *Twentieth-Century Music* (New York: Pantheon, 1967), 182.
17. Lawrence Morton, program note, Monday Evening Concerts (hereafter, MEC), 4 April 1977, Morton collection, UCLA. Between 1939 and 1954 and with many repeat performances Evenings on the Roof performed most of Bartók's chamber music, including all the string quartets except the first (Los Angeles or possibly West Coast premiere for the sixth); both violin sonatas; Rhapsody No. 2 for violin and piano; many of the Forty-Four Duos for violins; *Contrasts* for violin, clarinet, and piano (Los Angeles or West Coast premiere); Five Songs, Op. 16, and others. From the piano literature (most performed by Mullen) came the Piano Sonata; *Allegro barbaro;* much of *Mikrokosmos; For Children;* Rumanian Folk Dances (both the piano and violin-piano versions); Four Dirges; Suite, Op. 14 for piano; *Out of Doors;* Eight Improvisations on Hungarian Peasant Songs.
18. Between 1939–1954 Evenings on the Roof performed most of Schoenberg's chamber music (and repeated many of these works): the piano pieces Opp. 11, 19, 23, 33a & b, and Suite, Op. 25; the song cycle *The Book of the Hanging Gardens,* Op. 15 (five times), and songs (Opp. 2, 3, 6, 14, and 48); choral works Opp. 13, 27 (No. 3, *The New Classicism,* was given a world premiere); String Quartets Nos. 1, 2, and 4; *Pierrot lunaire* (four times); *Herzgewächse* (two times, the first a West Coast premiere); *Ode to Napoleon Buonaparte;* Wind Quintet (two times); *Verklärte Nacht;* String Trio, Op. 45; Serenade, Op. 24; Suite for Septet, Op. 29 (two times); Chamber Symphony No. 1; Violin Concerto, Op. 36 (world premiere of two movements); Cello Concerto after the Concerto for Harpsichord by Georg Mattias Monn (the concertos with piano reductions of orchestral score).
19. Yates, letter to Houston, n.d., postmarked 7 March 1934.
20. Yates, letter to Houston, 1 April 1935.
21. Yates, letter to Houston, n.d., postmarked 2 January 1936.
22. Yates, oral history, 66.
23. Yates, letter to Houston, postmarked 2 January 1936.
24. Yates, essay on Schoenberg, in letter to Houston, 29 December 1938–13 January 1939.
25. Yates, letter to Houston, 26 January–14 February 1939.
26. Yates, letter to Houston, 20 March–15 April 1939.
27. Yates, letter to Houston, 2–8 March 1940.
28. Yates, letter to Houston, 18 January–16 February 1940.
29. Yates, letter to Houston, 1–23 February 1940.
30. Yates, letter to Houston, 12 November–9 December 1940.
31. Yates, "Arnold Schoenberg: A note on the great composer as we await the recording of the *Pierrot lunaire,*" *California Arts and Architecture,* December 1940.

32. Yates, letter to Houston, 5–10 March 1948.
33. Yates, letter to Houston, 25 May 1948.
34. Yates, letter to Houston, 20–22 August 1949.
35. *New York Times* Magazine, 11 September 1949.
36. Arnold Schoenberg, letter to Yates, 16 September 1949, Yates collection, UCSD.
37. The recording was made through the generosity of the film composer Alfred Newman, who invited the Kolisch Quartet to record the Schoenberg quartets, sub rosa, at the United Artists' studio, during the period when Elizabeth Sprague Coolidge presented the Kolisch in four programs at UCLA's Royce Hall, in each of which a single Schoenberg quartet was combined with a Beethoven string quartet. The Schoenberg quartets recorded by the Kolisch Quartet have recently been reissued on an Archiphon compact disk.
38. Yates, letter to Houston, 15 July 1952.
39. Yates, letter to Houston, 16 September 1952.
40. Ibid. The performance was conducted by Robert Craft.
41. Yates, *Arts and Architecture,* January 1951.
42. Yates, *Arts and Architecture,* September 1952.
43. Yates, letter to Houston, 16 February 1961.
44. Yates, letter to Charles Ives, enclosed in letter to Houston, n.d. (April 1938).
45. In February 1944 Yates donated the scores and instrumental parts Ives sent him to the Los Angeles Central Library, except for the score of *Three Places in New England,* which Klemperer took on his first visit to the Roof and apparently never returned.
46. Yates did obtain scores from Strang and gave them to the Los Angeles Central Library in 1944.
47. Charles E. Ives, letter to Yates, 6 April 1938, copied in Yates letter to Houston, n.d. (April 1938).
48. Yates, letter to Houston, n.d., postmarked 28 March 1938.
49. Yates, letters to Houston, n.d., postmarked 16 July 1938 and 14 September 1938.
50. Yates, letter to Houston, 14 September 1938.
51. Yates, letter to Houston, n.d. (April 1938).
52. Yates, letter to Houston, 27 November 1938.
53. Yates, letter to Houston, 23 August–28 September 1940.
54. Houston, excerpt from "Concord: In Memory of C. I." published by Yates, in "Charles Ives—An American Composer," *Parnassus Poetry in Review* 3, no. 2 (Spring–Summer 1975): 318–28.
55. Yates, letter to Houston, n.d., postmarked 23 June 1939.

    A summary of performances of Ives's works on Evenings on the Roof, 1939–1954 includes Piano Sonata No. 2 (*Concord*) given its West Coast premiere and performed repeatedly (6–9 times) by Mullen; the four sonatas for violin and piano (West Coast premieres of movements from No. 2 and all of No. 3); West Coast premieres of String Quartet No. 2, *Aeschylus and Sophocles,* and *Hallowe'en;* many songs.

56. Yates, "Charles Ives," *California Arts and Architecture,* November 1940.
57. Yates, "For Charles Ives," in *A Smaller Poem Book,* 24, Morton collection, UCLA. The poem is copyrighted (1980) by Frances Mullen Yates and printed by permission.
58. Dorothy Norman, letter to Houston, 3 April 1941, Yates collection, UCSD.
59. Harmony Ives, letter to Yates, 12 August, no year, Yates collection, UCSD.
60. Yates, letter to Houston, 29 June 1941.
61. Yates, letter to Houston, 11 April–1 June 1943.
62. Lou Harrison, letter to Yates, n.d., Yates collection, UCSD. The date is probably late 1943 or early 1944, when Yates was preparing an article on Harrison, published February 1944 in *Arts and Architecture.*
63. Ibid.
64. Stuart Feder, *Charles Ives: "My Father's Song"* (New Haven: Yale University Press, 1992), 346.
65. Yates, letter to Houston, 5–7 October 1944.
66. H. H. Stuckenschmidt, *Arnold Schoenberg: His Life, World and Work,* trans. Humphrey Searle (New York: Schirmer Books, 1977), 440. Live Roof performances were broadcast at this time by Julius Toldi, an Austrian musician who organized regular broadcasts of contemporary music on KECA. In his oral history (153) Yates confirmed that *Pierrot* was broadcast a few days after the concert and mentioned other live broadcasts.
67. Yates, "Charles Ives—An American Composer," 323. In 1966 Yates stated that Sidney Cowell "said it was not possible that Ives could have come to that reception in 1933, so I have to take Schoenberg's memory against her denial" (Yates, oral history, 88).
68. Ives collection, Yale University.
69. Harmony Ives, letter to Gertrud Schoenberg, 25 November (no year), Arnold Schoenberg Institute, University of Southern California.
70. Harmony Ives, letter to Yates, 22 June 1946, Yates collection, UCSD.
71. Harmony Ives, letter to Yates, 13 April (no year, between 1946 and 1950), in Yates collection, UCSD.
72. Yates, letter to Houston, 12 November 1940.
73. Yates, letter to Houston, n.d. (November 1933).
74. Yates, letter to Houston, 9 January 1934.
75. Yates, letter to Houston, 12 November 1940.
76. Yates, "Twentieth-Century Symphonic Writing," *California Arts and Architecture,* June 1943.
77. Yates, letter to Houston, 11 May 1944.
78. Yates, letter to Houston, 9 May 1946.
79. Yates, letter to Houston, 17 December 1947.
80. Yates, letter to Houston, 17 May 1952.

81. Vera Stravinsky, *Dearest Bubushkin,* ed. Robert Craft, trans. Lucia Davidova (New York: Thames & Hudson, 1985), 144.
82. Leonard Stein, "Schoenberg and 'Kleine Modernsky,' " in *Confronting Stravinsky: Man, Musician, and Modernist,* ed. Jann Pasler (Berkeley: University of California Press, 1986), 315.
83. Morton, draft of section of his unfinished book on Stravinsky, Morton collection, UCLA.
84. Yates, letter to Houston, 17 February 1953.
85. Yates, letter to Houston, 3 February–3 March 1954.
86. Yates, letter to Houston, 23 June 1953.

A summary of performances at Evenings on the Roof of Stravinsky's works, 1939–1954, includes many performances by Babitz and Dahl, and, later, Craft: most of the works for violin, including *Duo concertant;* the Concerto in D for violin (with piano transcription of the orchestral score); Stravinsky's many transcriptions of his own works for violin and piano; most of the piano works, including *Piano-Rag-Music* (two performances), Tango, Concerto for Two Solo Pianos, Serenade in A, Piano Sonata, and Sonata for Two Pianos; also performed were *L'Histoire du soldat;* Three Pieces for String Quartet; Octet; Concertino for String Quartet; *Ragtime; Pribaoutki;* Cantata. The following received world premieres, Craft conducting: *Three Songs from William Shakespeare, Praeludium* for chamber orch., and Tango (1953 instrumentation). West Coast or Los Angeles premieres were given Three Pieces for Clarinet, *The Wedding* (version for 4 pianos and 6 percussionists), *Ebony Concerto, Elegy in Memory of Alphonse Onnou* for viola (or violin), *Renard,* and Septet (which received two performances).

87. Yates, letter to Houston, 24 January 1954.

CHAPTER FIVE

1. Peter Yates, letter to Houston, 15 November 1952.
2. Front page headline article, *Los Angeles Daily News,* 20 December 1937.
3. Yates, letter to Houston, 28 December 1937.
4. Yates, letter to Houston, 17 November 1938.
5. Yates, letters to Houston, 23 November 1941, and 12 November 1942.
6. Yates, letter to Houston, 11 October 1943–3 January 1944.
7. Ibid. Yates's first published book on music, *An Amateur at the Keyboard* (New York: Pantheon, 1964), reflects his exhaustive research into keyboard literature, as well as his very tangible enthusiasm and encouragement to the amateur to play (as he did) anything and everything, in privacy, without inhibition, but with full knowledge of the instruments and the periods being explored.

8. Yates dedicated *An Amateur at the Keyboard* to Kuhnle, who died before it was published.
9. 11 October 1927, in the Kuhnle repository, CSLB.
10. H.F. Peyser, *New York Telegram,* 11 October 1927, in Kuhnle repository, CSLB.
11. Clare G. Rayner, "The Wesley Kuhnle Repository at California State University, Long Beach," 21, Morton collection, UCLA. The fact is also stated in Pauline Alderman, *We Build a School of Music* (Los Angeles: University of Southern California, Alderman Book Committee, 1989), 190.
12. Harry Haskell, *The Early Music Revival: A History* (London: Thames & Hudson, 1988), 54.
13. *Principles of Extensions in Violin Fingering* (Philadelphia, 1947).
14. Sol Babitz, 1964 curriculum vitae, Sol Babitz collection, Music Library, University of California, Los Angeles (hereafter, Babitz collection, UCLA).
15. Joel Cohen and Herb Snitzer, *Reprise: The Extraordinary Revival of Early Music* (Boston: Little, Brown, 1985), 51.
16. Lawrence Morton, *Script,* October 1948.
17. Haskell, *The Early Music Revival,* 57.
18. Yates, letter to Houston, 17 March 1952.
19. *The Musical Quarterly* 38 (1952): 533–564.
20. Yates, letter to Virgil Thomson, 18 January 1950, Yates collection, UCSD.
21. Babitz, 23 February 1970 letter to members of his Early Music Laboratory apologizing for and withdrawing his publication, *The Great Baroque Hoax* (Los Angeles: Early Music Laboratory, 1970).
22. Yates, letter to Houston, 15 November 1952.
23. Babitz's subsequent article, "Identifying the Renaissance, Baroque, and Transition Violins," appeared in *The Strad* 15 (1965): 2.
24. Morton, correspondence with Sol and Mae Babitz, Morton collection, UCLA.
25. Babitz's personal papers, n.d., Babitz collection, UCLA.
26. Morton, *Script,* 4 December 1943.
27. Morton, note to Sol Babitz, July 1968, in Babitz collection, UCLA.
28. Yates, letter to Sol Babitz, 27 July 1970, Babitz collection, UCLA.
29. This material is derived from numerous documents in the Babitz collection, UCLA.
30. Yates, oral history, 165.
31. Yates, letter to Houston, 4 March 1938.
32. Yates, letter to Houston, 14 September 1938.
33. Frances Mullen Yates, letter to Morton, 27 October 1984, Morton collection, UCLA.
34. Yates, letter to Houston, 31 March 1940.

CHAPTER SIX

1. Vera Stravinsky, *Dearest Bubushkin,* ed. Robert Craft, trans. Lucia Davidova (New York: Thames & Hudson, 1985), 175. The letter is not dated but must have been written in late May or early June 1954.
2. Lawrence Morton, letter to Henry Leland Clarke, 25 November 1958. Morton collection, UCLA. Morton often kept carbon copies of his correspondence.
3. Morton, oral history, 89.
4. Morton, oral history, 119.
5. Ibid., 75–76, 79–80, 81, 115, 119, 140.
6. Ibid., 89.
7. Peter Yates, *Arts and Architecture,* October 1944.
8. Morton, *Script,* 4 March 1945. In this column he also argued against the appointments of the impresario L.E. Behymer, the conductor Alfred Wallenstein, and the composer Charles Wakefield Cadman to an advisory committee on music for the new Municipal Art Commission, to the exclusion of any composer who would represent progressive tendencies, or a representative from film and radio musicians, or a jazz musician.
9. Obituary for Morton, Burt Folkart, *Los Angeles Times,* 20 May 1987.
10. Morton, *Script,* 4 March 1944. In September 1944 the Musicians' Congress and UCLA co-sponsored a three-day conference, the Institute on Music in Contemporary Life, of which Morton (as chairman of the Musicians' Congress) was co-chair.
11. Morton, "Autobiographical Sketch" (1979), *Tempo* 164 (March 1988): 29.
12. Morton, letter to Marni Nixon, 28 July 1986, Morton collection, UCLA. In his 1959 application to the Guggenheim Foundation he reports having earned only $6,500 a year as theater organist, 1923–1928. He claimed to have earned $4,000 per year as arranger and composer for film and radio in Hollywood, 1940–1952.
13. Morton, "Stravinsky at Home," in *Confronting Stravinsky: Man, Musician, and Modernist,* ed. Jann Pasler (Berkeley: University of California Press, 1986), 332.
14. Morton, "Autobiographical Sketch," November 1978 talk for the School of Music, USC; in the Morton collection, UCLA.
15. A list of the publications in which Morton's writings appeared includes *Script,* 1940–1949; *Modern Music,* 1943–1946; *The Hollywood Quarterly* (later *Quarterly of Film, Radio & Television*), 1945–1950; *Notes,* 1948–1957; *The Musical Quarterly,* 1953–1958; *Ojai Festival Program Book,* 1948–1970; *Counterpoint* 1952–1953; *Film Music Notes,* 1948–1951; *Frontier,* 1951–1958; liner notes without signature for Alco, Crystal, and Capitol Records, and Columbia Masterworks, 1953–1959. In later years he contributed frequently to programs of the Los Angeles Philharmonic, the Coleman Chamber Concerts, and, of course, Monday Evening Concerts. Occasional articles appeared in *California Arts*

and Architecture, Sight and Sound, and *Tempo.* He contributed articles on Stravinsky to encyclopedias, symposia, and collections of essays on the composer.

16. Morton, foreword to *Film Composers in America,* compiled and edited by Clifford McCarty (Glendale, Calif.: Valentine, 1953), xiii.
17. Yates, *B'nai B'rith Messenger,* Friday, 18 April 1947.
18. Yates, *Arts and Architecture,* July 1954.
19. Burt Folkart, *Los Angeles Times,* 20 May 1987.
20. Morton, letters to Yates, 11 July and n.d. (1963), Yates collection, UCSD.
21. Robert Craft, letter to the author, 1 June 1989.
22. Michael Tilson Thomas, interview with the author, 1 July 1988, Laguna Beach, Calif.
23. Stravinsky program note for Columbia recording ML 6048, "Stravinsky conducts favorite short pieces" [1966 or 1967].
24. Pierre Boulez, interview with the author, 16 May 1989, Los Angeles.
25. Morton, "Autobiographical Sketch," 1978, Morton collection, UCLA.
26. Tilson Thomas, interview, 1 July 1988.
27. Morton, oral history, 27.
28. Morton, oral history, 148.
29. Yates, letter to Melissa Blake Levitzky, 24 May 1952, Yates collection, UCSD.
30. Morton, oral history, 160–65.
31. Oscar Moss, letter to Yates, 31 March 1954, Yates collection, UCSD.
32. Yates collection, UCSD.
33. Morton, correspondence with Yates, December 1953–April 1954, Yates collection, UCSD.
34. Morton, oral history, 161.
35. Morton, "Stravinsky at Home," in *Confronting Stravinsky,* 332. When patriots complained that Stravinsky had done violence to the anthem, Morton defended it in *Script,* 20 June 1942, with the sarcastic remark, "He is a very great musician—greater perhaps than Kate Smith," the country's favorite wartime interpreter of patriotic songs. In 1944, Boston banned Stravinsky's version, on the grounds he was "tampering with national property" (Eric Walter White, *Stravinsky: The Composer and His Works* [Berkeley: University of California Press, 1966], 547).
36. Robert Craft, "A Personal Preface," *The Score* 20 (June 1957): 12.
37. Morton, oral history, 168–69.
38. Albert Goldberg, *Los Angeles Times,* 21 September 1954.
39. Morton, oral history, 215.
40. Goldberg, *Los Angeles Times,* 21 September 1954.
41. Alma Gowdy, "Dylan Thomas Tribute Opens 'Monday' Series," *Los Angeles Herald Examiner,* 21 September 1954.
42. Morton, oral history, 169.

43. Marilyn Horne, radio interview with the author for "Backstage at Royce," for the University of California, Los Angeles, Center for the Performing Arts, on KUSC-FM, University of Southern California, 18 February 1988, Glendale, Calif.
44. Horne, letter to Morton, 24 February 1957, Morton collection, UCLA.
45. Horne, radio interview with the author, 18 February 1988.
46. Halsey Stevens, letter to Morton, 15 September 1954, in Morton collection, UCLA.
47. Morton, oral history, 173.
48. Morton, oral history, 174–76.
49. Morton, oral history, 177.
50. Horne, radio interview, 18 February 1988.
51. The hemiolas, switching from three- to two-beat rhythms, intrigued Stravinsky, as well as the "characterizations of the various participants in the drama, such as the four trombones for Herod" (Morton, oral history, 183–84). Stravinsky was flying to San Francisco to conduct *Petrushka* for a ballet company.
52. In 1991 Salamunovich was appointed a successor to his teacher and mentor, Roger Wagner, as conductor of the Los Angeles Master Chorale.
53. Morton, oral history, 197. Shortly afterward, the Monday Evening Concerts performers recorded them.
54. Marni Nixon, interview with the author, 30 December 1988, Santa Monica.
55. Morton, oral history, 194–95.
56. Luigi Dallapiccola, letters to Morton, 23 September 1954 and 30 September 1955, in Morton collection, UCLA.
57. Morton, oral history, 199.
58. Alexander Ringer, "Leon Kirchner," *The Musical Quarterly* 43, no. 1 (January 1957): 1.
59. In the early fifties Oscar Moss's underwriting amounted to $2,000–$3,000 annually (Oscar Moss, letter to Yates, 31 March 1954, Yates collection, UCSD).
60. Morton, oral history, 209, and "In Appreciation," memorial tribute to Oscar Moss in program for 3 October 1955, Morton collection, UCLA.
61. Stravinsky, letter for Emergency Committee for the Southern California Chamber Music Society, 24 August 1955, Morton collection, UCLA. Among the members of this committee were Artie Mason Carter, Ingolf Dahl, Mme. Alice Ehlers, Lukas Foss, Hugo Friedhofer, Ben Gould, Johnny Green, Ernst Krenek, David Raksin, Eudice Shapiro, Leonard Stein, Joseph Szigeti, John te Groen, and Peter Yates.
62. Sadye Moss's annual contribution of $2,000 remained constant until the dissolution of the Southern California Chamber Music Society in 1984.
63. Morton, oral history, 211.
64. *Aldous Huxley: A Memorial Volume,* ed. Julian Huxley (New York: Harper & Row, 1965), 36, 51–52, 61, 86.

65. From *Do What You Will,* quoted in Sybille Bedford, *Aldous Huxley* (New York: Harper & Row, 1974), 218.
66. Bedford, *Aldous Huxley,* 457.
67. *Aldous Huxley: A Memorial Volume,* 26.
68. Igor Stravinsky and Robert Craft, *Memories and Commentaries* (Berkeley: University of California Press, 1959), 154.
69. Horne, radio interview, 18 February 1988.
70. Goldberg, *Los Angeles Times,* 18 October 1955.
71. Bedford, *Aldous Huxley,* 587–88. Huxley subsequently wrote the liner notes for the first recording by Craft and the madrigal singers (who called themselves, for the recording, "The Singers of Ferrara"), by Sunset Records, 1956 (LP600). He published a long article on Gesualdo and the madrigals in *Esquire* magazine (January 1956).
72. Marilyn Horne (with Jane Scovell), *My Life* (New York: Atheneum, 1983), 86.
73. According to Craft's liner notes for Columbia LP ML 5341.
74. Grace-Lynne Martin, letter to Morton, 3 September 1985, Morton collection, UCLA.
75. *Time,* 10 September 1956.
76. André Previn, letter to Morton, 15 July 1984, Morton collection, UCLA.
77. Goldberg, *Los Angeles Times,* 18 October 1955.
78. *B'nai B'rith Messenger,* 28 October 1955.
79. Unsigned review, *Los Angeles Times,* 1 November 1955.
80. Leonard Stein, interview with the author, 7 July 1988, Santa Monica.
81. Morton, oral history, 223.
82. Morton, oral history, 227.
83. Morton, oral history, 230.
84. Goldberg, "Odd Piece Mystifies at Monday Concert," *Los Angeles Times,* 24 January 1956.
85. Craft, letter to the author, 1 June 1989.
86. Natalie Limonick, interview with the author, 12 May 1989, Los Angeles.
87. Morton, oral history, 232–33.
88. Goldberg, "Kontrapunkte No. 1 Fails to Impress," *Los Angeles Times,* 21 January 1956.
89. Craft, *Stravinsky: Chronicle of a Friendship, 1948–1971* (New York: Knopf, 1972), 48, 60, 65.
90. Boulez, interview with the author, 16 May 1989.
91. Patterson Greene, "Europe Rates L.A. as Music Center," *Los Angeles Herald Examiner,* Sunday, 21 October 1956.
92. Morton, oral history, 247–48.
93. Morton, oral history, 251–53.
94. Morton, oral history, 254.
95. Morton, oral history, 255–57.

96. Morton, MEC program note, 18 February 1957, Morton collection, UCLA.
97. Gregg Smith, interview with the author, 12 November 1987, Los Angeles.
98. Morton, oral history, 267–68.
99. Gregg Smith, interview with the author, 12 November 1987, Los Angeles.
100. C. Gayer, in Morton, "Boulez in Los Angeles: Recollections and Tributes," in conference booklet, *From Pierrot to Marteau,* ed. L. Stein (Arnold Schoenberg Institute, University of Southern California School of Music, 14–16 March 1987), 54.
101. William Kraft, in Morton, "Recollections of Boulez," 55.
102. William Kraft, interview with the author, 15 May 1988, Los Angeles.
103. Kraft, "Recollections of Boulez," 55.
104. Boulez, interview, 16 May 1989.
105. Morton, oral history, 272; and clippings, Morton collection, UCLA.
106. Morton, "Boulez in Los Angeles," 53.
107. Goldberg, "Strange Music Heard at Monday Concert," *Los Angeles Times,* 12 March 1957.
108. Morton, oral history, 281.
109. Morton, "Current Chronicle: Los Angeles," *The Musical Quarterly* 43, no. 4 (October 1957): 536.
110. Morton, oral history, 289.
111. Morton, oral history, 283.
112. Morton presented only one other work of Babbitt, the West Coast premiere of his Wind Quartet in 1960. In these years Babbitt, teaching at Princeton University, was a vastly influential force in East Coast music, but in a 1964 letter Morton asked Aaron Copland, "Do you know any new composers who don't have the Princeton Pox?" (Morton, letter to Aaron Copland, 16 March 1964, Morton collection, UCLA).
113. Copland, letter to Morton, 1 March 1957, Morton collection, UCLA. In this letter, Copland promised the premiere of the Piano Fantasy to MEC, but as the Dumbarton Oaks Foundation had commissioned the work, William Masselos gave the world premiere there, and this was the second performance.
114. Morton, letter to Copland, 13 January 1958, quoted in Copland and Vivian Perlis, *Copland Since 1943* (New York: St. Martin's Press, 1989), 246.
115. Morton, oral history, 289.
116. Ibid.
117. Gregg Smith, interview, 12 November 1987.
118. Nicolas Slonimsky, *Perfect Pitch* (New York: Oxford University Press, 1988), 140–41.
119. Morton, oral history, 293.
120. Morton, letter to Copland, 17 October 1958, in Morton collection, UCLA.
121. Morton, oral history, 295–96.
122. Goldberg, *Los Angeles Times,* 15 October 1958.

123. Morton, oral history, 296.
124. Morton, letter to Leonard Stein, 11 October 1958. I am indebted to Leonard Stein for providing access to this correspondence, which I read in the Arnold Schoenberg Institute, USC. Unfortunately, the present whereabouts of the correspondence is unknown.
125. Morton, oral history, 294.
126. Goldberg, *Los Angeles Times,* 3 December 1958.
127. Ernst Krenek, letter to Robert Craft, 14 February 1958, in Igor Stravinsky, *Selected Correspondence,* ed. R. Craft (New York: Knopf, 1984), 2:335.
128. Morton, oral history, 303.
129. Stein, letter to Morton, 24 July 1958, in Morton collection, UCLA.
130. Goldberg, *Los Angeles Times,* 14 December 1958.
131. Goldberg, *Los Angeles Times,* 21 January 1959.
132. Morton, oral history, 305.
133. 4 February 1959.
134. Morton, oral history, 311.
135. Paul Fromm, born in 1906 in Kitzingen, Bavaria, came to the United States in 1938. He started the Fromm Music Foundation in 1952; for many years he considered his commissioning "an extension of myself." In 1955 Aaron Copland involved him in the project that became Contemporary Music Week at Tanglewood. In 1972 he moved the foundation to Harvard University, so that his work would be carried on when he was no longer able to continue. In 1975, after a hiatus beginning with Lawrence Morton's retirement, he gave a Fromm Prize in Los Angeles, and the four finalists were honored by having their pieces played at a Monday Evening Concert at the Los Angeles County Museum. He recognized that "The Monday Evenings are the oldest contemporary music institution in the country. They were in existence long before similar groups were formed in other cities, and introduced the works of many young American composers, as well as by the masters like Schoenberg and Stravinsky" (Paul Fromm, 1975 interview in Deena Rosenberg and Bernard Rosenberg, *The Music Makers* [New York: Columbia University Press, 1979], 378–92). Fromm's first sponsorship for Monday Evening Concerts amounted to $500 (Morton, letter to Yates, 17 June 1958, Yates collection, UCSD). The last Fromm program at MEC, 27 April 1981, amounted to $5,000. Thereafter there were reduced general contributions, with $3,000 for the year 1984–85 the last recorded. Fromm died in 1987.
136. Krenek, letter to Robert Craft, 21 November 1957, in Stravinsky, *Selected Correspondence,* 2:329–31.
137. Yates, letter to John Cage, 22 May 1959, Cage archives, Northwestern University.
138. Nixon, interview, 30 December 1988.
139. "Season's Last Eve Concert Festive," *Los Angeles Times,* 23 March 1959.

140. Ibid.
141. Morton, letter Karl Kohn, 17 January 1959, Morton collection, UCLA.
142. Morton, oral history, 322.

CHAPTER SEVEN

1. Lawrence Morton, oral history, 237.
2. Albert Goldberg, *Los Angeles Times,* 7 October 1959.
3. Morton, oral history, 323.
4. Goldberg, *Los Angeles Times,* 21 October.
5. This work was performed by the clarinetist Kalman Bloch with Shapiro and Gottlieb on Evenings on the Roof, 16 May 1949.
6. Walter Arlen, *Los Angeles Times,* 4 November 1959.
7. Morton, letter to Paul Henry Lang, 29 January 1960, Morton collection, UCLA.
8. Morton, letter to Peter Yates, 10 January 1960, in Yates collection, UCSD.
9. Morton, letter to Leonard Stein, 8–9 December 1959.
10. Morton, letter to Stein, 26 January 1960 (the date of the concert).
11. Morton, letter to Stein, 9 February 1960.
12. Morton, letter to Stein, December 1959.
13. Morton, letter to Stein, 13 November 1959.
14. Stein, letter to Morton, 19 November 1959, Morton collection, UCLA.
15. Karlheinz Stockhausen, letter to Morton, 6 October 1960, Morton collection, UCLA.
16. Stein, letter to Morton, 30 April 1961, Morton collection, UCLA.
17. Stein, letter to Morton, 1 December 1959, Morton collection, UCLA.
18. Stein, letter to Morton, 25 November 1959, Morton collection, UCLA.
19. Yates, letter to John Cage, 12 May 1960, Cage archives, Northwestern University.
20. Ibid.
21. Yates, letter to Cage, 31 May 1960, Cage archives, Northwestern University.
22. Yates, draft of program notes, Yates collection, UCSD.
23. Lou Harrison, interview with the author, 13 January 1990, letter and cassette from Los Aptos, Calif.
24. Stein, letter to Morton, 16 February 1960, Morton collection, UCLA.
25. Goldberg, *Los Angeles Times,* 9 March 1960.
26. Goldberg, *Los Angeles Times,* 6 April 1960.
27. Goldberg, *Los Angeles Times,* 12 May 1960.
28. Yates, letter to Houston, 30 April–17 May 1960.
29. Stein, letter to Morton, 12 May 1960, Morton collection, UCLA.
30. Morton, letter to Stein, 2 June 1960.
31. Morton, letter to Stein, 11 July 1960.

32. Craft, letter to the author, 1 June 1989.
33. Stein, letters to Morton, July–August 1960, Morton collection, UCLA.
34. Morton, oral history, 338.
35. Stein, letter to Morton, 9 November 1960, Morton collection, UCLA.
36. Arlen, *Los Angeles Times,* 23 November 1960.
37. Stein, letter to Morton, 31 July 1960, Morton collection, UCLA.
38. Goldberg, *Los Angeles Times,* 18 January 1961.
39. William Kraft, interview with the author, 22 June 1988, Altadena, Calif.
40. Goldberg, *Los Angeles Times,* 22 February 1961.
41. Goldberg, *Los Angeles Times,* 8 March 1961.
42. Goldberg, *Los Angeles Times,* 5 April 1961.
43. Morton, oral history, 346.
44. Lukas Foss, interview with the author, 27 July 1988, Los Angeles.
45. Morton, oral history, 347–48.
46. Aaron Copland, letter to Leo Smit, n.d. (1961), Morton collection, UCLA.
47. Morton, oral history, 351–52.
48. Morton, letter to Stein, 30 May 1961.
49. Morton, 1975 interview, in Rosenberg and Rosenberg, *The Music Makers,* 395.
50. Morton, letter to Stein, 1 August 1961.
51. Morton, letter to Stein, 19 August 1961.
52. As early as 16 March 1961 he wrote to William Lichtenwanger to refuse the task of writing an article about Stravinsky for *Notes,* the journal of the Music Library Association, explaining that he felt he was losing material to the Stravinsky-Craft conversation books, was feeling threatened by the competition of other projects on Stravinsky, and did not want to publish any of his material prematurely.
53. Goldberg, *Los Angeles Times,* 18 October 1961.
54. Morton, oral history, 354.
55. Morton, oral history, 355–56. Stalvey's piece was a String Trio.
56. Arlen, *Los Angeles Times,* 1 November 1961, referring to the Duo for Clarinet and Piano.
57. Morton, oral history, 357.
58. Morton, oral history, 359.
59. Herbert Donaldson, *Los Angeles Examiner,* 6 December 1961.
60. Goldberg, *Los Angeles Times,* 6 December 1961.
61. Morton, oral history, 361.
62. Ibid., 363.
63. Goldberg, *Los Angeles Times,* 7 February 1962.
64. Leonard Stein, "The Performer's Point of View," *Perspectives of New Music* 1, no. 2 (Fall–Winter 1963): 71.
65. Morton, letter to Elliott Carter, 27 January 1962, Morton collection, UCLA. Morton usually called Stravinsky "Maestro." Stravinsky told him to use the patronymic form (Rosenberg and Rosenberg, *The Music Makers,* 396).

66. Elliott Carter, letter to Morton, 6 March 1962, Morton collection, UCLA. By permission of Elliott Carter. In the summer of 1955 Carter heard Karl and Margaret Kohn perform Bartók's Sonata for Two Pianos and Percussion in Sanders Theater at Harvard and told them that he had never heard it played well until then. Karl Kohn remembers Carter saying, "He had heard it early, and it had all seemed just baffling, and now it seemed totally clear" (Karl and Margaret Kohn, interview with the author, 22 February 1990, Santa Monica).
67. Boulez had found Cage's use of the prepared piano very striking in 1949, the year Boulez and Cage met in Paris and began their correspondence. In December 1950 Boulez wrote Cage of his intent, in *Polyphonie X,* that the performer exercise some choice and, further, "I shall also make use, as you do in the music you are in the process of writing, of sampled sonorities, i.e., sound aggregates, linked by a constant but movable within the scale of sonorities" (Jean-Jacquez Nattiez, ed., *The Boulez-Cage Correspondence,* trans. Robert Samuels [Cambridge: Cambridge University Press, 1993], 80, 85). But the following year Boulez rejected Cage's practice of using absolute chance (by tossing coins) and in 1957 wrote his article "Aléa" on the tensions between control and hazard to accompany the composition of his Third Piano Sonata the same year. Cage and the pianist David Tudor performed at Donaueschingen in 1954, and in 1958 Cage lectured on indeterminacy at Darmstadt. His lectures, performances, and book *Silence* (published in 1961) were causing a wide stir. At this time he also often traveled widely with Merce Cunningham's dance troupe.
68. Yates, letter to John Cage, 20 April 1960, Cage archives, Northwestern University.
69. John Cage, letter to Morton, 27 October 1961, Morton collection, UCLA.
70. Morton, letter to Cage, 9 January 1962, Morton collection, UCLA.
71. Cage, letter to Morton, 13 January 1962, Morton collection, UCLA.
72. Morton, letter to Cage, 25 January 1962, Morton collection, UCLA.
73. Goldberg, *Los Angeles Times,* 7 March 1962.
74. Morton, oral history, 370.
75. Goldberg, *Los Angeles Times,* 21 March 1962.
76. Morton, oral history, 373–75.
77. Morton, oral history, 378.
78. Goldberg, *Los Angeles Times,* 16 April 1962.
79. Yates, letter to Houston, 11 March 1962.
80. Morton, oral history, 378–79.
81. Morton, review of *Stravinsky: The Composer and His Works,* by Eric Walter White, *The Musical Quarterly* 53, no. 4 (October 1967): 593.
82. Morton, translation from Romaine Rolland, *Journal des années de guerre* (Paris: Albin Michel, 1952), 852, in Morton collection, UCLA.
83. Morton, letter to Sheldon Meyer, 30 July 1961, Morton collection.

84. Morton, "Notes on MEC for R.K.," in Morton collection, UCLA.
85. Laurence Lesser, interview with the author, 31 December 1987, Newton, Mass.
86. Kraft, interview, 22 June 1988.
87. Goldberg, *Los Angeles Times,* 3 October 1962.
88. Morton, oral history, 381.
89. Morton, oral history, 382.
90. Arlen, *Los Angeles Times,* 7 November 1962.
91. Morton, oral history, 384–85.
92. Arlen, *Los Angeles Times,* 12 November 1962.
93. Morton, oral history, 388.
94. Morton, oral history, 392.
95. Arlen, *Los Angeles Times,* 20 March 1963.
96. Pierre Boulez, letter to Morton, 7 February 1962, Morton collection, UCLA.
97. Morton, letters to Boulez, 7, 13–14, and 16 March 1963, Morton collection, UCLA. Morton kept carbon copies of most of his letters to Boulez. The originals are in the Sacher Foundation, Basel, Switzerland.
98. Boulez, letter to Morton, 17 November 1962, Morton collection, UCLA.
99. Goldberg, *Los Angeles Times,* 5 April 1963.
100. Morton, oral history, 394–95.

CHAPTER EIGHT

1. Albert Goldberg, *Los Angeles Times,* 23 October 1963.
2. Lawrence Morton, oral history, 400.
3. Walter Arlen, *Los Angeles Times,* 6 November 1963.
4. Morton, oral history, 407.
5. Karl Kohn and Margaret Kohn, interview, 22 February 1990, Santa Monica.
6. Morton, oral history, 411.
7. Morton, letter to the editor, *American Composers Alliance Bulletin* 11, nos. 2–4 (December 1963): 9 (Morton collection, UCLA).
8. Morton, letter to Aaron Copland, 16 March 1964, Morton collection, UCLA.
9. Copland, letter to Morton, 27 March 1964, Morton collection, UCLA.
10. Morton, oral history, 423.
11. Goldberg, *Los Angeles Times,* 8 April 1964.
12. Mitchell Lurie, letter to Morton, 18 October 1986, Morton collection, UCLA.
13. Morton, letter to Sheldon Meyer, 25 February 1973, in Morton collection, UCLA.
14. Jann Pasler, ed., *Confronting Stravinsky: Man, Musician, and Modernist* (Berkeley: University of California Press, 1986), 333.
15. Morton, letter to Boulez, 25 June 1964, Morton collection, UCLA.

16. Goldberg, *Los Angeles Times,* 7 October 1964.
17. Goldberg, review of Roberto Gerhard's *Nonet* (1956), *Los Angeles Times,* 1 May 1963.
18. Morton, oral history, 444–45.
19. Morton, oral history, 448.
20. Morton, oral history, 451.
21. Arlen, *Los Angeles Times,* n.d.
22. Laurence Lesser, interview with the author, 31 December 1987, Newton, Mass.
23. Michael Tilson Thomas, interview with the author, 1 July 1988, Laguna Beach.
24. Morton, oral history, 460–70.
25. Kristine McKenna, "The Sentimental Musical Tastes of Ed Ruscha," *Los Angeles Times,* 19 June 1988. Designs by Josef Albers, Morton's friend William Vanderhoef, and Frank Stella were used on subsequent seasons' programs.
26. Goldberg, *Los Angeles Times,* 17 March 1965.
27. Morton, oral history, 478.
28. Arlen, *Los Angeles Times,* 15 December 1965.
29. Martin Bernheimer, *Los Angeles Times,* 26 January 1966.
30. Morton, oral history, 495.
31. Morton, oral history, 496.
32. Goldberg, *Los Angeles Times,* 16 March 1966.
33. Morton, oral history, 497.
34. Bernheimer, *Los Angeles Times,* 20 April 1966.
35. Quincy Porter, "Laurel Leaf Award to Lawrence Morton," 18 May 1966, in Morton collection, UCLA.
36. Morton, letter to Boulez, 27 May 1966, Morton collection, UCLA.
37. Goldberg, *Los Angeles Times,* 5 October 1966.
38. Ingolf Dahl, notes copied by Morton, in Morton collection, UCLA.
39. Tilson Thomas, interview, 1 July 1988.
40. William Kraft, interview, 22 June 1988.
41. Arlen, *Los Angeles Times,* 2 November 1966.
42. Tilson Thomas, interview, 1 July 1988.
43. Bernheimer, *Los Angeles Times,* 8 March 1967.
44. Goldberg, *Los Angeles Times,* 29 March 1967.
45. Arlen, *Los Angeles Times,* 2 November 1966.
46. Peter Yates, letter to Houston, n.d., postmarked 26 December 1967.
47. Program note, 22 January 1968.
48. Goldberg, *Los Angeles Times,* 24 January 1968.
49. György Ligeti, letter to Morton, 26 February 1968, Morton collection, UCLA.
50. Ingolf Dahl, review of MEC's performance of Ligeti's *Aventures* and *Nouvelles Aventures,* 10 November 1969, for Southern California Chamber Music Society, Morton collection, UCLA.

51. *Los Angeles Times,* 7 February 1968.
52. Arlen, *Los Angeles Times,* 27 March 1968.
53. *Los Angeles Times,* 22 October 1968.
54. Yates, letter to Houston, 11 January 1967, Yates collection, UCSD.
55. *Los Angeles Times,* 22 October 1968.
56. Goldberg, *Los Angeles Times,* 29 January 1969.
57. Goldberg, *Los Angeles Times,* 11 December 1968.
58. Bernheimer, *Los Angeles Times,* 15 January 1969.
59. Arlen, *Los Angeles Times,* 19 February 1969.
60. Arlen, *Los Angeles Times,* 16 April 1969.
61. Sadye Moss, letter to members of Southern California Chamber Music Society (SCCMS), August 1969, Yates collection, UCSD.
62. Laurence Lesser, review for SCCMS, 12 January 1970, Morton collection, UCLA.
63. Yates, letter to Morton, 2 May 1970, Yates collection, UCSD.
64. *Los Angeles Times,* 22 October 1969.
65. Arlen, *Los Angeles Times,* 12 November 1969.
66. John Rockwell, *Los Angeles Times,* 25 February 1970.
67. Bernheimer, *Los Angeles Times,* 11 March 1970.
68. Arnold Schoenberg, "Preface to the Four String Quartets," quoted in program notes for 9 and 16 March 1970.
69. Alfred Schnittke, letter to Morton, 5 May 1970, Morton collection, UCLA.
70. Rockwell, *Los Angeles Times,* 15 April 1970.
71. Ibid.
72. Morton, letter to Yates, 18 February 1970, Yates collection, UCSD.
73. Morton, letter to Yates, 10 August 1970, Yates collection, UCSD.
74. Morton, letter to Yates, 7 December 1971, Yates collection, UCSD.
75. Morton, letter to Yates, 10 October 1971, Yates collection, UCSD.
76. Bernheimer, *Los Angeles Times,* 27 December 1970.
77. Bernheimer, *Los Angeles Times,* 20 November 1970.
78. Morton, letter to Yates, 11 April 1965, Yates collection, UCSD.
79. Morton, letter to Yates, 10 December 1970, Yates collection, UCSD.
80. Morton, letter to Yates, n.d., Yates collection, UCSD.
81. Bernheimer, *Los Angeles Times,* 6 October 1970.
82. Arlen, *Los Angeles Times,* 21 October 1970.
83. Rockwell, *Los Angeles Times,* 18 November 1970.
84. Bernheimer, *Los Angeles Times,* 9 December 1970.
85. Bernheimer, *Los Angeles Times,* 13 January 1971.
86. Bernheimer, *Los Angeles Times,* 10 February 1971.
87. Rockwell, *Los Angeles Times,* 24 February 1971. Ever ready to correct critics, Morton wrote a letter to the *Times* (25 February 1971) accusing Rockwell of listening "imperfectly" (Morton collection, UCLA).
88. Arlen, *Los Angeles Times,* 10 March 1971.

89. Morton, "A Very Personal Program Note," 3 May 1971, Morton collection, UCLA.
90. Ibid.
91. Ibid.

CHAPTER NINE

1. Lawrence Morton, "Parentheses," *Music Listener's Guide* (January 1958): 7. On the outside of this issue appears the year 1957, but the publisher prints 1958 on the inside title page and in the index of programs for January 1958.
2. Morton, *Script,* 26 October 1940.
3. Morton, address for the opening session of the Institute on Music in Contemporary Life, Morton collection, UCLA.
4. Morton, "Democracy and the Musician," talk for 1945 meeting of the Music Library Association at UCLA, Morton collection, UCLA.
5. *Fourth Report of the Senate Fact-Finding Committee On Un-American Activities: Communist Front Organizations* (Sacramento: California Senate, 1948), 310–17. Morton kept this historic book (which he seems to have obtained from Senator Jack B. Tenney, chair of the Fact-Finding Committee) and carefully underlined the appearances of his name. On the front cover he wrote, "see Index" (Morton collection, UCLA).
6. Ibid., 170–71.
7. Morton, "American Culture and the Serious Composer," *The Score* 4, no. 3 (May 1950): 8.
8. Morton, "Aaron Copland: Prophet of American Music," *Los Angeles Times,* Sunday, 8 November 1970.
9. Morton, review of Copland's Duo for Violin and Piano, *Notes* 7 (1950): 434.
10. Morton, record review, *Musical Quarterly* 40, no. 2 (April 1954): 294.
11. Morton, "The Spring Festivals," *Frontier,* August 1951.
12. Morton, *Script,* 10 May 1941.
13. Morton, letter to Virgil Thomson, 15 June 1947, Morton collection, UCLA.
14. Morton, "Mr. Schoenberg's Contribution," *Script,* September 1948.
15. See Leonard Stein, "Lawrence Morton (1904–1987)," *Journal of the Arnold Schoenberg Institute* 10, no. 1 (June 1987): 89–95.
16. Morton, "Arnold Schoenberg," *Frontier,* September 1951. Could Morton have been contradicting fellow critic Yates, who had so often used the word "love" in connection with Schoenberg?
17. Morton, "Evenings on the Roof," *Frontier,* January 1953.
18. Robert Craft, letter to the author, 1 June 1988.
19. Don Christlieb, *Remembrance of Lawrence Morton* (Los Angeles: privately printed, n.d.), 32–33.
20. Morton, *Script,* 25 October 1941 and 31 January 1942.

21. Robert Craft, *Present Perspectives* (New York: Knopf, 1984), 230.
22. Morton, *Script,* 18 January 1947.
23. Morton, *Script,* May 1948.
24. Craft, *Present Perspectives,* 230.
25. Robert Craft, "Assisting Stravinsky," *Atlantic Monthly,* December 1982, 71, 73.
26. Morton, oral history, 158–59.
27. Craft, letter to the author, 1 June 1988.
28. Robert Craft, "A Personal Preface," *The Score* 20 (June 1957): 7–13.
29. Craft, "Assisting Stravinsky," 74.
30. Here are the nine Stravinsky world premieres presented by Diaghilev:

Firebird	1910
Petrushka	1911
Le Sacre du printemps	1913
Chant du rossignol	1914
Renard	1922
Les Noces	1923
Pulcinella	1920
Mavra	1922
Oedipus Rex	1927

31. Stravinsky, program note for Columbia Record ML 6048, 1966.
32. Michael Tilson Thomas, interview with the author, 1 July 1988, Laguna Beach.
33. Morton, "Stravinsky in Los Angeles," 79.
34. Morton, "Stravinsky at Home," in *Confronting Stravinsky: Man, Musician and Modernist,* ed. Jann Pasler (Berkeley: University of California Press, 1986), 347.
35. Carol Rosenstiel, letter to Morton, 30 March 1985, Morton collection, UCLA.
36. Charles Fierro, letter to Morton, 25 March 1985, Morton collection, UCLA.
37. Grace-Lynne Martin Ingle, letter to Morton, 3 September 1985, Morton collection, UCLA.
38. Catherine Gayer, letter to Morton, 22 August 1985, Morton collection, UCLA.
39. Morton, "Stravinsky at Home," 343–44.
40. Craft, letter to the author, 1 June 1988.
41. Morton, "Los Angeles Letter," *Counterpoint,* November 1952, Morton collection, UCLA.
42. Robert Craft, *Prejudices in Disguise* (New York: Knopf, 1974), 208–9.
43. Igor Stravinsky, *Selected Correspondence,* ed. Robert Craft (New York: Knopf, 1984), 2:350.
44. Morton, notes for his book on Stravinsky, Morton collection, UCLA.

45. Section on post–World War II Paris (7, paragraph 3, which is anonymous) from article in *New Grove Dictionary of Music and Musicians,* 14:222.
46. Albert Goldberg, "Stockhausen a Dedicated Visionary of New Music," *Los Angeles Times,* 7 December 1958.
47. Robert Craft, "Boulez and Stockhausen," *The Score* (November 1958): 62.
48. Leonard Stein, letter to Morton, 12 May 1960, Morton collection, UCLA.
49. Luciano Berio, interview with Vivian Perlis, November 1971, New Haven, Conn., in oral history, American Music Project, School of Music, Yale University.
50. Cathy Berberian, letter to Morton, 22 December, n.y., Morton collection, UCLA.
51. Lukas Foss, interview with E. Grimes, 9–10 January 1988, revised 23 November 1988, in oral history, American Music Project, School of Music, Yale University.
52. Ibid.
53. Yates, letter to John Cage, 22 May 1959, Cage archives, Northwestern University.
54. Tilson Thomas, interview with the author, 1 July 1988. Robert Craft says Morton regarded Cage as a fraud (Craft, letter to the author, 1 June 1989).
55. Morton, letter to John Cage, 24 October 1961, Morton collection, UCLA.
56. Seymour Shifrin, letter to Morton, 12 December 1965, Morton collection, UCLA.
57. Leon Kirchner, letter to Morton, 4 December 1961, Morton collection, UCLA.
58. Morton, letter to Leonard Stein, 13 November 1959, Arnold Schoenberg Institute.
59. Luigi Nono, letter to Morton, 20 August 1960, Morton collection, UCLA. I am grateful to Nuria Schoenberg Nono for her comments on her husband's remark.
60. Morton, letter to Leonard Stein, 24 April 1961.
61. Quoted in Sybille Bedford, *Aldous Huxley* (New York: Harper & Row, 1974), 669–70; original emphasis.
62. The other composers whose chamber works played at Monday Evening Concerts resulted from Fromm commissions were Claudio Spies, Seymour Shifrin, Donald Martino, Charles Wuorinen, Mario Davidovsky, and Harvey Sollberger.
63. Paul Fromm, 1975 interview in Rosenberg and Rosenberg, *The Music Makers,* 378–84.
64. Quoted in Patrick Wilson, "William Kraft: On Conducting, Performance, and New Music," *Symphony* Magazine, December 1986, 71; original emphasis.
65. Tilson Thomas, interview with the author, 1 July 1988; original emphasis.

66. Ibid.
67. Anthony Linick, letter to the author, 6 January 1993. A portion of this passage is from Linick's unpublished biography, *Ingolf and Etta: a Biography of the Dahls* (1980), which he graciously granted me permission to quote.
68. Morton, oral history, 61, 45, 89. According to his students, Dahl—although an immigrant himself—became a convinced, almost chauvinist, advocate of American music in that period.
69. Ibid., 92.
70. Ibid., 557–58.

CHAPTER TEN

1. Readers' responses published in Albert Goldberg articles in the *Los Angeles Times:* "Avant-Garde Jab Strikes Responsive Chord," Sunday, 30 June 1963, and "The Debate Goes On: Avant-Garde Rebuttal," Sunday, 21 July 1963.
2. Lawrence Morton, quoted by Goldberg in "The Debate Goes On: Avant-Garde Rebuttal," *Los Angeles Times* Calendar, Sunday, 21 July 1963.
3. Morton, oral history, 527.
4. Harry Haskell, *The Early Music Revival: A History* (London: Thames and Hudson, 1968), 128.
5. Morton, "Articulated Baroque," *Counterpoint,* May 1952, 32–34.
6. Morton, autobiographical article (dated 13 May 1962), "The Patron Reminisces," 10, Morton collection, UCLA.
7. Aldous Huxley, "Variations on a Musical Theme," *Esquire,* January 1956, 43.
8. Peter Yates, letter to Melissa Levitzsky, 12 November 1953, Yates collection, UCSD.
9. Goldberg, "Ojai's Ninth Festival Attains Top Standard," *Los Angeles Times,* 23 May 1955.
10. Morton, oral history, 522.
11. Ibid., 106, 443.
12. Unfortunately, by 1965 she had lost Paul Hindemith's manuscript realization of some of these works, according to Morton (oral history, 476).
13. Morton, oral history, 521.
14. Malcolm Hamilton, interview with the author, 16 March 1993, Los Angeles. The hiatus in his performances was from April 1967 until the Dahl memorial concert, September 1970. He played once more for Morton, in the program alternating Bach with Webern, 22 February 1971.
15. Morton, oral history, 158.
16. Ibid., 51.
17. Robert Craft, letter to the author, 1 June 1989.

18. Morton, application (1959) for Guggenheim Foundation fellowship, Morton collection, UCLA.
19. Huxley, "Variations on a Musical Theme."
20. Morton, oral history, 213.
21. Ibid., 286.
22. Igor Stravinsky and Robert Craft, *Expositions and Developments* (Berkeley: University of California Press, 1981), 106.
23. Morton, oral history, 291.
24. Morton, draft of liner notes for Craft's recording of works of Schütz for Columbia Records, Morton collection, UCLA.
25. Morton, oral history, 223.
26. Ibid., 221.
27. Denis Stevens, letter to Morton, 25 September 1961, in Morton collection, UCLA. Stevens's own edition of the work, published by Novello, is dated 1961, and omits the "liturgically irrelevant" motets, a controversial stance attacked by other scholars. Another Monteverdi scholar, Denis Arnold, concludes, "It seems unlikely that there will ever be a final 'authentic' edition, either on paper or on record, and conductors have considerable freedom in producing their own versions" (Arnold, *Monteverdi Church Music* [London: British Broadcasting Corporation, 1982], 62).
28. Ibid., 389.
29. Ibid., 220.
30. Morton, "A Very Personal Program Note" for 3 May 1971 Monday Evening Concert.
31. Morton, "Parentheses," *Music Listener's Guide,* January 1958.

CHAPTER ELEVEN

1. Peter Yates, *An Amateur at the Keyboard* (New York: Pantheon, 1964), 241–42.
2. Barbara Joan Seitz, "The History and Significance of the Concert Series Evenings on the Roof, 1938–1954" (master's thesis, School of Music, Indiana University, 1971), 81.
3. Interview with Kurt Reher, 14 June 1971, Los Angeles, in ibid., 75.
4. Ibid., 75.
5. Ibid., 84.
6. Eudice Shapiro, interview with the author, 28 June 1988.
7. Lawrence Morton, oral history, 536.
8. Speeches, "Address to Dance Panel" on the background of the Musicians' Congress, 23 April 1944, and "Challenge to Music Education," 6 August

1944, for Musicians' Congress, 14 September 1944, UCLA; both in Morton collection, UCLA.

9. David Raksin, interview with the author, 11 March 1994, Santa Monica.
10. Robert Craft, interview with the author, 29 December 1993, New York City.
11. Raksin interview, 11 March 1994.
12. Marilyn Stalvey, interview with author, 19 March 1994, Los Angeles.
13. Craft interview, 29 December 1993.
14. Morton, "Expression X," n.d., in his collected speeches, Morton collection, UCLA.
15. Morton's letters to Dahl are in the possession of Anthony Linick.
16. Morton, letter to Henry Leland Clarke, 25 November 1958, Morton collection, UCLA.
17. Elliott Carter, letter to Yates, 8 June 1959, in Yates collection, UCSD. By permission of Elliott Carter.
18. Morton, oral history, 148–49, 151, 154.
19. James Decker, interview with the author, 21 April 1993, Los Angeles.
20. Morton, letter to *Los Angeles Times,* 19 December 1971, in response to music critic John Rockwell's description of him.
21. Morton, *Los Angeles Examiner,* 29 September 1957.
22. Morton, notes for Raymond Kendall's article on Monday Evening Concerts for the *Los Angeles Times* Calendar, 4 November 1962, Morton collection, UCLA.
23. Morton, oral history, 16.
24. Frederick Lesemann, interview with the author, 10 June 1992, Los Angeles.
25. Robert Craft, letter to the author, 1 June 1989.
26. Laurence Lesser, interview with the author, 31 December 1987, Newton, Mass.
27. Shapiro, interview, 28 June 1988, Studio City, Calif.
28. Gregg Smith, interview with the author, 12 November 1987, Los Angeles.
29. Michael Tilson Thomas, interview with the author, 1 July 1988, Laguna Beach.
30. Seitz, "History and Significance of Evenings on the Roof," 83.
31. Morton, "Tribute to Joseph Szigeti," 2 March 1973, written for the *Los Angeles Times* after Szigeti's death in Switzerland but not published (Morton collection, UCLA).
32. Morton, entry in *Who's Who in America,* 43d edition (Chicago: Marquis Who's Who, 1984–1985), 2:2337.
33. Marshall Bialosky, interview with the author, 6 August 1992, Los Angeles.
34. Karl Kohn, interview, 10 March 1994, Claremont, Calif.
35. Leonard Stein, interview with the author, 8 August 1992, Hollywood.
36. Dorrance Stalvey, letter to author, 1 April 1994.
37. Sadye Moss, letter to Earl A. Powell, III, 15 April 1985. This letter, and a collection of minutes, letters, and documents from the SCCMS board meet-

ings between 19 November 1982 and the completion of the dissolution of SCCMS, 31 July 1985, are in the Morton collection, UCLA.

38. Sadye Moss, letter to Earl A. Powell, III, 11 February 1985, Morton collection, UCLA.

39. Earl A. Powell, III, letter to Sadye Moss, 26 March 1985, Morton collection, UCLA.

SELECT BIBLIOGRAPHY

ARCHIVES

Arnold Schoenberg Institute, University of Southern California
Charles Ives collection, Yale University
Lawrence Morton collection, Department of Special Collections, University Research Library, University of California, Los Angeles
Los Angeles Public Library, Music division
Oral history, American Music Project, Yale University
Peter Yates collection, Mandeville Department of Special Collections, University Library, University of California, San Diego
Wesley Kuhnle repository, Special Collections, California State University, Long Beach

BOOKS AND ARTICLES

Alderman, Pauline. *We Build a School of Music.* Los Angeles: Alderman Book Committee, 1989.
Baum, Vicki. *It Was All Quite Different: The Memoirs of Vicki Baum.* New York: Funk & Wagnalls, 1964.
Bedford, Sybille. *Aldous Huxley.* New York: Knopf, 1974.
Behrdahl, James M. "Ingolf Dahl: His Life and Works." Ph.D. diss., University of Miami, 1975.
Craft, Robert. "A Personal Preface." *The Score* 20 (June 1957): 7–13.

———. *Stravinsky: Chronicle of a Friendship, 1948–1971.* New York: Knopf, 1972.
———. *Prejudices in Disguise.* New York: Knopf, 1974.
———. *Current Convictions.* New York: Knopf, 1977.
———. *A Stravinsky Scrapbook.* London: Thames & Hudson, 1983.
———. *Present Perspectives.* New York: Knopf, 1984.
Crawford, Dorothy L. "Peter Yates and the Performance of Schoenberg Chamber Music at 'Evenings on the Roof.'" *Journal of the Arnold Schoenberg Institute* 12, no. 2 (November 1989): 175–201.
Davis, Mike. *City of Quartz: Excavating the Future in Los Angeles.* New York: Vintage, 1992.
Dunaway, David King. *Huxley in Hollywood.* New York: Harper & Row, 1989.
Friedrich, Otto. *City of Nets: A Portrait of Hollywood in the 1940s.* New York: Harper & Row, 1986.
Fromm, Paul. *A Life for New Music: Selected Papers of Paul Fromm.* Ed. David Gable and Christoph Wolff. Cambridge, Mass.: Music Department of Harvard University, 1988.
Griffiths, Paul. *Modern Music: The Avant-garde since 1945.* New York: Braziller, 1981.
Hamm, Charles. *Music in the New World.* New York: Norton, 1983.
Haskell, Harry. *The Early Music Revival: A History.* London: Thames & Hudson, 1988.
Heibut, Anthony. *Exiled in Paradise.* New York: Viking, 1983.
Heyworth, Peter, ed. *Conversations with Klemperer.* London: Faber & Faber, 1985.
Hitchcock, H. Wiley. *Music in the United States: An Historical Introduction.* New Jersey: Prentice-Hall, 1969.
Howard, Orrin, ed. *Festival of Music Made in Los Angeles.* Los Angeles: Los Angeles Philharmonic Association, 1981.
Huxley, Aldous. "The Marriage of Poetry and Music Can Produce a Versatile Child: Variations on a Musical Theme." *Esquire,* January 1956.
Huxley, Julian, ed. *Aldous Huxley: 1894–1963.* New York: Harper & Row, 1965.
Jackman, Jarrell. "Exiles in Paradise: A Cultural History of German Émigrés in Southern California, 1939–1950." Ph.D. diss., University of California, Santa Barbara, 1977.
Libman, Lillian. *And Music at the Close: Stravinsky's Last Years.* New York: Norton, 1972.
McWilliams, Carey. *Southern California: An Island on the Land.* Santa Barbara: Peregrine Smith, 1973.
Mann, Katia. *Unwritten Memories.* Trans. Hunter and Hildegarde Hannum. New York: Knopf, 1975.
McFarlane, Henrietta. "They Shall Have Music." *California Arts and Architecture* 56 (December 1939).
Mead, Rita. *Henry Cowell's New Music: 1925–1936.* Studies in Musicology 40, University of Michigan. Ann Arbor: UMI Research Press, 1981.

Morton, Lawrence. "A Brief Resume of Musical Activity in Southern California: 1939–1945." Report for Office of War Information. Manuscript.
———. "Monday Evening Concerts." Transcript of 1966 oral history. Interview by Adelaide Tusler. Department of Special Collections, University Research Library, University of California, Los Angeles, 1973.
———. "Stravinsky in Los Angeles." Los Angeles: Los Angeles Philharmonic Association, 1982.
Nattiez, Jean-Jacques, ed. *The Boulez-Cage Correspondence.* Trans. Robert Samuels. Cambridge: Cambridge University Press, 1993.
Pasler, Jann, ed. *Confronting Stravinsky: Man, Musician, and Modernist.* Berkeley: University of California Press, 1986.
Reher, Sven. "We Must Go Farther Yet." Transcript of oral history. Interview by Thomas Bertonneau. Department of Special Collections, University Research Library, University of California, Los Angeles, 1981.
Reich, Willi. *Schoenberg: A Critical Biography.* Trans. Leo Black. New York: Praeger, 1971.
Rodriguez, J., ed. *Music and Dance in California.* Hollywood: Bureau of Musical Research, 1940.
"A Roof in Los Angeles." *Time,* 8 October 1951, 67.
Rubsamen, Walter H. "Schoenberg in America." *Musical Quarterly* 37 (October 1951): 469–89.
Saunders, Richard Drake, ed. *Music and Dance in California and the West.* Hollywood: Bureau of Musical Research, 1948.
Schoenberg, Arnold. *Letters.* Ed. Erwin Stein. Trans. Eithne Wilkins and Ernst Kaiser. Berkeley: University of California Press, 1987.
Seitz, Barbara Jean. "The History and Significance of the Concert Series, Evenings on the Roof 1938–54." Master's thesis, Indiana University, 1971.
Selwyn, Mary-Jeannette Brown. "A Lapse of Musical Memory in Los Angeles." February 1984 manuscript, author's collection.
Slonimsky, Nicolas. *Perfect Pitch.* New York: Oxford University Press, 1988.
Smith, Catherine Parsons, and Cynthia S. Richardson. *Mary Carr Moore, American Composer.* Ann Arbor: University of Michigan Press, 1987.
Sontag, Susan. "Pilgrimage." *The New Yorker,* 21 December 1987, 38.
Stevens, Halsey. "Los Angeles Scene." *American Composers Alliance Bulletin* 3 (Spring 1953): 11.
Stevenson, Robert M. "John Cage on his 70th birthday: West Coast Background." *Inter-American Music Review* 5, no. 1 (1982): 3.
———. "Los Angeles." In *New Grove Dictionary of American Music,* ed. H. Wiley Hitchcock and Stanley Sadie. New York: Macmillan, 1986.
Stravinsky, Igor. *Selected Correspondence.* Ed. Robert Craft. New York: Knopf, 1984.
Stravinsky, Igor, and Robert Craft. *Conversations with Igor Stravinsky.* Berkeley: University of California Press, 1980.
———. *Memories and Commentaries.* Berkeley: University of California Press, 1981.

———. *Expositions and Developments.* Berkeley: University of California Press, 1981.
———. *Dialogues.* Berkeley: University of California Press, 1982.
———. *Themes and Episodes.* New York: Knopf, 1984.
Stravinsky, Vera. *Dearest Bubushkin.* Ed. Robert Craft, trans. Lucia Davidova. New York: Thames & Hudson, 1985.
Stuckenschmidt, H. H. *Arnold Schoenberg: His Life, World and Work.* New York: Schirmer, 1978.
Swan, Howard. *Music in the Southwest.* San Marino, Calif.: Huntington Library, 1952.
Tawa, Nicholas E. *A Most Wondrous Babble: American Art Composers, Their Music, and the American Scene, 1950–85.* New York: Greenwood Press, 1987.
Taylor, John Russell. *Strangers in Paradise.* New York: Holt, 1983.
Weschler, Lawrence. *Seeing Is Forgetting the Name of the Thing One Sees: A Life of Contemporary Artist Robert Irwin.* Berkeley: University of California Press, 1982.
White, Eric Walter. *Stravinsky: The Composer and His Works.* Berkeley: University of California Press, 1966.
Yates, Peter. *Evenings on the Roof: Fourth Report.* Los Angeles: Roof Publications, 1946.
———. *A Smaller Poem Book.* Los Angeles: Roof Publications, 1946.
———. "The Demi-Wasteland." *Hi-Fidelity* 12 (January 1962): 39.
———. *An Amateur at the Keyboard.* New York: Pantheon, 1964.
———. *Twentieth Century Music.* New York: Pantheon, 1967.
———. "Evenings on the Roof, 1939–1954." Transcript of 1967 oral history. Interview by Adelaide Tusler. Department of Special Collections, University of California, Los Angeles, 1972.
———. "A Serpent on the Roof." *International Musician* 51 (November, 1952): 13.

INDEX

Compositor:	Impressions, a division of Edwards Brothers
Text:	12/14.5 Adobe Garamond
Display:	Perpetua and Adobe Garamond
Printer and Binder:	Edwards Brothers, Inc.